Adolescent Drug Abuse: Clinical Assessment and Therapeutic Interventions

Editors:

Elizabeth Rahdert, Ph.D.

Dorynne Czechowicz, M.D.

NIDA Research Monograph 156
1995

U.S. DEPARTMENT OF HEALTH AND HUMAN SERVICES
Public Health Service
National Institutes of Health

National Institute on Drug Abuse
Division of Clinical and Services Research
5600 Fishers Lane
Rockville, MD 20857

ACKNOWLEDGMENT

This monograph is based on the papers from a technical review on "Adolescent Drug Abuse: Clinical Assessment and Therapeutic Interventions" held on May 13-14, 1993. The review meeting was sponsored by the National Institute on Drug Abuse.

COPYRIGHT STATUS

The National Institute on Drug Abuse has obtained permission from the copyright holders to reproduce certain previously published material as noted in the text. Further reproduction of this copyrighted material is permitted only as part of a reprinting of the entire publication or chapter. For any other use, the copyright holder's permission is required. All other material in this volume except quoted passages from copyrighted sources is in the public domain and may be used or reproduced without permission from the Institute or the authors. Citation of the source is appreciated.

Opinions expressed in this volume are those of the authors and do not necessarily reflect the opinions or official policy of the National Institute on Drug Abuse or any other part of the U.S. Department of Health and Human Services.

The U.S. Government does not endorse or favor any specific commercial product or company. Trade, proprietary, or company names appearing in this publication are used only because they are considered essential in the context of the studies reported herein.

National Institute on Drug Abuse
NIH Publication No. 95-3908
Printed 1995

NIDA Research Monographs are indexed in the *Index Medicus*. They are selectively included in the coverage of *American Statistics Index, BioSciences Information Service, Chemical Abstracts, Current Contents, Psychological Abstracts,* and *Psychopharmacology Abstracts.*

Contents

Advances in Adolescent Drug Abuse Treatment 1
   Elizabeth Rahdert and Dorynne Czechowicz

Identifying High-Risk Youth: Prevalence and Patterns of
Adolescent Drug Abuse 7
   Michael D. Newcomb

Service Delivery Strategies for Treating High-Risk Youth:
Delinquents, Homeless, Runaways, and Sexual Minorities 39
   James A. Farrow

Adolescent Substance Use Disorder with Conduct Disorder
and Comorbid Conditions 49
   Thomas J. Crowley and Paula D. Riggs

Physical Health Problems Associated with Adolescent
Substance Abuse 112
   Patricia Kokotailo

AIDS, Drugs, and the Adolescent 130
   Elizabeth Steel

Current Issues and Future Needs in the Assessment of
Adolescent Drug Abuse 146
   Ken C. Winters and Randy D. Stinchfield

Cultural Competence in Assessing Hispanic Youths and Families:
Challenges in the Assessment of Treatment Needs and Treatment
Evaluation for Hispanic Drug-Abusing Adolescents 172
   William M. Kurtines and José Szapocznik

Therapeutic Communities for Adolescents 190
   Nancy Jainchill, Gauri Bhattacharya, and John Yagelka

Family-Based Treatment for Adolescent Drug Use:
State of the Science 218
   Howard A. Liddle and Gayle A. Dakof

Skills Training for Pregnant and Parenting Adolescents 255
   James A. Hall

Pharmacotherapy for Adolescents with Psychoactive
Substance Use Disorders 291
    Yifrah Kaminer

Youth Evaluation Services (YES): Assessment, Systems of Referral,
and Treatment Effects 325
    Frances K. Del Boca, Thomas F. Babor, and
    Margaret Anne McLaney

Posttreatment Services for Chemically Dependent Adolescents 341
    Sherilynn F. Spear and Sharon Y. Skala

Advances in Adolescent Drug Abuse Treatment

Elizabeth Rahdert and Dorynne Czechowicz

INTRODUCTION

Early in 1988 the National Institute on Drug Abuse (NIDA) published a research monograph entitled "Adolescent Drug Abuse: Analyses of Treatment Research" (Rahdert and Grabowski 1988). It was organized so as to highlight achievements in the areas of assessment, client-treatment matching, and theoretically based models of treatment. Since then, there has been an increased awareness of other important elements in the therapeutic process. One such element is initial case identification, especially as it pertains to targeting high-risk youth for early or moderately intensive intervention. Another is aftercare service, which is thought to be essential in supporting recovery and preventing relapse.

Advances leading to a better understanding of adolescent drug abuse have, in part, come about through a recognition of the multigenerational and multidimensional nature of the problem, its causes, consequences, and effective solutions (Newcomb 1992). For example, many developmental, psychological, physical, sociocultural, legal, and academic factors require attention during the assessment and treatment of an adolescent with a substance-use disorder. Likewise, drug use should be questioned when some other medical or psychiatric disorder is the primary diagnosis (U.S. Congress 1991).

Given a continued concern about adolescent drug abuse, it was deemed appropriate to present an update on research findings and provide an opportunity to identify prominent gaps in current knowledge. To meet these aims a Technical Review meeting, "Adolescent Drug Abuse: Clinical Assessment and Therapeutic Interventions," was held in Bethesda, Maryland, on May 13 and 14, 1993. The participants in the meeting (and subsequent monograph) included Crowley, Del Boca, Farrow, Hall, Jainchill, Kaminer, Kokotailo, Liddle, Newcomb, Spear, Steel, Szapocznik, and Winters. Below is a summary of the chapters that resulted from that meeting.

INITIAL CASE IDENTIFICATION

By way of furnishing a context within which to examine a broad range of issues, Newcomb reviewed what is currently known about the extent and patterns of teenage drug involvement, in particular the use of tobacco, alcohol, and marijuana. Although there had been a drop in use during the late 1980s, a recent upturn has been reported with some youngsters beginning experimentation with psychoactive drugs as early as the eighth grade. A small but clinically significant number of those children develop a lifestyle involving the regular and heavy use of psychoactive substances, including drugs known for their very serious psychological effects (e.g., cocaine, hallucinogens, inhalants).

To better understand the need for treatment, Newcomb discussed many probable environmental, interpersonal, and psychobehavioral causes and attributable outcomes associated with long-term drug use. Like other contributors to this monograph, Newcomb stressed the importance of identifying specific drug use patterns that predict a later need for treatment if less intensive, preventative intervention is not provided early on.

Of equal importance to the issue of escalating drug use among junior and senior high school students is the question of identifying drug abuse among young psychiatric patients. In the presentation and chapter coauthored with Riggs, Crowley illustrated this point and described the heavy drug use among adolescent patients diagnosed with a conduct disorder. Similarly, Kaminer reported on drug and alcohol use among teenagers admitted to treatment for a primary depressive disorder.

Several authors examined adolescent substance abuse among patients in treatment for serious physical health problems. Kokotailo reviewed morbidity and mortality rates for drug-related injuries from motor vehicle accidents, infectious disease states (e.g., sexually transmitted diseases (STDs), tuberculosis), and other physical conditions (e.g., pregnancy). From the perspective of a primary care physician and clinical investigator, Kokotailo observed that drug abuse and related problems often cluster (e.g., intoxication, unprotected sex, and rape). Therefore, a drug use history should always be part of the physical examination and treatment plan.

Steel emphasized this same point by presenting an update on the topic of acquired immunodeficiency syndrome (AIDS) and adolescents. That chapter discusses how drug abuse puts many teenagers at risk of exposure to human immunodeficiency virus (HIV) infection; Farrow concurred. Based upon a review of what is currently known about drug abuse, HIV transmission, and interrelated problems among homeless runaway youths, gay and lesbian teenagers, and adolescents who resort to prostitution, Farrow found that many of these teenagers will need therapeutic services that are sensitive to their particular lifestyles, environment, and economic realities.

SCREENING AND DIAGNOSTIC ASSESSMENT

The importance of having appropriate assessment tools available for use in gathering valid, accurate, and precise information for clinical research and practice can not be overstated. Psychometrically sound instruments are necessary to differentially describe persons in treatment and document clinically significant changes that come about (or do not come about) during and after therapy. To the degree that clinicians utilize less-than-adequate measures, they can not be sure to what extent and for whom their treatment is the most (and least) effective.

Over the past decade, Winters has been involved in developing and refining assessment tools designed specifically for adolescents. As noted in an earlier review on the topic (Winters and Henley 1988), most screening and diagnostic instruments available at the time were good for use only with adult populations. But progress has been made; a number of instruments have since been redesigned to be developmentally appropriate for use with adolescents. Other psychometrically sound measures have been newly constructed. Some identify alcohol and drug use only, while others are multidimensional in scope. Unfortunately, only a few of these measures have been validated in any but their English-language version.

Szapocznik and coworkers reported on accomplishments in responding to this need for culture- and language-appropriate tools. Their chapter describes several culturally appropriate tools developed for use with Hispanic adolescents and their families in treatment. The authors also discuss the challenge of creating different assessment methodologies for use with linguistically and culturally diverse clinic populations.

CLIENT/PATIENT TREATMENT MATCHING

Although an effective system for matching drug-abusing individuals with diagnostically appropriate programs has important implications in terms of the quality of health care delivery, few clinical investigators have critically assessed different strategies for matching clients to available treatment. Addressing this issue, Del Boca, Babor, and McLaney reported on their recent study that was aimed at evaluating a well-delineated, community-wide youth services program that included centralized assessment, systematic matching, and referral to local treatment and service providers. Preliminary results suggest treatment can be beneficial if the adolescents participate in programs that are selected on the basis of a comprehensive assessment and referral to specific services thought to meet their individual needs.

THERAPEUTIC INTERVENTIONS

Many clinical investigators have been involved with determining the efficacy of various types of treatment for drug-abusing youth. Although considerable progress has been made in regard to developing theoretically based psychosocial approaches for treating youths, far less has been achieved in terms of identifying effective medications. In the chapter on pharmacotherapy for adolescents with comorbid disorders, Kaminer reviewed the few empirical studies that have appeared in the literature. Kaminer concluded that some of the medications prescribed for this age group deserve substantially more attention then they have heretofore received.

Significant progress has been made in terms of several specific non-pharmacological methods of treatment. First, Liddle provided an overview of various models of family-based therapy for adolescent drug abuse. Many appear to hold more immediate promise for positive outcomes. Hall followed with a review of recent work in developing a peer-group skills training program for drug-abusing pregnant and parenting teenage girls. Then Jainchill and colleagues described treatment in an adolescent-oriented program in a residential therapeutic community.

AFTERCARE SERVICES

Spear's chapter stresses the importance of providing effective posttreatment services as a necessary extension of a continuum of care for drug-abusing adolescents. Recognizing the scarcity of empirically based research in this area of treatment research, Spear urged clinical investigators to develop and critically evaluate a range of aftercare service that can help recovering adolescents sustain the progress they make in treatment.

CONCLUSION

Statistics from the 1985 annual High School Senior Survey (Rahdert and Grabowski 1988) indicated a steady decline in most types of drug use among teenagers. Unfortunately, that trend was transient. As previosly noted, an increasing number of children and young adolescents are using illicit drugs and starting to do so at an earlier age. Although not all will continue or accelerate their use, an early start predicts polydrug abuse and multiple related problems later on for a clinically significant number.

For older, more troubled adolescents, a statement made in the 1988 monograph is still relevant: "Different types of therapeutic interventions will be necessary to treat [the] more severely affected youth" (Rahdert 1988). This statement is important because it identifies at least two important advances that have been made since then: First, the recognition that drug-abusing adolescents most in need of treatment experience multiple problems; and second, the acknowledgement that a wide variety and various combinations of effective therapeutic approaches must be available to meet each teenager's individual needs.

Thanks go to the authors who, by contributing to this monograph, may advance the areas of assessment and therapeutic interventions. All participants provided thoughtful and thorough reviews of progress made in specific therapeutic areas. Many also discussed methodological issues associated with conducting studies and made recommendations for future research. All insights and shared experiences are greatly appreciated and will make invaluable contributions to the field of adolescent drug abuse research.

REFERENCES

Newcomb, M.D. Understanding the multidimensional nature of drug use and abuse: The role of consumption, risk factors, and protective factors. In: Glantz, M., and Pickens, R., eds. *Vulnerability to Drug Abuse*. Washington, DC: American Psychological Association 1992. pp. 255-297.

Rahdert, E. Treatment services for adolescent drug abusers: Introduction and overview. In: Rahdert, E., and Grabowski, J., eds. *Adolescent Drug Abuse: Analyses of Treatment Research*. DHHS Pub. No. (ADM)88-1523. Washington, DC: Supt. of Docs., U.S. Govt. Print. Off., 1988. pp. 1-3.

Rahdert, E., and Grabowski, J., eds. *Adolescent Drug Abuse: Analyses of Treatment Research*. DHHS Pub. No. (ADM)88-1523. Washington, DC: Supt. of Docs., U.S. Govt. Print. Off., 1988.

U.S. Congress, Office of Technology Assessment. *Adolescent Health. Vol. 2, Background and the Effectiveness of Selected Prevention and Treatment Services* (OTA-H-466). Washington, DC: Supt. of Docs., U.S. Govt. Print. Off., 1991.

Winters, K.C., and Henley, G. Assessing adolescents who abuse chemicals: The chemical depencency adolescent assessment project. In: Rahdert, E., and Grabowski, J., eds. *Adolescent Drug Abuse: Analyses of Treatment Research*. DHHS Pub. No. (ADM)88-1523. Washington, DC: Supt. of Docs., U.S. Govt. Print. Off., 1988. pp. 4-18.

AUTHORS

Elizabeth Rahdert, Ph.D.
Research Psychologist

Dorynne Czechowicz, M.D.
Medical Officer

Division of Clinical and Services Research
National Institute on Drug Abuse
5600 Fishers Lane
Parklawn Building, Room 10A-10
Rockville, MD 20857

Identifying High-Risk Youth: Prevalence and Patterns of Adolescent Drug Abuse

Michael D. Newcomb

INTRODUCTION

Most researchers and clinicians agree that substance use disorders among adolescents share many similarities as well as several important differences when compared with other psychiatric syndromes that occur during the teenage years (Newcomb and Richardson, in press). The similarities include impairment of these individuals, dysfunctions within the family and social network, and potential mortality (as with dysphoric affective disorders). It is important to understand, prevent, and treat these problems from a biopsychosocial perspective.

Drug and alcohol abuse and dependence are unlike most other mental disorders in at least two ways. First, they are pathoplastic disorders; their existence and prevalence require an external agent (the drug) and vary according to the availability and potency of these agents. Second, drug abuse disorders involve a willing host (the abuser) who is an active participant in generating these disorders. If individuals did not choose to ingest these substances or the drugs were not available, there would be no disorder. However, many drugs are widely available to teenagers and most adolescents are willing to ingest at least some of them (Newcomb and Bentler 1989).

The similarities and differences between drug abuse and other types of mental disorders must be carefully understood and appreciated. Prevention and treatment strategies designed for depression, adjustment disorders, or other types of psychological dysfunction cannot be indiscriminately used for intervention in problems of drug abuse. This is one way in which epidemiological and etiological research can inform and guide the unique and specific components of drug abuse prevention and intervention to ensure greater success.

Several issues must be kept in mind when trying to assess, understand, or intervene in the use of drugs by teenagers. These include, but are certainly not limited to: what should be considered substance use in contrast to drug abuse and dependence disorders in teenagers; appreciation that drug abuse disorders among teenagers are not a homogeneous group of syndromes; the ramifications of treating such disorders (however defined); consideration of the larger context of attitudes, behaviors, and social relationships within which youthful drug use occurs; and the importance of considering the epidemiological and etiological factors associated with drug and alcohol use and abuse among teenagers.

For instance, there is no generally accepted criteria for deciding what constitutes drug use versus drug abuse among teenagers. Although the "Diagnostic and Statistical Manual of Mental Disorders," 4th ed. (DSM-IV) (American Psychiatric Association 1994) provides diagnostic criteria for various types of drug abuse and drug dependence, these criteria may not be completely appropriate for adolescents (Newcomb and Richardson, in press). Use of a drug by a teenager may represent experimentation with prohibited behaviors, reflecting what some might consider a typical feature of adolescent development (Peele 1987). At what point does this drug involvement reflect abuse, dependence, or a disorder that may destroy a life? Where along this continuum should prevention or treatment be targeted? Might aggressive intervention at low levels of drug involvement exacerbate the problem rather than help it? Should specific criteria be developed for assessing drug abuse and problems among teenagers?

This chapter focuses on four topics related to teenage drug involvement from epidemiological and etiological perspectives: extent of the problem, causes of drug involvement, drug use and other problem behaviors, and course and patterns of drug involvement.

EXTENT OF THE PROBLEM

Until recently, the most extensive surveys of drug use among U.S. adolescents have been annual assessments conducted by the National Institute on Drug Abuse: One called Monitoring the Future (Johnston et al. 1993), and the other the National Household Survey of Drug Use (NIDA 1991) that includes drug assessments of 12- to 17-year-olds. Until the last 2 years, Monitoring the Future only surveyed high school seniors; in 1991 the study began annual assessments of 8th and 10th graders as well. These surveys provide the best data available for prevalence estimates of drug use among teenagers in this country. Nevertheless, they have several important limitations including underrepresentation of truants and school dropouts, limited access to adolescents considered at particularly high risk for substance abuse (such as the homeless, throwaway teenagers, and innercity gang members), and restrictions to measures of drug use frequency and quantity which certainly result in imprecise approximations of drug abuse or dependence.

These national surveys and other local studies yield a fairly clear understanding of drug use patterns among adolescents, although the extent of drug abuse and dependence among teenagers is more poorly documented. There is clear evidence of widespread tobacco use (62 percent lifetime prevalence in 1992) and alcohol use (nearly 90 percent) among high school seniors (Johnston et al. 1993) and inferences that abuse of these substances may be common. For instance, over one-quarter of American high school seniors reported having five or more drinks on at least one occasion in the 2 weeks before survey participation, and one out of 10 leave high school addicted to cigarettes and smoking a half-pack or more per day.

One of the primary causes of death among teenagers in the United States is drunk driving, accounting for more than 20 percent of all mortalities (Julien 1992). The effects of tobacco smoking (e.g., heart disease, lung cancer) are the leading cause of death among all Americans and will probably be responsible for killing more current children and teenagers later in their life than any other single cause (Julien 1992). There are clearly substantial reasons for concern regarding the abuse of tobacco and alcohol among teenagers, although clear focus on these drugs is conspicuously missing in the current War on Drugs (Newcomb 1992*a*).

The use and abuse of all other drugs currently lags far behind these socially approved drugs. Marijuana is by far the most commonly used illicit substance, with a 33 percent lifetime prevalence rate among high school seniors in 1992, whereas 2 percent reported daily marijuana use (compared with over 10 percent only a decade ago). About 17 percent of high school seniors also reported that they had tried inhalants, 14 percent had tried stimulants, 6 percent had tried cocaine (powder or crack), and 9 percent had tried hallucinogens at some time in their lives (Johnston et al. 1993; Oetting and Beauvais 1990).

However, these national survey data document a fairly steady decrease in drug use for most types of illicit drugs since the early- to mid-1980s (including marijuana, cocaine, stimulants, and sedatives), with less dramatic changes in cigarette and alcohol use (Johnston et al. 1993). At the same time, though, the use of inhalants and hallucinogens has leveled off or shown a modest increase since the mid-1980s among older adolescents. Further, an alarmingly high number of young people continue to experiment with both legal and illicit drugs at very early ages; many may progress to drug abuse.

There are serious causes for concern based on the report (Johnson et al. 1993) from the Monitoring the Future Study released in April 1993. These findings include:

- Reduction in perceived risk and harm from using marijuana and cocaine
- Rates of tobacco use have showed little change in the past 2 years
- Based on two annual waves of 8th grade survey data, significant increases have been found in the use of marijuana, cocaine, crack, lysergic acid diethylamide (LSD), other hallucinogens, stimulants, and inhalants.

Although no national data are available that can yield true prevalence rates of drug abuse and dependence among teenagers as defined in the DSM-IV, estimates can be made from local surveys. For instance, Lewinsohn and colleagues (1993) determined the lifetime prevalence rates for various diagnoses among a group of Oregon adolescents. Alcohol abuse or dependence was found among 5.9 percent of the girls and 6.6 percent of the boys. Cannabis use disorder was found among 5.3 percent of the girls and 7.9 percent of the boys, whereas analogous figures were substantially smaller for amphetamine (2.5 percent for girls and 1.3 percent for boys) and for cocaine (0.5 percent for girls and 0.7 percent for boys). No information was provided for tobacco abuse and dependence.

Comorbidity of alcohol and other drug abuse is also an important issue that was documented nationally in the Epidemiologic Catchment Area Study (Regier et al. 1990), although these data did not include anyone under 18 years of age. However, the Oregon data (Lewinsohn et al. 1993) corroborate these high rates of comorbidity of alcohol and other drug abuse with other mental disorders among adolescents. In these data from teenagers, substance use disorders were most commonly associated with diagnoses of disruptive behavior and eating disorders.

Survey reports also suggest interesting trends in substance use related to demographic characteristics. Roughly equivalent rates of use are reported across all social classes in many surveys (Brook et al. 1983; Johnston et al. 1993). Nonetheless, socioeconomic status (SES) may function as a mediating variable; lower SES adolescents are at greater risk because lower SES increases the impact of other negative influences (Tolan 1988).

Available evidence regarding the impact of family structure (i.e., intact versus broken families), however, is more equivocal. Still, most investigators argue that greater adolescent drug use is observed within disrupted families (Needle et al. 1990; Newcomb and Bentler 1988*c*).

National surveys suggest some reduction in regional differences in drug use in the 1980s. However, there is still greater drug use in the West and Northeast compared with the North Central and Southern United States and only marginal differences in reported rates of drug use in rural compared to urban settings, though drugs of choice may differ dramatically in rural versus urban contexts (Johnston et al. 1993).

Gender differences in rates of drug use are typically found in these surveys. Except for cigarettes, boys tend to initiate drug use before girls and to use slightly greater quantities, a differential that is maintained throughout high school (Johnston et al. 1993; Newcomb et al. 1987). Girls, however, tend to surpass the boys' use of pills with age and there appears to be a trend toward convergence between genders for use of all drugs over the past decade.

Although African Americans and Hispanics are apparently overrepresented among drug-abusing populations (Medina et al. 1982), this may be an artifact of who uses public health services. Most recent local and national nontreatment surveys suggest moderately higher rates of illicit drug use among white and Hispanic adolescents compared with African-American and Asian adolescents (Johnston et al. 1993; Maddahian et al. 1986). The author must conclude that, nationwide, there is little compelling or convincing evidence for substantial differences in overall patterns of use as a function of ethnicity. Nonetheless, ethnic minorities (particularly African Americans and Hispanics) are currently far more likely than other adolescent groups to be targeted for attention from law enforcement officials as a function of drug involvement. Some suggest that although the prevalence of drug use may be similar across ethnic groups, there may be different rates of drug abuse among users from different ethnic populations (Kandel, in press).

CAUSES OF THE DISORDER

The influences that generate drug use and abuse are many, varied, and far from clearly understood. While most drug use initiation occurs with friends or peers also using drugs, the stage has been set for this event much earlier by parents, the community, and society at large (Newcomb 1992a, 1994a).

Myriad variables have been studied for their ability to predict drug involvement. These can be conceptualized as reflecting several domains or areas (Lettieri 1985): cultural/societal environment; interpersonal forces (i.e., school, peers, and family); psychobehavioral factors (e.g., personality, attitudes, activities); and biogenetic influences. An individual can be considered at risk because of factors or forces within each of these areas.

Hawkins and colleagues (1992) reviewed the possible risk factors for youthful drug use and identified 17 potential causes. These 17 factors reflect the four general areas listed above and are depicted in table 1.

Included among cultural/societal factors are laws and norms favorable toward drug use, availability of drugs, extreme economic deprivation, and neighborhood disorganization. Interpersonal forces include family alcohol and drug behavior and attitudes, poor and inconsistent family management practices, family conflict, peer rejection in elementary grades, and association with drug-using peers. Psychobehavioral influences include early and persistent problem behaviors, academic failure, low degree of commitment to school, alienation and rebelliousness, attitudes favorable to drug use, and early onset of drug use. Biogenetic factors include potential heritability of drug abuse and psychophysiological susceptibility to the effects of drugs.

Additional influences not directly addressed in their review include psychological and emotional factors such as anxiety, need for excitement, depression, psychopathology, low constraint or antisocial personality, and contextual factors such as physical or sexual abuse or stressful life events (Harrison et al. 1989; Johnson and Kaplan 1990; Labouvie et al. 1990;

TABLE 1. *Summary of risk factors for drug use.*

Domain	Risk Factor
Culture and Society	- laws favorable to drug use - social norms favorable to drug use - availability of drugs - extreme economic deprivations - neighborhood disorganization
Interpersonal	- parent and family drug use - positive family attitudes toward drug use - poor/inconsistent family management practices - family conflict and disruption - peer rejection - association with drug-using peers
Psychobehavioral	- early/persistent problem behavior - academic failure - low commitment to school - alienation - rebelliousness - favorable attitudes toward drug use - early onset of drug use
Biogenetic	- inherited susceptibility to drug abuse - psychophysiological vulnerability to drug effects

Newcomb and Harlow 1986; Newcomb and McGee 1991; Zucker and Gomberg 1986).

Although also not specifically mentioned by Hawkins and colleagues (1992), certainly the *best* predictor of future behavior is past behavior. Therefore, the strongest predictor of current drug use is past drug use. Peer influences such as modeling drug use, provision of drugs, and attitudes and behavior that encourage drug use are generally viewed as secondary only to prior experience with drugs.

Another obvious factor related to drug use initiation is the age of the adolescent. The risk of initiating drug use increases for most drugs to a peak during mid-to-late adolescence and decreases thereafter (Kandel and Logan 1984). Typically tobacco has the youngest age of peak vulnerability. Increased likelihood for beginning use of alcohol, marijuana, and psychedelics occur next. Whereas initial cocaine use typically occurs in young adulthood, this pattern may be changing due to the insurgence of crack, the inexpensive and smokable form of cocaine, which may be more alluring and available to teenagers. Nevertheless, Kandel and Yamaguchi (1993) have demonstrated that use of crack cocaine typically occurs subsequent to use of licit drugs (alcohol and tobacco) as well as marijuana. These patterns may vary when examining specific and homogenous populations such as innercity gang members.

Some types of alcohol and drug abuse may have a genetic component. However, for initiation of drug use and progression to drug abuse, environmental, social, and psychological factors have received the most attention. Although biogenetic influences certainly affect the potential emergence of drug abuse, they are clearly shaped and modified by other personal attributes and environmental conditions (Marlatt et al. 1988).

Despite the compelling notion that the causes of drug use may be different from the causes of drug abuse and dependence, until quite recently little systematic research has addressed this important issue (Glantz and Pickens 1992). This vital research agenda was directly thwarted by political demands to make no distinctions between use and abuse of drugs. Nevertheless, several investigators have found that most drug use occurs due to social influences, whereas the abuse of drugs is more strongly tied to psychological factors and processes such as self-medication against emotional distress (Carman 1979; Newcomb and Bentler 1990; Paton et al. 1977).

Family Influences

Family influences on alcohol and drug use among teenagers, although often excluded from prevention efforts, must be a critical component in adolescent drug treatment programs. Although biogenetic factors certainly represent one type of parental influence on the drug abuse susceptibility of children, parents and other family members affect drug use patterns in other important ways. These factors typically represent socialization processes related to parental modeling of drug-using behaviors, youths' imitation of parents' behaviors, social reinforcement related to internalization of values and behaviors within the family, and social control aspects of parenting and disciplinary activities. Considerable attention has been given to the important factors of family disruption, quality of parent-child relationships, parental support, parents as socialization agents and value inculcators, and parental use of and attitudes towards drugs (Johnson and Pandina 1991; Needle et al. 1990; Newcomb and Bentler 1988*b*, 1988*c*).

In general, familial factors have a greater influence on drug-using behaviors during preadolescence; in adolescence, peer and friendship networks become more prominent factors (Huba and Bentler 1980). Many suggest that parental influences contribute in a substantial manner even at later ages since they create the basis on which the child constructs his/her social world (Johnson and Pandina 1991; Newcomb 1994*a*). Although parents may lose their direct effect on their child's drug use as he/she matures through adolescence, they have already established the trajectory of their child's development and can be considered to have an indirect influence on nearly all later outcomes of the child's life.

Nondrug aspects of parent and family functioning may also affect the likelihood of child drug use. Hawkins and colleagues (1992) categorized these more general familial conditions into three groups: poor and inconsistent family management practices, family conflict, and low bonding to family. Chances of adolescent involvement with drugs are heightened by inconsistent discipline and overly authoritative parenting practices, low and poor quality of parent interaction and involvement with their children, and low aspirations and expectations for their children. Family conflict as reflected in marital distress, divorce and separation, and general family discord also increase the likelihood that children may turn to drugs in attempts to cope with such stress and instability (Newcomb and Harlow 1986; Richardson 1993). These characteristics often prevent secure bonding of the child to the family and as a result also contribute to youthful drug use (Jessor and Jessor 1977; Kandel 1980). Conversely, close, supportive, involved, but not overly intrusive family relationships may protect children from the allure of drugs.

Multiple Risk and Protective Factors

The various influences discussed above have been related to involvement with drug use or abuse, but none has ever been found to be the primary factor that causes drug use or abuse. Because the range of variables leading to initial drug involvement is so large, recent views of this phenomenon have emphasized the risk factor notion often used in medical epidemiology (Bry et al. 1982; Newcomb et al. 1986, 1987; Scheier and Newcomb 1991b). As might be expected, these risk factors include environmental, behavioral, psychological, and social attributes. It seems highly unlikely that any one factor or even a few factors will ever be identified as accounting fully and totally for all variations of drug involvement. Rather, adolescent drug involvement is multiply determined; the more risk factors that encourage drug use one is exposed to, the more likely one will use or abuse drugs. Exposure to more risk factors is not only a reliable correlate of drug use; it increases drug use over time, implying a true etiological role (Newcomb and Felix-Ortiz 1992; Newcomb et al. 1986; Scheier and Newcomb 1991a). This view implies that drug use is but one of several coping responses that can be used when the individual is exposed to an increasing number of vulnerability conditions. The particular factors are not as important as the simple accumulation of vulnerability conditions in the person's life.

The flip side of risk factors for drug use are protective factors that reduce the likelihood and level of drug use and abuse. Protective factors are those psychosocial influences that have a direct effect on limiting or reducing drug involvement (Newcomb 1992b). Very recently, the risk factors approach to the study of drug use and abuse has been expanded to test for multiple protective factors as well (Newcomb 1992b; Newcomb and Feliz-Ortiz 1992).

Protective factors may also operate in a different manner or process than simply having a direct effect on reducing drug involvement. Protective factors may, in fact, buffer or moderate the association between risk factors and drug use and abuse (Brook et al. 1992; Newcomb and Felix-Ortiz 1992; Stacy et al. 1992). Protective factors that moderate the relationship between risk for drug use or abuse can involve aspects of the environment such as maternal affection, sibling personality or behavior, family support, and peers (Brook et al. 1986, 1989, 1991; Stacy et al. 1992; Wills et al. 1992) or the individual, including characteristics of introversion, self-acceptance, or low aggression (Brook et al. 1992; Stacy et al. 1992).

For instance, Stacy and colleagues (1992) found that a high degree of self-acceptance moderated the relationship between peer use of hard drugs and an individual's use of hard drugs; a strong relationship between these variables existed for those low in self-acceptance, but little association was found between these variables in those with high self-acceptance. Similarly, Wills and colleagues (1992) found that both high instrumental (i.e., behavioral or problem-focused) and emotional support reduced the association between major negative events and substance use, compared with those who had low levels of instrumental and emotional support. Newcomb and Felix-Ortiz (1992) have also tested the buffering effects of multiple protective factors on the relationship between multiple risk factors and drug use and abuse. Several significant interaction or moderator effects were noted, primarily for illicit drugs.

An Empirical Example of Multiple Risk and Protective Factors. The findings of Newcomb and Felix-Ortiz (1992) provide a concrete example of these multiple influences. Their paper was based on data from a long-term prospective study of drug use beginning in early adolescence (Newcomb and Bentler 1988*a*, 1988*b*, 1988*c*). The analyses presented here are from the fourth wave of data collection that occurred during mid- to late adolescence. At that time, data were gathered from 896 teenagers (291 males and 605 females) throughout Los Angeles County who had begun participation in the study when they were in the 7th, 8th, and 9th grades. Fourteen items or scales were selected from this database as possible risk or protective factors for drug use. Very few teenagers should have many risk or protective factors (Newcomb and Felix-Ortiz 1992), so the upper and lower 20 percent of the distribution of each factor were specified as either risk or protection. In this way, two variables were created from each factor, one capturing the 20 percent at risk and the other the 20 percent protected. An empirical method was used to assign each factor to either the risk or protective index. These 28 variables (two for each factor) were correlated with five frequency of drug use scales (cigarettes, alcohol, cannabis, cocaine, and other hard drugs). The average correlation (AC) was calculated across the five drugs for each of the 28 variables. A factor was assigned to the risk index if the AC was greater for the risk version of that factor when compared to the AC for the protected version of that factor. If the AC of a factor's protected version was larger than the risk version, the factor was assigned to the protective index.

In this manner seven factors were assigned to the risk index and seven factors to the protective index. These are presented in table 2.

There appears to be a general conceptual distinction between the risk and protective factors based on these empirical results. The protective factor seems to be more psychological, attitudinal, and home related, whereas

TABLE 2. *Cutpoints for the protective and risk factors.*

Factors	Variable Range	Cutpoint for Index	Percent of Sample
		Protective Factors	
Grade point average	1-4	A - F	11.8[a]
Law abidance	4-20	>16	21.1
Religiosity	4-20	>19	18.3
Depression	4-20	= 4	18.9
Self-acceptance	4-20	>18	24.6
Home relationships	8-40	>36	21.0
Sanctions against drug use	6-30	>23	21.9
		Risk Factors	
Educational aspiration	1-6	<3	15.1
Perceived opportunity	3-15	<10	16.6
Deviance	0-42	>6	20.8
Important people/ community support	12-53	>27	21.1
Perceived adult drug use	9-34	>19	20.5
Perceived peer drug use	9-35	>20	18.5
Availability of drugs	6-30	>28	21.0

KEY: [a] = Cutoff closest to 20 percent given the variable's distribution; N=896.

the risk factors appear to be more environmentally embedded. In other words, in terms of these factors examined, risk emerges from the outside or perceived external conditions of the teenager, whereas protective forces are those within the adolescent.

Each of the seven risk factors (scored "0" for no risk and "1" for at risk) was summed in to a multiple risk factor index. Similarly, each of the protective factors (score "0" for no protection and "1" for protected) was summed into a multiple protector factor index. As expected, most teenagers (over 60 percent) received 0 to 1 on each of these indices. Very few received 6 or 7, and therefore were collapsed into the grouping of 5 or more.

One very important question concerns whether risk and protection are simply the opposite ends of a single continuum. This notion would predict that the risk and protection factor indices should be highly negatively correlated. In fact, the correlation between these two indices was a significant, but modest, $r = -0.33$. These two indices are plotted in figure 1, and although there appears to be a linear relationship between the number of risk and protective factors, the association is far from perfect. In fact, there is less than 15 percent variance between the number

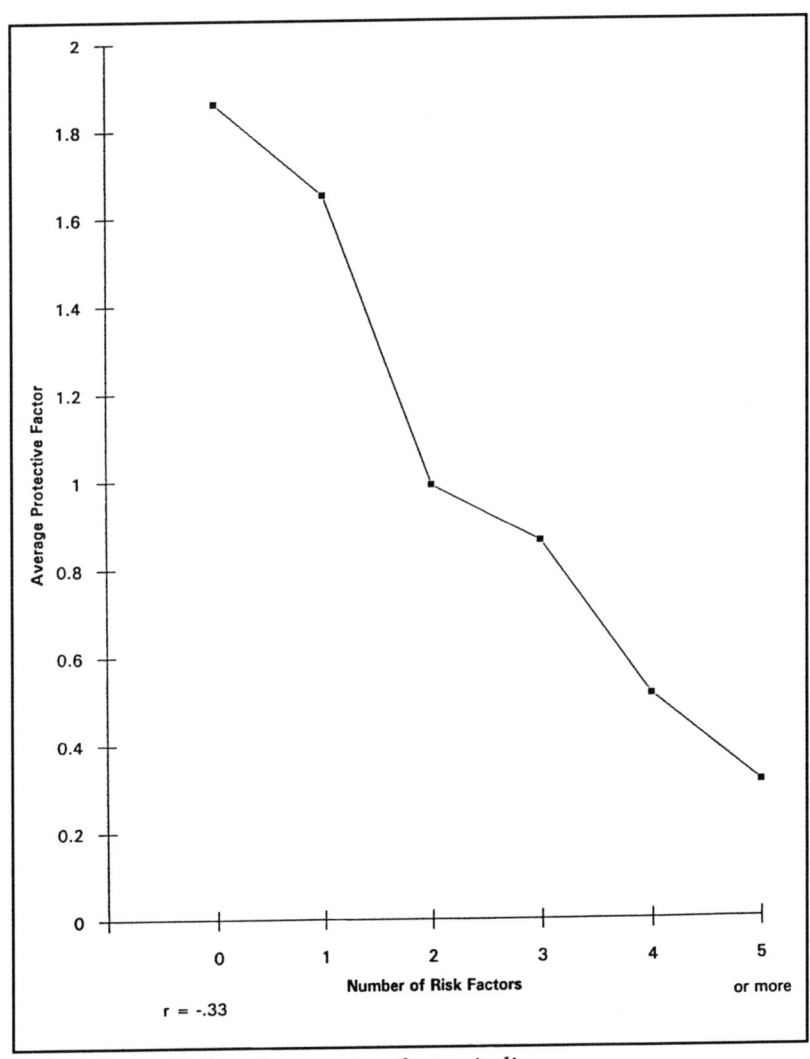

FIGURE 1. *Risk and protection factor indices.*

of risk and protective factors. Based on this empirical determination of risk and protection, they capture both unique conceptual domains and are moderately independent.

Next, these indices were correlated with each of the five drug use scales. All correlations were highly significant in the expected directions (positive for the risk factor index and negative for the protection factor index). These indices are presented in table 3.

TABLE 3. *Correlations between risk and protective factor indices and drug use.*

	Risk Factor Index	Protective Factor Index	Z-difference between Correlations
Cigarettes			
- frequency	0.41	-0.25	4.48
- quantity	0.36	-0.20	4.38
Alcohol			
- frequency	0.51	-0.31	5.91
- quantity	0.43	-0.28	4.26
Cannabis			
- frequency	0.62	-0.29	10.26
- quantity	0.58	-0.26	9.64
Cocaine			
- frequency	0.55	-0.21	9.96
Other hard drugs			
- frequency	0.51	-0.21	8.64

NOTE: All correlations and z-differences are significant ($p < 0.001$).

The Duncan-Clark test was used to compare the magnitude of the absolute value of the correlations for each index. These tests revealed that the apparently greater correlations with the risk index were, in fact, significantly larger when compared to the analogous correlation with the protection index. This risk index correlation indicates that this group of risk factors is significantly more associated with drug use than is this group of protective factors. Nevertheless, when both indices were used to predict drug use in multiple regression analyses, each index contributed significant and unique variance to explaining drug use scores (Newcomb and Felix-Ortiz 1992).

The associations between number of risk factors and frequency of drug use are depicted in figure 2. Similarly, the associations between number of protective factors and drug use frequencies are depicted in figure 3.

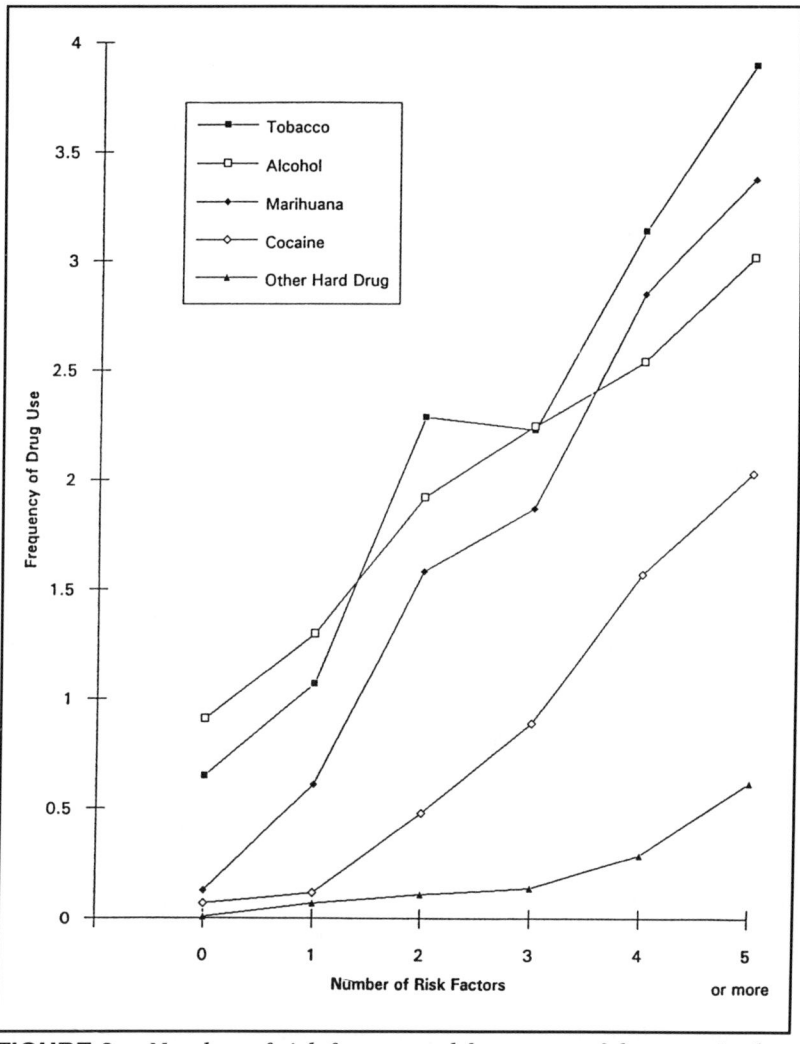

FIGURE 2. *Number of risk factors and frequency of drug use in the past 6 months.*

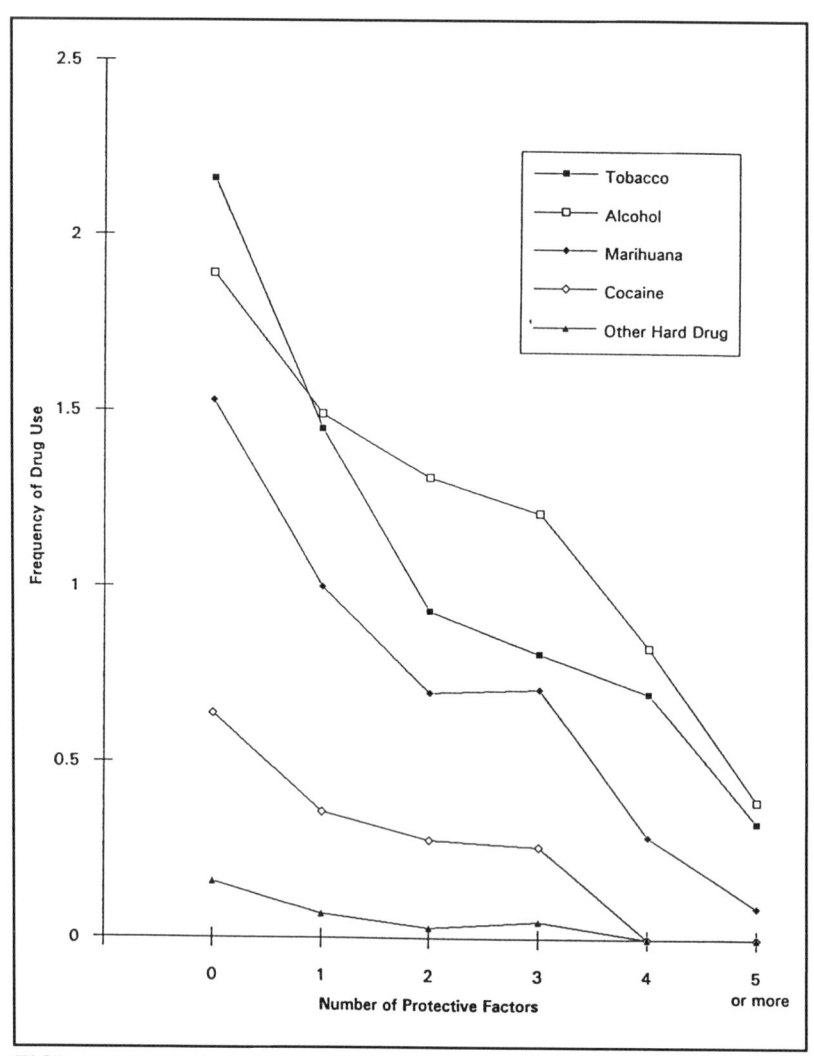

FIGURE 3. *Number of protective factors and drug use frequency in the past 6 months.*

These figures clearly document the positive correlations between the risk factor index and drug use scales (figure 2) and the negative correlations between the protective factor index and the drug use scales (figure 3).

A further concern is how these two indices relate to heavy levels of drug involvement or drug abuse. Quantity of drug use measures were used to generate prevalence rates of tobacco abuse (1/2 pack or more per day), alcohol abuse (5 or more drinks per typical occasion), and marijuana abuse (two or more joints smoked per occasion). These prevalence rates were calculated for each level of the risk or protection factor index and then converted to a hazard rate. A hazard rate of 100 indicated average degree of abuse across the sample. The results for the risk factors are presented in figure 4 and the analogous results for the protective factors are shown in figure 5.

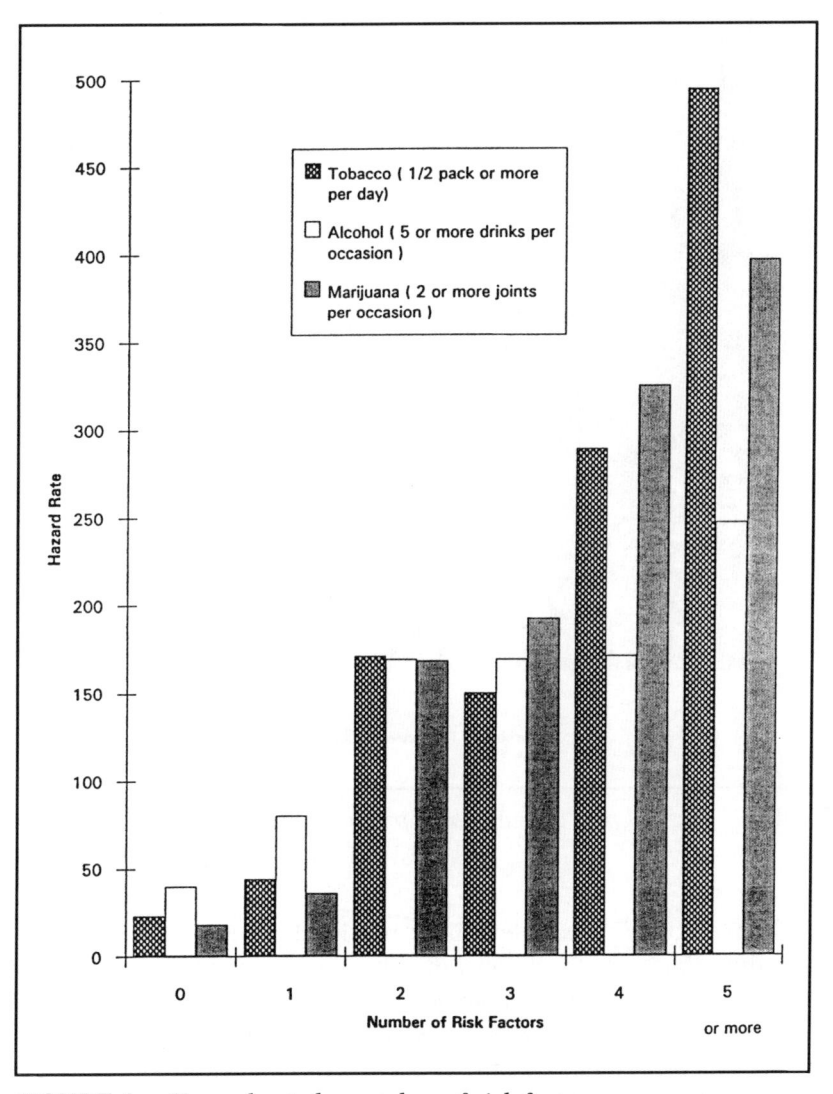

FIGURE 4. *Hazard rate by number of risk factors.*

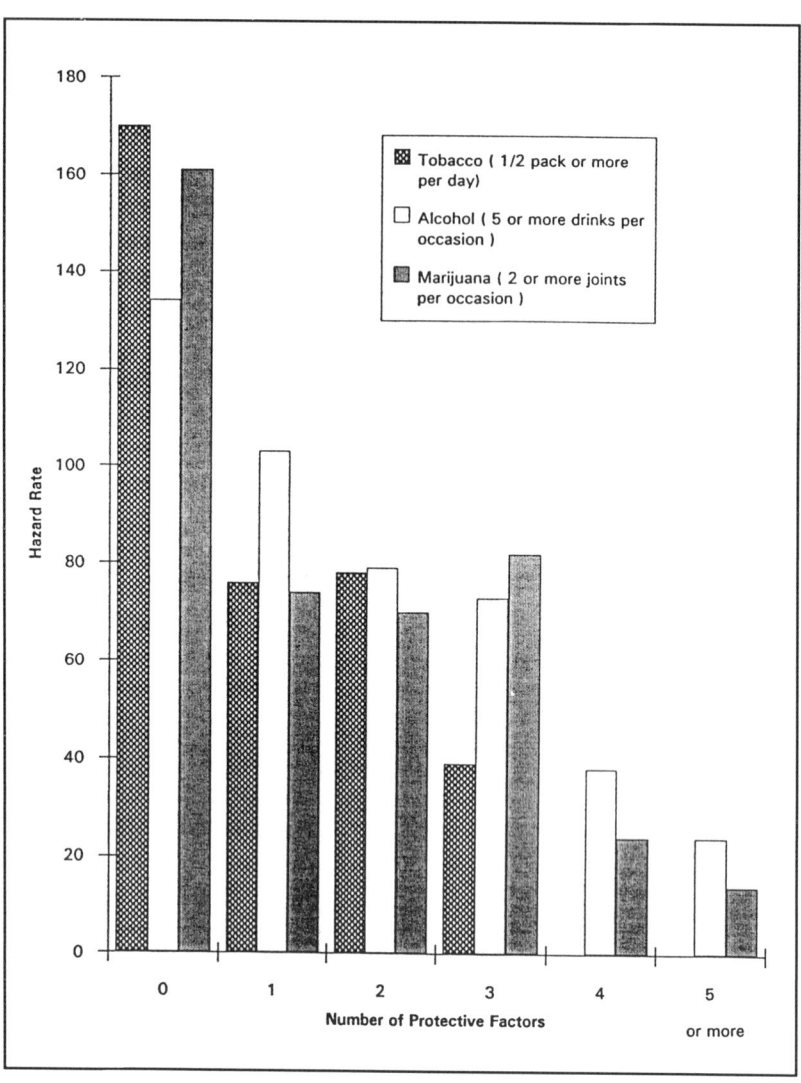

FIGURE 5. *Hazard rate by number of protective factors.*

Both of these figures show a clear linear relationship between the hazard rates for drug abuse and the number of risk factors or number of protective factors, paralleling the frequency of drug use findings. What is interesting, however, is the severe vulnerability to both tobacco and marijuana abuse at high levels of risk, and conversely the extremely low hazard rates for abusing these drugs at high levels of protection. Those with five or more risk factors are nearly five times more likely to abuse tobacco than the average of this sample. On the other hand, virtually no one with five or more protective factors abuses tobacco. Similarly, those with five or more protective factors are over 20 times less likely to abuse marijuana than the general sample.

A final issue involves the buffering role of multiple protective factors when exposed to multiple risk conditions. Does high protection moderate the relationship between risk and drug use? There were several significant interaction effects between multiple risk and protection indices in the Newcomb and Felix-Ortiz (1992) study. The author presents two examples: one for cigarette quantity and the other for hard drug use frequency.

Figure 6 plots the significant interaction effect for cigarette quantity, whereas figure 7 presents the significant interaction effect for hard drug frequency. Both figures show that those with low risk indices had a slightly lower level of drug use in conjunction with high protective indices as compared with those who had low protective indices. On the other hand, those at high risk for drug use reported much greater drug involvement if they had low protective indices compared with those with high protective indices. In other words, protective factors for these two drugs are most important among those at high risk for drug use.

Drug Use and Other Problem Behaviors

Drug use and abuse do not occur as isolated events or as distinct aspects of an individual's behavior. They are typically only aspects or symptoms of a cluster of behaviors and attitudes that form a syndrome or lifestyle of problem behavior or general deviance (McGee and Newcomb 1992; Newcomb and McGee 1991). Problem behavior theory (Jessor and Jessor 1977) provides a valuable conceptualization to understand how teenage drug use reflects one aspect of a deviance-prone lifestyle. Adolescent substance use is only one facet of a constellation of attitudes and behavior that are considered problematic, unconven-tional, or nontraditional for a specific developmental stage. More generally, this syndrome involves "Behavior that is socially defined as a problem, a source of concern, or as undesirable by the norms of conventional society ... and its occurrence usually elicits some kind of social control response" (Jessor and Jessor 1977, p. 33). For adolescents, these deviant behaviors include alcohol abuse, illicit drug use, precocious sexual involvement, academic problems, frequency of various sexual activities, deviant attitudes, and delinquent behavior.

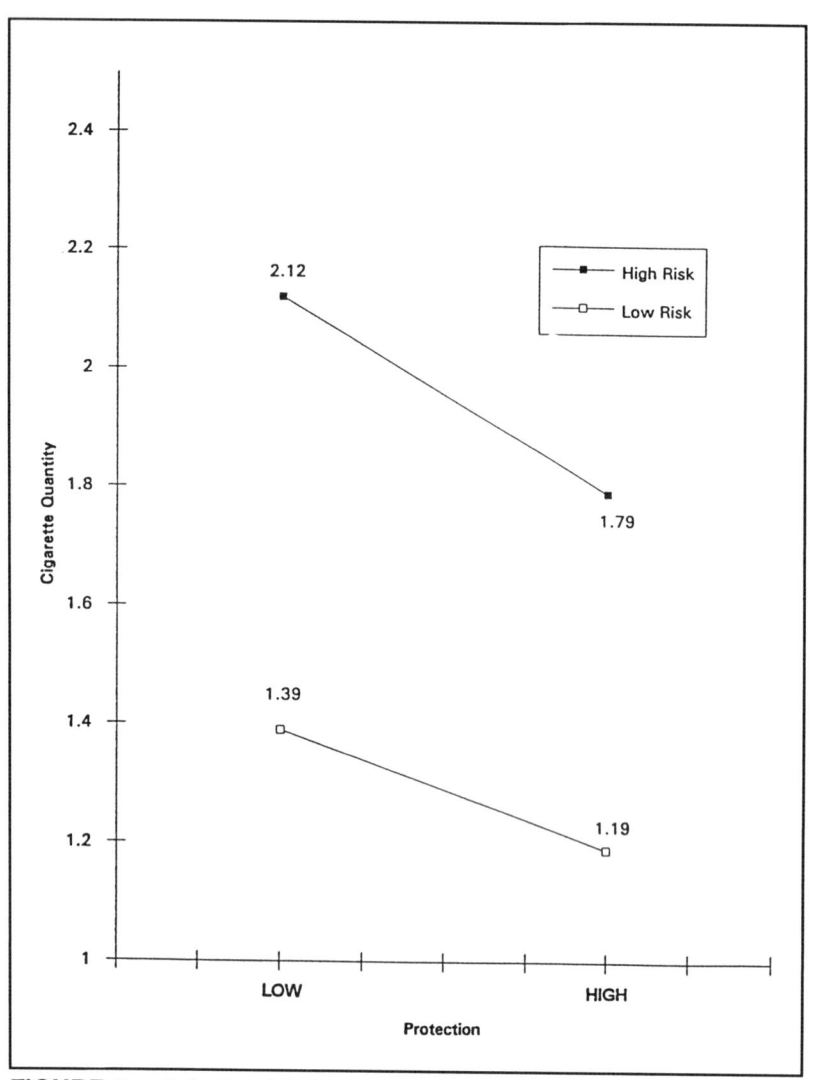

FIGURE 6. *Relationship between protective factors and cigarette use.*

Several studies have confirmed a syndrome of problem behaviors among adolescents and young adults by revealing that either one common latent factor accounts for the correlations among several indicators of problem behavior or that all of these constructs were highly correlated (Donovan and Jessor 1985; McGee and Newcomb 1992; Newcomb and Bentler 1988*a*; Newcomb and McGee 1991). For instance, Newcomb and

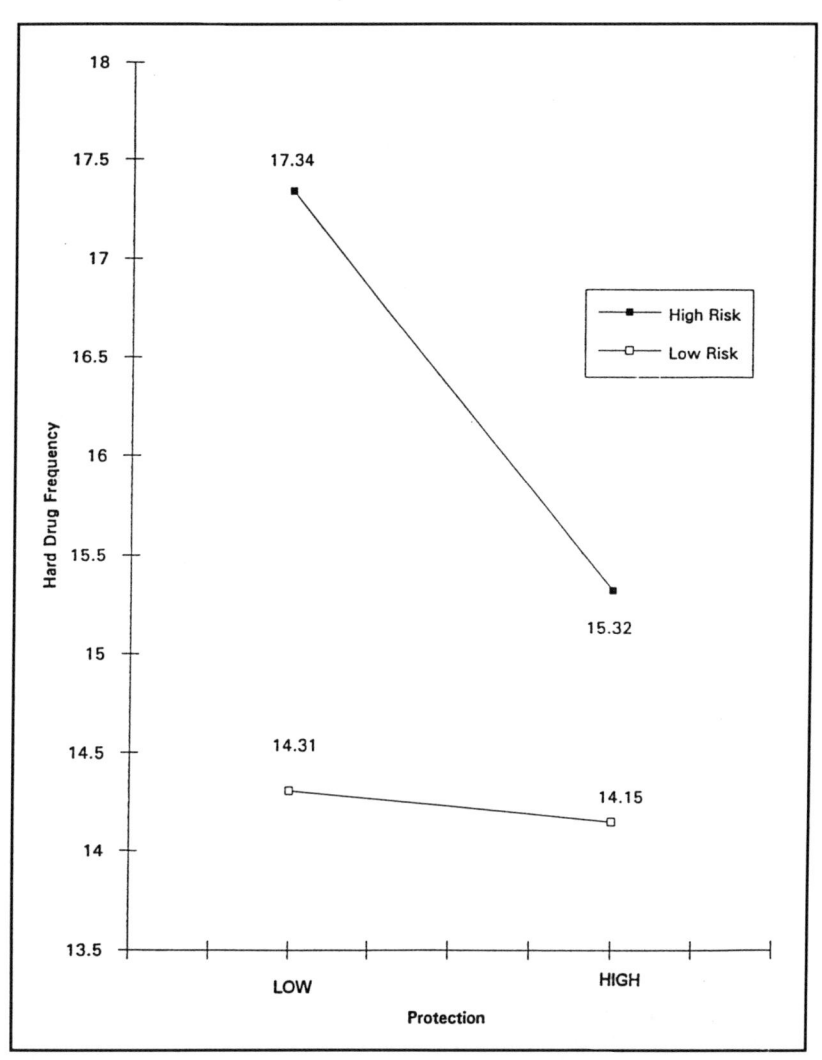

FIGURE 7. *Relationship between protective factors and hard drug use.*

Bentler (1988a) found that teenage polydrug use was highly correlated with low social conformity, criminal activities, deviant friendship network, early sexual involvement, and low academic potential. McGee and Newcomb (1992) used higher-order confirmatory factor analyses to examine the construct of general deviance at four ages from early adolescence to adulthood and found that the construct was highly reliable at early and late adolescence.

An example of this syndrome is depicted in figure 8 as a latent-factor model and represents late adolescence (McGee and Newcomb 1992). A second-order construct of general deviance accounted for significant and substantial portions of variance among five first-order constructs.

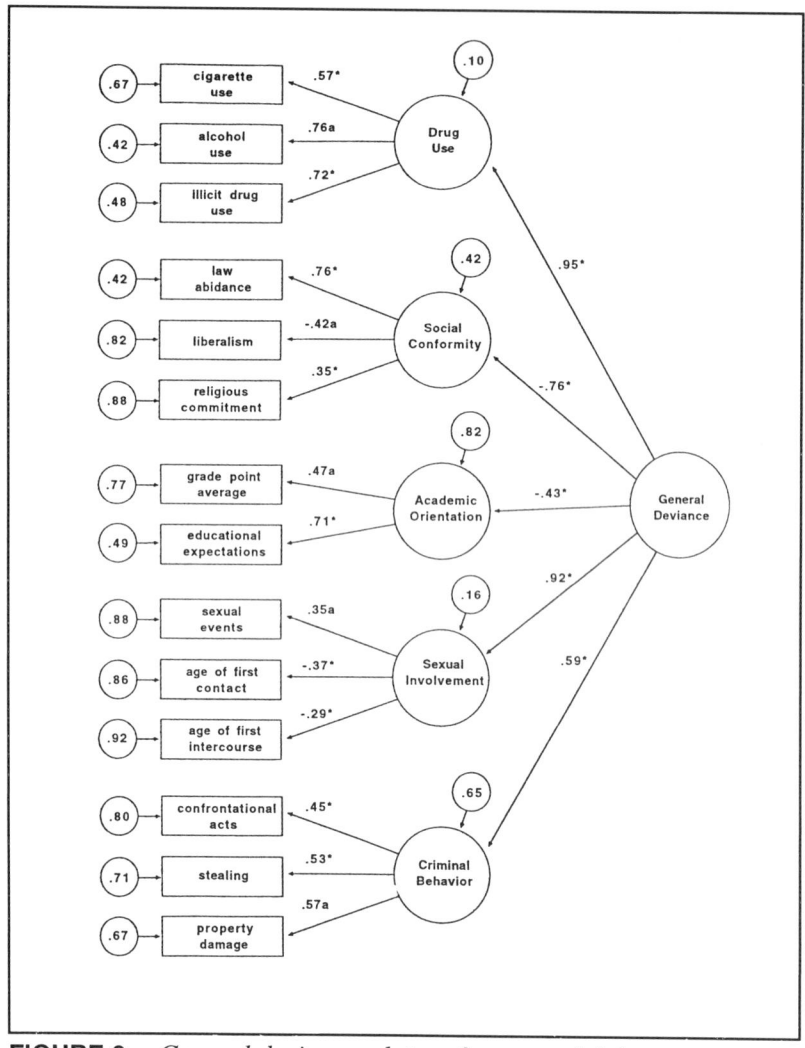

FIGURE 8. *General deviance—latent-factor model, late adolescence.*

KEY: * = p < 0.001; a = fixed at 1.0 in the nonstandard matrix to identify the factor.

General deviance was most represented by the constructs of drug use (90 percent) and sexual involvement (84 percent). The attitudinal construct of low social conformity contributed the third largest variance to general deviance (58 percent), followed by criminal behavior (35 percent) and academic orientation (18 percent).

In short, the concept of problem behavior appears to adequately describe a set of factors that encourage and coexist with adolescent drug use. In terms of prevention and treatment, the implications of this syndrome are clear. Adolescent drug use cannot be prevented or treated without consideration of and attention to the other types of deviance and problems of adolescence. They form an interwoven net of attitudes and behavior that must not be addressed by focusing on single strands without including the total fabric.

Course and Patterns of Drug Involvement

Most teenage users of alcohol or other substances do not become addicted or abusers (Johnston et al. 1991; Kandel and Logan 1984). Even many of those who indulge heavily as teenagers do not develop substance use disorders later in life, although this may vary by type of drug. In one study, the associations between the extent of consumption and abuse (negative consequences) were examined for alcohol, marijuana, and cocaine (Newcomb 1992*b*). There was a substantial association between consumption and abuse consequences for alcohol, a higher degree of association for marijuana, and a perfect association for cocaine. Although no similar study has been conducted for tobacco, it may also rank very high for addictive, if not abuse, potential.

In their review of adolescent drug use studies, Clayton and Ritter (1985, p. 83) found that "More often than not, the persons who are using drugs frequently, are multiple drug users." For instance, in at least one study, cocaine users reported significantly higher prevalence rates for all other types of drugs including cigarettes, alcohol, cannabis, over-the-counter medications, hypnotics, stimulants, psychedelics, inhalants, narcotics, and PCP compared with those who had not used cocaine (Newcomb and Bentler 1986*a*). These large differences were evident for both females and males as adolescents and young adults (Newcomb and Bentler 1986*b*). The association among various types of drug use are so high for teenagers that latent constructs of general polydrug use have been identified distinctly and reliably (Bentler and Newcomb 1986; Newcomb and Bentler 1988 *a,b*).

Another approach to understanding drug involvement is the progression or stage theory. One of the first researchers to investigate this hypothesis found that teenagers initiate drug use with beer, wine, or cigarettes, progress to the use of hard liquor, may then transition to marijuana, and finally may proceed to the use of other illicit drugs (Kandel 1975). Of course, these shifts from a lower stage to a higher stage are not guaranteed, but are probable (Newcomb and Bentler 1989). Involvement at one stage does not necessarily lead to involvement at the next stage, but involvement at a later stage is unlikely without prior involvement at the earlier stage. This notion has been tested in various studies with some important variations. Donovan and Jessor (1983) found that problem drinking occurred later in the progression than general alcohol use. On the other hand, Newcomb and Bentler (1986c) found that several mini-sequences accounted for drug involvement from early adolescence to young adulthood when the roles of cigarettes and nonprescription medications were considered. The mechanisms that drives such staging (e.g., availability, anxiety reduction, peer groups norms, or physiological vulnerability) are not clearly established, though there are some hints that these factors may not be consistently as important at all stages. For example, psychopathology has been implicated primarily at later stages or higher levels of drug involvement and not at initiation.

From a different perspective, accumulating evidence attests to the short- and long-term adverse consequences of teenage drug involvement (Newcomb 1994b). Although some may simply assume that drug use by teenagers always has deleterious outcomes, scientists and clinicians cannot make such unfounded and undocumented conclusions. Although researchers are all too familiar with the tragedies associated with acute drug intoxication of teenagers that include driving injuries and fatalities, likelihood of violence and criminal activities, and estrangement from traditional institutions, the later outcomes of continued drug involvement and mechanisms describing such subsequent consequences are poorly understood (Newcomb and Bentler 1988a). The author has observed that adolescent drug abusers accelerate their development into adulthood but do not acquire the necessary skills and abilities normally acquired during adolescence that permits them to successfully transition into adult life and competently engage in adult behaviors. Others have characterized this deviation in normal maturation as a hiatus in development (Baumrind and Mosselle 1985), continuation of general problem behavior (Newcomb and McGee 1991), or simply impairment of psychosocial functioning (Newcomb and Bentler 1988a, 1988b). Nevertheless, it is unclear what extent of drug use during adolescence and what possibly mediating factors contribute to these potential dysfunctions later in life.

The author concludes that the course of youthful drug use is unclear and not fully understood due to the variations in drugs, drug use patterns, biological vulnerability, and exposure to psychosocial risk and protective factors. It seems prudent to directly confront the use of drugs by youths without overreacting to what may be a typical and (for many) benign experimentation with experiences that characterizes adolescence. Although most adult alcoholics and drug abusers began their patterns of abuse in their youth, most youths who try drugs do not progress to abuse or suffer severe consequences.

Consistent across several studies of the course of youthful drug use is the finding that those adolescents who develop a lifestyle involved with regular and heavy use of drugs experience severe and even tragic outcomes attributable to this abuse either immediately or later in life (Newcomb 1994*b*; Newcomb and Bentler 1988*a*, 1988*b*). Although this area of research is relatively new, there is evidence (Newcomb and Bentler 1987, 1988*a*, 1988*b*) that a linear relationship exists between the level of teenage drug use and later negative consequences. In other words, the more seriously teenagers are involved with drugs, the more adverse the consequences they experience in later life across several domains including educational pursuits, work and job conditions, emotional health, social integration, criminal activities, and family establishment and stability.

There are only two exceptions to this general pattern. First, teenage use of alcohol to the exclusion of all other drugs has been found to have a few positive effects on later life, limited to social relationships and self-feelings (Kandel et al. 1986). Second, Schedler and Block (1990) reported that those who simply tried or experimented with drugs were psychologically healthier than those adolescents who totally abstained (and who were also less well adjusted, more rigid) and those who were heavily involved with drugs (the most poorly adjusted group).

CONCLUSIONS

- There is cause for concern regarding the upturn in drug use among eighth graders, particularly those illicit drugs that may have serious psychological effects (i.e., hallucinogens).

- Not all types of teenage drug use may need prevention or treatment efforts. Targets of such intervention must be carefully determined.

- Teenage drug use is not generated by a single factor or even a few distinct factors. To prevent teenage drug abuse, many of these contributing influences must be confronted and modified. Effective treatment of adolescent drug abuse must also alter the predisposing factors that exist in all domains of the teenager's life including attitudes, behaviors, family, school, peers, and community norms and expectations.

- Teenage drug use does not occur in isolation, but is embedded in a syndrome of other problem behaviors that must be included in prevention and treatment interventions.

- The expected course of adolescent drug involvement is not precisely known, although both immediate and long-term severe problems can occur with heavy involvement or abuse.

- The typical or likely consequences of teenage drug use must be incorporated into both immediate and long-term treatment approaches, since the deficits accrued due to drug involvement may be serious and far-reaching.

- Finally, tobacco and alcohol are the most widely used, abused, and deadly drugs ingested by teenagers. These should top the list of priorities for prevention and treatment.

REFERENCES

American Psychiatric Association. *Diagnostic and Statistical Manual of Mental Disorders.* 4th ed. Washington, DC: American Psychiatric Association, 1994.

Baumrind, D., and Moselle, K.A. A developmental perspective on adolescent drug use. *Adv Alcohol Subst Abuse* 5:41-67, 1985.

Bentler, P.M., and Newcomb, M.D. Personality, sexual behavior, and drug use revealed through latent variable methods. *Clin Psychol Rev* 6:363-385, 1986.

Brook, J.S.; Cohen, P.; Whiteman, M.; and Gordon, A.S. Psychosocial risk factors in the transition from moderate to heavy use or abuse of drugs. In: Glantz, M.D., and Pickens, R., eds. *Vulnerability to Drug Abuse*. Washington, DC: American Psychological Association, 1992. pp. 359-388.

Brook, J.S.; Nomura, C.; and Cohen, P. Prenatal, perinatal, and early childhood risk factors and drug involvement in adolescence. *Genet Soc Gen Psychol Monog* 115(2):221-241, 1989.

Brook, J.S.; Whiteman, M.; Brook, D.W.; and Gordon, A.S. Sibling influences on adolescent drug use: Older brothers on younger brothers. *J Am Acad Child Adoles Psychiatry* 30(6):958-966, 1991.

Brook, J.S.; Whiteman, M.; and Gordon, A.S. Stages of drug use in adolescence: Personality, peer, and family correlates. *Dev Psychol* 19:269-277, 1983.

Brook, J.S.; Whiteman, M.; Gordon, A.S.; and Cohen, P. Dynamics of childhood and adolescent personality traits and adolescent drug use. *Dev Psychol* 19:269-277, 1986.

Bry, B.H.; McKeon, P.; and Pandina, R. Extent of drug use as a function of number of risk factors. *J Abnorm Psychol* 91:273-279, 1982.

Carman, R.S. Motivations for drug use and problematic outcomes among rural junior high school students. *Addict Behav* 4:91-93, 1979.

Clayton, R.R., and Ritter, C. The epidemiology of alcohol and drug abuse among adolescents. *Adv Alcohol Subst Abuse* 4:69-97, 1985.

Donovan, J.E., and Jessor, R. Problem drinking and the dimensions of involvement with drugs: A Guttman scalogram analysis of adolescent drug use. *Am J Pub Health* 73:543-552, 1983.

Donovan, J.E., and Jessor, R. Structure of problem behavior in adolescence and young adulthood. *J Consult Clin Psychol* 53:890-904, 1985.

Glantz, M., and Pickens, R., eds. *Vulnerability to Drug Abuse*. Washington, DC: American Psychological Association, 1992.

Harrison, P.; Hoffmann, N.G.; and Edwall, G.E. Sexual abuse correlates: Similarities between male and female adolescents in chemical dependency treatment. *J Adoles Res* 4:385-399, 1989.

Hawkins, J.D.; Catalano, R.F.; and Miller, J.Y. Risk and protective factors for alcohol and other drug problems in adolescence and early adulthood: Implications for substance abuse problems. *Psychol Bull* 112:64-105, 1992.

Huba, G.J., and Bentler, P.M. The role of peer and adult models for drug taking at different stages in adolescence. *J Youth Adoles* 9:449-465, 1980.

Jessor, R., and Jessor, S.L. *Problem Behavior and Psychosocial Development.* New York: Academic Press, 1977.

Johnson, L.D.; O'Malley, P.M.; and Bachman, J.G. *Drug Use Among American High School Seniors, College Students and Young Adults.* Rockville, MD: National Institute on Drug Abuse, 1991.

Johnson, L.D.; O'Malley, P.M.; and Bachman, J.G. *National Survey Results on Drug Use from the Monitoring the Future Study, 1975-1992.* Vol. I. *Secondary School Students.* Rockville, MD: National Institute on Drug Abuse, 1993.

Johnson, R.I., and Kaplan, H.B. Stability of psychological symptoms: Drug use consequences and intervening processes. *J Health Soc Behav* 31:277-291, 1990.

Johnson, V., and Pandina, R.J. Effects of the family environment on adolescent substance use, delinquency, and coping styles. *Am J Drug Alcohol Abuse* 17:71-88, 1991.

Julien, R.M. *A Primer of Drug Action.* 6th ed. New York: Freeman and Co., 1992.

Kandel, D.B. Stages in adolescent involvement in drug use. *Science* 190:912-914, 1975.

Kandel, D.B. Drug and drinking behavior among youth. *Ann Rev Sociol* 6:235-285, 1980.

Kandel, D.B. Ethnic differences in drug use: Patterns and paradoxes. In: Botvin, G.J., ed. *Multi-Ethnic Drug Abuse Prevention,* in press.

Kandel, D.B., and Logan, J.A. Patterns of drug use from adolescence to young adulthood: I. Periods of risk for initiation, continued use, and discontinuation. *Am J Pub Health* 74:660-666, 1984.

Kandel, D.B., and Yamaguchi, K. From beer to crack: Developmental patterns of drug involvement. *Am J Public Health* 83:851-855, 1993.

Kandel, D.B.; Davies, M.; Karus, D.; and Yamaguchi, K. The consequences in young adulthood of adolescent drug involvement. *Arch Gen Psychiatry* 43:746-754, 1986.

Labouvie, E.W.; Pandina, R.J.; White, H.R.; and Johnson, V. Risk factors of adolescent drug use: An affect-based interpretation. *J Subst Abuse* 2:265-285, 1990.

Lettieri, D.J. Drug abuse: A review of explanations and models of explanations. *Adv Alcohol Subst Abuse* 4:9-40, 1985.

Lewinsohn, P.M.; Hops, H.; Roberts, R.E.; Seeley, J.R.; and Andrews, J.A. Adolescent psychopathology: I. Prevalence and incidence of depression and other DSM-III-R disorders in high school students. *J Abnorm Psychology* 102(1):133-144, 1993.

Marlatt, G.A.; Baer, J.S.; Donovan, D.M.; and Kivlahan, D.R. Addictive behaviors: Etiology and treatment. *Ann Rev Psychol* 3:223-252, 1988.

Maddahian, E.; Newcomb, M.D.; and Bentler, P.M. Adolescent's substance use: Impact of ethnicity, income, and availability. *Adv Alcohol Subst Abuse* 5:63-78, 1986.

McGee, L., and Newcomb, M.D. General deviance syndrome: Expanded hierarchical evaluations at four ages from early adolescence to adulthood. *J Consult Clin Psychol* 60:766-776, 1992.

Medina, A.S.; Wallace, H.M.; Ralph, N.R.; and Goldstein, H. Adolescent health in Alameda County. *J Adolesc Health Care* 2:175-182, 1982.

National Institute on Drug Abuse. *National Household Survey on Drug Abuse: Main Findings*. Rockville, MD: National Institute on Drug Abuse, 1991.

Needle, R.H.; Su, S.S.; and Doherty, W.J. Divorce, remarriage, and adolescent substance use: A prospective longitudinal study. *J Marriage Fam* 52:157-169, 1990.

Newcomb, M.D. Substance abuse and control in the United States: Ethical and legal issues. *Soc Sci Med* 35:471-479, 1992*a*.

Newcomb, M.D. Understanding the multidimensional nature of drug use and abuse: The role of consumption, risk factors, and protective factors. In: Glantz, M.D., and Pickens, R., eds. *Vulnerability to Drug Abuse*. Washington, DC: American Psychological Association, 1992*b*. pp. 255-297.

Newcomb, M.D. Drug use and intimate relationships among women and men: Separating specific from general effects in prospective data using structural equations models. *J Consult Clin Psychol* 62:463-476, 1994*a*.

Newcomb, M.D. Families, peers, and adolescent alcohol abuse: A paradigm to study multiple causes, mechanisms, and outcomes. In: Zucker, R.A.; Boyd, G.M.; and Howard, J., eds. *Development of Alcohol Problems: Exploring the Biopsychosocial Matrix of Risk.* National Institute on Alcohol Abuse and Alcoholism Research Monograph No. 26. Rockville, MD: National Institute on Alcohol Abuse and Alcoholism, 1994*b*. pp. 157-168.

Newcomb, M.D., and Bentler, P.M. Cocaine use among adolescents: Longitudinal associations with social context, psychopathology, and use of other substances. *Addict Behav* 11:263-273, 1986*a*.

Newcomb, M.D., and Bentler, P.M. Cocaine use among young adults. *Adv Alcohol Subst Abuse* 6:73-96, 1986*b*.

Newcomb, M.D., and Bentler, P.M. Frequency and sequence of drug use. A longitudinal study from early adolescence to young adulthood. *J Drug Educ* 16:101-120, 1986*c*.

Newcomb, M.D., and Bentler, P.M. The impact of late adolescent substance use on young adult health status and utilization of health services: A structural equation model over four years. *Soc Sci Med* 24:71-82, 1987.

Newcomb, M.D., and Bentler, P.M. *Consequences of Adolescent Drug Use: Impact on the Lives of Young Adults.* Beverly Hills, CA: Sage, 1988a.

Newcomb, M.D., and Bentler, P.M. Impact of adolescent drug use and social support on problems of young adults: A longitudinal study. *J Abnorm Psychol* 97:64-75, 1988b.

Newcomb, M.D., and Bentler, P.M. The impact of family context, deviant attitudes, and emotional distress on adolescent drug use: Longitudinal latent variable analyses of mothers and their children. *J Res Pers* 22:154-176, 1988c.

Newcomb, M.D., and Bentler, P.M. Substance use and abuse among children and teenagers. *Am Psychol* 44:242-248, 1989.

Newcomb, M.D., and Bentler, P.M. Antecedents and consequences of cocaine use: An eight-year study from early adolescence to young adulthood. In: Robins, L., ed. *Straight and Devious Pathways from Childhood to Adulthood.* New York: Cambridge Press, 1990. pp. 158-181.

Newcomb, M.D., and Felix-Ortiz, M. Multiple protective and risk factors for drug use and abuse: Cross-sectional and prospective findings. *J Pers Soc Psychol* 63:280-296, 1992.

Newcomb, M.D., and Harlow, L.L. Life events and substance use among adolescents: Mediating effects of perceived loss of control and meaninglessness in life. *J Pers Soc Psychol* 51:564-577, 1986.

Newcomb, M.D., and McGee, L. The influence of sensation seeking on general deviance and specific problem behaviors from adolescence to young adulthood. *J Pers Soc Psychol* 61:614-628, 1991.

Newcomb, M.D., and Richardson, M.A. Substance use disorders. In: Hersen, M., and Ammerman, R.T., eds. *Advanced Abnormal Child Psychology.* Hillsdale, NJ: Erlbaum, in press.

Newcomb, M.D.; Maddahian, E.; and Bentler, P.M. Risk factors for drug use among adolescents: Concurrent and longitudinal analyses. *Am J Pub Health* 76:525-531, 1986.

Newcomb, M.D.; Maddahian, E.; Skager, R.; and Bentler, P.M. Substance abuse and psychosocial risk factors among teenagers: Associations with sex, age, ethnicity, and type of school. *Am J Drug Alcohol Abuse* 13:413-433, 1987.

Oetting, E.R., and Beauvais, F. Adolescent drug use: Findings of national and local surveys. *J Consult Clin Psychol* 58:385-394, 1990.

Paton, S.; Kessler, R.C.; and Kandel, D.B. Depressive mood and illegal drug use: A longitudinal analysis. *J Genet Psychol* 131:267-289, 1977.

Peele, S. What can we expect from treatment of adolescent drug and alcohol abuse? *Pediatrician* 14:62-69, 1987.

Regier, D.A.; Farmer, M.E.; Rae, D.S.; Locke, B.Z.; Keith, S.J.; Judd, L.L.; and Goodwin, F.K. Comorbidity of mental disorders with alcohol and other drug abuse. *JAMA* 264(19):2511-2518, 1990.

Richardson, M.A. *"Psychosocial Predictors and Consequences of Recent Drug Use Among Anglo and Hispanic Children and Adolescents."* Unpublished doctoral dissertation, University of California, Los Angeles, 1993.

Scheier, L.M., and Newcomb, M.D. Differentiation of early adolescent predictors of drug use versus abuse: A developmental risk factor model. *J Subst Abuse* 3:277-299, 1991*a*.

Scheier, L.M., and Newcomb, M.D. Psychosocial predictors of drug use initiation and escalation: An expansion of the multiple risk factors hypothesis using longitudinal data. *Contemp Drug Probl* 18:31-73, 1991*b*.

Shedler, J., and Block, J. Adolescent drug use and psychological health: A longitudinal inquiry. *Am Psychol* 45:612-630, 1990.

Stacy, A.W.; Newcomb, M.D.; and Bentler, P.M. Interactive and higher-order effects of social influences on drug use. *J Health Soc Behav* 33:226-241, 1992.

Tolan, P. Socioeconomic, family, and social stress correlates of adolescent antisocial and delinquent behavior. *J Abnorm Child Psychol* 16:317-331, 1988.

Wills, T.A.; Vaccaro, D.; and McNamara, G. The role of life events, family support, and competence in adolescent substance use: A test of vulnerability and protective factors. *Am J Community Psychol* 20(3):349-374, 1992.

Zucker, R.A., and Gomberg, E.S.L. Etiology of alcoholism reconsidered: The case for a biopsychosocial approach. *Am Psychol* 41:783-793, 1986.

ACKNOWLEDGMENT

Preparation of this report was supported by grant DA 01070 from the National Institute on Drug Abuse.

AUTHOR

Michael D. Newcomb, Ph.D.
Professor and Chairperson
Division of Counseling
University of Southern California
Los Angeles, CA 90089-0031

Service Delivery Strategies for Treating High-Risk Youth: Delinquents, Homeless, Runaways, and Sexual Minorities

James A. Farrow

INTRODUCTION

Some populations of adolescents with significant drug- and alcohol-related problems are especially hard to reach. These are children and adolescents who are alienated from family and society: youth in the juvenile justice system, gang members, runaway and homeless youth, and gay or lesbian adolescents. Ample evidence supports the fact that these populations of youth have substance abuse problems and treatment needs. Because these young people are outside of the mainstream social system, special service delivery strategies for identifying, assessing, and treating these high-risk youth are indicated.

HOMELESS/STREET YOUTH

It is very difficult to count the number of runaways in the United States. The best estimates place their numbers at half a million runaways and approximately a third that many "throwaways" in this country (Finkelhor et al. 1990). These estimates go as high as 2 million, however. There seems to be a fairly even gender distribution among runaways, although the number of females is frequently higher in shelters, while young males are more likely to travel farther from home (National Network of Runaway and Youth Services 1991). The median age of runaway youth is between 14 and 16 years (Farber 1987). Since many publicly funded programs will not accept youth over 18 years of age, runaways who do not have contact with shelters are particularly difficult to track. Most runaways come from within a 50-mile radius of home and are highly transient within a particular urban area. Many wander between urban centers along highly traveled corridors. The racial and ethnic makeup of runaways and street youth is similar to that of the nearby community (Administration on Children, Youth and Families 1988).

Impaired relationships with parents or guardians are the main reason for running away from home. A number of studies have shown that fewer than one third of runaways come from homes with both parents present (Kufeldt and Nimmo 1987; Palenski and Launer 1987). Physical and sexual abuse are also major factors; 60 to 75 percent of runaways report serious physical abuse, and the prevalence of sexual abuse is especially high among young women (Powers et al. 1990; Rotheram-Borus and Koopman 1991).

The reasons for the high level of substance abuse and alcoholism in this population are many. For many of these adolescents, drugs play a functional survival role: deadening emotional pain and helping them cope with the uncertainty and the instability of their living situation. Clinical reports indicate that drug dependence also serves to destabilize their lives, making it more difficult for them to utilize services, be reunited with family, or transition to a more stable living situation. In addition, drug abuse increases their risk for health problems, including trauma, sexually transmitted diseases (STDs), and other infections such as human immunodeficiency virus (HIV) and tuberculosis (TB) (Kipke 1991).

In a study of youth in shelters (van Houten and Golembiewski 1978), 76 percent of the youth in 16 shelters surveyed were regular problematic users of alcohol. In a similar study by Schaffer and Caton (1984), a large percentage of shelter users admitted to being significantly intoxicated at least once per week. In a study at a free youth clinic in Los Angeles (Kipke 1991), 69 percent of outpatients reported alcohol use in the past 24 hours. Robertson (1989), in a study focused on Hollywood, CA, runaways and homeless youth, reported that alcohol use began at an early age and that these youth experienced severe social impairment and practiced exaggerated consumption patterns, a pattern and level of substance abuse that was identical to homeless adults on Los Angeles' skid row. Several researchers have noted that, in selected samples of homeless street youth who abused drugs, up to 40 percent met diagnostic criteria for chemical dependency as defined in the "Diagnostic and Statistical Manual of Mental Disorders," 3d. ed. (DSM-III) (Robertson 1989).

In some urban areas, juvenile prostitution and serious drug abuse go hand in hand. In an unpublished survey of adolescent intravenous (IV) drug users in the Seattle-King County Juvenile Detention Center, more than 90 percent of the IV drug users were female (Farrow, unpublished data). In the same survey, more than half of the juvenile females arrested were charged with prostitution. The reasons for this relationship are several and include young adult males controlling young women by promoting prostitution and/or exchanging drugs for sex.

Several studies also point to the comorbidity of alcohol abuse and mental illness in this population. In one Los Angeles study, 11 percent of the homeless youth had major depression and alcohol abuse. It was also noted that major depression, conduct disorder, and posttraumatic stress disorder were diagnosed three times more often than in the nonhomeless population (Robertson 1989).

Service Delivery Strategies for Homeless/Runaways

The most common and urgent need for these young people is stabilization of their living situation. To the extent possible, easy access to shelters and outreach to draw these youth into services are critical. Services are often more acceptable to these youth when they are framed in a health care context. Services should be part of a more comprehensive health service where these youth can receive a variety of assistance in a one-stop, shopping-service center format. There should be no access barriers due to such factors as location, financing, or paperwork.

The storefront triage model of placing a chemical dependency worker in a runaway dropin center or shelter has proven to be a workable model. Programs that use paid peer counselors may be helpful in creating the necessary bonding with the suspicious and alienated youth of the street.

One example of such a program is the DePaul Homeless/Street Youth Day Treatment Project in Portland, OR. The program consists of a pretreatment program that is linked with a street clinic for homeless youth in an urban area. The street clinic adjoins a shelter that provides housing for youth. The DePaul Program provides alcohol and drug assessments, group and individual counseling, and support groups, and meets daily with youth. The program sponsors weekly drug-free social/recreational activities for homeless youth as a referral network for inpatient adolescent treatment. The program also provides transportation, including pickups on street corners. The key features of the model that are important to its success include use of trained peer counselors and outreach workers, transportation, shelter, and on-site assessment (Ingram, unpublished observations).

DELINQUENT/INCARCERATED POPULATIONS

There is significant concern about whether drug abuse among juvenile delinquents represents a public health problem or a criminal justice problem. Because delinquent behavior is so closely associated with drug use and abuse, treatment and rehabilitation for underlying chemical dependency in these populations is often difficult to access and may be nonexistent in some areas of the country. According to Ewing (1993, p. 155),

> Juvenile offenders are likely to be drug and alcohol users and offenders, as well as to suffer from serious emotional disturbance for mental illness. Second, they are likely to have received little or no evaluation, assessment or diagnosis. Third, these youth are likely to have had no appropriate interventions or to have failed in a number of interventions that were not culturally, socially, psychologically, educationally, economically, or developmentally appropriate. Fourth, the families of these youth are not likely to have been involved in any treatment planning or consultation. Fifth, there are no quick fixes. Knowledge concerning the relationship between substance use, substance abuse and criminality remain quite limited.

The interface between substance abuse and criminal behavior has been hotly debated (Farrow and French 1986). Some researchers adamantly hold that there is no causal relationship between substance abuse and criminality (Rosenthal and Nakkash 1982). Others maintain that substance use contributes to some criminal acts but not others (Weitzel and Blount 1982). Some researchers believe that only certain substances contribute to some criminal acts. Yet others maintain that substance use and gender best predict certain criminal behaviors (Miller 1984; Windle and Barnes 1988). Others point out that street drug cultures distinguish themselves by high rates of assault, robbery, and homicide; both users and dealers are continuously victimized by their peers and rivals. Research does suggest a major role for substance abuse in conduct disorders, antisocial personality disorder, and other psychiatric disorders (Kellam et al. 1982; McCord 1979). Some researchers cite substance use as an indicator of a generalized social deviant syndrome that might include psychiatric disorders (Donovan and Jessor 1985; Jessor and Jessor 1977). Many believe that both criminality and drug addiction are manifestations of a defiant lifestyle in which drug use is a form of socialization (Rosenthal and Nakkash 1982). Of course, each of these positions suggests a different treatment perspective.

When substance abuse is viewed as part of generalized deviant behavior, then removing the drug will effectively limit or stop the criminal behavior. This criminal approach teaches prosocial behavior. In contrast, 12-step programs (e.g., Narcotics Anonymous) may isolate one substance (such as cocaine) and specifically target behavior (abstinence) related to that substance. This approach does not claim to affect any behaviors other than dependency or use, emphasizing that responsibility for other destructive conduct rests with the individual. Another viewpoint is that treatment of adolescents must address substance abuse and other underlying problems in the context of concurrent psychiatric diagnoses, learning disorders, family interactions, internal conflicts, and developmental issues. In essence, it sees the problem as both a symptom and a specific disorder.

Strategies With Incarcerated Delinquents

The approach to assessment and treatment of incarcerated youth depends significantly on the size of the facility and the duration of the stay. In short-term facilities an educational model has generally been proposed and 12-step programs implemented. Some educational models have been expanded to include aspects of social learning theory and effective education that have been more traditionally used in therapeutic communities. One example is the Paradigm Program in the Seattle-King County Youth Detention Center. In this program, preadjudicated youth stay in a special "straight-ahead" unit. More intensive intervention necessitates separating these youth from the corrections subculture, which considers active involvement and treatment to be a sign of weakness. The program involves an intensive approach to education and focuses on the development of self-esteem through values clarification and the enhancement of personal skills and decisionmaking techniques. The program also targets general life skills relevant to the use and sale of drugs including financial aspects, family effects, and risk of HIV infection. Youth receive individual and group education as well as drug and alcohol counseling, assessment, and access to on-site mental health, physical health, and HIV diagnostic services. The program has the capacity to diagnose chemical dependency and offer residential drug and alcohol treatment as an alternative to incarceration.

In long-term State-run juvenile correction facilities, actual 60- to 90-day comprehensive residential programs have been designed.

Key Strategies for Incarcerated Youth

In short-term facilities, screening, detoxification with medical monitoring, formal assessment, and basic cognitive behavioral group education should be components of a detention-based program. A beginning 12-step group should be offered to those who want to remain drug free for longer periods of time. To date there is no clear evidence that court-ordered referral to treatment is any more effective than treatment that is not court ordered. However, it may be that for those youth with few social supports and inadequate housing, court referrals allow access to treatment. Long-term facilities should include the family in treatment and provide specialized services that address contributory problems such as domestic violence and parental neglect. Long-term facilities should also provide more extensive transitional services as the adolescents reenter their home community.

SEXUAL MINORITY YOUTH

Studies have noted high rates of suicide in association with drug abuse among homosexual youth. In one study (Remafedi et al. 1991) that reviewed psychosocial characteristics of gay adolescents who attempted suicide, a high degree of illicit drug use (85 percent) was noted. There were reports of runaway behavior, multiple arrests, prostitution, and alcohol use among this same population. The results also indicated that 22 percent of attempted suicides had undergone chemical dependency treatment. Explanations for the association between depression, suicide, and substance abuse in this population are many. One reason directs attention to the turmoil over the "coming out" process, especially with the child's disclosure to the parents. Another suggests a connection between "sexual milestones" and suicide attempts. Additionally, suicide and substance abuse in this population appear to be aggravated by societal discrimination, violence, loss of friendships, and current personal attitudes toward homosexuality. While suicide in adolescent sexual minority populations was not significantly associated with runaway behavior, drug abuse was. In the Remafedi and Farrow sample, bisexuality, homosexuality, and sexual concerns were not associated with suicide, while other research points to a stronger relationship between substance abuse and homosexual self-identity (Horvitz and White 1987).

For many lesbian and gay young adults, the socialization process includes frequenting establishments in areas where alcohol and drug use are part of the lifestyle and the social experience. In addition, there are known relationships between sexual and substance abuse as well as runaway behavior and substance abuse. Both of these victimization factors are overrepresented among gay and lesbian youth (Remafedi and Farrow 1991).

SERVICE DELIVERY STRATEGIES FOR SEXUAL MINORITY YOUTH

Specialized drug and alcohol assessment and treatment programs have been developed for adult sexual minority groups, some of which derive from programs traditionally designed for mental patients. Many of these programs provided services to adolescents within the context of outpatient and inpatient treatment programs sensitive to sexual minority concerns. These programs recognized that these youth often lack parental and peer support for recovery; therefore, these youth are paired with recovering sponsors who are gay or lesbian to help the youth maintain abstinence and a healthier lifestyle after treatment.

One such program is Stonewall Recovery Services, which provides treatment at a variety of sites. These youth treatment programs have considerable flexibility, providing services in centrally located treatment facilities as well as offering outreach education, assessment, and group treatment in schools and dropin centers.

OVERALL RECOMMENDATIONS FOR RESEARCH CONCERNING HIGH-RISK YOUTH

1. Ethnographic studies are needed to look at treatment experiences of these populations and the environmental and intrapersonal reasons for dropout.

2. There is a need to test "streetside or detention-based" brief interventions, especially those using peer counseling strategies.

3. There is a need to study day treatment models especially in juvenile detention centers, shelters for homeless youth, and dropin centers for gay and lesbian youth.

4. Systems and health policy research are needed to promote chemical dependency rehabilitation within the juvenile justice system.

5. There is a need to develop public financing strategies for adolescent treatment. There are many more high-risk youth without resources who need treatment.

6. Interactive computer models need to be tested with high-risk populations to promote healthier behaviors and limit drug use and drug-related risk behavior.

7. General descriptions of treatment techniques and outcomes are needed for the drug/alcohol dependence and criminality of adolescents with conduct disorders. Almost nothing is known about how these youth are treated. Researchers have almost no outcome studies, even considering nonscientific reports.

REFERENCES

Administration on Children, Youth and Families (ACYF). *Annual Report to the Congress on the Runaway Homeless Youth Program, Fiscal Year 1988.* Washington, DC: U.S. Department of Health and Human Services, 1988.

Donovan, J.E., and Jessor, R. Structure of problem behavior in adolescence and young adulthood. *J Consult Clin Psychol* 53(6):890-904, 1985.

Ewing, J. Substance abuse programs. In: Thompson, L.S., and Farrow, J.A., eds. *Hard Time, Healing Hands: Developing Primary Health Care Services for Incarcerated Youth.* Arlington, VA: National Center for Education in Maternal and Child Health, 1993.

Farber, E. The adolescent who runs. In: Brown, B.S., and Mills, A.R., eds. *Youth at High Risk for Substance Abuse.* Rockville, MD: National Institute on Drug Abuse, 1987.

Farrow, J.A., and French, J. The drug abuse-delinquency connection revisited. *Adolescence* 21(84):951-960, 1986.

Finkelhor, D.; Hotaling, G.; and Sedlak, A. *Missing, Abducted, Runaway and Throwaway Children in America: First Report: Numbers and Characteristics: National Incidence Studies.* Washington, DC: Office of Juvenile Justice and Delinquency Prevention, Office of Justice Programs, U.S. Department of Justice. Washington, DC: Supt. of Docs., U.S. Govt. Print. Off., 1990.

Horvitz, A.V., and White, H.R. Gender role orientations and styles of pathology among adolescents. *J Health Soc Behav* 28:158-170, 1987.

Jessor, R., and Jessor, S.L. *Problem Behavior and Psychosocial Development: A Longitudinal Study of Youth.* New York: Academic Press, 1977.

Kellam, S.G.; Stevenson, D.L.; and Rubin, B.R. How specific are the early predictors of teenage drug use? In: Harris, L.S., ed. *Problems of Drug Dependence, 1981.* National Institute on Drug Abuse Research Monograph No. 41. Washington, DC: Supt. of Docs., U.S. Govt. Print. Off., 1982.

Kipke, M.D. "HIV and Substance Abuse Among Homeless Youth." Paper presented at the annual American Public Health Association Conference, Atlanta, GA, October 1991.

Kufeldt, K., and Nimmo, M. Youth on the street: Abuse and neglect in the eighties. *Child Abuse Negl* 11:531-543, 1987.

McCord, J. Some child-rearing antecedents of criminal behavior in adult men. *J Pers Soc Psychol* 37:1477-1486, 1979.

Miller, R.E. Nationwide profile of female inmate substance involvement. *J Psychoactive Drugs* 16(4):319-326, 1984.

National Network of Runaway and Youth Services, Inc. *To Whom Do They Belong? Runaway, Homeless and Other Youth in High-Risk Situations in the 1990's.* Washington, DC: National Network of Runaway and Youth Services, Inc., 1991.

Palenski, J., and Launer, H. The "process" of running away: A redefinition. *Adolescence* 22:347-462, 1987.

Powers, J.; Eckenrode, J.; and Jaklitsch, B. Maltreatment among runaway and homeless youth. *Child Abuse Negl* 14:87-98, 1990.

Remafedi, G.; Farrow, J.A.; and Deisher, R.W. Risk factors for attempted suicide in gay and bisexual youth. *Pediatrics* 87(6):869-875, 1991.

Robertson, M.J. *Homeless Youth: Patterns of Alcohol Use.* Report prepared for the National Institute on Alcohol Abuse and Alcoholism. Berkeley, CA: Alcohol Research Group, 1989.

Rosenthal, B.J., and Nakkash, K. Drug addiction and criminality: A model for predicting the incidence of crime among a treatment population. *J Drug Issues* 3:293-303, 1982.

Rotheram-Borus, M., and Koopman, C. Sexual risk behaviors, AIDS knowledge, and beliefs about AIDS among runaways. *Am J Public Health* 81:208-210, 1991.

Schaffer, D., and Caton, C.L.M. Runaway and Homeless Youth in New York City: A Report to the Ittleson Foundation. New York: Division of Child Psychiatry, New York State Psychiatric Institute and Columbia University College of Physicians and Surgeons, 1984.

van Houten, T., and Golembiewski, G. *Life Stress as a Predictor of Alcohol Abuse and/or Runaway Behavior.* Washington DC: American Youth Work Center, 1978.

Weitzel, S.L., and Blount, W.R. Incarcerated female felons and substance abuse. *J Drug Issues* 3:259-273, 1982.

Windle, M., and Barnes, G.M. Similarities and differences in correlates of alcohol consumption and problem behaviors among male and female adolescents. *Int J Addict* 23(7):707-728, 1988.

AUTHOR

James A. Farrow, M.D.
Director
Division of Adolescent Medicine
University of Washington, WJ-10
Seattle, WA 98195

Adolescent Substance Use Disorder with Conduct Disorder and Comorbid Conditions

Thomas J. Crowley and Paula D. Riggs

INTRODUCTION

A syndrome of general deviance characterizes adolescents who become involved with drugs, and those with diagnoses of conduct disorder (CD) epitomize that deviance. CD frequently is comorbid with substance use disorders. Although CD appears to be very common among youths entering substance treatment programs, the condition apparently is infrequently recognized in that setting. This chapter aims to familiarize substance clinicians and researchers with CD and its comorbid conditions. Antisocial personality disorder (ASPD) does not occur in the absence of CD in childhood, although perhaps half of children with CD do not develop adult ASPD. ASPD occurs in 2 to 3 percent of adult Americans, and CD apparently is somewhat more common than this in children; it is more prevalent among boys. Numerous family and social problems are strongly associated with CD, and probably contribute to the number and severity of symptoms. However, there is growing evidence that personality characteristics of CD, impulsiveness and aggressiveness, also are under genetic control, and CD-ASPD strongly tend to run in families. Numerous studies indicate that CD is favorably influenced during treatment in childhood or adolescence. In the short run, both medications and psychosocial treatments are beneficial. But no studies have demonstrated a long-term effect on the symptoms of CD after treatment ends.

Perhaps one-third to one-half of children with CD also have attention deficit-hyperactivity disorder (ADHD). Children with ADHD and CD are significantly more likely than children with either disorder alone to have family members with ASPD and/or substance use disorders. They apparently have more severe CD with a greater likelihood of continuing on to ASPD, and their risk for substance use disorders is elevated. Major depressive disorder (and perhaps dysthymia) may occur in 15 to 20 percent of adolescents with CD who are admitted to substance abuse treatment programs. Suicidal thoughts and a history of suicide attempts also are common in these adolescents. Few substance abuse treatment programs apparently diagnose, or focus treatment on, comorbid depression in these youths. CD and ASPD are associated frequently with, and usually predate, substance use disorders. Such heavy drug use in adolescence is serious and may increase mortality rates as much as fivefold. No particular CD symptom is especially predictive of drug use, but the total number of such symptoms is strongly associated with the probability of drug use and with earlier onset of substance problems.

Substance use and related problems are not randomly distributed among adolescents. Certain traits are associated with earlier, heavier, and more problematic substance use. These risk factors, many identified by Jessor and Jessor (1977), include peer drug use, school suspensions, law infringements, truancy, conflict with parents, and regular smoking (Swadi 1992; Vaillant 1983), lower school aspirations, more school failures, emotional distress and life dissatisfaction, depression, impulsiveness, restlessness and rebelliousness with unconventional attitudes, diminished verbal proficiency, and less church attendance (Adlaf and Smart 1985; Kandel and Raveis 1989; Knop et al. 1985; Newcomb and Felix-Ortiz 1992; Rydelius 1983*a, b*; Smith and Fogg 1978). Other associated traits include aggression, especially when combined with shyness (Goodwin et al. 1975; Kellam et al. 1983) and high novelty-seeking with low harm avoidance (Cloninger et al. 1988). For example, among boys followed prospectively into their thirties, those characterized in adolescence by rebelliousness, hostility, unconventionality, limit-testing, negativism, and being undercontrolled were at significant risk to become problem drinkers in adulthood (Block 1971; Jones 1968). Bry (1983) showed that such risk factors have a cumulative effect, and that the presence of more factors raises the risk of drug (including alcohol) abuse.

Jessor and Jessor (1977) found that behaviors of general deviance were associated with current drug use in high school students, and when the students were followed up 7 years later (Donovan et al. 1983) the high school measures of those traits still predicted problem drinking. What distinguished the adolescents headed toward problem drinking, those authors concluded, "Appears not to be specific predisposition toward problems with alcohol, but rather a generalized proneness toward problem behavior in adolescence" (Donovan et al. 1983, p. 133).

Indeed, adolescent drug use, together with low academic orientation, low social conformity, criminality, and early sexual involvement may comprise a general deviance syndrome, and the greater a youth's problems in one of these areas, the greater the risk of problems in the others (Donovan et al. 1988; Hundleby et al. 1982; McGee and Newcomb 1992).

Youths who display the extremes of these characteristics may seek or be sent to treatment. Whether such youths are viewed as being at one end of a dimensional antisocial spectrum or as having a unique disorder, clinicians deal with youths at the extreme. Such youths usually qualify for diagnoses of CD. Table 1 lists CD diagnostic criteria from the "Diagnostic and Statistical Manual of Mental Disorders" (3d ed. rev.) (DSM-III-R) (American Psychiatric Association 1987), together with new criteria from DSM-IV (American Psychiatric Association 1994).

In addition to these diagnostic symptoms of CD, Dishion and colleagues (1984) found that delinquent youths (most of whom probably have CD) have associated wide-ranging skill deficits in school and in interpersonal competence, interpersonal problem solving, reading achievement and verbal intelligence, homework skills, and in accomplishing chores.

"Conduct disorders are complex conditions for which as yet there are no adequate explanations or predictably reliable treatments" (O'Donnell 1985, p. 250). Kazdin and colleagues (1987*b*, p. 76) stated that this kind of antisocial behavior among children and adolescents:

> [Particularly aggressive acts] are relatively prevalent among community samples, serve as the basis for one-third to one-half of clinical referrals among children, are relatively stable over the course of development, often portend major dysfunction in adulthood (e.g., criminal behavior, alcoholism, antisocial personality), and are likely to be transmitted to one's offspring ... to date few treatments have been shown to alter antisocial behavior in clinical samples [of youths]; none has been shown to controvert the poor long-term prognosis.

Sturdy predictors of adult antisocial behavior were found by Robins (1978) in youths followed into adulthood. Adult antisocial behavior was virtually nonexistent without previous childhood antisocial behavior. However, half or more of antisocial children (those with CD in current terminology) did not become antisocial adults. The overall number and variety of childhood antisocial characteristics predicted adult antisocial

TABLE 1. *Diagnosis of conduct disorder, arranged in order of DSM-III-R criteria.*

DSM-III-R	DSM-IV
A. A disturbance of conduct lasting at least 6 months, during which at least three of the following have been present:	A. A repetitive and persistent pattern of behavior in which the basic rights of others or major age-appropriate societal norms or rules are violated, as manifested by the presence of three (or more) of the following criteria in the past 12 months, with at least one criterion present in the past 6 months:
(1) has stolen without confrontation of a victim on more than one occasion (including forgery)	(12) has stolen items of nontrivial value without confronting a victim (e.g., shoplifting, burglary, forgery)
(2) has run away from home overnight at least twice while living in parental or parental surrogate home (or once without returning)	(14) has run away from home overnight at least twice while living in parental or parental surrogate home (or once without returning for a lengthy period)
(3) often lies (other than to avoid physical or sexual abuse)	(11) often lies to obtain goods or favors or to avoid obligations (i.e., "cons" others)
(4) has deliberately engaged in fire setting	(8) has deliberately engaged in fire setting with the intention of causing serious damage
(5) is often truant from school (for older person, absent from work)	(15) is often truant from school, beginning before age 13 years
(6) has broken into someone else's house, building, or car	(10) identical
(7) has deliberately destroyed others' property	(9) identical

52

TABLE 1. *Diagnosis of conduct disorder, arranged in order of DSM-III-R criteria (continued).*

DSM-III-R	DSM-IV
(8) has been physically cruel to animals (other than by fire setting)	(5) identical
(9) has forced someone into sexual activity with him or her	(7) has forced someone into sexual activity
(10) has used a weapon in more than one fight	(3) has used a weapon that can cause serious physical harm to others (e.g., a bat, brick, broken bottle, knife, gun)
(11) often initiates physical fights	(2) identical
(12) has stolen with confrontation of a victim (e.g., mugging, purse snatching, extortion, armed robbery)	(6) has stolen while confronting a victim (e.g., mugging, purse snatching, extortion, armed robbery)
(13) has been physically cruel to people	(4) identical
(-) No corresponding item	(1) often bullies, threatens, or intimidates others
(-) No corresponding item	(13) often stays out at night despite parental prohibitions, beginning before age 13 years
(-) No corresponding item	B. The disturbance in behavior causes clinically significant impairment in social, academic, or occupational functioning.
B. If 18 or older, does not meet criteria for Antisocial Personality Disorder.	C. If 18 years or older, criteria not met for Antisocial Personality Disorder.

behavior better than any particular childhood behavior. Neither family background nor social class were better predictors than the childhood behavior. Having been placed out of the home, poverty, and number of years living with both parents did tend to predict which youths would become antisocial adults, but the children's behaviors were better predictors. Although many conduct-disordered youths recovered, the relationship with adult antisocial behavior was still so strong that Robins concluded, "Severe adult antisocial behavior is a syndrome and so is severe childhood antisocial behavior, and ... the two are closely interconnected, probably part of a single process" (Robins 1978, p. 617).

Since CD probably is the acme of a general deviance syndrome, and since substance problems are common in the latter, they may be in the former as well. A review by Bukstein and colleagues (1989, p. 1136) concluded that "The association [on the one hand] of substance abuse and [on the other] CD in adolescents and Antisocial Personality Disorder in adults appears well established."

Although good descriptions of CD are available (Kazdin 1985; O'Donnell 1985; Quay 1986; Rutter and Hersov 1985), many drug-abuse clinicians and researchers remain unfamiliar with the condition. For example, a massive substance abuse textbook (Lowinson et al. 1992) does not list CD in its extensive index. Complicating matters, ADHD and mood disorder often are comorbid with CD. This chapter reviews the comorbid relationships of CD and other psychiatric illnesses to clarify their relationships to substance use disorders, and ends by summarizing certain gaps in the knowledge of these disorders.

CASE DESCRIPTION

Clinical History

A 16-year-old Hispanic boy was referred to a residential treatment program by a social service department after probation revocation. He had two assault charges, another for brandishing a knife, charges for trespassing, repeated parole violations, and extensive truancy. The referring agency also was concerned about problems resulting from use of alcohol, cannabis, and inhalants.

The youth had begun drinking at age 14, and very soon was consuming about 9 beers and a pint of cheap wine each day. Some of the drinking was with his alcoholic mother. At the same age he began inhaling paint fumes and soon was doing so about 3 days per week, all day. At 15 years he began marijuana use, quickly escalating to about 4 joints daily.

The boy's father, mother, all 4 grandparents, and various aunts and uncles all were alcoholic. The father also used heroin and marijuana. The parents had divorced when the youth was 6 years old. The children stayed with the father until the boy was 10, when they were taken by social services because of the sexual abuse of a younger sister by the patient's father and older brother; that brother also had fondled the patient. The father then attempted suicide, but after 90 days in jail he got the children back. Meanwhile, the father was unemployed and supported his drug habit with his welfare checks and by stealing. The patient was placed in a foster home for a year at age 12 because of the continued family problems, and in a group home at age 15 because of his gang involvement and fights with family members. He was referred to the authors' residential treatment program because of the parole violations.

The boy ran from the open program on the third day and lived on the streets until he was arrested 6 months later. He then said he wanted treatment because he was tired of being intoxicated all the time. His DSM-III-R diagnoses upon admission were CD, alcohol dependence, cannabis abuse, and inhalant abuse (about 20 percent of admissions to the authors' treatment program also have diagnoses of major depression or dysthymia, but this boy did not.) On the peak aggression scale (the authors' modification of a scale by Lewis et al. 1982) he scored 7, which requires at least one of the following: fight-related injuries to others requiring medical attention, rape, attempted murder, injury-arson, armed robberies, gun or knife or blunt weapon fights. The program's special education teacher measured the patient's mathematics skills at grade level 2 to 3 and his reading skills at grade 6.

During treatment he made slow, steady gains in social skills, and during about a year of structured residential treatment he never was violent and never used drugs or alcohol. His father then claimed to be substance free, but this claim could not be verified because the father was so irregular in attending family therapy. The mother was on the streets drinking throughout this time. The youth suffered a major setback in treatment when a beloved older brother was killed in a gang fight. The boy later wanted a pass to visit the gravesite when his family drove there, but his father said that he could not go along because the father had too many dirty clothes in the car. A counselor had to drive the youth about 100 miles to the cemetery.

At this writing the youth is 18 years old and lives in a lightly supervised emancipation apartment which he rents from the program. He continues in outpatient treatment and attends the program's special school, where he is expected to obtain a high school equivalency diploma in a few months. He works two part-time jobs and has remained substance free and nonviolent. When asked by a group of visiting legislators why he had stayed after the second admission he answered, "Because they care about you here."

Comment on History

Disorders of this kind are catastrophic and potentially life-threatening for the individual and those around him. The authors and colleagues try to evaluate contributors to patients' substance problems according to widely demonstrated risk factors (figure 1). Drugs were easily available to this patient, and drug use was well accepted by his family and peers (in this chapter the term "drugs" always includes alcohol and nicotine). Alcohol pharmacologically reinforces its own self-administration (Crowley et al. 1992). The prevalence and persistence of frequent marijuana use among youths with CD suggests that its use is also reinforcing to them, although neither marijuana nor tetrahydrocannabinol (THC) usually reinforce self-administration in animals.

Risk taking and rule breaking characterize all youths with CD (table 1). This patient reported 4 CD symptoms on the Diagnostic Interview Schedule for Children (DISC) (Shaffer et al. 1990); only 3 are required for the diagnosis. The peak aggression score was 7, and there can be little doubt that this young man had severe problems of risk taking and rule breaking.

Personal and family history of substance use, gender, and age are all important predictors of further substance problems. This patient's extensive substance use history, with one diagnosis of full-blown dependence and two of abuse; the extraordinary family history of alcoholism (together with paternal heroin and marijuana problems); the male gender; and late adolescent age all suggest a high relapse risk.

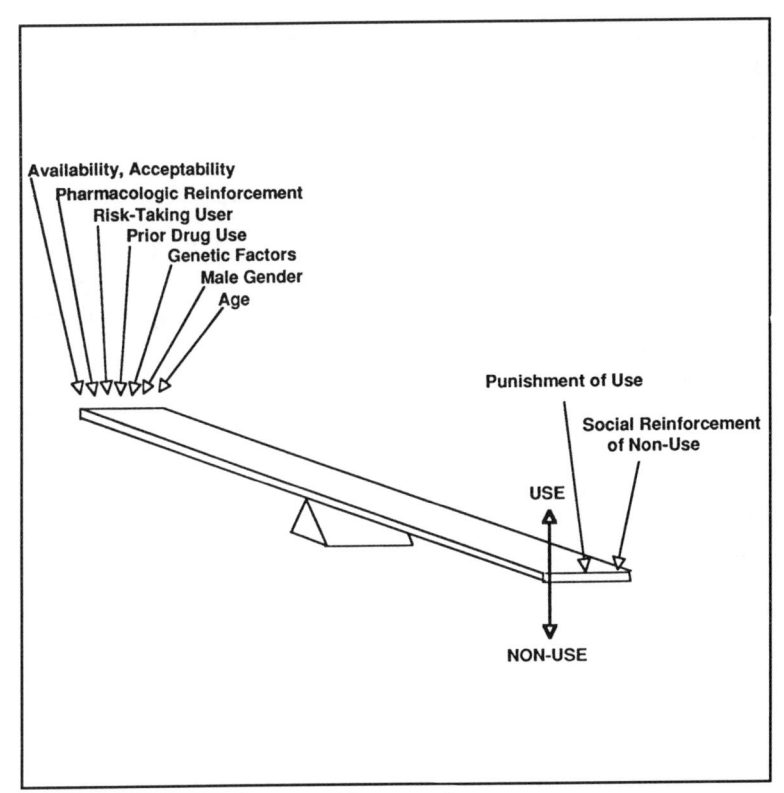

FIGURE 1. *Predictors of future substance use.*

SOURCE: Modified from Crowley 1988.

Finally, this boy (like nearly all in the authors' program) had experienced few reinforcements for drug abstinence and few punishments for drug use, factors that might have counterbalanced the pharmacologic reinforcement of drug taking. The program's main initial contribution may have been to break the cycle of drug use by reducing drug availability, surrounding the youth with staff and patients who did not accept drug use, and providing consistent reinforcement for abstinence with clearly stated plans to punish renewed drug use through immediate social consequences.

CONDUCT DISORDER AND ANTISOCIAL PERSONALITY DISORDER

Diagnosis

The relatively small changes in diagnostic criteria for CD from DSM-III-R to DSM-IV (table 1) probably will have little impact on clinical practice. However, changes in fine details, such as having used a weapon in more than one fight versus ever having used a weapon that can seriously harm others, will complicate the administration and scoring of structured interviews that are used widely in research.

DSM-III-R criteria for the diagnosis of adult ASPD require that the person be at least 18 years of age and have displayed at least 3 of 12 CD symptoms before age 15 (break-ins were excluded from the 12-symptom list). In addition, since age 15 the person must have shown at least four of the following: an inability to work consistently at school or job, criminal activity, fighting or assaults, defaulting on debts, transiency, lying or conning, serious risk taking, parental irresponsibility, no monogamous relationship lasting more than a year, and a lack of remorse. The criteria for ASPD in DSM-IV are almost identical to those used in DSM-III-R.

ASPD is defined as a life-long disorder, since it requires both childhood CD and adult antisocial behavior. An ASPD diagnosis cannot be made in the absence of a childhood history of CD. Why? Robins (1978) reviewed four studies of males who grew up in different eras and areas, and who were followed into adulthood. These studies each showed that antisocial behavior in adulthood consistently was preceded by antisocial behavior in childhood. Robins (1978, p. 611) concluded that "Adult antisocial behavior virtually requires childhood antisocial behavior," but added that "Most antisocial children do not become antisocial adults." More than half of the children with antisocial behavior did not become antisocial in adulthood, but nearly all antisocial adults had been antisocial in childhood. Social class or family background were weaker predictors of adult antisocial behaviors than childhood antisocial behavior.

Loeber (1991) recently questioned the proposition that many antisocial children avoid adult antisocial problems. That review suggests that those conduct-disordered youngsters who also show hyperactivity and inattention are less likely to outgrow their conduct problems. Loeber indicated that having conduct symptoms in a greater range or frequency, occurrence of symptoms in multiple settings, or earlier symptom onset each tend to predict persistence into adulthood (and thus, ASPD).

Prevalence of CD

Based on structured interviews of some 20,000 adults, it is estimated that 2.6 percent of Americans have ASPD (Regier et al. 1990), and all of them must have had childhood CD to qualify for the ASPD diagnosis. O'Donnell (1985) estimated the general population prevalence for CD at 3 to 4 percent, and a survey in New Zealand found that 3.4 percent of 11-year-old children did have CD with a male to female ratio of 3.2:1 (Anderson et al. 1987). A similar survey in Puerto Rico (Bird et al. 1988) made this diagnosis in 1.5 percent of 4- to 16-year-old children. A checklist rating procedure found CD in 9 percent of boys and 2 percent of girls 4 to 16 years of age in an Ontario sample (Boyle et al. 1992).

Etiology

What causes CD? Certain parent-child interactions, such as chronic conflict or child neglect, are commonly associated with disruptive child behavior (Loeber and Stouthamer-Loeber 1986). For example, Van Voorhis and colleagues (1988) examined youths' delinquency in relation to their family structure (one- versus two-parent homes), experience of conflict or abuse, enjoyment of the home, parental supervision, and other factors. Family structure had almost no relationship to delinquency, while the other characteristics did. The authors concluded that " 'Bad homes' not 'broken homes' place youth at risk" (Van Voorhis et al. 1988, p. 258). Similar findings were reported by Cernkovich and Giordano (1987). Loeber and Stouthamer-Loeber (1986) further suggested that disruptions in the continuity of child caretakers in the preschool period may be associated with CD.

A prospective longitudinal survey of over 400 inner-city London boys found that high levels of aggression at age 8 predicted later violent delinquency. Violent delinquents were significantly more likely to have cold, harsh, cruel, disharmonious, poorly supervising, and criminal parents (Farrington 1978). Rutter (1980) reviewed numerous influences on adolescent problem behavior: family discord and disharmony, family communication patterns, parental criminality and psychiatric disorder, poverty and low social status, violent films and television, poor schools, the community structure, and other variables. Such factors appear to be very important in determining whether vulnerable youths meet or remain below the threshold for a diagnosis of CD, and the number or intensity of their antisocial acts.

Home atmosphere is strongly associated with the subsequent development of criminality. Using data from a social work intervention project with inner-city youths conducted from 1939 to 1945, McCord (1979) related maternal affection, supervision, parental conflict, parental aggression, mother's self-confidence, father's deviance (alcoholism or criminality), and paternal absence to the occurrence (by 1975 to 1976) of convictions for major crimes among those adults who had received the intervention as children. Each family atmosphere variable was associated with subsequent criminality, and using all variables in a discriminate function permitted accurate prediction of criminality or noncriminality for three-fourths of the subjects. On this basis, one might conclude that problematic parenting causes CD.

However, these problems run in families, and that leads researchers to nature-nurture questions. For example, nearly a half-century ago Glueck and Glueck (1950), comparing 500 delinquent boys with 500 controls, found significantly more criminality and drunkenness in the delinquents' fathers and mothers, in the families of their fathers and mothers, and in the delinquents' siblings. Evidence continues to mount that the mothers of boys with CD have antisocial psychological characteristics (Frick et al. 1989; Lahey et al. 1989). Frick and colleagues (1992) reviewed and supported a growing literature (Biederman et al. 1987; Lahey et al. 1988*b*; Reeves et al. 1987) reporting high rates of ASPD and substance problems in the parents of boys referred to clinics for antisocial or aggressive behavior. Frick and colleagues (1992, p. 54) concluded that "The importance of [parental ASPD] as a risk factor for child CD suggests that future research should focus on unraveling the mechanisms involved in the link between parental ASPD and child CD." Might there be a *genetic influence* on such familial behavior?

The familial influence could be entirely genetic: parents with ASPD producing offspring with CD, those children then maturing into adults with ASPD. The chronic family conflict or child neglect could be a mere byproduct of genetically determined antisocial behavior. On the other hand, the psychological effects of neglect and abuse by antisocial parents could generate CD in children, who then might grow up to be antisocial themselves, abusing their own children and continuing the cycle. Of course, both genetics and environment could contribute to developing antisocial behavior.

This research challenge was highlighted by Frick and colleagues (1992) who found that, in comparison with controls, boys with CD were significantly more likely to have mothers who provided poor supervision and inconsistent discipline. In addition, these boys were significantly more likely to have fathers with ASPD; but when that paternal influence was controlled statistically, the maternal behaviors contributed little to the risk of developing CD, leaving the question clouded.

Crowe (1972) attempted to clarify the question of nature and nurture in examining criminal records of 25-year-old, adopted-out offspring of imprisoned women, comparing them with adopted-out controls whose mothers had not been imprisoned. Significantly more probands had arrest records, convictions, and incarcerations in comparison with controls. Such data strongly support the view that the offsprings' criminality was biologically influenced by the mothers' criminality, since the mothers had little psychological influence on their adopted-out children.

A study of 14,000 adoptees examined court records of biological parents, adoptive parents, and adoptees as adults. Adoptees with convictions were much more likely to have biological parents with convictions than to have adoptive parents with convictions (Mednick et al. 1984), again strongly suggesting a genetic influence on antisocial behavior.

Grove and colleagues (1990) examined identical twins who were reared apart beginning early in life, counting the number of antisocial symptoms that these people reported both in childhood and adulthood. There were significant correlations within twin pairs; if one twin had numerous antisocial behaviors, the other was likely to follow suit. Since the twins were raised apart, such correlations probably could not arise from a shared environment. Grove and colleagues (1990, p. 1301) concluded, "Present data demonstrate that antisocial behavior, defined much more broadly than just commissioned criminal acts, is heritable," to which the authors of this chapter would add "at least in part."

In an even more powerful design, Tellegen and colleagues (1988) examined both monozygotic and dizygotic twins, some pairs reared apart and some together. Such data permit detailed assessments of the influence of genetics, shared environments (e.g., the shared family environment of twins raised together), and of unshared environments (e.g., the separate family environments of twins raised apart, or friends not shared by a twin pair). One psychological variable assessed in this study was constraint, in which high scorers described themselves as restrained, cautious, avoiding dangerous kinds of excitement and thrills, deferential, and conventional, while low scorers reported impulsiveness, fearless sensation seeking, and rejection of conventional strictures on their behavior. These differences are highly relevant in discussions of ASPD and CD, although this sample of twins was not selected on the basis of criminality or antisocial problems. Among these adult twins, 58 percent of the measured diversity in constraint could be attributed to genetic diversity, 43 percent resulted from unshared environmental influences (which also include measurement error and the influence of transient states), while none of the diversity was attributable to the influence of shared environment. The data strongly suggest that among adults there is very little persisting influence of childhood family environment on constraint versus impulsiveness. Similarly, for aggression, 44 percent of the diversity appeared to be genetic, 56 percent arose from unshared environmental influences, and none from shared environmental influences. Moreover, four other studies of twins raised apart (cited in Carey and DiLalla 1994) generally support these findings.

One might argue that CD is a distinct pathologic entity, not simply one end of the population distribution of constraint versus impulsivity and thus that the genetics of that distribution are irrelevant to CD. But a review by Plomin (1989) strongly suggests that delinquent and criminal behavior also are under some genetic control.

Sociological research may support suggestions that the effect of "shared environment" (including parental influence) on children's behavior may be less persistent than the influence of peers (who comprise much of the nonfamily, "unshared environment"). Jessor and Jessor (1977) found that adolescents likely to engage in problem behavior perceived less compatibility between the expectations that their parents and friends held for them, acknowledged greater influence of friends relative to parents, perceived greater support for problem behavior among their friends, and had more friends who provide models for engaging in problem behavior.

However, some adoption studies suggest that environment should not be discounted as a cause of antisocial behavior. Cadoret (1978) studied 246 persons adopted out early in life and found that the intensity of antisocial behavior in adoptees was significantly predicted by having biological parents who were either antisocial or alcoholic, but it was predicted more strongly by having an adoptive parent with psychiatric problems. Later, Cadoret and colleagues (1983) counted CD symptoms during adolescence in adopted-away youths. They compared those counts with information about antisocial behavior and alcoholism in the youths' biological parents and to the presence of an adverse environment in the adoptive home (usually depression in the adoptive mother or antisocial behavior in an adoptive sibling). Youths whose biological parents and adoptive homes lacked adverse influences averaged only about one adolescent CD symptom, and so did those who had adversity either in the biological parents or in the adoptive home. But the mean symptom count rose to almost 4 in youths who had adversity both in their biological parents and adoptive homes. These data may suggest that genes have a "permissive" influence on adolescent antisocial behavior; such behavior may need certain genes and environmental adversity.

The twins in the study by Tellegen and colleagues (1988) were adults who showed little persistent effect of childhood home environments. Cadoret and colleagues (1983) studied late adolescent adoptees whose home environments still were influencing them. It may be that antisocial behavior *is* increased or decreased by the home environment, but that the influence wanes and inborn propensities are more fully expressed when the youth leaves home.

The review by Offord (1990, p. 280) concluded that genetics overall were not powerful contributors to the development of CD, but that they "May be a significant causal variable in certain cases ... of criminal adults with persistent antisocial behavior, which probably began in childhood in the majority of cases." The adolescents with CD and substance problems addressed in this review appeared at high risk of becoming criminal adults. The present authors conclude that available evidence currently supports an important role of genetics in the etiology of these cases.

Prevention and Treatment

Previous extensive reviews (Joffe and Offord 1987; Kazdin 1985; O'Donnell 1985; Offord 1987, 1990; Rutter and Giller 1983) indicate that no prevention or treatment effort in young children has been shown to prevent the development of CD and its comorbid conditions in adolescents, and no prevention or treatment effort among adolescents with CD has been demonstrated to prevent the subsequent development of ASPD. However, prospective studies consistently indicate that many children with CD do not progress to adult ASPD, suggesting a high natural remission rate. Further, to the authors' knowledge, no program has targeted youths with CD for prevention or treatment of substance abuse or dependence.

Psychological and Social Programs. A general problem is highlighted in a review of the potential impact of intervening on one or more risk factors associated with the development of CD (Boyle and Offord 1990). General population surveys show, for example, that one versus two parents in the home, low family income, family on welfare, a dysfunctional family, and school failure by the child are all risk factors for CD. Boyle and Offord (1990) estimated the advantage and disadvantage of intervening on one or more of these variables to reduce conduct problems. However, it is unclear whether such factors really cause CD, or are merely associated with it. As noted above, family environment actually may contribute little to persisting impulsivity and aggression, whereas nonfamily (unshared) environmental influences apparently have considerable impact. Thus, family characteristics may be invaluable flags marking vulnerable families and youths in need of prevention or treatment, but those characteristics may not be the variables to target in such interventions. Many currently identified risk factors for CD may only be associated factors, correlated but not causal, thus complicating the design of preventive interventions.

Kellam and colleagues (1983) found that shy, aggressive elementary school boys have an enhanced risk of developing substance problems in adolescence. These "loners who break rules and fight" are said to be "very much like the DSM-III under-socialized Conduct Disorder" children (Dolan et al. 1993, p. 320). Accordingly, efforts are underway (Dolan et al. 1993; Hawkins et al. 1991; Werthamer-Larsson et al. 1991) to help such boys with behavioral interventions aimed at reducing aggression and shyness. Studies show that aggression in such children is influenced significantly by the classroom environment; high-risk children in poorly behaving classes are significantly more aggressive than high-risk children in well-behaved classes. The investigators attempt, then, to reduce overall classroom aggression in order to reduce aggression by the highest risk boys. Whether these efforts will have lasting effects is a question for further research, but the data do show that aggression, an important component of CD, apparently is under environmental control, suggesting that youths with CD may be more or less aggressive in keeping with their classmates.

One example of a clear failure of psychosocial interventions with delinquents comes from the Seattle Atlantic Street Center Delinquency

Prevention Experiment (Berleman et al. 1972), which compared experimental and control groups of youths at high risk for delinquency. The experimental group received intensive casework by degreed (M.S.W.) social workers for up to 2 years, on an average of 6 times per month, for individual, group, and family counseling as well as various recreational and community activities. Controls received no comparable intervention. Very detailed followup of school, police, and court-related records found no difference in delinquency between the two groups.

Because of their emphasis on careful evaluation, behavioral therapists have been in the forefront of research on psychosocial treatments for CD youths. Ollendick (1986) extensively reviewed operant-based, modeling-based, and cognitive-based behavioral treatments for these youths. The various interventions reviewed generally effected improvement during the course of treatment, but few studies employing an active treatment control or comparison group succeeded in showing long-term differences in outcome, including institutional recidivism. Moreover, many of the most promising treatments, such as parent-training procedures, may be inapplicable to youths whose parents are heavy substance abusers, neglectful, and unmotivated for treatment participation.

Achievement Place was the first of many "teaching family programs" for predelinquent or delinquent youth. In this model, a married couple is taught behavioral principles including a point-motivation system, a self-government system, daily family conferences, selection of a peer manager, teaching of social skills, academic tutoring, and monitoring of performance in school. The couple then takes 6 to 8 youths into their home for many months of group-home living. Thereafter, the youths return to their natural homes or foster placement. The various behavioral elements have been carefully studied, and they clearly and favorably influence behavior in the program (Fixsen et al. 1973; Phillips 1968; Phillips et al. 1973). Moreover, during treatment in teaching family programs, youths were less delinquent than youths in group homes without that orientation. Unfortunately, 1 year after discharge the two groups were indistinguishable in delinquent acts (Kirigin et al. 1982; Weinrott et al. 1982).

Weinrott and colleagues noted that "The literature documents nearly as many instances of harmful effects as it does positive outcomes" from community-based placements of delinquent youth (Weinrott et al. 1982, p. 174). In their large evaluation of Achievement Place and comparison homes, they found that only 45 percent of youths in both samples completed all phases of the programs. The remaining 55 percent failed to function adequately in the programs (13 percent), eloped (10 percent), were removed by court for serious or repeated offenses (9 percent), or left for other reasons (23 percent). This study also found few differences between program completers and dropouts 2 to 3 years after discharge. About 40 percent of youths in both samples were committed to a closed institution at least once during the 3-year followup; one-third of these youths had fully completed the group-home treatment. Weinrott and colleagues (1982) concluded that it may be best to screen out high-risk youth characterized by prior institutionalization, chronic school failure, a history of drug use, and three or more felony arrests. However, these are the characteristics of the earlier clinical history described in this chapter, and are typical of most patients presenting for intensive treatment. Screening out high-risk youth is not a solution for the clinicians who must treat them.

Recent work by Kazdin and colleagues (1987*a, b*) is more encouraging. In two separate studies these authors examined behavioral treatments for aggressive children (ages 7 to 13). Problemsolving skills training, a cognitive-behavioral treatment, was provided for the experimental study children. In one study many parents were absent, neglectful, or had given up custody, so parents were not included. In the other, parents received parent management training. Appropriate control groups received other treatments. In both studies the children receiving problemsolving skills training did significantly better at home and school 1 month and 12 months following treatment compared with control groups. The magnitude of behavioral change was sufficient to remove many experimental children from the clinically disturbed classification. Although the studies are quite promising, these children were younger than the adolescents discussed in this chapter, apparently substance abuse was not yet a major problem for them, and long-term results remain unknown.

Pharmacological Treatments. Lithium may have a specific antiaggressive effect. Sheard and colleagues (1976) examined lithium versus placebo in 41 inmates of a medium security correctional institution. The subjects had committed serious aggressive crimes and continued their impulsive, aggressive acts in the institution. Most had been incarcerated between ages 12 and 18, and the group averaged 19 years of age when studied. They were considered to have non-psychotic personality disorders. Lithium-treated subjects had significant, progressive reductions in major and minor rule infractions over the 4 months of drug administration, and immediately rebounded to pretreatment levels after treatment ended. Placebo-treated controls remained unchanged. Campbell and colleagues (1984) studied hospitalized aggressive children with CD ranging in age from 6 to 13 years. The subjects received placebo, haloperidol, or lithium carbonate treatment for 4 weeks following 2 weeks of placebo treatment. Hyperactivity, aggression, hostility, and unresponsiveness improved with either lithium or haloperidol.

Siassi (1982) reported a substantial reduction in aggression during an open-label trial of lithium among 14 institutionalized aggressive children, and reviews (Campbell and Spencer 1988; O'Donnell 1985; Sargent 1989) concur that lithium seems to reduce aggression in CD. Lithium treatment appears to be safe in youngsters. Among 196 children treated with lithium for various psychiatric disorders, only one child experienced a moderate adverse effect: mild goiter without chemical hypothyroidism (DeLong and Aldershof 1987).

A number of open-label trials and a few double-blind trials indicate a possible effectiveness of carbamazepine in children, adolescents, and adults with aggressive and impulsive disorders (Alessi and Whittekindt 1989; Gardner and Cowdry 1986; Israel and Beaudry 1988; Mattes et al. 1984; O'Donnell 1985; Sheard 1988). The central nervous system (CNS) focus of carbamazepine's anticonvulsant activity is believed to be primarily limbic, and the limbic system is important in CNS regulation of impulsiveness and aggression. Reports of open-label trials suggest benefits of carbamazepine treatment in residual ADHD, alcohol and drug abuse, and CD (Mattes 1984).

In summary, the literature reveals no clearly efficacious primary or secondary long-term prevention for CD (Joffe and Offord 1987), although many cases apparently remit spontaneously. Certain treatments, both psychosocial and pharmacologic, may alleviate symptoms of CD. Structured environments with immediate rewards and punishments and with few peer inducements for antisocial activities reduce antisocial behavior. None of these treatments has been shown to permanently reverse the course of the disorder. However, given the often life-threatening nature of severe CD, even temporary alleviation may be beneficial. Studies (cited above) that have assessed both genetic and environmental influences on CD suggest that future research should examine changing the extrafamilial environment of CD youths, since peers and other nonfamily environment may play a very important role in determining CD's severity and prognosis.

Course and Prognosis

Stewart and colleagues (1988) reported an earlier onset of CD in children with antisocial or substance-abusing parents. Aggression, a central characteristic of CD, apparently is a very stable trait. The review by Olweus (1979) showed that assessments of aggression first made in prepubertal children or adolescents continue to predict levels of aggression for years. Boys can reliably be rated on differences in aggression by age 2 to 4, and ratings taken at age 2 strongly predict aggression as much as 21 years later.

O'Neal and Robins (1958) studied adults who had been examined in a children's psychiatric clinic some 30 years earlier. Adult psychiatric disorders were considerably more prevalent among these probands than among controls, and 37 percent of youths adjudicated as delinquent had developed sociopathic personality (now called ASPD) in adulthood. This study first underscored the tragic stability of antisocial behavior.

Within a smaller timeframe as well, earlier antisocial behavior predicts later antisocial problems. Farrington (1973) examined 405 normal schoolboys prospectively with questionnaires. Boys reporting more antisocial acts at ages 14 to 15 were more likely to achieve juvenile criminal status by ages 17 to 18; those with the most such acts achieved that status earliest. Similarly, among a group of 159 adolescents already identified as delinquent, 40 had a diagnosis of CD; that diagnosis significantly predicted rearrest for property crime within a few years (Weisz et al. 1991).

Aggression is not the only predictive or stable antisocial trait. In a British survey parents were asked to rate certain behaviors of their children ages 5 to 15. Parental reports of stealing, lying, destructiveness, or wandering from home significantly predicted criminality over the next 15 years of the children's lives; if the teachers concurred in these ratings, the probability of multiple court appearances by the child increased (Mitchell and Rosa 1981).

Despite these significant predictive correlations, many children with CD will not develop adult ASPD. Loeber (1982) examined characteristics that might predict those children whose antisocial behavior would continue. Those showing antisocial behaviors in multiple settings, a greater variety of antisocial behaviors, and an earlier onset of such behaviors were most likely to continue the behaviors.

Kelso and Stewart (1986) calculated that if an antisocial youth experienced out-of-home placement, severe poverty, and growing up without either parent, 89 percent would become antisocial adults; if all three factors were absent, 85 percent escaped an antisocial adulthood. In their 2-year followup of 91 CD boys ages 5 to 16, unfavorable outcome was also predicted by the number of different CD symptoms, fewer marriages by mother, firesetting, earlier age of CD onset, more treatment for accidents before age 6, familial alcoholism or antisocial behavior, number of children at home, and more quarrels with peers.

Despite numerous reports that early aggression, lying, theft, and other behaviors tend to be stable over time and to predict later antisocial behavior, one study suggests that the diagnosis of CD may not be stable. Among children evaluated after referral to a speech clinic, Cantwell and Baker (1989) found 9 with CD (mean age of 5.7 years). At followup 4 to 5 years later, only one child still had that diagnosis, although three had diagnoses of ADHD. The authors pointed out several possible reasons, including the unusual sample of children with speech problems from which these subjects were drawn and the very young age at which initial diagnoses were made (meaning that school or court records would not yet have been available).

Considering all of the reported data, there is strong evidence that a diagnosis of CD or the presence of various CD symptoms in middle childhood or adolescence significantly predict the later occurrence of antisocial or criminal behavior, although it is clear that the problem spontaneously remits in some children.

ADHD WITH CD

Diagnosis, Epidemiology, and Comorbidity with CD

A review by Taylor (1985, p. 424) noted that "Hyperactivity is a shorthand term for a cluster of complaints about a child's behavior; restlessness, inattentiveness, excitability, overactivity, impulsiveness, fidgetiness, distractedness and disruptiveness are the most prominent." Taylor noted that, while differences in the tempo of life are common among normal children, a syndrome of impaired attention and pervasive hyperactivity can be extremely disruptive to a child's life and the "recognition and treatment of this syndrome is a useful task for child psychiatry." That proposition was controversial until a general population study on the Isle of Wight found about 2 percent of children showing "pervasive hyperactivity" at home and at school, which commonly was associated with problems of conduct and of emotions (Schachar et al. 1981).

Table 2 lists diagnostic criteria for ADHD from DSM-III-R and DSM-IV. While DSM-III-R gave a single list of 14 symptoms, DSM-IV subdivides the symptoms into those of inattention and those of hyperactivity-impulsivity, and subtypes the disorder into prominently inattentive type, prominently hyperactive-impulsive type, or combined type.

The hyperactivity of these children is truly generalized hypermotility, and not merely inappropriately directed behavior. Porrino and colleagues (1983*a, b*) used an electronic monitor to study motility of hyperactive boys as they went about their daily lives. The hyperactive boys were significantly more active than classmate controls in nearly all situations, but especially in quiet tasks such as reading classes, mathematics classes, or during sleep. The hyperactives' motility counts fell significantly during double-blind treatment with dextroamphetamine.

General population surveys suggest that the prevalence of ADHD in children is about 5 to 7 percent, with a male-to-female ratio of about 5:1 (Anderson et al. 1987; Bird et al. 1988; Boyle et al. 1992). CD and ADHD are much more frequently comorbid than could be expected by chance, with the conditions co-occurring in 30 to 50 percent of cases in both epidemiologic and clinical samples (Biederman et al. 1991). Indeed, some experts suggest that CD and ADHD are comorbid so frequently that differentiating them is not useful, although most authorities deny this.

As noted by Alterman and Tarter (1983), earlier studies did not clearly distinguish the disorders. For example, Morrison and Stewart (1971) found that the parents of hyperactive children, in comparison with controls, were much more likely to have diagnoses of ASPD, alcoholism, or hysteria (an older diagnosis most related to somatization disorder), and to have been hyperactive as children. Cantwell (1972) found similar results, and Stewart and colleagues (1980), in comparing hyperactive boys to boys with other disorders in the same clinic, found more

TABLE 2. *Diagnostic criteria for ADHD, arranged in order of DSM-IV items.*

DSM-III-R	DSM-IV
A. A disturbance of at least 6 months during which at least eight of the following are present:	A. Either (1) or (2): 1. Six (or more) of the following symptoms of *inattention* have persisted for at least 6 months to a degree that is maladaptive and inconsistent with developmental level: *Inattention*
(-) No comparable item	(a) often fails to give close attention to details or makes careless mistakes in schoolwork, work, or other activities
(7) has difficulty sustaining attention in tasks or play activities	(b) often has difficulty sustaining attention in tasks or play activities
(12) identical	(c) often does not seem to listen when spoken to directly
(6) has difficulty following through on instructions from others (not due to oppositional behavior or failure of comprehension), e.g., fails to finish chores	(d) often does not follow through on instructions and fails to finish schoolwork, chores, or duties in the workplace (not due to oppositional behavior or failure to understand the instructions)
(8) often shifts from one uncompleted activity to another	(e) often has difficulties organizing tasks and activities

TABLE 2. *Diagnostic criteria for ADHD, arranged in order of DSM-IV items (continued).*

DSM-III-R	DSM-IV
(-) No comparable item	(f) often avoids, dislikes, or is reluctant to engage in tasks that require sustained mental effort (such as schoolwork or homework)
(13) often loses things necessary for tasks or activities at school or at home (e.g., toys, pencils, books, assignments)	(g) often loses things necessary for tasks or activities (e.g., toys, school assignments, pencils, books, or tools)
(3) is easily distracted by extraneous stimuli	(h) is often easily distracted by extraneous stimuli
(-) No comparable item	(i) is often forgetful in daily activities
	(2) six (or more) of the following symptoms of *hyperactivity-impulsivity* have persisted for at least 6 months to a degree that is maladaptive and inconsistent with developmental level:
	Hyperactivity
(1) often fidgets with hands or feet or squirms in seat (in adolescents, may be limited to subjective feelings of restlessness)	(a) often fidgets with hands or feet or squirms in seat
(2) has difficulty remaining seated when required to do so	(b) often leaves seat in classroom or in other situations in which remaining seated is expected

TABLE 2. *Diagnostic criteria for ADHD, arranged in order of DSM-IV items (continued).*

DSM-III-R	DSM-IV
(-) No comparable item	(c) often runs about or climbs excessively in situations in which it is inappropriate (in adolescents or adults, may be limited to subjective feelings of restlessness)
(9) has difficulty playing quietly	(d) often has difficulty playing or engaging in leisure activities quietly
(14) often engages in physically dangerous activities without considering possible consequences (not for thrill-seeking), e.g., runs into street without looking	(e) is often "on the go" or often acts as if "driven by a motor"
(10) often talks excessively	(f) identical
	Impulsivity
(5) often blurts out answers to questions before questions have been completed	(g) often blurts out answers before questions have been completed
(4) has difficulty awaiting turn in games or group situations	(h) often has difficulty awaiting turns
(11) often interrupts or intrudes on others, e.g., butts into other children's games	(i) often interrupts or intrudes on others (e.g., butts into conversations or games)
B. Onset before the age of 7	B. Some hyperactive-impulsive or inattentive symptoms that caused impairment were present before age 7 years

TABLE 2. *Diagnostic criteria for ADHD, arranged in order of DSM-IV items (continued).*

DSM-III-R	DSM-IV
	C. Some impairment from the symptoms is present in two or more settings (e.g., at school [or work] and at home)
	D. There must be clear evidence of clinically significant impairment in social, academic, or occupational functioning.
C. Does not meet the criteria for a Pervasive Developmental Disorder	E. The symptoms do not occur exclusively during the course of a Pervasive Developmental Disorder, Schizophrenia, or other Psychotic Disorder and are not better accounted for by another mental disorder (e.g., Mood Disorder, Anxiety Disorder, Dissociative Disorder, or a Personality Disorder).

alcoholism in the fathers of the hyperactive boys. However, none of these studies distinguished between the hyperactive children who did or did not have CD, leaving open the question of whether CD or the ADHD itself was associated with the parental pathology.

Reeves and colleagues (1987) subsequently compared boys with ADHD who either did or did not have comorbid CD or oppositional defiant disorder, which may be a milder version of CD. The boys who had CD or oppositional defiant disorder in addition to ADHD had worse social histories and their fathers had more alcoholism and ASPD than ADHD boys without CD. Walker and colleagues (1987), comparing boys who had only CD with boys who had CD plus ADHD, found that the latter were more aggressive and antisocial.

Lahey and colleagues (1988*b*) studied the parents of some boys who had ADHD, some who had CD, and others who had both disorders. ADHD alone was not associated with parental ASPD or substance use disorders, while CD alone was. Moreover, the parents of children who had both CD and ADHD were especially likely to have ASPD and/or substance use disorders. For example, 24 percent of fathers of CD+ADHD boys had a history of drug abuse, while 15 percent of fathers of CD-only boys and no fathers of ADHD boys had this history. Similarly, half of the CD+ADHD fathers had received prison sentences, while only about 10 percent of the other fathers had. Biederman and colleagues (1987, 1990) found that ASPD or CD were much more common not just in parents, but in all first-degree relatives of ADHD+CD children, when compared with relatives of ADHD-only children or normal controls.

So CD and ADHD commonly occur together. ADHD children who also have CD have more relatives with substance use disorders or ASPD, and accordingly experience more adverse family circumstances than ADHD-only children. The outcome of ADHD also is influenced by comorbid CD (see below). Hyperactivity itself may be a link in this comorbidity. Lahey and colleagues (1987) compared children with attentional disorder without hyperactivity against those with ADHD, and found that those with hyperactivity had much more severe conduct problems.

Etiology

The etiology of most cases of ADHD is unknown. However, the disorder is common in families with a rare genetic disease, generalized resistance to thyroid hormone (GRTH). This disorder is inherited as an autosomal dominant, and family members affected with GRTH are much more likely than unaffected relatives to also have ADHD (Hauser et al. 1993). This finding raises the possibility that thyroxin may play some role in ADHD.

Prevention and Treatment

Although the prevention and treatment of ADHD generally are beyond the scope of this review, the authors find no well-demonstrated procedures for prevention of ADHD. Both hyperactivity and inattentiveness are favorably influenced by psychotropic medications such as dextroamphetamine, methylphenidate, pemoline, or imipramine (Zametkin and Rapoport 1987). In the treatment of young children with ADHD, potentially addictive stimulant drugs usually are said not to produce later substance dependence (e.g., Hechtman et al. 1984*a*).

However, the use of stimulant drugs in adolescents with comorbid ADHD, CD, and substance dependence may seem unwise, although the authors are unaware of studies of pharmacological treatments for such patients.

Prognosis

The long-term prognosis in ADHD is becoming clearer. A few studies prospectively and repeatedly have examined ADHD patients from childhood until adulthood (see review of Klein and Mannuzza 1991). A Montreal group (Hechtman and Weiss 1984 *a, b*, 1986; Weiss et al. 1971, 1979) found that children with ADHD first seen at ages 6 to 13 years of age still showed (on average) excessive distractibility, aggression, restlessness, antisocial behavior, and academic problems 5 years later. In a 10-year followup, hyperactive youths had more alcohol and drug use and more contacts with courts and police than matched controls. The authors suggested that average outcomes inadequately reflected the existence of a subgroup of hyperactive children who were particularly prone to both substance problems and antisocial behaviors. At 15-year followup, trends toward more drug use among probands continued, and there were significantly more cases of severe antisocial behavior and ASPD among probands. Those with adult ASPD all had early childhood antisocial behavior. Predictors of later antisocial problems among these hyperactive children included early aggression, a lack of emotional stability, low frustration tolerance, adverse emotional climate in the home, and either overprotectiveness or a lack of control by the parents. In brief, among children with ADHD, symptoms of comorbid CD at ages 6 to 13 were associated years later with trends (at least) toward more drug problems, and with more cases of adult ASPD.

New York boys diagnosed as hyperactive at ages 6 to 12 years, together with controls, were followed to a mean age of 26 years (Gittelman et al. 1985; Mannuzza et al. 1988, 1989, 1993). At age 16 almost half of the boys had continuing ADHD, and rates of both CD and ADHD were significantly higher than among controls; the CD had developed despite an initial effort to exclude boys with marked aggression. Probands who continued to have ADHD at age 16 were much more likely than probands who no longer had ADHD to have antisocial behaviors or substance problems. Continuing ADHD seemed necessary for CD to occur, and the CD (or ASPD in older subjects) seemed necessary for substance use disorders to occur. The onset of CD always antedated onset of a substance use disorder. On the other hand, boys without ADHD symptoms in late adolescence were no more likely than controls to have CD or substance use disorders.

This New York cohort was again assessed at a mean age of 26 years. Many fewer probands had ADHD symptoms then as compared with late adolescence, but such symptoms still were significantly more common in probands than in controls. Similarly, the prevalence of CD or ASPD had dropped from 25 percent in adolescence to 18 percent at the adult followup, but was only 2 percent among controls. Substance use disorders also were significantly more common in probands (16 versus 4 percent), and antisocial persons were most likely to have substance use disorders. In the adolescent assessment, antisocial and drug disorders usually had occurred among subjects with continuing ADHD symptoms, but ADHD largely had disappeared by age 26 even among those with continuing antisocial and drug disorders. In both Montreal and New York, ADHD probands without ASPD in adulthood were no more likely than controls to have substance problems. Finally, in the New York probands, average occupational and educational advancements were significantly slower in comparison with controls.

Figure 2 summarizes some aspects of the comorbid relationship of CD and ADHD. Perhaps 30 to 50 percent of children who have one of these disorders at ages 5 to 12 also have the other; proportions vary in different samples. Children who have only ADHD tend to have relatives with childhood histories of ADHD. ADHD by itself impairs later educational and occupational achievement, but the outcome does not include excess risk for substance use disorders.

Children who have only CD have relatives with an excess prevalence of ASPD and substance use disorders (figure 2). Although the authors are unaware of long-term prospective studies of children who have CD without ADHD, retrospective studies indicate that these children face, in adulthood, an excess prevalence of both ASPD and substance use disorders.

Finally, children who have both ADHD and CD (figure 2) appear to have the highest levels of childhood aggression and hyperactivity. Their relatives have the greatest excess of ASPD and substance use disorders, as well as an excess prevalence of ADHD. And these children differ from ADHD-only children in that, when grown, they have an excess prevalence of ASPD and substance use disorders, as well as some cases of persisting residual ADHD.

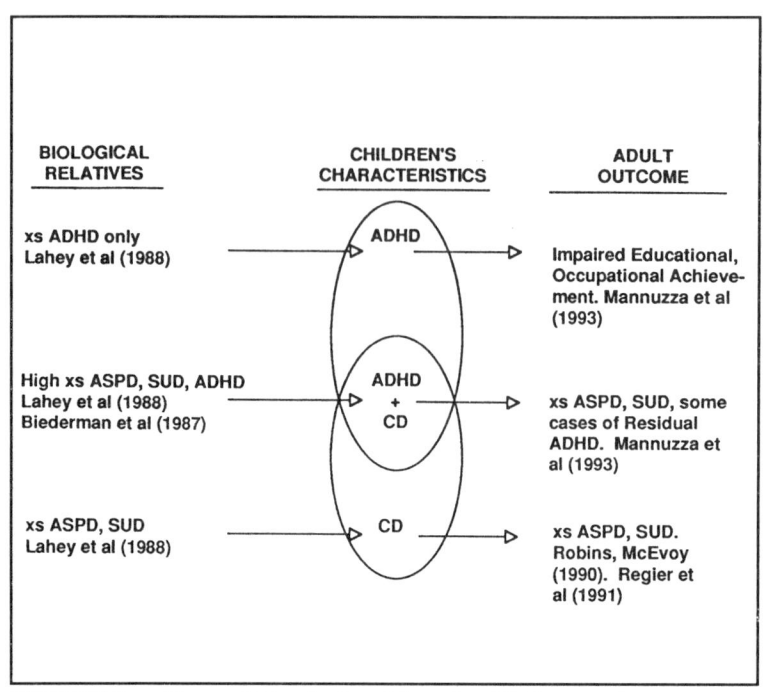

```
BIOLOGICAL              CHILDREN'S              ADULT
RELATIVES               CHARACTERISTICS         OUTCOME

xs ADHD only            ADHD                    Impaired Educational,
Lahey et al (1988)                              Occupational Achieve-
                                                ment. Mannuzza et al
                                                (1993)

High xs ASPD, SUD, ADHD ADHD                    xs ASPD, SUD, some
Lahey et al (1988)       +                      cases of Residual
Biederman et al (1987)  CD                      ADHD. Mannuzza et
                                                al (1993)

xs ASPD, SUD            CD                      xs ASPD, SUD.
Lahey et al (1988)                              Robins, McEvoy
                                                (1990). Regier et
                                                al (1991)
```

FIGURE 2. *Comorbid relationships, familiality, and outcome.*

KEY: xs = excess prevalence; ASPD = antisocial personality disorder; ADHD = attention deficit-hyperactivity disorder; CD = conduct disorder; SUD = substance use disorder.

DEPRESSION

Diagnosis, Epidemiology, and Comorbidity with CD

Most studies addressing comorbid depression in children and adolescents with CD have used structured instruments to assess major depression. A few assessed dysthymia (Kashani et al. 1987; Marriage et al. 1986), a less severe but more chronic form of depression (American Psychiatric Association 1987). Bipolar disorder is difficult to assess in children and adolescents since the manic symptoms necessary for this diagnosis rarely occur before age 15 (Akiskal et al. 1985). Therefore, this discussion is confined to major depression unless otherwise specified.

Criteria for diagnosis of depression are almost identical in DSM-III-R and DSM-IV; they include depressed mood, loss of interest or pleasure in activities, weight loss or gain, sleep changes, psychomotor agitation or retardation, fatigue or energy loss, feelings of worthlessness or guilt, inability to concentrate or indecisiveness, and thoughts of death or suicide.

Depression does occur in children and adolescents with comorbid CD. Alessi and colleagues (1984) found that 15 percent of 71 serious juvenile offenders in a training program met criteria for major depression by structured interview. In a similar population of delinquent boys, Kashani and colleagues (1982) reported an 18 percent prevalence of major depression, again using structured interviews. Chiles and colleagues (1980) found that 23 percent of 120 felonious youth ages 13 to 15 in a coeducational correctional facility met criteria for major depression, again using strict diagnostic criteria. Depression not only appears to be a valid diagnosis in such youth, but epidemiological studies indicate that depression occurs with higher frequency in youth who have CD (15 to 24 percent) than in youth without CD (2 to 8 percent) (Bird et al. 1988; Burke et al. 1990; Graham and Rutter 1973; Kovacs et al. 1988; Marriage et al. 1986; Robins and McEvoy 1990; Zoccolillo 1992). Kashani and Sherman (1989) further estimated, from a general population study, that the prevalence of depression is 1.9 percent in schoolage children and 4.7 percent in adolescents.

Several studies have sought to characterize differences between depression in youth with and without CD. Robins and Price (1991) have shown that depression comorbid with CD begins more often in preadolescence versus an age of onset between 18 and 26 in most general population studies (Weissman et al. 1991; Zoccolillo 1992). Marriage and colleagues (1986) suggested that youth with CD and depressive disorder have been dysphoric longer than those with major depression alone (25 months versus 7.8 months). Carlson and Cantwell (1980) characterized depression with comorbid CD as more severe than in youth without CD. Puig-Antich and colleagues (1989) compared depressed preadolescents (ages 6 to 11) with and without comorbid CD. The depressions of those with CD were characterized by less mania/hypomania, less hypersomnia, lower anxiety, fewer obsessive-compulsive symptoms, more suicidal ideation, and less fatigue than those without CD. Further, those without CD had higher rates of psychosis and family history of depression or bipolar disorder.

Other studies did not find significant differences in depressive symptom profiles of youth with or without CD. Kovacs and colleagues (1988) found that self-ratings for depression severity and course of depression did not differ among youth with CD plus major depression, compared with those with major depression alone. Harrington and colleagues (1991) examined 63 depressed children and adolescents and 68 nondepressed controls who were followed into adulthood. Depressives with CD could not be distinguished on the basis of depressive symptomatology from those without CD. Those with CD and depression had poorer short-term outcomes, but adult outcomes were similar to youth with uncomplicated CD.

Etiology

There are few data on the etiology of depression in youth with CD. Chiles and colleagues (1980) speculated that earlier onset and higher prevalence of depression in youth with CD may be related to a higher incidence of affective disorder among first-degree relatives, very chaotic households characterized by poor parenting and discipline, and a higher prevalence of substance abuse and ASPD in the parents (Cipaldi 1991). However, Puig-Antich and colleagues (1989) did not find a higher prevalence of affective disorder among first-degree relatives in depressed CD preadolescents.

Substance abuse and dependence certainly are associated with CD (Robins 1966). Do substance use disorders cause depression in youth with CD? Substance abuse and dependence are associated with increased prevalence of depressive and anxiety disorders in adults (Anthony and Helzer 1991; Ryan et al. 1986), but epidemiological studies reviewed by Zoccolillo (1992) indicated that the onset of both depression and CD precede substance abuse in the majority of delinquent adolescents (see also Robins and McEvoy 1990), suggesting that the drug involvement does not cause depression in most youths with CD.

On the other hand, there is some evidence that depressed delinquents may use substances to self-medicate their depression. Chiles and colleagues (1980) studied 120 felonious youths, and 61 percent of the clinically depressed delinquents said they dealt with depression by using more drugs, whereas only 13 percent of the nondepressed reported this.

Treatment

Little is known about treatment of depression in youth with CD. Puig-Antich (1982) reported that in a small number of prepubertal youth with CD and depression, imipramine improved both the depression and the conduct symptoms. Kovacs and colleagues (1988), however, have shown that CD persists after major depression resolves in many youths with CD. Ryan and colleagues (1986), in a study of 34 adolescents who met criteria for major depression, found a poor response of depression to imipramine. They hypothesized that high levels of sex hormones during adolescence and young adulthood may interfere with imipramine's antidepressant effects and recommended trials of other types of antidepressants in adolescents.

Zubieta and Alessi (1993) proposed that serotonergic agents may play a future role in treating depressions comorbid with disruptive behavior disorders like CD. They reviewed recent studies which implicate serotonergic systems not only in depression, but also in modulating aggressive-impulsive behavior in animals and in human adults and children. Serotonin systems also appear to partially regulate attention, suggesting a possible utility for serotonergic agents in treating ADHD, which often is also comorbid with CD (Biederman et al. 1991; Zubieta and Alessi 1993).

A practical treatment problem also arises. Youths with CD and major depression often are referred for residential placement or punitive custodial care (Alessi et al. 1984; Chiles et al. 1980; Kashani et al. 1982). Their CD, in the absence of systematic psychiatric evaluations, may override other considerations, making any evaluation and treatment of their depressions unlikely (Chiles et al. 1980; Kashani et al. 1982).

Prognosis

Data on the prognosis of affective disorder in youth with CD are inconsistent and contradictory. Harrington and colleagues (1991) reported that youth with CD plus depression had worse short-term outcomes but lower rates of depression in adulthood when compared with depressed children without CD. But Graham and Rutter (1973) reported that among youths with CD at ages 10 to 11, more do, than do not, develop depression or anxiety (comorbid with CD) by age 14 to 15 years.

Results of the Epidemiologic Catchment Area (ECA) Study (Regier and Eaton 1984), the Christchurch Psychiatric Epidemiology Study (Joyce et al. 1989), and the Zurich Longitudinal Study (Angst 1990) all indicate that CD or conduct symptoms in childhood are associated with increased risk of major depression and anxiety disorders in childhood, and perhaps in adulthood as well. The ECA data, in particular, showed that anxiety and depressive disorders are two to five times more common in both men and women with ASPD, all of whom must have had CD in childhood (Robins and Price 1991). The lack of consistency in outcome data may reflect multiple etiologies or subtypes of CD or researchers' lack of understanding of interrelations of CD with other comorbid conditions such as ADHD. Currently very little is known about factors that may contribute to spontaneous remission of CD, depression, or both in adults who had these disorders as children.

SUBSTANCE USE DISORDERS: COMORBIDITY WITH CD

Heavy adolescent drug use is neither trivial nor fleeting. Holmberg (1985) obtained drug-use information from a survey of 9th graders and followed the course of the more frequent users for 11 years in public records. The heavy users needed more health care; had much more drug addiction, alcoholism, and other mental disorders; and died at a rate fivefold greater than age mates from the general population.

Diagnosis, Epidemiology, and Comorbidity

Diagnostic criteria for substance dependence (the more serious substance use disorder) and for substance abuse (the less serious form) from DSM-III-R and DSM-IV appear in table 3. The DSM-IV field trials examined prevalence of abuse and dependence (as assessed by DSM-III-R or DSM-IV criteria) among about 1,000 persons (including some adolescents), some from substance treatment programs and some from community samples. Table 4 (calculated from data in Cottler et al., in press) examines changes in prevalence of diagnoses from DSM-III-R to DSM-IV. Among those in the field trial who had used any particular drug at least 5 times, the percentage diagnosed with dependence by DSM-IV criteria declined somewhat in comparison with DSM-III-R for all drugs, the percentage with abuse declined for most drugs, and the percentage with no diagnosis increased for all drugs except alcohol.

TABLE 3. *Diagnostic criteria for substance dependence or abuse, arranged in order of appearance in DSM-III-R.*

DSM-III-R	DSM-IV
A. At least three of the following:	A. A maladaptive pattern of substance use leading to clinically significant impairment or distress, as manifested by 3 (or more) of the following, occurring at any time in the same 12-month period:
(1) Substance often taken in larger amounts or over a longer period than the person intended	(3) The substance is often taken in larger amounts or over a longer period than was intended
(2) Persistent desire or one or more unsuccessful efforts to cut down or control substance use	(4) There is a persistent desire or unsuccessful effort to cut down or control substance use
(3) A great deal of time spent in activities necessary to get the substance (e.g., theft), taking the substance (e.g., chain-smoking), or recovering from its effects	(5) A great deal of time is spent in activities necessary to obtain the substance (e.g., visiting multiple doctors or driving long distances), use the substance (e.g., chain-smoking), or recover from its effects
(4) Frequent intoxication or withdrawal symptoms when expected to fulfill major role obligations at work, school, or home (e.g., does not go to work because hung over, goes to school or work "high," intoxicated while taking care of his or her children), or when substance use is physically hazardous (e.g., drives when intoxicated)	(-) See Abuse items 1 and 2 in DSM-IV

TABLE 3. *Diagnostic criteria for substance dependence or abuse, arranged in order of appearance in DSM-III-R (continued).*

DSM-III-R	DSM-IV
(5) Important social, occupational, or recreational activities are given up or reduced because of substance use	(6) Identical
(6) Continued substance use despite knowledge of having a persistent or recurrent social, psychological, or physical problem that is caused or exacerbated by the use of the substance (e.g., keeps using heroin despite family arguments about it, cocaine-induced depression, or having an ulcer made worse by drinking)	(7) The substance use is continued despite knowledge of having a persistent or recurrent physical or psychological problem that is likely to have been caused or exacerbated by the substance (e.g., current cocaine use despite recognition of cocaine-induced depression, or continued drinking despite recognition that an ulcer was made worse by alcohol consumption)
(7) Marked tolerance: need for markedly increased amounts of the substance (i.e., at least a 50 percent increase) in order to achieve intoxication or desired effect, or markedly diminished effect with continued use of the same amount	(1) Tolerance, as defined by either of the following: (a) A need for markedly increased amounts of the substance to achieve intoxication or desired effect (b) Markedly diminished effect with continued use of the same amount of the substance

TABLE 3. *Diagnostic criteria for substance dependence or abuse, arranged in order of appearance in DSM-III-R (continued).*

DSM-III-R	DSM-IV
(8) Characteristic withdrawal symptoms (9) Substance often taken to relieve or avoid withdrawal symptoms B. Some symptoms of the disturbance have persisted for at least 1 month, or have occurred repeatedly over a longer period of time.	(2) Withdrawal, as manifested by either of the following: (a) The characteristic withdrawal syndrome for the substance (b) The same (or a closely related) substance is taken to relieve or avoid withdrawal symptoms (-) No comparable item

ABUSE	
A. A maladaptive pattern of psychoactive substance use indicated by at least one of the following: (1) Continued use despite knowledge of having a persistent or recurrent social, occupational, psychological, or physical problem that is caused or exacerbated by use of the psychoactive substance	A. A maladaptive pattern of substance use leading to clinically significant impairment or distress, as manifested by 1 (or more) of the following, occurring within a 12-month period: (4) Continued substance use despite having persistent or recurrent social or interpersonal problems caused or exacerbated by the effects of the substance (e.g., arguments with spouse about consequences of intoxication, physical fights)

TABLE 3. *Diagnostic criteria for substance dependence or abuse, arranged in order of appearance in DSM-III-R (continued).*

ABUSE	
(2) Recurrent use in situations in which use is physically hazardous (e.g., driving while intoxicated)	(2) Recurrent substance use in situations in which it is physically hazardous (e.g., driving an automobile or operating a machine when impaired by substance use)
(-) No comparable item	(1) Recurrent substance use resulting in a failure to fulfill major role obligations at work, school, or home (e.g., repeated absences or poor work performance related to substance use: substance-related absences, suspensions, or expulsions from school; neglect of children or household) [cf., Dependence Item 4 in DSM-III-R]
(-) No comparable item	(3) Recurrent substance-related legal problems (e.g., arrests for substance-related disorderly conduct) [This item includes part of the "social" consequences of DSM-III-R Dependence Item 5]
B. Some symptoms of the disturbance have persisted for at least one month, or have occurred repeatedly over a longer period of time	(-) No comparable item in DSM-IV
C. Never met the criteria for Psychoactive Substance Dependence for this substance	B. The symptoms have never met criteria for Substance Dependence for this class of substance

TABLE 4. *Users (at least 5 times) with diagnoses.*

	Percent diagnosed in DSM-IV minus percent in DSM-III-R		
	Dependence	Abuse	No Diagnosis
Alcohol	-10	10	0
Amphetamine	-5	-19	24
Cannabis	-8	-11	18
Cocaine	-3	-5	7
Hallucinogen	-10	-15	24
Inhalant	-9	-6	15
Opioid	-8	-1	9
PCP	-8	-13	21
Sedative-Hyp	-6	0	6
Nicotine	-5	NA	6

SOURCE: Adapted from Cottler et al., in press.

Data reviewed above suggest, first, that children with CD are at high risk to develop adult ASPD. Second, both CD and ASPD are associated frequently with substance use disorders (Alterman and Tarter 1986). Third, some children with ADHD are at high risk to develop ASPD and substance use disorders, but this elevated risk appears to be due to the comorbidity of ADHD and CD; that is, the ADHD children who also have CD may be at especially high risk to develop ASPD and substance use disorders. Fourth, depressed youngsters with CD and substance involvement usually report that the CD antedated both the depression and the drug use. The following paragraphs further examine two of these points.

CD + ASPD frequently are comorbid with substance use disorders.
The ECA study interviewed some 20,000 American adults for psychiatric diagnoses. The rate of comorbidity of ASPD and substance use disorders was stunning. Seventeen percent of the general population, but

84 percent of persons with ASPD, reported a substance use disorder at some time in their lives (Regier et al. 1990). So the large majority of persons with ASPD also have substance use disorders, and all of them had had CD as youngsters.

Robins and McEvoy (1990) examined adult ECA respondents' reports of their childhood CD symptoms in relation to their problems with drugs. In comparison with the general population, drug users were more than twice as likely to have a history of CD; as the number of CD symptoms increased in an individual, so did the probability of that person being a drug user. No particular CD symptom was especially predictive of drug use, but the total number of conduct symptoms was strongly associated with the probability of drug use. Persons with more CD symptoms had problems with more categories of drugs.

Moreover, Robins and McEvoy (1990) showed that the larger the number of conduct symptoms, the younger was the age of first drug use or first drunkenness; the earlier the first drug use or drunkenness, the greater was the risk for problems from drugs or alcohol. They also related the well-established gender differences in prevalence of substance use disorder to presence of CD symptoms. Although girls generally have fewer CD symptoms and also have a lower prevalence of substance problems, girls with, for example, four CD symptoms, are just as likely to develop substance problems as boys with four CD symptoms. Robins and McEvoy (1990, p. 198) concluded that "In this general population of drug users, substance abuse virtually required both having at least some early behavior problems and beginning use of substances before age 20."

Further support for the relationship between childhood antisocial behavior and drug use comes from Nurco and colleagues (1993), who asked adult heroin addicts for retrospective reports of their antisocial or criminal behavior at age 11 and again at ages 12 to 14. Controls were nonaddicts who had been children in the same neighborhoods at the same time. The addicts reported significantly more criminal involvement at age 11 (before their addictions began) than did controls, and the differences persisted at ages 12 to 14. Youths with more severe criminal histories also started using drugs earlier. After controlling for the influence of the neighborhood and the era, this study shows that antisocial behavior antedates and predicts drug addiction.

Van Kammen and colleagues (1991) surveyed both substance use and antisocial behaviors among 2,500 first, fourth, and seventh grade boys.

Those who had used marijuana or hard liquor were significantly more likely to have committed a large variety of antisocial acts than were those with no use, or only beer drinking.

Other studies link childhood antisocial behavior with later substance use disorders. O'Neal and Robins (1958) examined adults who, as children, had been evaluated in a psychiatric clinic. Of those with court appearances for delinquency in childhood, over a third had sociopathic personality (an older name for ASPD) in adulthood, and many of them had excessive alcohol intake. Another quarter of the delinquents were said to have alcoholism without ASPD.

Persons with CD develop alcoholism earlier than alcoholics without CD. Rosenberg (1969) compared the childhood histories of alcoholics with earlier (under 30 years of age) or later alcoholism treatment. Those with younger onset had significantly more incidents of youthful stealing, running away, truancy, and vandalism, and their fathers were significantly more likely to have been alcoholic. Significantly more of them also abused other drugs. Alcoholics with ASPD also had stronger family histories of alcoholism than non-ASPD alcoholics (Alterman 1988).

Similarly, Cloninger and colleagues (1988) reanalyzed a prospective study which used teacher descriptions of 11-year-old children who subsequently were assessed for alcoholism at the age of 27 years. Measures at age 11 of risk taking (low harm avoidance) and high novelty seeking, thought to be characteristics of CD + ASPD, were strongly associated with the occurrence of alcoholism by age 27.

Rydelius (1983a, b) examined psychological profiles and substance use among 18-year-old recruits to the Swedish army. Heavy drinkers, compared with nondrinkers, were much more likely to have committed various antisocial legal offenses, to have experienced precocious drunkenness, to be users of other drugs, to have alcoholic parents, and to be suspicious, impulsive, aggressive, and irritable.

So one group in whom substance use disorders commonly arise are those with "The general pattern of deviant behavior which we call 'conduct disorder' when it occurs in children and 'antisocial personality' when it occurs in adults" (Robins 1980, p. 18); Vaillant (1983) concurred. A second, nonantisocial group had later onset of substance problems and a different background of disturbance in relatives. Such parsing was the basis for the important genetic studies reviewed next.

ADHD without comorbid CD does not produce substance use disorders. It was noted earlier that ADHD, in the absence of CD, does not lead to substance use disorders (Mannuzza et al. 1993). The Ontario Child Health Study (Boyle et al. 1992) examined 12- to 16-year-olds in 1983 and followed them again in 1987. A CD diagnosis in 1983 predicted the development of marijuana and hard drug use (after statistically controlling for comorbid ADHD), while ADHD did not significantly predict such drug use. These studies concurred that CD with or without ADHD, and not ADHD alone, is an important antecedent of drug problems.

Earlier studies had associated substance problems and ADHD (which had been known as the hyperactive child syndrome, minimal brain dysfunction, or simply childhood hyperactivity) (Alterman et al. 1985; Goodwin et al. 1975; Tarter et al. 1977; Wood et al. 1983). However, in assessing hyperactivity, such studies often included criteria now used to diagnose CD, such as lying, truancy, fighting, stealing, vandalism, overaggressiveness, and destructiveness (Tarter et al. 1977). Those earlier studies probably included many children with CD in their hyperactive groups, and those CD children would have loaded the samples toward substance problems.

Etiology

Cloninger and colleagues (1981) studied 862 men who were adopted out early in infancy, some from alcoholic and some from nonalcoholic biological parents. Some were raised in alcoholic homes, but most were not. Among these adoptees followed into early adulthood, having an alcoholic biological father raised fourfold the chance for alcoholism. The sons of fathers who were both antisocial and alcoholic were much more likely to develop alcoholism, to have an earlier onset, and to display antisocial behaviors themselves. Cloninger called this male-limited or type II alcoholism, contrasted with milieu-limited or type I alcoholism, which had later onset and was not associated with antisocial behavior in the offspring or their biological fathers.

Cadoret and colleagues (1986) studied nonalcohol drug abuse in late adolescents or young adults who had been adopted away early in infancy. Their drug abuse appeared to arise in three ways. First, alcoholism in biological parents was associated with drug abuse among probands. Second, disturbances in the adoptive home, such as mental illness, alcoholism, or divorce, appeared independently to lead to drug abuse.

And third, relevant to the present authors' thesis, antisocial biological parents tended to produce offspring with CD and ASPD, and that in turn led to drug abuse.

Identical twins raised apart have identical genes but dissimilar environmental backgrounds, so their similarities likely are due to genetic influences, while their dissimilarities reflect environmental influences. Grove and colleagues (1990) found that twin pairs raised apart were very likely to be concordant for antisocial behavior (in other words, if one twin was or was not antisocial, the other was likely to be the same), both during childhood and later. If one twin abused drugs, the other was also likely to do so. Moreover, there was a significant likelihood that the more antisocial twin pairs would also abuse drugs. This study suggested that common genes influence antisocial behavior, excessive drinking, and drug use.

While identical twins have identical genes, fraternal twins are no more closely related than any two siblings. Thus, for a characteristic largely determined by genetics, many more identical twin pairs than fraternal twin pairs should be concordant. To the extent that environment also determines a characteristic, the difference in concordance rates of identical and fraternal twins will become smaller. From concordance rates, appropriate statistics can determine the amount of genetic influence, the amount of influence from shared environment (e.g., the child-raising practices of the parents of a twin pair) and from unshared environment (e.g., behavior of the twins' different spouses). With these techniques, Pickens and colleagues (1991) confirmed previous suggestions of significant genetic influence in alcohol dependence, clarified earlier suggestions (Bohman et al. 1981; Cloninger et al. 1981) that the genetic influence is stronger in males than in females, and provided evidence that abuse or dependence on drugs other than alcohol also is genetically influenced. While alcohol dependence was definitely under genetic influence among males, among females it was not, and alcohol abuse showed no evidence of genetic control in either sex. Unfortunately, these authors did not comment on whether ASPD interacted with these heritabilities.

In summary, it appears that the antisocial disorders ASPD and CD are caused at least partially by genes, and that these disorders are antecedent to many cases of dependence on alcohol, other drugs, or both.

Treatment

Adolescent drug abusers referred for treatment probably have, on average, more serious problems than those not referred, and the data reviewed above strongly suggest that those with more serious problems are likely to include a sizable proportion with CD. But most studies of adolescent substance treatment populations have not made this diagnosis (Friedman and Glickman 1987). The present authors' residential program for substance-dependent delinquents has a prevalence of comorbid CD approaching 100 percent, and Skuse and Burrell (1982) found CD in 42 percent of an outpatient population of adolescent inhalant users.

Large numbers of adolescents are in treatment. In 1982 about 36,000 persons under the age of 20 entered federally sponsored drug treatment programs in the United States, with alcohol and marijuana being the substances most commonly involved. Beschner (1985, p. 8) wrote of those admissions that "In spite of findings that traditional drug treatment programs are effective in treating adult drug abusers, insufficient evidence exists to show that they are effective with adolescent clients."

Judging from delinquency rates, CD diagnoses probably are frequent among these admissions, especially in residential programs. About 70 percent of adolescent male, and 60 percent of female, admissions report "predatory illegal activity," and about one-quarter of these youths reported more than 10 illegal acts in the year preceding admission (Hubbard et al. 1985).

About a third of the youths studied by Hubbard and colleagues prematurely left treatment within 1 month. Comparing reports of pre- versus posttreatment behavior, Hubbard and colleagues (1985) reported sizable gains from residential treatment programs, and those staying longest had the best outcomes. Outpatient treatment gave more mixed results. Hubbard and colleagues concluded that multiple drug use was the rule, although it is unclear whether the youths had substance abuse or dependence. Reports of suicidal thoughts or attempts were common, as were predatory crimes. Delinquency, substance problems, and depression combined to make the residential patients a difficult population to treat, and particular mention was made that specific treatment for alcohol problems had been absent in most drug treatment programs.

The authors are unaware of controlled studies of treatments for adolescent substance abusers. Specialized treatments for substance use disorders in youths with CD apparently are not even described in any detail, and the authors know of no controlled studies of treatment for these important comorbid conditions. Skuse and Burrell (1982) minimally described a treatment for inhalant users, 42 percent of whom had CD; some subsets of the sample were said to have improved by some criteria. The whole area of treatment for this very important population remains largely unexplored.

FUTURE RESEARCH NEEDS

1. The remarkable comorbidity of CD, ADHD, major depression, and substance abuse/dependence in adolescents may suggest a common pathobiology. Zubieta and Alessi (1993) extensively reviewed animal and (mostly adult) human clinical data indicating that hypoactivity of CNS serotonin increases motor activity, aggression, and impulsivity. They noted that serotonin-related studies of children and adolescents have been rare and often flawed, but that the best available child data mainly are in agreement with the adult information. Moreover, serotonin hypoactivity appears to cause some cases of depression, leading to the recent introduction of several selective serotonin reuptake inhibitors that increase CNS serotonin activity. These drugs are antidepressant in adults and also reduce drinking in alcoholics and in certain animal models of alcoholism. Zubieta and Alessi (1993) called for much more research on the possible role of serotonin in CD and ADHD.

   Among children with disruptive behavior disorders, reduced cerebrospinal fluid (CSF) levels of 5-hydroxyindole acetic acid (5-HIAA), a serotonin metabolite, correlate significantly with measures of aggression (Kruesi et al. 1990) and predict subsequent aggression (Kruesi et al. 1992). But the invasiveness of CSF measures for assessing CNS serotonin activity no doubt have limited such studies in children. Fortunately, the availability of neuro-hormone challenges for serotonin assessment, challenges which are only modestly invasive, offers promise for more intensive work in this area (Mann et al. 1992). For example, although fenfluramine does not reduce hyperactivity in ADHD (Donnelly et al. 1989), it does elevate prolactin levels through a CNS serotonin pathway. Among adult substance abusers, Fishbein and colleagues (1989) reported that the prolactin increase was greater in more aggressive and impulsive subjects.

Others report that adults with either personality disorder or major depression have reduced prolactin response to fenfluramine, and that the reduction is significantly related to past suicide attempts and ratings of impulsive aggression (Coccaro et al. 1989; O'Keane et al. 1992). Moss and colleagues (1990), using a different challenge drug, also found reduced prolactin response among adult ASPD subjects overall, and the response was most suppressed in those reporting assaultive aggression and negative affect. In children with disruptive behavior disorders there is good test-retest reliability to fenfluramine challenge (Stoff et al. 1992), and despite some discrepant findings the procedure deserves research application among adolescents with CD and its comorbid conditions.

2. There is a need for treatment trials of selective serotonin reuptake inhibitors for the aggression, impulsiveness, depression, and substance problems of adolescents with CD and substance use disorders. In addition, lithium, tricyclic antidepressants, and carbamazepine have been reported to benefit the symptoms often shown by these patients; these drugs should be further assessed.

3. Current evidence supports a role of genetics in the etiology of CD. However, environmental factors such as availability of drugs, availability of weapons, organized juvenile gangs in the neighborhood, and a home environment with reasonable discipline almost certainly influence the life course of youths vulnerable to CD. Sophisticated research designs addressing CD symptoms and environmental characteristics among youths from clinical samples (and their relatives) will be essential for sorting out the genetic and environmental contributors to CD. Understanding the role of such environmental factors will be crucial to developing better prevention and treatment programs.

4. Current evidence suggests that unshared or nonfamily environment may be quite important in determining impulsiveness and aggression. Treatment efforts focused on providing sustained influences to change such factors as peer relationships, gang membership, and weapon use warrant further investigation.

5. The literature suggests that among preadolescent children with diagnoses of CD, many will spontaneously remit before adulthood. However, of those whose CD persists into middle adolescence, how many will escape an antisocial adulthood? This is the time when most such youths come in contact with substance treatment programs, but very little is known about spontaneous remission rates at midado-lescence and beyond. Longitudinal prospective studies are urgently needed.

6. Almost no studies have used modern diagnostic criteria in assessing adolescents with CD and substance use disorders. Researchers really do not know what proportion of adolescents entering substance treatment programs have CD. Although these youths usually are loosely referred to as "substance abusers," it is unclear whether they meet formal criteria for substance abuse or substance dependence. Does a diagnosis of abuse versus dependence make a difference in outcome among adolescents? Researchers do not know.

7. It is widely held that treatment of ADHD with stimulant drugs does not lead to problems of substance abuse or dependence. However, children with ADHD and CD appear to be at high risk for developing substance use disorders. In that group with CD+ADHD, might exposure to stimulants increase the subsequent risk for substance use disorders, or conversely, might adequate anti-ADHD treatment reduce that risk? If ADHD is identified in an adolescent with CD and a substance use disorder, is the course improved with medication treatment for the ADHD? Which medication might benefit such patients without becoming a drug of abuse? Research is clearly needed here.

8. ADHD comorbid with CD apparently worsens the risk and pattern of substance problems. Substance treatment clinicians need better tools for diagnosing comorbid ADHD in substance-using adolescent patients. In the frequently disturbed families of these patients, it may be impossible to get information from parents about the child's hyperactivity. Can clinicians rely on adolescents' self-reports for this information? What assessment tools are most useful? Is direct and automatic monitoring of motility useful in this regard?

9. ADHD occurs with increased frequency in families with a rare genetic disorder, GRTH. Is CD also more common in these

families? Is ADHD associated with an increased risk of substance use problems? Does this co-occurrence suggest that thyroid hormone plays some role in ADHD generally?

10. Research on girls with CD and substance use disorders is extremely limited. Outcomes of conduct-disordered girls treated in a psychiatric hospital reportedly are bleak (Zoccolillo and Rogers 1991). Fewer girls than boys enter substance treatment programs, and those that do reportedly have much higher rates of attempted suicide (Hubbard et al. 1985). In what other ways do these girls differ from boys? Do patterns of drug initiation or drug use differ by gender? Do levels of violence differ by gender in these aggressive and delinquent youths? What are the special needs, such as birth control information, that distinguish girls from boys? How many of these girls are teen mothers, and what are the implications of motherhood for treatment needs? Do treatment outcomes differ by gender?

11. Clinically severe, diagnosable depression is common among adolescents with CD and substance use disorders. How does any one of these disorders modify the course of the comorbid disorders? For example, does depression increase the use of drugs among youths with CD? Does drug abstinence alleviate the depression? Do any antidepressant drugs (which ones) help with depression in these youngsters, and does antidepressant treatment favorably influence the substance use disorder or CD?

12. Although few studies of youths admitted for substance treatment have made formal diagnoses of CD, the literature suggests that the condition is extremely prevalent in such programs. This evidence seems so strong that it is important to ask whether any youths without CD enter substance treatment, and if so, whether any other diagnoses are comorbid with substance use disorders among such adolescents.

13. Very little is known about the patterns of drug use among youths in treatment. At what ages do they start using drugs? With what drugs do they typically start? By what routes of administration do they use drugs, and are they at risk for human immunodeficiency virus (HIV) through needle use? What medical or psychological problems specifically result from the substance use, and what problems are related to the CD?

14. What specific antisubstance treatments used with adults should be extended to adolescents? Would they benefit from disulfiram, naltrexone, methadone, or nicotine patches? How applicable are Alcoholics Anonymous, Narcotics Anonymous, or Cocaine Anonymous programs? Is outcome improved by residential treatment?

15. The data of Hubbard and colleagues (1985) indicated that retention in treatment is a major problem in the management of adolescents with substance use disorders, and that those who remain in treatment tend to benefit more. What can be done to improve retention of adolescents in treatment?

16. What is the outcome of these youths' substance problems? How many become chronic patients (e.g., in adult methadone maintenance programs)? How many die prematurely from drug use? How many recover? Prospective assessments are desperately needed.

17. The abuse liability of most drugs in humans is well predicted by the propensity of animals to self-administer the drugs. However, while animals do not consistently take marijuana or tetrahydrocannabinol, the prevalence and intensity of marijuana use among adolescents with CD suggests that the drug is highly reinforcing to them. Researchers might better understand the processes of drug reinforcement if this discrepancy were understood.

REFERENCES

Adlaf, E.M., and Smart, R.G. Drug use and religious affiliation, feelings and behaviour. *Br J Addict* 80:163-171, 1985.

Akiskal, H.S.; Downs, J.; Watson, S.; Jordan, P.; Daugherty, D.; and Pruitt, D. Affective disorders in referred children and younger siblings of manic-depressives: Mode of onset and prospective course. *Arch Gen Psychiatry* 42:996-1003, 1985.

Alessi, N.E., and Wittekindt, J. Childhood aggressive behavior. *Pediatr Ann* 8:94-101, 1989.

Alessi, N.E.; McManus, M.; Grapentine, W.L.; and Brickman, A. The characterization of depressive disorders in serious juvenile offenders. *J Affect Disord* 6:9-17, 1984.

Alterman, A.I. Patterns of familial alcoholism, alcoholism severity, and psychopathology. *J Nerv Ment Dis* 176(3):167-175, 1988.

Alterman, A.I., and Tarter, R.E. The transmission of psychological vulnerability: Implications for alcoholism etiology. *J Nerv Ment Dis* 171:147-154, 1983.

Alterman, A.I., and Tarter, R.E. An examination of selected topologies: Hyperactivity, familial, and antisocial alcoholism. In: Galanter, M., ed. *Recent Developments in Alcoholism.* Vol. 4. New York: Plenum Press, 1986. pp. 169-189.

Alterman, A.I.; Tarter, R.E.; Baughman, T.G.; Bober, B.A.; and Fabian, S.A. Differentiation of alcoholics high and low in childhood hyperactivity. *Drug Alcohol Depend* 15:111-121, 1985.

American Psychiatric Association. *Diagnostic and Statistical Manual of Mental Disorders.* 3d ed. rev. Washington, DC: American Psychiatric Association, 1987.

American Psychiatric Association. *Diagnostic and Statistical Manual of Mental Disorders.* 4th ed. Washington, DC: American Psychiatric Association, 1994.

Anderson, J.C.; Williams, S.; McGee, R.; and Silva, P.A. DSM-III disorders in preadolescent children. *Arch Gen Psychiatry* 44:69-76, 1987.

Angst, J. Recurrent brief depression: A new concept of depression. *Pharmacopsychiatry* 23:63-66, 1990.

Anthony, J., and Helzer, J. Syndromes of drug abuse and dependence. In: Robins, L.N., and Regier, P., eds. *Psychiatric Disorders in America.* New York: Plenum Press, 1991.

Berleman, W.C.; Seaberg, J.R.; and Steinburn, T.W. The delinquency prevention experiment of the Seattle Atlantic Street Center: A final evaluation. *Soc Sci Rev* 46:323-346, 1972.

Beschner, G. The problem of adolescent drug abuse: An introduction to intervention strategies. In: Friedman, A.S., and Beschner, G.M., eds. *Treatment Services for Adolescent Substance Abusers.* Rockville, MD: U.S. Department of Health and Human Services, 1985. pp. 1-12.

Biederman, J.; Munir, K.; and Knee, D. Conduct and oppositional disorder in clinically referred children with attention deficit disorder: A controlled family study. *J Am Acad Child Adolesc Psychiatry* 26(5):724-727, 1987.

Biederman, J.; Faraone, S.V.; Keenan, K.; Knee, D.; and Tsuang, M.T. Family-genetic and psychosocial risk factors in DSM-III attention deficit disorder. *J Am Acad Child Adolesc Psychiatry* 29(4):526-533, 1990.

Biederman, J.; Newcorn, J.; and Sprich, S. Comorbidity of attention deficit hyperactivity disorder with conduct, depressive, anxiety, and other disorders. *Am J Psychiatry* 148:564-577, 1991.

Bird, H.R.; Canino, G.; Rubio-Stipec, M.; Gould, M.S.; Ribera, J.; Sesman, M.; Woodbury, M.; Huertas-Goldman, S.; Pagan, A.; Sanchez-Lacay, A.; and Moscoso, M. Estimates of the prevalence of childhood maladjustment in a community survey in Puerto Rico: The use of combined measures. *Arch Gen Psychiatry* 45:1120-1126, 1988.

Block, J. *Lives Through Time.* Berkeley, CA: Bancroft Books, 1971.

Bohman, M.; Sigvardsson, S.; and Cloninger, R. Maternal inheritance of alcohol abuse: Cross-fostering analysis of adopted women. *Arch Gen Psychiatry* 38:965-969, 1981.

Boyle, M.H., and Offord, D.R. Primary prevention of conduct disorder: Issues and prospects. *J Am Acad Child Adolesc Psychiatry* 29(2):227-233, 1990.

Boyle, M.H.; Offord, D.R.; Racine, Y.A.; Szatmari, P.; Fleming, J.E.; and Links, P.S. Predicting substance use in late adolescence: Results from the Ontario child health study follow-up. *Am J Psychiatry* 149:761-767, 1992.

Bry, B.H. Predicting drug abuse: Review and reformulation. *Int J Addict* 18:223-233, 1983.

Bukstein, O.G.; Brent, D.A.; and Kaminer, Y. Comorbidity of substance abuse and other psychiatric disorders in adolescents. *Am J Psychiatry* 146(9):1131-1141, 1989.

Burke, K.C.; Burke, J.D.; Regier, D.A.; and Rae, D.S. Age of onset of selected mental disorders in five community populations. *Arch Gen Psychiatry* 47:511-518, 1990.

Cadoret, R.J. Psychopathology in adopted-away offspring of biologic parents with antisocial behavior. *Arch Gen Psychiatry* 35:176-184, 1978.

Cadoret, R.J.; Cain, C.A.; and Crowe, R.R. Evidence for gene-environment interaction in the development of adolescent antisocial behavior. *Behav Genet* 13(3):301-310, 1983.

Cadoret, R.J.; Troughton, E.; O'Gorman, T.W.; and Heywood, E. An adoption study of genetic and environmental factors in drug abuse. *Arch Gen Psychiatry* 43:1131-1136, 1986.

Campbell, M., and Spencer, E.K. Psychopharmacology in child and adolescent psychiatry: A review of the past five years. *J Am Acad Child Adolesc Psychiatry* 27:269-279, 1988.

Campbell, M.; Small, A.M.; Green, W.H.; Jennings, S.J.; Perry, R.; Bennett, W.G.; and Anderson, L. Behavioral efficacy of haloperidol and lithium carbonate. *Arch Gen Psychiatry* 41:650-656, 1984.

Cantwell, D.P. Psychiatric illness in the families of hyperactive children. *Arch Gen Psychiatry* 27:414-417, 1972.

Cantwell, D.P., and Baker, L. Stability and natural history of DSM-III childhood diagnoses. *J Am Acad Child Adolesc Psychiatry* 28(5):691-700, 1989.

Carey, G., and DiLalla, D.L. Personality and psychopathology: Genetic perspectives. *J Abnorm Psychol* 103:32-43, 1994.

Carlson, G.A., and Cantwell, D.P. Unmasking masked depression in children and adolescents. *Am J Psychiatry* 137(4):445-449, 1980.

Cernkovich, S.A., and Giordano, P.C. Family relationships and delinquency. *Criminology* 25(2):295-319, 1987.

Chiles, J.A.; Miller, M.L.; and Cox, G.B. Depression in an adolescent delinquent population. *Arch Gen Psychiatry* 37:1179-1184, 1980.

Cipaldi, D.M. Co-occurrence of conduct problems and depressive symptoms in early adolescent boys: I. Familial factors and general adjustment at grade 6. *Dev Psychopathol* 3:277-300, 1991.

Cloninger, C.R.; Bohman, M.; and Sigvardsson, S. Inheritance of alcohol abuse: Cross-fostering analysis of adopted men. *Arch Gen Psychiatry* 38:861-868, 1981.

Cloninger, C.R.; Sigvardsson, S.; and Bohman, M. Childhood personality predicts alcohol abuse in young adults. *Alcohol Clin Exp Res* 12(4):494-505, 1988.

Coccaro, E.F.; Siever, L.J.; Klar, H.M.; Maurer, G.; Cochrane, K.; Cooper, T.B.; Mohs, R.C.; and Davis, K.L. Serotonergic studies in patients with affective and personality disorders. *Arch Gen Psychiatry* 46:587-599, 1989.

Cottler, L.B.; Schuckit, M.A.; Helzer, J.E.; Crowley, T.; Woody, G.; and Nathan, P. The DSM-IV field trial for substance use disorders: Major results. *Drug Alcohol Depend,* in press.

Crowe, R.R. The adopted offspring of women criminal offenders. *Arch Gen Psychiatry* 27:600-603, 1972.

Crowley, T.J. Learning and unlearning drug abuse in the real world: Clinical treatment and public policy. In: Ray, B., ed. *Learning Factors in Substance Abuse*. National Institute on Drug Abuse Research Monograph No. 84. DHHS Pub. No. (ADM)88-1576. Washington, DC: Supt. of Docs., U.S. Govt. Print. Off., 1988. pp. 100-121.

Crowley, T.J.; Mikulich, S.K.; Williams, E.A.; Zerbe, G.O.; and Ingersoll, N. Cocaine, social behavior, and alcohol-solution drinking in monkeys. *Drug Alcohol Depend* 29:205-223, 1992.

DeLong, G.R., and Aldershof, A.L. Long-term experience with lithium treatment in childhood: Correlation with clinical diagnosis. *J Am Acad Child Adolesc Psychiatry* 26:389-394, 1987.

Dishion, T.J.; Loeber, R.; Stouthamer-Loeber, M.; and Patterson, G.R. Skill deficits and male adolescent delinquency. *J Abnorm Child Psychol* 12(1):37-54, 1984.

Dolan, L.J.; Kellam, S.G.; Brown, C.H.; Werthamer-Larsson, L.; Rebok, G.W.; Mayer, L.S.; Laudolff, J.; Turkhan, J.S.; Ford, C.; and Wheeler, L. The short-term impact of two classroom-based preventive interventions on aggressive and shy behaviors and poor achievement. *J Appl Dev Psychol* 14:317-345, 1993.

Donnelly, M.; Rapoport, J.L.; Potter, W.Z.; Oliver, J.; Keysor, C.S.; and Murphy, D.L. Fenfluramine and dextroamphetamine treatment of childhood hyperactivity: Clinical and biochemical findings. *Arch Gen Psychiatry* 46:205-212, 1989.

Donovan, J.E.; Jessor, R.; and Jessor, L. Problem drinking in adolescence and young adulthood. *J Stud Alcohol* 44(1):109-137, 1983.

Donovan, J.E.; Jessor, R.; and Costa, F.M. Syndrome of problem behavior in adolescence: A replication. *J Consult Clin Psychol* 56(5):762-765, 1988.

Farrington, D.P. Self-reports of deviant behavior: Predictive and stable? *J Crim Law Criminol* 64(1):99-110, 1973.

Farrington, D.P. The family backgrounds of aggressive youths. In: Hersov, L.A.; Berger, M.; and Shaffer, D., eds. *Aggression and Anti-Social Behaviour in Childhood and Adolescence.* New York: Pergamon Press, 1978. pp. 73-93.

Fishbein, D.H.; Lozovsky, D.; and Jaffe, J.H. Impulsivity, aggression, and neuroendocrine responses to serotonergic stimulation in substance abusers. *Biol Psychiatry* 25:1049-1066, 1989.

Fixsen, D.L.; Phillips, E.L.; and Wolf, M.M. Achievement Place: Experiments in self-government with pre-delinquents. *J Appl Behav Anal* 6:31-47, 1973.

Frick, P.J.; Lahey, B.B.; Hartdagen, S.; and Hynd, G.W. Conduct problems in boys: Relations to maternal personality, marital satisfaction, and socioeconomic status. *J Consult Clin Psychol* 18(2):114-120, 1989.

Frick, P.J.; Lahey, B.B.; Loeber, R.; Stouthamer-Loeber, M.; Christ, M.A.G.; and Hanson, K. Familial risk factors to oppositional defiant disorder and CD: Parental psychopathology and maternal parenting. *J Consult Clin Psychol* 60(1):49-55, 1992.

Friedman, A.S., and Glickman, N.W. Effects of psychiatric symptomatology on treatment outcome for adolescent male drug abusers. *J Nerv Ment Dis* 175(7):425-430, 1987.

Gardner, D.L., and Cowdry, R.W. Positive effects of carbamazepine on behavioral dyscontrol in borderline personality disorder. *Am J Psychiatry* 143:519-522, 1986.

Gittelman, R.; Mannuzza, S.; Shenker, R.; and Bonagura, N. Hyperactive boys almost grown up. I. Psychiatric status. *Arch Gen Psychiatry* 42:937-947, 1985.

Glueck, S., and Glueck, E. *Unraveling Juvenile Delinquency.* Cambridge, MA: Harvard University Press, 1950.

Goodwin, D.W.; Schulsinger, F.; Hermansen, L.; Guze, S.B.; and Winokur, G. Alcoholism and the hyperactive child syndrome. *J Nerv Ment Dis* 160(5):349-353, 1975.

Graham, P., and Rutter, M. Psychiatric disorder in the young adolescent: A follow-up study. *Proc R Soc Med* 66:58-61, 1973.

Grove, W.M.; Eckert, E.D.; Heston, L.; Bouchard, T.J.; Segal, N.; and Lykken, D.T. Heritability of substance abuse and antisocial behavior: A study of monozygotic twins reared apart. *Biol Psychiatry* 27:1293-1304, 1990.

Harrington, R., Fudge, H.; Rutter, M.; Pickles, A.; and Hill, J. Adult outcome of childhood and adolescent depression: II. Links with antisocial disorders. *J Am Acad Child Adolesc Psychiatry* 30:434-439, 1991.

Hauser, P.; Zametkin, A.J.; Martinez, P.; Vitiello, B.; Matochik, J.A.; Mixson, A.J.; and Weintraub, B.D. Attention deficit-hyperactivity disorder in people with generalized resistance to thyroid hormone. *N Engl J Med* 328(14):997-1001, 1993.

Hawkins, J.D.; Von Cleve, E.; and Catalano, R.F. Reducing early childhood aggression: Results of a primary prevention program. *J Am Acad Child Adolesc Psychiatry* 30(2):208-217, 1991.

Hechtman, L., and Weiss, G. Controlled prospective fifteen year follow-up of hyperactives as young adults: Non-medical drug and alcohol use and anti-social behaviour. *Can J Psychiatry* 31:557-567, 1986.

Hechtman, L.; Weiss, G.; and Perlman, T. Hyperactives as young adults: Past and current substance abuse and antisocial behavior. *Am J Orthopsychiatry* 54(3):415-425, 1984*a*.

Hechtman, L.; Weiss, G.; Perlman, T.; and Amsel, R. Hyperactives as young adults: Initial predictors of adult outcome. *J Am Acad Child Adolesc Psychiatry* 23(3):250-260, 1984*b*.

Holmberg, M.B. Longitudinal studies of drug abuse in a fifteen-year-old population. 2. Antecedents and consequences. *Acta Psychiatr Scand* 71:80-91, 1985.

Hubbard, R.L.; Cavanaugh, E.R.; Craddock, S.G.; and Rachal, J.V. Characteristics, behaviors, and outcomes for youth in the TOPS. In: Friedman, A.S., and Beschner, G.M., eds. *Treatment Services for Adolescent Substance Abusers*. Rockville, MD: U.S. Department of Health and Human Services, 1985. pp. 49-65.

Hundleby, J.D.; Carpenter, R.A.; Ross, R.A.J.; and Mercer, G.W. Adolescent drug use and other behaviors. *J Child Psychol Psychiatry* 23(1):61-68, 1982.

Israel, M., and Beaudry, P. Carbamazepine in psychiatry: A review. *Can J Psychiatry* 33:577-584, 1988.

Jessor, R., and Jessor, S.L. *Problem Behavior and Psychosocial Development: A Longitudinal Study of Youth*. New York: Academic Press, 1977.

Joffe, R.T., and Offord, D.R. The primary prevention of antisocial behavior. *J Preventive Psychiatry* 3(3):251-259, 1987.

Jones, M.C. Personality correlates and antecedents of drinking patterns in adult males. *J Consult Clin Psychol* 32(1):2-12, 1968.

Joyce, P.R.; Bushnell, J.A.; Oakley-Browne, M.A.; Wells, J.E.; and Hornblow, A.R. The epidemiology of panic symptomatology and agoraphobic avoidance. *Compr Psychiatry* 30:303-312, 1989.

Kandel, D.B., and Raveis, V.H. Cessation of illicit drug use in young adulthood. *Arch Gen Psychiatry* 46:109-116, 1989.

Kashani, J.H., and Sherman, D.D. Mood disorders in children and adolescents. In: Tasman, A.; Hales, R.E.; and Frances, A.J., eds. *American Psychiatric Press Review of Psychiatry*. Vol. 8. Washington, DC: American Psychiatric Press, 1989. pp. 197-216.

Kashani, J.H.; Beck, N.C.; and Hoeper, E.W. Psychiatric disorders in a community sample of adolescents. *Am J Psychiatry* 144:584-589, 1987.

Kashani, J.H.I.; Henrichs, T.F.; Reid, J.C.; and Huff, C. Depression in diagnostic subtypes of delinquent boys. *Adolescence* 17:943-949, 1982.

Kazdin, A.E. *Treatment of Antisocial Behavior in Children and Adolescents*. Homewood, IL: Dorsey Press, 1985.

Kazdin, A.E.; Esveldt-Dawson, K.; French, N.H.; and Unis, A.S. Effects of parent management training and problem-solving skills training combined in the treatment of antisocial child behavior. *J Am Acad Child Adolesc Psychiatry* 26:416-424, 1987a.

Kazdin, A.E.; Esveldt-Dawson, K.; French, N.H.; and Unis, A.S. Problem-solving skills training and relationship therapy in the treatment of antisocial child behavior. *J Consult Clin Psychol* 55:76-85, 1987b.

Kellam, S.G.; Brown, C.H.; Rubin, B.R.; and Ensminger, M.E. Paths leading to teenage psychiatric symptoms and substance use: Developmental epidemiological studies in Woodlawn. In: Guze, S.B.; Earls, F.J.; and Barrett, J.E., eds. *Childhood Psychopathology and Development.* New York: Raven Press, 1983. pp. 17-51.

Kelso, J., and Stewart, M.A. Factors which predict the persistence of aggressive CD. *J Child Psychol Psychiatry* 27:77-86, 1986.

Kirigin, K.A.; Braukmann, C.J.; Atwater, J.D.; and Wolf, M.M. An evaluation of teaching-family (Achievement Place) group homes for juvenile offenders. *J Appl Behav Anal* 15:1-16, 1982.

Klein, R.G., and Mannuzza, S. Long-term outcome of hyperactive children: A review. *J Am Acad Child Adolesc Psychiatry* 30(3):383-387, 1991.

Knop, J.; Teasdale, T.W.; Schulsinger, F.; and Goodwin, D.W. A prospective study of young men at high risk for alcoholism: School behavior and achievement. *J Stud Alcohol* 46:273-278, 1985.

Kovacs, M.; Paulauskas, S.; Gatsonis, C.; and Richards, C. Depressive disorders in childhood: III. A longitudinal study of comorbidity with and risk for conduct disorders. *J Affect Disord* 15:205-217, 1988.

Kruesi, M.J.P.; Rapoport, J.L.; Hamburger, S.; Hibbs, E.; Potter, W.Z.; Lenane, M.; and Brown, G.L. CSF monoamine metabolites, aggression and impulsivity in disruptive behavior disorders of children and adolescents. *Arch Gen Psychiatry* 47:419-426, 1990.

Kruesi, M.J.; Hibbs, E.D.; Zahn, T.P.; Keysor, C.S.; Hamburger, S.D.; Bartko, J.J.; and Rapoport, J.L. A 2-year prospective follow-up study of children and adolescents with disruptive behavior disorders. *Arch Gen Psychiatry* 49:429-435, 1992.

Lahey, B.B.; Hartdagen, S.E.; Frick, P.J.; McBurnett, K.; Connor, R.; and Hynd, G. Conduct disorder: Parsing the confounded relation to parental divorce and antisocial personality. *J Abnorm Psychol* 97(3):334-337, 1988*a.*

Lahey, B.B.; Piacentini, J.C.; McBurnett, K.; Stone, P.; Hartdagen, S.; and Hynd, G. Psychopathology in the parents of children with conduct disorder and hyperactivity. *J Am Acad Child Adolesc Psychiatry* 27(2):163-170, 1988*b.*

Lahey, B.B.; Russo, M.F.; Walker, J.L.; and Piacentini, J.C. Personality characteristics of the mothers of children with disruptive behavior disorders. *J Consult Clin Psychol* 57(4):512-515, 1989.

Lahey, B.B.; Schaughency, E.A.; Hynd, G.W.; Carlson, C.L.; and Nieves, N. Attention deficit disorder with and without hyperactivity: Comparison of behavioral characteristics of clinic-referred children. *J Am Acad Child Adolesc Psychiatry* 26(5):718-723, 1987.

Lewis, D.O.; Pincus, J.H.; Shanok, S.S.; and Glaser, G.H. Psychomotor epilepsy and violence in a group of incarcerated adolescent boys. *Am J Psychiatry* 139:882-887, 1982.

Loeber, R. The stability of antisocial and delinquent child behavior: A review. *Child Dev* 53:1431-1446, 1982.

Loeber, R., and Stouthamer-Loeber, M. Family factors as correlates and predictors of juvenile conduct problems and delinquency. In: Tonry, M., and Morris, N., eds. *Crime and Justice: An Annual Review of Research.* Vol. 7. Chicago: The University of Chicago Press, 1986. pp. 29-150.

Loeber, R. Antisocial behavior: More enduring than changeable? *J Am Acad Child Adolesc Psychiatry* 30(3):393-397, 1991.

Lowinson, J.H.; Ruiz, P.; Millman, R.B.; and Langrod, J.G. *Substance Abuse: A Comprehensive Textbook.* 2d ed. Baltimore: Williams and Wilkins, 1992.

Mann, J.J.; McBride, P.A.; Brown, R.P.; Linnoila, M.; Leon, A.C.; DeMeo, M.; Mieczkowski, T.; Myers, J.E.; and Stanley, M. Relationship between central and peripheral serotonin indexes in depressed and suicidal psychiatric inpatients. *Arch Gen Psychiatry* 49:442-446, 1992.

Mannuzza, S.; Klein, R.G.; Bessler, A.; Malloy, P.; and LaPadula, M. Adult outcome of hyperactive boys: Educational achievement, occupational rank, and psychiatric status. *Arch Gen Psychiatry* 50:565-576, 1993.

Mannuzza, S.; Klein, R.; Bonagura, N.; Konig, P.; and Shenker, R. Hyperactive boys almost grown up: II. Status of subjects without a mental disorder. *Arch Gen Psychiatry* 45:13-18, 1988.

Mannuzza, S.; Klein, R.; Konig, P.; and Giampino, T.L. Hyperactive boys almost grown up: IV. Criminality and its relationship to psychiatric status. *Arch Gen Psychiatry* 46:1073-1079, 1989.

Marriage, K.; Fine, S.; Morett, M.; and Haley, G. Relationship between depression and conduct disorder in children and adolescents. *J Am Acad Child Adolesc Psychiatry* 27:342-348, 1986.

Mattes, J.A. Carbamazepine for uncontrolled rage outbursts. *Lancet* 2:1164-1165, 1984.

Mattes, J.A.; Rosenberg, J.; and Mays, D. Carbamazepine vs. propranolol in patients with uncontrolled rage outbursts: A random assignment study. *Psychopharmacol Bull* 20:98-100, 1984.

McCord, J. Some child-rearing antecedents of criminal behavior in adult men. *J Pers Soc Psychol* 37(9):1477-1486, 1979.

McGee, L., and Newcomb, M.D. General deviance syndrome: Expanded hierarchical evaluations at four ages from early adolescence to adulthood. *J Consult Clin Psychol* 60(5):766-776, 1992.

Mednick, S.A.; Gabrielli, W.F.; and Hutchings, B. Genetic influences in criminal convictions: Evidence from an adoption cohort. *Science* 224:891-893, 1984.

Mitchell, S., and Rosa, P. Boyhood behaviour problems as precursors of criminality: A fifteen-year follow-up study. *J Child Psychol Psychiatry* 22:19-33, 1981.

Morrison, J.R., and Stewart, M.A. A family study of the hyperactive child syndrome. *Biol Psychiatry* 3:189-195, 1971.

Moss, H.B.; Yao, J.K.; and Panzak, G.L. Serotonergic responsivity and behavioral dimensions in antisocial personality disorder with substance abuse. *Biol Psychiatry* 28:325-338, 1990.

Newcomb, M.D., and Felix-Ortiz, M. Multiple protective and risk factors for drug use and abuse: Cross-sectional and prospective findings. *J Pers Soc Psychol* 63(2):280-296, 1992.

Nurco, D.N.; Kinlock, T.; and Balter, M.B. The severity of preaddiction criminal behavior among urban, male narcotic addicts and two nonaddicted control groups. *J Res Crime Delinq* 30(3):293-316, 1993.

O'Donnell, D.J. CDs. In: Wiener, J.M., ed. *Diagnoses in Psychopharmacology of Childhood and Adolescent Disorders*. New York: Wiley and Sons, 1985. pp. 250-287.

Offord, D.R. Prevention of behavioral and emotional disorders in children. *J Child Psychol Psychiatry* 28(1):9-19, 1987.

Offord, D.R. Conduct disorder: Risk factors and prevention. In: Shaffer, D.; Philips, I.; and Enzer, N.D., eds. *Prevention of Mental Disorders, Alcohol and Other Drug Use in Children and Adolescents*. Office of Substance Abuse Prevention Monograph 2. Rockville, MD: U.S. Department of Health and Human Services, 1990. pp. 273-297.

O'Keane, V.; Moloney, E.; O'Neill, H.; O'Connor, A.; Smith, C.; and Dinan, T.G. Blunted prolactin responses to d-fenfluramine in sociopathy: Evidence for subsensitivity of central serotonergic function. *Br J Psychiatry* 160:643-646, 1992.

Ollendick, T.H. Child and adolescent behavior therapy. In: Garfield, S.L., and Bergin, A.E., eds. *Handbook of Psychotherapy and Behavior Change*. 3d ed. New York: Wiley & Sons, 1986. pp. 525-564.

Olweus, D. Stability of aggressive reaction patterns in males: A review. *Psychol Bull* 86(4):852-875, 1979.

O'Neal, P., and Robins, L.N. The relation of childhood behavior problems to adult psychiatric status: A 30-year follow-up study of 150 subjects. *Am J Psychiatry* 114:961-969, 1958.

Phillips, E.L. Achievement Place: Token reinforcement procedures in a home-style rehabilitation setting for "pre-delinquent" boys. *J Appl Behav Anal* 1:213-223, 1968.

Phillips, E.L.; Phillips, E.A.; Wolf, M.M.; and Fixsen, D.L. Achievement Place: Development of the elected manager system. *J Appl Behav Anal* 6:541-561, 1973.

Pickens, R.W.; Svikis, D.S.; McGue, M.; Lykken, D.T.; Heston, L.L.; and Clayton, P.J. Heterogeneity in the inheritance of alcoholism: A study of male and female twins. *Arch Gen Psychiatry* 48:19-28, 1991.

Plomin, R. Environment and genes: Determinants of behavior. *Am Psychol* 44(2):105-111, 1989.

Porrino, L.J.; Rapoport, J.L.; Behar, D.; Sceery, W.; Ismond, D.R.; and Bunney, W.E. A naturalistic assessment of the motor activity of hyperactive boys: I. Comparison with normal controls. *Arch Gen Psychiatry* 40:681-687, 1983*a*.

Porrino, L.J.; Rapoport, J.L.; Behar, D.; Ismond, D.R.; and Bunney, W.E. A naturalistic assessment of the motor activity of hyperactive boys: II. Stimulant drug effects. *Arch Gen Psychiatry* 40:688-693, 1983*b*.

Puig-Antich, J. Major depression and conduct disorder in prepuberty. *J Am Acad Child Adolesc Psychiatry* 21:118-128, 1982.

Puig-Antich, J.; Goet, D.; and Davies, M. A controlled family history study of prepubertal major depressive disorder. *Arch Gen Psychiatry* 46:406-418, 1989.

Quay, H.C. Conduct disorders. In: Quay, H.C., and Werry, J.S., eds. *Psychopathological Disorders of Childhood*. 3d ed. New York: Wiley & Sons, 1986. pp. 35-72.

Reeves, J.C.; Werry, J.S.; Elkind, G.S.; and Zametkin, A. Attention deficit, conduct, oppositional, and anxiety disorders in children: II. Clinical characteristics. *J Am Acad Child Adolesc Psychiatry* 26(2):144-155, 1987.

Regier, D.A., and Eaton, R.L. The NIMH epidemiologic catchment area program. *Arch Gen Psychiatry* 41:934-941, 1984.

Regier, D.A.; Farmer, M.E.; Rae, D.S.; Locke, B.Z.; Keith, S.J.; Judd, L.L.; and Goodwin, F.K. Comorbidity of mental disorders with alcohol and other drug abuse: Results from the Epidemiologic Catchment Area (ECA) study. *JAMA* 264(19):2511-2518, 1990.

Robins, L.N. *Deviant Children Grown Up*. Baltimore: Williams and Wilkins, 1966.

Robins, L.N. Sturdy childhood predictors of adult antisocial behaviour: Replications from longitudinal studies. *Psychol Med* 8:611-622, 1978.

Robins, L.N. The natural history of drug abuse. Supplement. *Acta Psychiatr Scand* 284(62):7-20, 1980.

Robins, L.N., and McEvoy, L. Conduct problems as predictors of substance abuse. In: Robins, L.N., and Rutter, M., eds. *Straight and Devious Pathways from Childhood to Adulthood.* Cambridge: Cambridge University Press, 1990. pp. 182-204.

Robins, L.N., and Price, R.K. Adult disorders predicted by childhood conduct problems: Results from the NIMH epidemiologic catchment area project. *Psychiatry* 54:113-132, 1991.

Rosenberg, C.M. Young alcoholics. *Br J Psychiatry* 115:181-188, 1969.

Rutter, M. Influences on adolescent behavior. In: Rutter, M., ed. *Changing Youth in a Changing Society.* Cambridge, MA: Harvard University Press, 1980. pp. 145-192.

Rutter, M., and Giller, H. Prevention and intervention. In: Rutter, M., and Giller, H., eds. *Juvenile Delinquency: Trends and Perspectives.* New York: Penguin Books, 1983. pp. 267-362.

Rutter, M., and Hersov, L. *Child and Adolescent Psychiatry: Modern Approaches.* 2d ed. London: Blackwell Scientific Publications, 1985.

Ryan, N.D.; Puig-Antich, J.; Cooper, T.; Rubinovich, H.; Ambrosini, P.; Davies, M.; King, J.; Torres, D.; and Fried, J. Imipramine in adolescent major depression: Plasma level and clinical response. *Acta Psychiatr Scand* 73:275-288, 1986.

Rydelius, P.A. Alcohol-abusing teenage boys: Testing a hypothesis on alcohol abuse and personality factors, using a personality inventory. *Acta Psychiatr Scand* 68:381-385, 1983*a*.

Rydelius, P.A. Alcohol-abusing teenage boys: Testing a hypothesis on the relationship between alcohol abuse and social background factors, criminality and personality in teenage boys. *Acta Psychiatr Scand* 68:368-380, 1983*b*.

Sargent, M. Treating nonaffect disorders with lithium. *Hosp Community Psychiatry* 40:579-581, 1989.

Schachar, R.; Rutter, M.; and Smith, A. The characteristics of situationally and pervasively hyperactive children: Implications for syndrome definition. *J Child Psychol Psychiatry* 22(4):375-392, 1981.

Shaffer, D.; Fisher, P.; Piacentini, J.; Schwab-Stone, M.; and Wicks, J. *Diagnostic Interview Schedule for Children 2.1.* Available from Prudence Fisher, Division of Child and Adolescent Psychiatry, New York State Psychiatric Institute, 722 West 168th Street, New York, NY 10032, 1990.

Sheard, M.H. Clinical pharmacology of aggressive behavior. *Clin Neuropharmacol* 11:483-492, 1988.

Sheard, M.H.; Marini, J.L.; Bridges, C.I.; and Wagner, E. The effect of lithium on impulsive aggressive behavior in man. *Am J Psychiatry* 133:1409-1413, 1976.

Siassi, I. Lithium treatment of impulsive behavior in children. *J Clin Psychiatry* 43:482-484, 1982.

Skuse, D., and Burrell, S. A review of solvent abusers and their management by a child psychiatric out-patient service. *Hum Toxicol* 1:321-329, 1982.

Smith, G.M., and Fogg, C.P. Psychological predictors of early use, late use, and nonuse of marihuana among teenage students. In: Kandel, D.B., ed. *Longitudinal Research on Drug Use: Empirical Findings and Methodological Issues.* Washington, DC: Hemisphere Publishing Corp., 1978. pp. 101-113.

Stewart, M.A.; Copeland, L.E.; and deBlois, C.S. Age of onset of aggressive conduct disorder: A pilot study. *Child Psychiatry Hum Dev* 19(2):126-131, 1988.

Stewart, M.A.; DeBlois, C.S.; and Cummings, C. Psychiatric disorder in the parents of hyperactive boys and those with conduct disorder. *J Child Psychol Psychiatry* 21:283-292, 1980.

Stoff, D.M.; Pasatiempo, A.P.; Yeung, J.H.; Bridger, W.H.; and Rabinovich, H. Test-retest reliability of the prolactin and cortisol responses to d,l-fenfluramine challenge in disruptive behavior disorders. *Psychiatry Res* 42:65-72, 1992.

Swadi, H. Relative risk factors in detecting adolescent drug abuse. *Drug Alcohol Depend* 29:253-254, 1992.

Tarter, R.E.; McBride, H.; Buonpane, N.; and Schneider, D.U. Differentiation of alcoholics: Childhood history of minimal brain dysfunction, family history, and drinking pattern. *Arch Gen Psychiatry* 34:761-768, 1977.

Taylor, E. Syndrome of overactivity and attention deficit. In: Rutter, M., and Hersov, L., ed. *Child and Adolescent Psychiatry: Modern Approaches.* 2d ed. London: Blackwell Scientific Publications, 1985. pp. 424-443.

Tellegen, A.; Lykken, D.T.; Bouchard, T.J.; Wilcox, K.J.; Segal, N.L.; and Rich, S. Personality similarity in twins reared apart and together. *J Pers Soc Psychol* 5(6):1031-1039, 1988.

Vaillant, G.E. Natural history of male alcoholism. V. Is alcoholism the cart or the horse to sociopathy? *Br J Addict* 78:317-326, 1983.

Van Kammen, W.B.; Loeber, R.; and Stouthamer-Loeber, M. Substance use and its relationship to conduct problems and delinquency in young boys. *J Youth Adolesc* 20(4):399-413, 1991.

Van Voorhis, P.; Cullen, F.T.; Mathers, R.A.; and Garner, C.C. The impact of family structure and quality of delinquency: A comparative assessment of structural and functional factors. *Criminology* 26(2):235-261, 1988.

Walker, J.L.; Lahey, B.B.; Hynd, G.W.; and Frame, C.L. Comparison of specific patterns of antisocial behavior in children with conduct disorder with or without coexisting hyperactivity. *J Consult Clin Psychol* 55(6):910-913, 1987.

Weinrott, M.R.; Jones, R.R.; and Howard, J.R. Cost-effectiveness of teaching family programs for delinquents: Results of a national evaluation. *Evaluation Rev* 6:173-201, 1982.

Weiss, G.; Minde, K.; Werry, J.S.; Douglas, V.; and Nemeth, E. Studies on the hyperactive child: VIII. Five-year follow-up. *Arch Gen Psychiatry* 24:409-414, 1971.

Weiss, G.; Hechtman, L.; Perlman, T.; Hopkins, J.; and Wener, A. Hyperactives as young adults: A controlled prospective ten-year follow-up of 75 children. *Arch Gen Psychiatry* 36:675-681, 1979.

Weissman, M.M.; Bruce, M.L.; Leaf, P.J.; Florio, L.P.; and Holzer, C. Affective disorders. In: Robins, L.N., and Regier, D.A., eds. *Psychiatric Disorders in America*. New York: The Free Press, 1991. pp. 53-80.

Weisz, J.R.; Martin, S.L.; Walter, B.R.; and Fernandez, G.A. Differential prediction of young adult arrests for property and personal crimes: Findings of a cohort follow-up study of violent boys from North Carolina's Willie M program. *J Child Psychol Psychiatry* 32(5):783-792, 1991.

Werthamer-Larsson, L.; Kellam, S.; and Wheeler, L. Effect of first-grade classroom environment on shy behavior, aggressive behavior, and concentration problems. *Am J Community Psychol* 19(4):585-602, 1991.

Wood, D.; Wender, P.H.; and Reimherr, F.W. The prevalence of attention deficit disorder, residual type, or minimal brain dysfunction, in a population of male alcoholic patients. *Am J Psychiatry* 140:95-98, 1983.

Zametkin, A.J., and Rapoport, J.L. Neurobiology of attention deficit disorder with hyperactivity: Where have we come in 50 years? *J Am Acad Child Adolesc Psychiatry* 26:676-686, 1987.

Zoccolillo, M. Co-occurrence of conduct disorder and its adult outcomes with depressive and anxiety disorders: A review. *J Am Acad Child Adolesc Psychiatry* 31:547-555, 1992.

Zoccolillo, M., and Rogers, K. Characteristics and outcome of hospitalized adolescent girls with conduct disorder. *J Am Acad Child Adolesc Psychiatry* 30:973-981, 1991.

Zubieta, J.K., and Alessi, N.E. Is there a role of serotonin in the disruptive behavior disorders? A literature review. *J Child Adolesc Psychopharmacol* 3(1):11-35, 1993.

ACKNOWLEDGMENT

Preparation of this review was supported in part by grant DA06941 from the National Institute on Drug Abuse.

AUTHORS

Thomas J. Crowley, M.D.
Professor of Psychiatry

Paula D. Riggs, M.D.
Instructor in Psychiatry
University of Colorado School of Medicine
4200 East Ninth Avenue, C268-35
Denver, CO 80262

Physical Health Problems Associated with Adolescent Substance Abuse

Patricia Kokotailo

INTRODUCTION

Adolescence is normally thought of as a healthy time of life with low morbidity and mortality rates as compared with other times of life. Teenagers and young adults make fewer physician visits than any other age group and have relatively low levels of disability, illness, and death (National Center for Health Statistics 1994*a*).

Although the adolescent mortality rate is quite low compared with that of adults, there is a striking increase in the death rate over the course of adolescence, with 15- to 19-year-olds having an overall death rate 3 times that of 10- to 14-year-olds—the single largest increase in mortality rates between any two age groups in the life cycle (National Center for Health Statistics 1992). Adolescents of all ages experience their highest rates of mortality from unintentional injuries, homicide, and suicide. Unintentional injuries were the leading cause of death for young people of all racial groups aged 15 to 24 years in 1989-91 except for black youth, for whom homicide was the leading cause of death. Deaths from motor vehicle accidents (MVAs) accounted for 76 to 79 percent of all unintentional injuries among Hispanic, Asian, and white youth, and 66 to 71 percent of the injuries among black and Native American youth (National Center for Health Statistics 1994*a*). Unintentional and intentional injuries accounted for approximately three quarters of the more than 40,000 deaths in the 10- to 24-year-old age group in the United States, with 37 percent of all deaths resulting from MVAs, 14 percent from homicides, 12 percent from suicides, and 12 percent from other injuries such as drowning, poisoning, and burns (Centers for Disease Control and Prevention (CDC) 1993*a*).

In a CDC report analyzing mortality data from 1979 to 1988 (CDC 1993*a*), overall death rates for 10- to 24-year-olds decreased 11.7 percent over this time, but suicide rates increased by 75 percent for 10- to 14-year-olds and by 34.5 percent for 15- to 19-year-olds. Homicide rates increased for the 10- to 24-year-old group, with the largest increase (41.7 percent) among the 10- to 14-year-old subgroup.

Traditional views and measures of morbidity and mortality are often disease related and adult focused, and underestimate the health risk behaviors initiated during adolescence that are responsible for short-term and long-term negative physical and psychosocial consequences (Ryan and Irwin 1992). During adolescence the primary causes of illness, injury, and disability are behaviorally generated. Ryan and Irwin (1992) stated that more than 50 percent of the morbidity in adolescents stems from three behaviors: sexual activity, alcohol and other drug (AOD) use and abuse, and recreation/motor vehicle use. These three behaviors generally have their onset in adolescence; are common among all socioeconomic, racial, and age groups; and share a common theme—*risk taking*.

RELATED RISK-TAKING BEHAVIOR

Although AOD use had shown documented declines among secondary school students over the past two decades, the use of illicit drugs rose sharply in 1993 for 8th, 10th, and 12th graders, while attitudes of disapproval and perceived risk declined (Johnston et al. 1994). Johnston and colleagues (1994) found that by 8th grade, 67 percent of young people report having tried alcohol and 26 percent report having already been drunk at least once. Cigarettes had been tried by nearly half of 8th graders with just over half indicating they thought there is great risk associated with being a pack-a-day smoker. Marijuana had been tried by 13 percent of 8th graders and inhalants used by 19 percent. Inhalants are the only class of drugs for which use is substantially higher at the 8th grade level than at the 10th or 12th grade level.

As shown in many studies (Chewning et al. 1988; Donovan et al. 1988; Jessor and Jessor 1977; Mott and Haurin 1988; Zabin 1984), risk-taking behaviors have been noted to cluster in adolescents. Jessor and Jessor's work (1977) found the four problem behaviors of alcohol abuse, marijuana use, delinquent behavior, and sexual intercourse to be significantly correlated, with more frequent involvement in one behavior associated with a higher frequency of involvement in other problem behaviors. An interrelationship has also been shown between these behaviors and cigarette smoking. Based on current longitudinal studies, it is not entirely clear whether covariation of risk behavior represents the causal effect of one behavior on the initiation of a second behavior, or the fact that the behaviors result from a common set of risk factors (Ryan and Irwin 1992). One risk behavior, however, may serve as a warning sign that an individual is engaged or intending to engage in other related risk behaviors. Although a certain amount of risk-taking behavior or experimentation is a normal part of adolescent development, it is important and extremely challenging for medical providers to screen and evaluate adolescents to determine when experimentation has progressed to risk-taking behaviors that may be detrimental to the adolescent.

Health consequences of at-risk behaviors are also interrelated and can include unwanted pregnancy, sexually transmitted diseases (STDs), trauma, and AOD abuse. Although the health consequences of some at-risk behaviors may be immediately apparent, such as the relationship between intravenous (IV) drug use and the acquisition of blood-borne pathogens such as human immunodeficiency virus (HIV) and hepatitis B, other consequences may be less immediately apparent. For example, unwanted sexual activity may take place when adolescents are intoxicated, drugs may be exchanged for sexual favors, and adolescents may have difficulty using safer sexual practices or contraception if they are high or drunk.

This chapter focuses on four major areas of adolescent health—pregnancy, STDs, tuberculosis, and trauma—and the relationship to AOD use.

AOD USE AMONG PREGNANT ADOLESCENTS

Significant use of cigarettes and AOD have been found in multiple samples of pregnant adolescents (Amaro et al. 1989; Gilcrest et al. 1990; Kokotailo and Adger 1991; Kokotailo et al. 1992; Lohr et al. 1992; Pletch 1988), but use estimates have varied based on the age of the sample and the method of determining use. Estimates of use have also varied based on whether data were obtained by self-report, medical provider report, urine drug metabolite screening, or a combination of methods, as well as whether use was throughout gestation or at a specific time in pregnancy.

Amaro and colleagues (1989) examined a sample of 253 pregnant adolescents with a mean age of 17.7 years. The sample, described as predominantly poor, urban, unmarried black and Hispanic young women, used AOD during pregnancy as determined by a combination of interviews and urine screenings. Within the previous year 65 percent used alcohol, 41 percent used marijuana, and 17 percent used cocaine. Use during pregnancy was 52 percent for alcohol, 32 percent for marijuana, and 14 percent for cocaine.

Lohr and colleagues (1992) reported initial results of a longitudinal study of a racially mixed group of 241 pregnant and parenting schoolage urban adolescents with a mean age of 16 years. In this study, use during pregnancy was considered to be use in the prior 30 days as determined by interview, with a 50 percent random urine drug screening sample showing misclassification in only 3 percent. Respondents were 28 weeks pregnant on average, and 22 percent reported the use of alcohol or another drug during the prior month while pregnant. Of those who reported use, 70 percent used alcohol, 61 percent used marijuana, 13 percent used cocaine, and 6 percent used other drugs. Almost one-half of the patients used two or more drugs, with alcohol and marijuana used separately or together having the highest incidence of use.

In two separate studies, Kokotailo and colleagues (1992, 1994) found that alcohol and marijuana were the most often used drugs in both schoolage and older pregnant adolescents. In both studies, current (past 30 days) use was determined by self-report on a questionnaire, medical provider report as documented in the medical record, and urine screening for drug metabolites at the initial prenatal visit. In the first study sample of 212 primarily African-American, inner-city, schoolage adolescents (mean age of 16 years), 17 percent of patients were positive for current AOD use determined by one or more of the methods described above. Seven percent of patients were positive for alcohol use, 8 percent for marijuana use, and 6 percent for other drug use. Urine screenings for drug metabolites were positive in 8 percent of the patients, with 55 percent of the metabolites being those of marijuana, 25 percent cocaine, 15 percent opiates, and 5 percent benzodiazepines.

In the second study, using similar methods, a sample of 117 older (mean age of 18 years), primarily Caucasian, small-city adolescents and young women, 35 percent of patients were positive for current AOD use. Alcohol was used by 25 percent of patients and other drugs by 21 percent, nearly all of which was marijuana. At the initial visit, 13 percent of patients were positive (urine screening) for at least one drug metabolite, with the predominant metabolite again being for marijuana (88 percent of all metabolites found).

Many of these recent studies (Amaro et al. 1989; Kokotailo et al. 1992, 1994; Lohr et al. 1992) have examined risk factors associated with AOD use by pregnant adolescents. Common risk factors determined include the patient's history of an STD, patient's previous use of AOD, partner's AOD use and its consequences, patient being intoxicated at school, the lack of a parent in the home, patient with a prior pregnancy, patient's and friend's use of cigarettes, the lack of perceived harm of cigarette and AOD use in pregnancy, and being a school dropout. Determination of such risk factors may be very useful in improving identification of adolescents who use AOD during pregnancy and in improving interventions targeting these young women.

Although there have been few longitudinal studies of AOD use by pregnant adolescents, there have been favorable indications in the study by Lohr and colleagues (1992) and the longitudinal Monitoring the Future Study (Johnston et al. 1991) that pregnant adolescents and young women may sometimes decrease or stop their use of AOD during pregnancy. Lohr and colleagues' (1992) sample demonstrated a high rate of prepregnancy AOD use, but reported a significant drop in use during pregnancy. Johnston and colleagues (1991), in analyzing self-report data comparing use by pregnant young adult women with nonpregnant young adult women (both of whom reported use as teenagers), found substantially higher quitting rates among the pregnant women than the nonpregnant women. These higher rates were found for cigarette use as well as for alcohol, marijuana, and cocaine use.

However, a substantial number of adolescents continue to use during pregnancy. Based upon third trimester urine drug metabolite screenings in the Kokotailo and colleagues' studies (1992, 1994), adolescents continued to use (8 percent positive at both initial and third trimester screen in the younger, urban adolescents; 13 percent positive at initial and 10 percent positive at third trimester screens in the older, small-city adolescents). Lohr and colleagues (1992) also reported a substantial minority of patients who continue to use AOD while pregnant; of these users, almost one-half used more than one substance.

The challenge remains to detect AOD use during pregnancy, to intervene to help young women quit use during pregnancy, and to continue AOD abstinence postpartum.

STDs AND AOD USE AMONG ADOLESCENTS

STDs are not only prevalent in adolescents, they also carry the possibility of lifelong sequelae including chronic pain, infertility (Hatcher et al. 1990), and death. Although the actual number of STD cases are highest in the 20- to 24-year-old age group, younger adolescents have the highest rates of STDs when rates are adjusted to include only those who are sexually active (Neinstein 1991).

Neisseria gonnorhoeae and *Chlamydia trachomatis* are the two most common bacterial STDs in the United States today. Approximately 175,000 cases of gonorrhea in teenagers were reported to the CDC in 1989, while chlamydia infections are estimated to be at least twice as common as gonorrheal infections (Cates 1990). Viral STDs are also common. In office-based, fee-for-service practices, the number of visits by women aged 15 to 19 years increased from 15,000 yearly visits in 1966 to 125,000 visits in 1988. Obviously, these visits to private clinicians represent only a small proportion of total disease (Cates 1990). The prevalence of human papilloma virus (HPV) has been shown to be as high as 38 to 46 percent in urban and college youth, arguably making it the most common STD (Rosenfeld et al. 1989). HIV and the resultant acquired immunodeficiency syndrome (AIDS) are great risks to adolescents and are covered briefly in the section on tuberculosis. Rates of all STDs are generally considered underestimates due to under-reporting as well as the lack of required reporting in some States for many diseases, including chlamydia and many sexually transmitted viral infections such as herpes and HPV.

Shafer and Boyer (1991) described an increased risk of exposure to STDs as largely a result of adolescents' sexual activities and their use of drugs and alcohol. Specifically, adolescents increase their risk of exposure from sexual activities by having their first intercourse at an early age, having multiple sexual partners, and engaging in anal intercourse. Risk is also increased through the inadequate use of barrier contraceptives. Use of AOD has been associated with early first intercourse, inadequate use of contraception, and exchange of sexual activity for drugs.

Shafer and Boyer (1991) further investigated the relationship of AOD use and STD risk behavior in a study of 540 ninth-grade urban students in California by the use of a self-report questionnaire. Sexual risk behaviors investigated included forced sex, sex with gay or bisexual males, history of one or more STD, history of pregnancy, and infrequent condom use.

The investigators found that students' perceptions that peers were not engaging in preventive behaviors and a strong peer affiliation were linked to AOD use by the youth. AOD use was the best predictor of sexual risk behaviors, while lower STD/AIDS knowledge and perceptions that peers are not engaging in preventive behaviors predicted nonuse of condoms.

Strunin and Hingson (1992) also investigated the relationship between AOD use and adolescent sexual behavior in a 1990 study of 1,152 16- to 19-year-olds in Massachusetts by a random digit-dial telephone survey. In this study, 66 percent of adolescents reported engaging in sexual intercourse, with 64 percent reporting intercourse after drinking and 15 percent reporting intercourse after other drug use. Forty-nine percent of the respondents reported being more likely to have sex if they and their partner had used alcohol, and 32 percent reported being more likely to have sex if they and their partner had used drugs. Only 37 percent of the respondents reported always using condoms, 17 percent used condoms less often after drinking, and 10 percent used them less after other drug use.

The authors concluded that since so few adolescents consistently used condoms under any circumstances, the greatest risk for HIV, STDs, and unwanted pregnancy is the *increased* likelihood of having sex after drinking or drug use, *not* the *decreased* likelihood of condom use after drinking and drug use.

Other associations between AOD use and STDs include the finding that adolescent patients with syphilis have been shown to be more likely to have a history of substance abuse when compared with sex-matched controls (Cox et al. 1992). This finding represents a newly recognized risk factor for an old disease and demonstrates the need for a high index of suspicion for syphilis in sexually active AOD abusers. A history of STDs and sexual risk factors have also been associated with adolescent crack cocaine use, which may be influenced by the perception of crack as an aphrodisiac as well as the exchange of crack for sex (Fullilove et al. 1990). High rates of both sexual activity and STDs have also been found in AOD treatment center youth (Jenkins and Simmons 1990).

TUBERCULOSIS AND HIV/AIDS AMONG ADOLESCENTS

The incidence of tuberculosis (TB) in adolescents has been increasing since 1985, paralleling trends in the general population. The rise has generally been attributed to the influx of new cases from foreign-born immigrants as well as the resurgence of cases in areas where HIV infection is prevalent (Mayers 1992). Tuberculosis is a well-known complication of immunosuppression, and HIV infection appears to be an important risk factor for TB.

Until recently, TB was one of the few respiratory diseases that was curable. The recent unfortunate emergence of drug-resistant TB has become a major concern in the United States. In New York City in 1991, 33 percent of TB cases were reported to be resistant to at least one drug, with 19 percent resistant to both isoniazid and rifampin, the two drugs considered most effective for treating TB (CDC 1993*b*). Cases of TB resistant to one or more drugs have been reported to the CDC from all regions across the United States, and outbreaks of multidrug-resistant TB have occurred in a variety of institutional settings including hospitals and prisons. These outbreaks have been characterized by a high prevalence of HIV infection (ranging from 20 to 100 percent) among those affected (CDC 1993*b*).

The prevalence of HIV is approximately one million cases in the U.S. population (National Center for Health Statistics 1994*b*). Although less than 1 percent of AIDS cases are in 13- to 19-year-old adolescents, approximately 19 percent of all cases are in 20- to 29-year-olds. As of June 1994, 1,768 AIDS cases had been reported in 13- to 19-year-olds in the United States and 15,204 cases had been reported in 20- to 24-year-olds (CDC 1994*a*). Given the long latency period of this disease, it is likely that many of these 20- to 29-year-olds were infected as teenagers. Use of injection drugs as well as sexual contact with injection drug users are well-documented methods of HIV transmission.

TB is associated with HIV infection in several important ways. It is estimated that approximately 4 percent of AIDS cases appear on the TB registries nationwide, but the percentage is higher in some areas. HIV seroprevalence in TB patients has ranged from 23 to 29 percent in several studies. The finding that TB often precedes other opportunistic diseases included in the national surveillance definition of AIDS suggests that latent, subclinical TB infection may often progress to clinical TB early in the course of HIV-induced immunosuppression. Therefore, AIDS patients known to have TB may represent only a small proportion of HIV-associated TB (CDC 1989).

Implications of these findings for adolescents include the increased need for medical providers to screen for TB in high-risk youth, especially those who are known to use drugs. The converse is also true: medical providers should screen for AOD use in adolescents who test positive for TB. If an adolescent's TB test is positive, health providers will also need to provide close followup to ensure treatment compliance and evaluate for other health risk factors. Because the administration of a single drug to treat TB often leads to the development of a bacterial population resistant to that drug, treatment regimens with multiple drugs to which the organisms are susceptible are recommended.

A four-drug regimen including isoniazid, rifampin, pyrazinamide, and ethambutol or streptomycin is now recommended by the CDC for initial treatment of TB. The regimen can be altered when results of the organism's drug susceptibility testing are available. Infants and children with TB should be treated with the same regimens as adults, although drug dosages may need to be altered. Because a major cause of drug-resistant TB and treatment failure is patient noncompliance with prescribed treatment, direct observed therapy (DOT) should be considered for all patients. DOT can be conducted with regimens given once a day, two or three times per week. This approach has been shown to increase adherence in both urban and rural settings and provide complete and effective treatment for TB (CDC 1993*b*).

PHYSICAL TRAUMA, VIOLENCE, AND DRUG USE AMONG ADOLESCENTS

Violence, including unintentional injuries, homicide, and suicide, accounts for the majority of deaths of 15- to 24-year-olds in the United States (CDC 1992). Components of the unintentional injury category include MVAs, drowning, poisonings, firearm injuries, burns, and falls. Unintentional injuries account for approximately half of the deaths of 15- to 24-year-olds in the United States, and approximately 75 percent of these deaths involve motor vehicles (CDC 1991). Forty-five percent of those MVAs are related to alcohol use, making MVAs resulting from driving under the influence of alcohol the leading cause of death in this age group. For adolescents under the age of 21, 51 percent of deaths from MVAs are alcohol related (McKenzie 1992).

The National Highway Traffic Safety Administration considers a fatal traffic crash to be alcohol related if either a driver or a nonoccupant (i.e., a pedestrian) had a blood alcohol concentration (BAC) of greater than or equal to 0.01 grams per deciliter (g/dL) in a police-reported traffic crash. (A blood alcohol concentration of ≥ 0.10 g/dL is the legal level of intoxication in most States). The good news about adolescents, alcohol, and MVAs is that the percentage of alcohol-related traffic fatalities among 15- to 24-year-olds decreased from 1982 to 1989, with 15- to 17-year-olds showing the greatest decrease (31 percent reduction). Unfortunately, alcohol-impaired driving still remains a major public health problem; about 7,000 15- to 24-year-old youths in the United States died in alcohol-related crashes in 1989 (CDC 1991).

Factors that may have contributed to the reduction in alcohol-related traffic fatalities include: increases in the minimum drinking age in 37 States from 1982 to 1988, with all 50 States and the District of Columbia now having minimum drinking ages of 21 years; educational efforts and programs for young people aimed at reducing drinking and driving; formation of student groups against drinking and driving; and changes in State laws penalizing drivers with lower blood alcohol levels (CDC 1991).

Although alcohol use increases the risk for an MVA for drivers of all ages, for young drivers the risk begins to increase at very low BACs. At all BACs, the relative risk for crash involvement is greater for younger than older drinking drivers. Prevalence of intoxication in drivers involved in fatal crashes increased with age, with 54 percent of 15- to 17-year-old alcohol-impaired drivers involved in fatal crashes compared with 68 percent of 18- to 20-year-olds, 77 percent of 21- to 24-year-olds, and 79 percent of those over 25 years old in 1989 (CDC 1991) (figure 1).

Less information is available on drug use and its relationship with unintentional injuries. In one of the first studies done in this area, Williams and colleagues (1985) analyzed blood samples of 440 male drivers aged 15 to 34 years old killed in MVAs in California from 1982 to 1983. One or more drugs were found in 81 percent of victims, and two or more in 43 percent. Alcohol was found in 70 percent of drivers, cannabinoids in 37 percent, and cocaine in 11 percent. Nineteen percent of the sample (N = 83) was 15 to 19 years old. Of these adolescents, 35 percent had one or more drugs, and in 37 percent two or more drugs were detected. Alcohol was the most prevalent drug detected in 63 percent of drivers, with marijuana found in 37 percent, and cocaine in 4 percent.

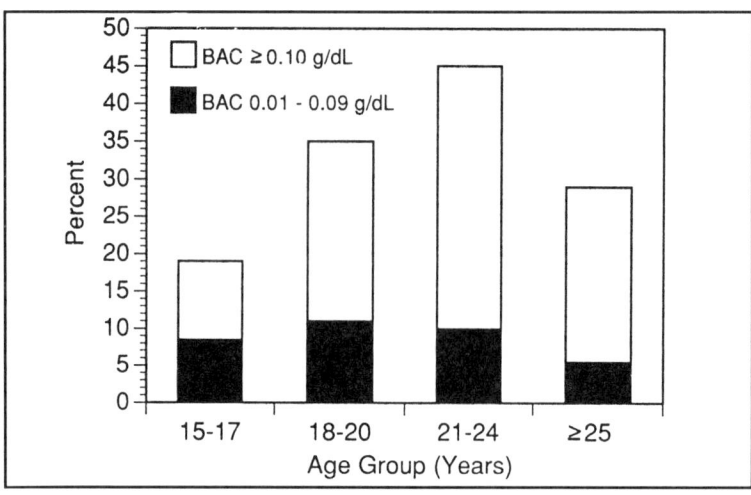

FIGURE 1. *BAC levels of alcohol-impaired drivers* involved in fatal crashes, United States 1989.*

KEY: * = Regardless of whether driver was killed.

SOURCE: CDC 1991.

Drug use in relation to trauma was also examined in an urban Philadelphia study (Lindenbaum et al. 1989), where investigators tested blood and urine samples for alcohol and other drug metabolites in a random sample of trauma patients with both unintentional and violent crime injuries. The sample consisted of 169 patients aged 14 to 85 years old, 80 percent of whom were male, with a mean age of 28.7 years. Positive blood and urine screening results for illicit drugs or prescription drugs with abuse potential were found in 75 percent of all patients, and 36 percent of patients tested positive for alcohol. Alcohol and at least one other drug were found in 28 percent, and two or more drugs were found in 24 percent of samples analyzed. Young people aged 10 to 20 years old accounted for 18 percent of the positive drug screens and 19 percent of the positive alcohol screens. From these results, drug use and alcohol use appear to have an important association with trauma in young people.

Statistics are more difficult to obtain for suicide and homicide, but it is generally thought that alcohol is involved in about 40 percent of suicides and homicides in the 15- to 24-year-old age group (McKenzie 1992).

FUTURE DIRECTIONS

In dealing with the medical problems related to adolescent AOD use and abuse as well as the AOD problems themselves, one must return to the commonality of the risk behaviors. These risk behaviors tend to cluster in adolescents, and techniques and solutions for dealing with these problems, as well as future directions in these research areas, have much in common.

Prevention and early intervention programs should concentrate on all of the common adolescent risk behaviors, be biopsychosocial in nature, and utilize the young person's environment through community-based or school-based programs.

Research focused on evaluating the use of peer methods should be a priority. Peer education and counseling appear to be especially promising prevention techniques for adolescents and very developmentally appropriate, based on the importance of peers in this age group (Bangert-Drowns 1988; Jay et al. 1984; Rubenstein and Panzarine 1990; Tobler 1986).

Development of easy-to-use, reliable, validated, gender-neutral, developmentally and culturally appropriate screening tools should be a continuing priority. Improved screening of adolescents and early intervention for problem behaviors is essential for all of these risk behaviors. As discussed, recent studies have focused on risk factors associated with AOD use among pregnant adolescents and other high-risk teenage groups that should be identified. Research should continue in the development and implementation of accurate and efficient screening methods for these groups, as well as adolescent screening in primary care settings and by medical providers such as nurses and nurse practitioners, social workers, athletic trainers, and mental health providers who deal with adolescents.

Interactive computers and video appear to hold great potential for screening (Paperny et al. 1990) and teaching adolescents (Chewning 1993; Gustafson et al. 1987; Kuhnen and Chewning 1983; Levenson and Morrow 1987; Levenson et al. 1984). Ever-expanding technical developments may further improve a technique especially attractive to adolescents; ongoing evaluation of such techniques is essential.

Evaluation and research in educational strategies should continue. Based on the 1992 Youth Risk Behavior Survey, conducted as part of the 1992 National Health Interview Survey, at least one-fourth of all 12- to 13-year-olds engage in at least one health-risk behavior such as failure to wear safety belts, physical fighting, tobacco use, or alcohol use (CDC 1994*b*). Such findings emphasize the importance of initiating prevention measures early, such as in elementary school, and reinforcing measures in both middle school and high school. Comprehensive school health education should focus on assisting students to avoid or reduce health-risk behaviors, and should be provided from kindergarten through 12th grade (CDC 1994*b*). An example of comprehensive school health guidelines that have been developed for health-risk behavior prevention are the CDC "Guidelines for School Health Programs to Prevent Tobacco Use and Addiction" (CDC 1994*c*).

It is recommended that additional interventions that focus on skills to promote healthy behaviors be made available to young people who are in the workplace and in postsecondary institutions (CDC 1994*b*). Development of medical and psychosocial outreach programs for adolescents both in and out of school may serve the dual purposes of providing needed health and reproductive care as well as engaging adolescents to deal with other psychosocial problems such as AOD abuse. Primary health care providers, in their practices or through medical outreach programs, may also be in a position to address the AOD abuse needs of special populations of adolescents. Such groups would include pregnant, homeless, homosexual, and truant adolescents.

More research is necessary that focuses on the extremely important role of primary care physicians in initially screening and identifying AOD involvement in their adolescent patients, appropriately referring patients to drug abuse treatment programs and/or participating in treatment, and monitoring patient progress in aftercare settings. After the public schools, the health care system may be the most likely site for identification and intervention with adolescent AOD problems. Early intervention programs in the health care system include screening, assessment and referral services, and brief interventions by physicians (Klitzner et al. 1993).

To address these physician issues, the Health Resources Services Administration, in association with the Society for Teachers of Family Medicine (Fleming et al. 1992, 1994), the Ambulatory Pediatric Association, and the Society for General Internal Medicine has organized faculty development teaching programs and curricula in AOD screening and assessment for physicians involved in teaching medical students and residents. Such faculty training and curriculum development should continue and include other medical providers such as nurses and nurse practitioners, social workers, athletic trainers, and mental health providers who deal with adolescents. Further research must also include the evaluation of early intervention programs as well as treatment programs for AOD abuse in adolescents.

REFERENCES

Amaro, H.; Zuckerman, B.; and Cabral, J. Drug use among adolescent mothers: Profile of risk. *Pediatrics* 84:144-151, 1989.

Bangert-Drowns, R.L. The effects of school-based substance abuse education—A meta-analysis. *J Drug Educ* 18:253-264, 1988.

Cates, W. The epidemiology and control of sexually transmitted diseases in adolescents. *Adoles Med* 1(3):409-427, 1990.

Centers for Disease Control and Prevention. Tuberculosis and human immunodeficiency virus infection: Recommendations of the Advisory Committee for the Elimination of Tuberculosis (ACET). *MMWR* 38(14):236-250, 1989.

Centers for Disease Control and Prevention. Alcohol-related traffic fatalities among youth and young adults—United States, 1982-1989. *MMWR* 40(11):148-187, 1991.

Centers for Disease Control and Prevention. Homicide surveillance United States, 1979-1988. *MMWR CDC Surveill Summ* 41(No. SS-3):16-17, 1992.

Centers for Disease Control and Prevention. Mortality trends and the leading causes of death among adolescents and young adults—United States, 1979-1988. *MMWR* 42(23):459-462, 1993*a*.

Centers for Disease Control and Prevention. Initial therapy for tuberculosis in the era of multidrug resistance. Recommendations of the Advisory Council for the Elimination of Tuberculosis. *MMWR* 42(No. RR-7):1-8, 1993*b*.

Centers for Disease Control and Prevention. *HIV/AIDS Surveill Rep* 6(No. 1):5-27, 1994*a*.

Centers for Disease Control and Prevention. Health-risk behaviors among persons aged 12-21 years—United States, 1992. *MMWR* 43(13):231-235, 1994*b*.

Centers for Disease Control and Prevention. Guidelines for school health programs to prevent tobacco use and addiction. *MMWR* 43(No. RR-2):1-18, 1994c.

Chewning, B. Evaluating the computer as a data camera in family planning research. *Adv Popul* 1:85-103, 1993.

Chewning, B.A.; Vankoningsveld, R.; Hawkins, R.; Bosworth, K.; Gustafson, D.; and Moore, J. *"Adolescent Sexual Risk Taking Antecedents and Sequelae."* Final report prepared for the Office of Population Affairs under grant no. APR000937-01-0, 1988.

Cox, J.M.; D'Angelo, L.J.; and Silber, T.J. Substance abuse and syphilis in urban adolescents: A new risk factor for an old disease. *J Adolesc Health* 13(6):483-486, 1992.

Donovan, J.E.; Jessor, R.; and Costa, F.M. Syndrome of problem behaviors in adolescence: A replication. *J Consult Clin Psychol* 56:762-765, 1988.

Fleming, M.; Barry, K.; Davis, A.; Kahn, R.; and Rivo, M. Faculty development in addiction medicine: Project SAEFP, a one year follow-up. *Fam Med* 26:221-225, 1994.

Fleming, M.F.; Clark, K.; Davis, A.; Brown, R.; Finch, J.; Henry, R.; Sherwood, R.; and Politzer, R. National model of faculty development in addiction medicine. *Acad Med* 67(10):691-693, 1992.

Fullilove, R.E.; Fullilove, M.T.; Bowser, B.P.; and Gross, S.A. Risk of sexually transmitted disease among black adolescent crack users in Oakland and San Francisco, Calif. *JAMA* 263(6):851-855, 1990.

Gilcrest, L.D.; Gillmore, M.R.; and Lohr, M.J. Drug use among pregnant adolescents. *J Consult Clin Psychol* 58(4):402-407, 1990.

Gustafson, D.H.; Bosworth, K.; Chewning, B.; and Hawkins, R.P. Computer-based health promotion: Combining technological advances with problem-solving techniques to effect successful health behavior changes. *Ann Rev Public Health* 8:387-415, 1987.

Hatcher, R.A.; Stewart, F.; Trussell, J.; Kowal, D.; Guest, F.; Stewart, G.K.; and Cates, W. *Contraceptive Technology.* New York: Irvington Publishers, Inc., 1990. pp. 91-129.

Jay, M.S.; DuRant, R.H.; Shofitt, T.; Linder, C.W.; and Litt, I.F. Effect of peer counselors on adolescent compliance in use of oral contraceptives. *Pediatrics* 73:126-131, 1984.

Jenkins, S.C., and Simmons, P.S. Survey of genitourinary organisms in a population of sexually active adolescent males admitted to a chemical dependency unit. *J Adolesc Health Care* 11(3):223-226, 1990.

Jessor, R., and Jessor, S.L. *Problem Behavior and Psychosocial Development: A Longitudinal Study of Youth.* New York: Academic Press, 1977.

Johnston, L.D.; O'Malley, P.M.; and Bachman, J.G. *Drug Use Among American High School Seniors, College Students and Young Adults, 1975-1990.* Vol. 1. High School Seniors. DHHS Pub. No. (ADM) 91-1813. Rockville, MD: National Institute on Drug Abuse, 1991.

Johnston, L.D.; O'Malley, P.M.; and Bachman, J.G. *National Survey Results on Drug Use from the Monitoring the Future Study, 1975-1993.* Vol. 1. Secondary School Students. NIH Pub. No. 94-3809. Rockville, MD: National Institute on Drug Abuse, 1994.

Klitzner, M.; Fisher, D.; Stewart, K.; and Gilbert, S. *Substance Abuse: Early Intervention for Adolescents.* Princeton, NJ: Robert Wood Johnson Foundation, 1993.

Kokotailo, P.K., and Adger, H. Substance use by pregnant adolescents. *Clin Perinatol* 18(1):125-138, 1991.

Kokotailo, P.K.; Adger, H.; Duggan, A.K.; Repke, J.; and Joffe, A. Cigarette, alcohol and other drug use by school age pregnant adolescents: Prevalence, detection and associated risk factors. *Pediatrics* 90:328-334, 1992.

Kokotailo, P.K.; Langhough, R.E.; Smith Cox, N.; Davidson, S.R.; and Fleming, M.F. Cigarette, alcohol and other drug use among small city pregnant adolescents. *J Adolesc Health* 15:366-373, 1994.

Kuhnen, K., and Chewning, B. BARNY: A computer who cares about adolescents' sex education. *Am J Mat Child Nurs* 8:350, 1983.

Levenson, P.M., and Morrow, J.R. Learner characteristics associated with responses to film and interactive video lessons on smokeless tobacco. *Prev Med* 16:52-62, 1987.

Levenson, P.M.; Morrow, J.R.; and Smith, P. Instructional design strategies for developing an interactive video educational program for pregnant teens. *Patient Educ Couns* 6:149-154, 1984.

Lindenbaum, G.A.; Carroll, S.F.; Daskal, I.; and Kapusnick, R. Patterns of alcohol and drug abuse in an urban trauma center: The increasing rate of cocaine abuse. *J Trauma* 29(12):1654-1658, 1989.

Lohr, M.J.; Gillmore, M.R.; Gilchrist, L.D.; and Butler, S.S. Factors related to substance use by pregnant school-age adolescents. *J Adolesc Health* 13(6):475-482, 1992.

Mayers, M.M. Tuberculosis. In: Friedman, S.B.; Fisher, M.; and Schonberg, S.K., eds. *Comprehensive Adolescent Health Care.* St. Louis, MO: Quality Medical Publishing, Inc., 1992.

McKenzie, R.G. Substance use and abuse. In: Friedman, S.B.; Fisher, M.; and Schonberg, S.K., eds. *Comprehensive Adolescent Health Care.* St. Louis, MO: Quality Medical Publishing, Inc., 1992.

Mott, F.L., and Haurin, R.J. Linkages between sexual activity and alcohol and drug use among American adolescents. *Fam Plann Perspect* 20:128-136, 1988.

National Center for Health Statistics. Advance report of final mortality statistics, 1989. *Vital Health Stat* [2] 40(8):15, 1992.

National Center for Health Statistics. *Health, United States, 1993.* DHHS Pub. No. (PHS) 94-1232. Hyattsville, MD: Public Health Service, 1994*a*.

National Center for Health Statistics. *Healthy People 2000 Review, 1993.* DHHS Pub. No. (PHS) 94-1232-1. Hyattsville, MD: Public Health Service, 1994*b*.

Neinstein, L.S. *Adolescent Health Care: A Practical Guide.* Baltimore: Urban and Schwarzenberg, 1991.

Paperny, D.M.; Aono, J.Y.; Lehman, R.M.; Hammar, S.L.; and Risser, J. Computer-assisted detection and intervention in adolescent high-risk health behaviors. *J Pediatr* 116(3):456-462, 1990.

Pletch, P.K. Substance use and health activities of pregnant adolescents. *J Adolesc Health Care* 9:38-45, 1988.

Rosenfeld, W.D.; Vermund, S.H.; Wentz, S.J.; and Burk, R.D. High prevalence rate of human papillomavirus infection and association with abnormal Papanicolaou smears in sexually active adolescents. *Am J Dis Child* 143:1443-1447, 1989.

Rubenstein, E.M., and Panzarine, S. Peer counseling with adolescent mothers: A pilot program. *Fam Soc* 71:136-141, 1990.

Ryan, S.A., and Irwin, C.E. Risk behavior. In: Friedman, S.B.; Fisher, M.; and Schonberg, S.K., eds. *Comprehensive Adolescent Health Care*. St. Louis, MO: Quality Medical Publishing, Inc., 1992.

Shafer, M.A., and Boyer, C.B. Psychosocial and behavioral factors associated with risk of sexually transmitted diseases, including human immunodeficiency virus infection, among urban high school students. *J Pediatr* 119(5):826-833, 1991.

Strunin, L., and Hingson, R. Alcohol, drugs, and adolescent sexual behavior. *Int J Addict* 27(2):129-146, 1992.

Tobler, N.S. Meta-analysis of 143 adolescent drug prevention programs: Quantitative outcome results of program participants compared to a control or comparison group. *J Drug Issues* 16:537-567, 1986.

Williams, A.F.; Peat, M.A.; Crouch, D.J.; Wells, J.K.; and Finkle, B.S. Drugs in fatally injured young male drivers. *Pub Health Rep* 100(1):19-25, 1985.

Zabin, L.S. The association between smoking and sexual behavior among teens in US contraceptive clinics. *Am J Public Health* 74:261-263, 1984.

AUTHOR

Patricia Kokotailo, M.D., M.P.H.
Assistant Professor of Pediatrics
Director of Pediatric Medical Education
Department of Pediatrics
The University of Wisconsin-Madison
CSC H6/440
600 Highland Avenue
Madison, WI 53792-4116

AIDS, Drugs, and the Adolescent

Elizabeth Steel

INTRODUCTION

Drug abuse is a major factor in the spread of human immunodeficiency virus (HIV) in the United States. The direct injection of infected blood is an extremely efficient way to transmit pathogens. People who share equipment for injecting drugs are at risk for contracting acquired immunodeficiency syndrome (AIDS) whenever HIV is present in the local population of drug injectors. In addition, drug use contributes to the transmission of AIDS and other sexually transmitted diseases (STDs). Many drugs (including alcohol) are disinhibiting, so users are more likely than nonusers to engage in unprotected sex. Also, the need to obtain drugs may become so urgent that the user feels impelled to trade sex for drugs or for money to purchase drugs. Under such circumstances, multiple high-risk sex acts with many partners have been noted.

AIDS was first identified in adults; therefore, early AIDS research was conducted using adult subjects. Later, a research focus on children under the age of 13 developed. More recently, adolescents have begun to be viewed as a population with specific needs in terms of HIV prevention and treatment.

This chapter reviews what is known about drug abuse-related AIDS and adolescents. Since there is such a long period of time between HIV infection and the onset of symptoms, the extent of the illness in young adults and in teenagers is reviewed. Issues of prevention and access to care as they relate to teens are addressed. Barriers to conducting research in this population are also noted.

BACKGROUND

Adolescence is a time of great change. The young person defines him- or herself to him- or herself and to the world, drawing on internal and external experiences in the process. The body changes, developing attributes that characterize the sexually mature male and female. This individual begins to identify as a heterosexual or homosexual person. He or she accepts or disavows some of the norms and values of the people who raised him or her. Given a reasonably healthy mind, body, and environment, the adolescent uses the years between 13 and 18 to establish the personal identity that will frame life as an adult (Springhall and Collins 1984).

Nature has provided the adolescent with characteristics that are functional in that they facilitate transition to adulthood. The youth is willing to experiment, to take risks, and is relatively oblivious to the dangers implicit in risk taking. Potential consequences of actions for either the long or the short term are far from the mind. He or she is even relatively unaware of personal mortality, as any parent of a teenaged driver can confirm.

These same characteristics that allow transition from childhood to adulthood also make the adolescent particularly vulnerable to drug experimentation and to diseases such as AIDS. The boy who is willing to test himself against the dangers of the football field may also be willing to share the syringe full of steroids that is passed by a locker room buddy. The girl who competes for attention from a popular boy may be willing to engage in unprotected sex in order to hold him.

In even more danger of contracting and transmitting AIDS are those young people who are outside the societal mainstream: runaway children, throwaway children, and youngsters who are homeless and living on the streets. Many come from dysfunctional families, and a history of physical or sexual abuse is common. These youngsters are often in high-risk situations and may engage in multiple high-risk behaviors (Hein 1991). Some in these groups trade sex for money that is used to pay for necessities (survival sex). Others engage in prostitution to pay for the drugs that provide them with some escape from the unpleasant realities of their lives (Rickel and Hendren 1993).

EXTENT OF THE PROBLEM

Population Data

The United States had a total of 248.8 million people at the end of 1989 (U.S. Bureau of the Census 1991). Of these, 24.4 million (or just under 10 percent) were between the ages of 13 and 19. Males made up 48.8 percent of the total population and 51.2 percent of the adolescents. Whites, who account for 84.1 percent of the total population, made up

80.3 percent of the adolescent population. Blacks, who comprised 12.4 percent of the total population, accounted for 15.6 percent of adolescents (U.S. Bureau of the Census 1991).

At the same time, another 16.4 percent of the population was between the ages of 20 and 29. Half this group were male, 83 percent were white, and 13.6 percent were black (U.S. Bureau of the Census 1991).

Cases of AIDS

By the end of December 1993, a total of 361,164 cases of AIDS in the United States had been reported to the Centers for Disease Control and Prevention (CDC). Less than 1 percent (N = 1,554) of these cases were reported in adolescents between the ages of 13 and 19. On the other hand, 19 percent (N = 68,483) of all cases were reported in young adults between the ages of 20 and 29 (CDC 1994). The long incubation period between HIV infection and the onset of AIDS makes it reasonable to assume that many young adults were infected with HIV during their teen years but did not exhibit symptoms until much later.

In terms of race and ethnicity, whites between the ages of 13 and 29 accounted for 47 percent of the total AIDS cases in people of those ages. Another 32.6 percent of the cases was diagnosed in blacks. Hispanics, who made up about 8.3 percent of the U.S. population in 1989, accounted for 19 percent of the AIDS cases diagnosed in people aged 13 to 29 through December 1993 (CDC 1994).

Injecting drug use has been accepted as a risk factor for the transmission of HIV since 1983. The possible relationship of HIV transmission with noninjecting drug use was recognized later, but the CDC HIV/AIDS surveillance reports do not track these data. However, some studies have addressed this issue. The CDC's 1990 Youth Risk Behavior Survey found a relationship between the use of marijuana, cocaine, and other illicit drugs (and, to some extent, alcohol and tobacco) and an increased likelihood of engaging in unsafe sexual behaviors (Lowry et al. 1994). Cooper and colleagues (1994) randomly sampled 1,259 sexually active adolescents and found that substance abuse was associated with increased sexual risk taking at first intercourse and at first intercourse with the most recent sexual partner. Butcher and colleagues (1991) studied the intersection between alcohol intoxication and sexual intercourse. Of 243 single, heterosexual 17- to 24-year-old students, 47 percent of the men and 57 percent of the women stated that they had had sexual intercourse between 1 and 5 times primarily because they were intoxicated. Additionally, Boyer and Kegeles (1991) noted that several studies have correlated sexual intercourse while under the influence of alcohol and drugs with high-risk sexual activities in adults, both homosexual men and heterosexual men and women.

Injecting drug use by an individual, sexual partner, or a parent was identified as the HIV exposure category for 35 percent of all AIDS cases reported through December 1993. For 13- to 19-year-olds with AIDS, 14 percent of cases were related to the individual's injecting drug use. A full 24 percent of cases were related to injecting drug use by the individual or by a sexual partner. (No individuals with perinatally acquired infection were given an AIDS diagnosis during adolescence.) Remembering that AIDS cases reflect events that occurred many years before symptoms appear, 24 percent is a surprisingly high figure to be related to injecting drug use.

Overall, seven times as many males as females have been diagnosed with AIDS in this country. On the other hand, for 13- to 19-year-olds, the ratio is 2.2 males to 1 female. Among blacks teens with AIDS, the ratio is only 1.1 males to each female (CDC 1994).

Adolescent women show a particular vulnerability to acquiring HIV through heterosexual contact. Fifty-two percent of those diagnosed with AIDS have a history of such contact as compared with 35 percent of the cases in all women. For both adolescent men and all men, heterosexual contact accounts for only 2 percent of the AIDS cases (CDC 1994).

HIV Infection

Less is known about the prevalence of HIV infection among Americans in general than is known about their rates of diagnosed AIDS. HIV seropositivity has recently become reportable in 26 States (only pediatric cases are reportable in Connecticut) (CDC 1994). In addition, many people have not been tested for HIV. However, data from a variety of sources yield some idea of the extent of the epidemic in certain populations of young people.

Adolescents accounted for 3.5 percent of the 55,649 HIV infection cases (not AIDS) reported to CDC through December 1993 (CDC 1994). In female adolescents, 19.5 percent of HIV infections were related to personal injecting drug use or sexual relations with an injecting drug user (IDU). For males, this proportion was 12.9 percent.

Two national surveys drew on populations of adolescents applying to enter the Job Corps and the military. By looking at these broad groups, it was possible to identify some differences in seropositivity related to geography that would not be picked up in smaller surveys. Note, however, that self-selection factors make the military's numbers, in particular, probably underrepresentative of the total population of adolescents who might otherwise apply for admission.

Burke and colleagues (1990) tested sera from more than one million applicants to the U.S. military between October 1985 and March 1989. They found an overall seropositivity rate of 0.34 per 1,000 (about 1 positive test for every 3,000 teenagers tested). The highest rates were noted in youth from the District of Columbia and urban counties in New York, Maryland, and Texas. Rates in males were similar to those in females, with 17- and 18-year-old females having even higher rates than were found in males of the same ages. Black youth had higher prevalence rates (1.06 per 1,000) than did Hispanics (0.31/1,000) or whites (0.18/1,000). No information about individual risk behaviors was available for these subjects.

St. Louis and colleagues (1991) studied 137,209 adolescents who applied to the U.S. Job Corps between October 1987 and February 1990. These youngsters, unlike the military recruits, were considered to be socioeconomically disadvantaged. Their overall seropositivity rate was found to be 3.6 per 1,000, more than 10 times that found in the Burke and colleagues (1990) study. The highest overall rates were found in the Northeast, which is primarily urban. When the data were analyzed in terms of metropolitan statistical area (MSA) size, however, the seroprevalence rates for rural areas and smaller cities were higher in the South than in the Northeast. The overall seroprevalence rate in males was 3.7 per 1,000; in females, 3.2 per 1,000. In younger subjects ages 16 and 17, rates in females were higher than those in males. The rates for females from the South (Florida and Georgia) were nearly twice the rates for males from any State, from New York City, or from the District of Columbia. As in the study of military recruits, no data about individual risk factors were provided. However, it was noted that a history of substance abuse would not preclude admission to the Job Corps.

As one might expect, HIV seroprevalence has been found to be higher in groups of adolescents from the high-risk end of the spectrum than in the broader samples of adolescents drawn from such populations as military recruits and Job Corps applicants. One study (Stricof et al. 1991) reported that 5.3 percent of 2,667 young people tested in a facility for runaway and homeless adolescents in New York City were positive for HIV. Another study was conducted by D'Angelo and colleagues (1991) of all adolescents (ages 13 to 19) receiving outpatient care at Children's National Medical Center in the District of Columbia. They found an overall seroprevalence rate of 0.37 percent in blood samples drawn for other reasons. A subset of these adolescents who were considered to be at high risk were offered HIV testing during the study period; of those who accepted, 4.1 percent were found to be HIV positive.

Drug Use in Adolescence

A major survey of adolescent drug use has been conducted for the National Institute on Drug Abuse (NIDA) annually since 1975. Originally designed to follow high school seniors, the survey was expanded in 1991 to include 8th and 10th graders. The expanded survey provides information about younger students and reaches some youngsters who might not remain in school until the senior year (Johnson et al. 1992).

A decrease in illicit drug use among mainstream youngsters has been noted for some time. For example, 40.7 percent of students in the graduating class of 1992 admitted to having used an illicit drug at least once in their lifetime. This compares with 44.1 percent in the class of 1991, and 65.6 percent in the class of 1981. The lifetime use of cocaine was down among seniors (7.8 percent in 1991; 6.1 percent in 1992). However, an increase was seen among 8th graders (2.3 percent in 1991; 2.9 percent in 1992) (Johnson et al. 1992). This is particularly worrisome since cocaine is a short-acting drug, and frequent doses may be taken in order to maintain a high. For this reason, it has been shown that individuals who inject cocaine are at greater risk for HIV infection than persons who inject only heroin (Chaisson et al. 1989).

Since 1977, a subset of the youngsters surveyed as high school seniors has been followed for several years into college. A downward trend in illicit drug use has been seen, with 29.2 percent of the 1991 sample reporting use of an illicit substance within the preceding year, down from 33.3 percent in 1990. Past year cocaine use was reported by 3.6 percent of the college students in 1991, and 0.5 percent used cocaine in the form of crack. Only 0.1 percent reported past year use of heroin. No indication is given of whether the noncrack-cocaine and the heroin were injected or taken by some other route (Johnson et al. 1992).

Another large survey addressed people who live in households, again perhaps missing those at highest risk for drug-related AIDS. The 1992 National Household Survey on Drug Abuse found that more than 4 million youngsters aged 12 to 17 (20.1 percent) had tried an illicit drug at least once in their lives. More than 490,000 had tried cocaine, and about 51,000 used it at least weekly. More than 1 million used alcohol once a week or more, and the impaired judgment that may accompany such use makes it an important risk factor for AIDS (NIDA 1992).

IDUs are difficult to identify and to count. Their behavior is both illegal and stigmatized, and they often live in unstable or transient situations. However, there are a few studies of adolescent IDUs, and three are noted here.

DuRant and colleagues (1993) surveyed 1,881 students in Richmond County, Georgia. They found that 6.5 percent of the males and 1.9 percent of the females reported using anabolic steroids illicitly. A quarter of these reported sharing needles for drug injection within the preceding 30 days. The research group found a significant association between the use of anabolic steroids and the use of other drugs including marijuana, cocaine, and alcohol.

In studying a probability sample of all 9th through 12th graders in the United States, Holtzman and colleagues (1991) found that 2.7 percent had a history of drug injection and 0.8 percent had shared needles. By extrapolating to population figures, they estimated that 102,200 youngsters may have already engaged in the type of sharing behavior that can effectively transmit HIV.

Finally, the CDC recently reported data on IDUs among students participating in State and local school-based components of the Youth Risk Behavior Surveillance System (CDC 1993). A range of 1 percent to 4 percent of injectors were self-reported by students in grades 9 to 12, with a national prevalence of 2 percent. At all sites, 5 percent or less of males and females reported injecting drugs.

Drug-Related Sexual Risk Factors

A full discussion of sexual risk factors is beyond the scope of this chapter. However, some issues that relate drug abuse to sexual risk should be noted.

Boyer and Ellen (1994) reported that adolescents are engaging in sexual intercourse at early ages, and some engage in serial or sequential relationships with a number of partners. Anal intercourse is not rare, and is sometimes used as a form of birth control. STDs and pregnancy rates are high. The prevalence of condom use is unclear, but probably low.

As stated earlier, sex and drugs are related in a number of ways. Drugs may be used as disinhibitors. Sex may be traded for drugs or the money to pay for drugs, and certain drugs may have an aphrodisiac effect. Additional drug-related sexual risks may be inferred from social and environmental factors. Sexual abuse, which has been related to drug-using behaviors in adolescents, may also be related to drug or alcohol problems in their abusers. Runaway or throwaway youngsters who resort to prostitution may have fled from parents who are alcoholic or dependent on illicit drugs. Adolescents who are incarcerated for drug-related crimes (12 percent of the juveniles in custody in 1989) (Morris et al. 1992) may be subject to sexual attacks or may participate in unprotected sex when condoms are not available. Some studies report that rape is prevalent among runaway and homeless youth (Sowder 1991). Indeed, Sondheimer (1992) noted that the rate of sexual abuse among homeless women is 20 times the rate among all women, and 50 percent of all rape victims are under age 18. Finally, gay and lesbian youth who are unsure of their sexual orientation or ashamed to be different from the majority may use drugs to overcome their sexual inhibitions.

Summary

Blood and blood products are basically safe in the United States, and AIDS cases related to hemophilia or the receipt of blood transfusion, blood components, or tissue are declining from 3 percent of cumulative adult AIDS cases to 2 percent of cases reported in 1993 alone and from 10 percent of cumulative pediatric AIDS cases to 5 percent of pediatric cases reported in 1993 alone (CDC 1994). Adolescents, like everyone else, are most at risk for AIDS if they engage in risky sexual or injection behaviors with HIV-infected people. Both factors must be present—the virus, and the opportunity to pass it from one person to another. The likelihood of becoming infected through a single encounter with the virus is unknown. However, the more often one engages in high-risk behaviors, the more likely one is to encounter the virus.

It is important to remember that adolescent drug abusers are not a single homogeneous group. These youth are of differing races, religions, and ethnic backgrounds and have differing interests and social network patterns. They live in various parts of the country, and in geographic areas with differing population densities. Some live in traditional settings with their families and face risks that may differ in kind and intensity from those facing street youth. The busy high school student may be at risk only on Saturday night at a party where liquor is available and condoms are not. Other youngsters may be as marginal as the displaced and undocumented Latino youth who arrive at San Francisco's Larkin Street Youth Center with no money, possessions, or connections (Kennedy and Van Houten 1992). These adolescents may be at daily risk when they engage in prostitution to acquire money for food and shelter, and perhaps for drugs.

Penetrative sexual acts and injecting drug use are the activities that now put adolescents at highest risk for acquiring HIV. Noninjecting drug use, and particularly the use of crack cocaine, is also of concern.

IMPLICATIONS FOR DRUG ABUSE TREATMENT

Drug abuse treatment has been found to be an effective means of limiting the spread of HIV in adults (Ball et al. 1988; Metzger et al. 1993; Novick et al. 1990). It is also an important component of comprehensive care for some people who are HIV infected. For an adolescent who is already dependent on drugs, treatment may help diminish high-risk sexual or injecting behaviors and thus protect the youth from acquiring HIV. For those who are both HIV seropositive and drug dependent, drug abuse treatment may improve the quality of their lives and help them to avoid high-risk behaviors and pregnancy, thus limiting the spread of HIV to others.

Surgeon General Joycelyn Elders has written that "Contemporary threats to adolescent health are largely the result of social environment and/or behavior" (Elders and Hui 1993). Two of the most urgent conditions threatening adolescents are AIDS and drug abuse. Unfortunately, both are major public health problems that have social, behavioral, moral, and legal aspects in addition to their impact on physical health. As a result, there are gaps in researchers' knowledge of these conditions in all populations, and particularly in adolescents. Consequently, barriers are encountered in trying to ensure that people with these problems have adequate access to assessment and care (Dougherty et al. 1992; Steel and Haverkos 1992).

Among the gaps in knowledge is a full understanding of the antecedents to drug use. The reasons why adolescents use drugs are varied and include social, biological, and behavioral influences. Peer pressure explains some drug use. Some teens use drugs to escape from unpleasant realities or to build courage for experimenting with sex. Some depressed youngsters may self-medicate with street drugs (Rotheram-Borus et al. 1989). Researchers need to know more about the range of adolescents' sexual behaviors, their antecedents, and their relationship to drug abuse.

One major barrier to providing care for adolescents is the limited pool of providers who are skilled in assessment. Even those youngsters who are identified as troubled by school personnel or others may not receive an adequate assessment for substance abuse or for HIV risk. Primary health care providers may have little training in the signs and symptoms of substance abuse. If adolescents are referred to drug treatment personnel, those counselors may have gaps in their understanding of the medical sequelae of drug abuse, including AIDS. Providers who do have knowledge of both conditions may still encounter subtle pressure to deny the existence of a stigmatized problem such as substance abuse. This denial may be on the individual patient level ("My patient is the son of a middle-class professional and therefore would not use cocaine or be at risk for HIV infection."). It may also be on the community level ("Kids shouldn't drink, of course, but sometimes they sneak a few beers. Anyway, we all like to have a good time around here, and we certainly don't have any alcoholics in this good part of town."). Provider resistance to assessing teen clients for HIV and drug abuse must be overcome. Cross-training of primary health care, substance abuse, and mental health providers is one way to address this problem.

Another barrier to care is locating appropriate drug treatment programs for teenagers. Millstein and colleagues (1993) noted that in promoting adolescent health, the cultural and social contexts in which the adolescents live need to be considered. And Rotheram-Borus and colleagues (1994) have pointed out that Maslow's hierarchy of needs provides a foundation. A teenager who presents as hungry, cold, sick, and frightened is not likely to be able to consider and benefit from drug abuse treatment. In cases when there is coexisting mental or physical illness, access to drug abuse treatment may be even more limited. In a recent review of adolescent-focused HIV prevention and service delivery programs funded by the Health Resources and Services Administration, it was noted that referrals for drug treatment have been among the most difficult to make (Conviser 1992).

An important issue is the need to determine what types of drug treatment programs would be useful in reducing HIV transmission in adolescent populations. Studies involving adults have been conducted in methadone maintenance clinics. More must be learned about the types of youngsters who inject drugs, the types of treatment programs that will be most effective in reaching them, and the likelihood that such programs will reduce their HIV risk behaviors and their acquisition of HIV. Similarly, more must be known about noninjecting drug abuse in adolescents, its relationship to the transmission of HIV, and the types of drug abuse treatment programs that will effectively reduce HIV risk behaviors.

Logistical, Financial, and Legal Problems

Logistical, financial, and legal problems are other barriers to drug abuse treatment. HIV-positive, drug-abusing youngsters often lack the kind of network that provides informal support to their functional peers. Even when family support is present, the majority of adolescents come from families with working parents who cannot afford the loss of salary that would result from accompanying the youngster to treatment. In areas where there is no public transportation, an adolescent without a drivers license or an adult available to provide transportation would be unable to participate in treatment. For teenage mothers, a lack of child care would represent a significant barrier.

Many adolescents lack health insurance (1 of 7, or 4.6 million) or Medicaid coverage (1 of 3 poor adolescents, or 1.76 million) (Dougherty et al. 1992). When insurance is available, it does not always cover drug abuse treatment or treatment for HIV/AIDS. Underage youth may need parental consent for treatment, so that even in the presence of adequate financing, access to health care may be limited. There are exceptions to the consent requirements, but these vary from locality to locality and "Even with any given state, laws governing consent and confidentiality frequently seem to lack a coherent rationale" (Dougherty et al. 1992, p. 172).

More information is needed about the efficacy of case management or care coordination in ensuring that adolescents with HIV and drug abuse problems receive appropriate drug abuse treatment. What other types of interventions might serve the same purpose? Can outreach and advocacy workers help youngsters to negotiate the systems that should lead them to services?

In summary, much needs to be done before the conditions that lead to drug abuse-related HIV infection in adolescents are understood. Drug abuse treatment is probably an important method for reducing AIDS risk behaviors in adolescents. It should be linked with primary health care and mental health services. Social services, when indicated, should also be available. Further studies will help researchers develop specific treatment recommendations for identifying teens in need of care, designing the most effective modalities for treating them, and ensuring that they have access to care once the need has been identified.

RESEARCH NEEDS

It is clear that drug abuse plays a major role in the acquisition of HIV. It has also been shown that drug abuse treatment can have an important role in preventing the acquisition of HIV in adults. Beyond that, there are gaps in knowledge. Many questions about adolescents, AIDS, and drug abuse remain to be answered. Some of these are as follows:

1. Adult studies that indicate that drug abuse treatment is useful for preventing AIDS have been conducted in methadone maintenance programs. Does drug treatment also reduce the transmission of HIV in adolescent populations? What kinds of treatment are most effective?

2. Who are the youngsters who inject drugs? What predisposes adolescents to engage in high-risk drug use and sexual behaviors? What type of drug abuse treatment is most likely to diminish such behaviors?

3. How can drug treatment providers, primary health care providers, and mental health practitioners be trained to identify, refer, and treat teenagers with HIV (or at risk for HIV) and substance abuse problems?

4. How can communities be encouraged to initiate or expand drug treatment programs that meet the needs of adolescents with or at risk for HIV?

5. What role do prior sexual abuse and other factors related to family dysfunction play in the development of teens at risk for AIDS? What interventions at the family or network level might be useful in reducing this risk?

6. What are the actual behaviors that place teens at risk, and why do they engage in them (e.g., anal intercourse to preserve virginity or prevent conception; taking drugs to self-medicate for depression)? What interventions might reduce the frequency of these behaviors?

7. How can research be conducted on populations of legal minors when there are concerns about confidentiality and alienation from parents? Do adolescents have legal access to the services that are needed? How can research be adapted to conform with the widely varying State and local laws that affect youngsters?

These questions are not an exhaustive list of issues to be resolved, but they do identify some of the research areas to be addressed in curbing the terrible epidemic of AIDS. Drug abuse has always been a threat to the lives of young people. Now drug abuse-related AIDS has become a major killer of people in their most productive years. Researchers must do all they can to reduce its impact.

REFERENCES

Ball, J.C.; Myers, C.P.; and Friedman, S.R. Reducing the risk of AIDS through methadone maintenance treatment. *J Health Soc Behav* 28(3):213-215, 1988.

Boyer, C.B., and Ellen, J.M. HIV risk in adolescents: The role of sexual activity and substance use behaviors. In: Battjes, R.J.; Sloboda, Z.; and Grace, W.C., eds. *The Context of HIV Risk Among Drug Users and Their Sexual Partners*. National Institute on Drug Abuse Research Monograph No. 143. NIH Pub. No. 94-3750. Washington, DC: Supt. of Docs., U.S. Govt. Print. Off., 1994.

Boyer, C.B., and Kegeles, S.M. AIDS risk and prevention among adolescents. *Soc Sci Med* 33(1):11-23, 1991.

Burke, D.S.; Brundage, M.C.; Goldenbaum, M.S.; Gardner, L.I.; Peterson, M.; Visintine, R.; Redfield, R.R.; and the Walter Reed Retrovirus Research Group. Human immunodeficiency virus infections in teenagers: Seroprevalence among applicants for US military service. *JAMA* 263(15):2074-2077, 1990.

Butcher, A.H.; Manning, D.T.; and O'Neal, E.C. HIV-related sexual behaviors of college students. *J Am Coll Health* 40(3):115-118, 1991.

Centers for Disease Control and Prevention. Selected behaviors that increase risk for HIV infection, other sexually transmitted diseases, and unintended pregnancy among high school students—United States, 1991. *JAMA* 269(3):329-330, 1993.

Centers for Disease Control and Prevention. *HIV/AIDS Surveillance Report* 5(no. 4):8-25, 1994.

Chaisson, R.E.; Bacchetti, P.; and Brodie, B. Cocaine use and HIV infection in intravenous drug users in San Francisco Medical Service, San Francisco General Hospital. *JAMA* 262(11):1471-1472, 1989.

Conviser, R. "Serving Young People At Risk for HIV Infection: Case Studies of Adolescent-Focused HIV Prevention and Service Delivery Programs." Report prepared for the National Pediatric HIV Resource Center, 1992.

Cooper, M.L.; Pierce, R.S.; and Huselid, R.F. Substance use and sexual risk taking among black adolescents and white adolescents. *Health Psychol* 13(3):251-262, 1994.

D'Angelo, L.J.; Getson, P.R.; Luban, N.L.C.; and Gayle, H.D. Human immunodeficiency virus infection in urban adolescents: Can we predict who is at risk? *Pediatrics* 88(5):982-986, 1991.

Dougherty, D.; Eden, J.; Kemp, K.B.; Metcalf, K.; Rowe, K.; Ruby, G.; Strobel, P.; and Solarz, A. Adolescent health: A report to the U.S. Congress. *J School Health* 62(5):167-174, 1992.

DuRant, R.H.; Rickert, V.I.; Ashworth, C.S.; Newman, C.; and Slavens, G. Use of multiple drugs among adolescents who use anabolic steroids. *N Engl J Med* 328(13):922-926, 1993.

Elders, M.J., and Hui, J. Making a difference in adolescent health. [Editorial] *JAMA* 269(11):1425-1426, 1993.

Hein, K. Risky business: Adolescents and human immunodeficiency virus. *Pediatrics* 88(5):1052-1054, 1991.

Holtzman, D.; Anderson, J.E.; Kann, L.; Arday, S.L.; Truman, B.I.; and Kolbe, L.J. HIV instruction, HIV knowledge, and drug injection among high school students in the United States. *Am J Public Health* 81(12):1596-1601, 1991.

Johnson, L.D.; O'Malky, P.M.; and Bachman, J.G. *National Survey Results on Drug Use from the Monitoring the Future Study, 1975-1992.* Vol. 1. Secondary School Students. NIH Pub. No. 94-3809. Rockville, MD: National Institute on Drug Abuse, 1992.

Kennedy, M., and Van Houten, C. Comprehensive services for homeless Latino immigrant and refugee youth in San Francisco. In: Bond, L.S., ed. *A Portfolio of AIDS/STD Behavioral Interventions and Research.* Washington, DC: Pan American Health Organization, 1992. pp. 65-69.

Lowry R.; Holtzman, D.; Truman, B.I.; Kann, L.; Collins, J.L.; and Kolbe, L.J. Substance use and HIV-related sexual behaviors among US high school students: Are they related? *Am J Public Health* 84:1116-1120, 1994.

Metzger, D.S.; Woody, G.E.; McLellan, A.T.; O'Brien, C.P.; Druley, P.; Navaline, H.; DePhilippis, D.; Stolley, P.; and Abrutyn, E. Human immunodeficiency virus seroconversion among intravenous drug users in- and out-of-treatment: An 18-month prospective follow-up. *J AIDS* 6(9):1049-1056, 1993.

Millstein, S.G.; Nightingale, E.O.; Petersen, A.C.; Mortimer, A.M.; and Hamburg, D.A. Promoting the healthy development of adolescents. *JAMA* 269(11):1413-1415, 1993.

Morris, R.E.; Baker, C.J.; and Huscroft, S. Incarcerated youth at risk for HIV infection. In: DiClemente, R., ed. *Adolescents and AIDS: A Generation in Jeopardy.* Newbury Park, CA: Sage Publications, Inc., 1992. pp. 52-70.

National Institute on Drug Abuse. *National Household Survey on Drug Abuse: Main Findings 1990.* Rockville, MD: National Institute on Drug Abuse, 1992.

Novick, D.M.; Joseph, H.; Croxson, T.S.; Salsitz, E.A.; Wang, G.; Richman, B.L.; Poretsky, L.; Keefe, J.B.; and Whimbey, E. Absence of antibody to human immunodeficiency virus in long-term, socially rehabilitated methadone maintenance patients. *Arch Intern Med* 150(1):97-99, 1990.

Rickel, A.U., and Hendren, M.C. Aberrant sexual experiences in adolescence. In: Gulotta, T.B.; Adams, G.R.; and Montemayor, R., eds. *Adolescent Sexuality.* Newbury Park, CA: Sage Publications, 1993. pp. 141-160.

Rotheram-Borus, M.J.; Luna, G.C.; Marotta, T.; and Kelly, H. Going nowhere fast: Methamphetamine use and HIV infection. In: Battjes, R.J.; Sloboda, Z.; and Grace, W.C., eds. *The Context of HIV Risk Among Drug Users and Their Sexual Partners.* National Institute on Drug Abuse Research Monograph No. 143. NIH Pub. No. 94-3750. Washington, DC: Supt. of Docs., U.S. Govt. Print. Off., 1994.

Rotheram-Borus, M.J.; Koopman, C.; and Bradley, J.S. Barriers to successful AIDS prevention programs with runaway youth. In: Woodruff, J.O.; Doherty, D.; and Athey, J.G., eds. *Troubled Adolescents and HIV Infection: Issues in Prevention and Treatment.* Washington, DC: CASSP Technical Assistance Center, 1989.

Sondheimer, D.L. HIV infection and disease among homeless adolescents. In: DiClemente, R., ed. *Adolescents and AIDS: A Generation in Jeopardy.* Newbury Park, CA: Sage Publications, Inc., 1992. pp. 71-88.

Sowder, B.J. "Runaway and Homeless Youth: A Summary of Selective Literature." Report prepared for National Institute on Drug Abuse under contract 271-90-8402, 1991.

Springhall, N.A., and Collins, W.A. *Adolescent Psychology: A Developmental View.* Reading, MA: Addison-Wesley Publishing Co., 1984. pp. 29-55.

Steel, E., and Haverkos, H.W. AIDS and drug abuse in rural America. *J Rural Health* 8(1):70-73, 1992.

St. Louis, M.E.; Conway, G.A.; Hayman, C.R.; Miller, C.; Petersen, L.R.; and Dondero, T.J. Human immunodeficiency virus infection in disadvantaged adolescents. *JAMA* 266(17):2387-2391, 1991.

Stricof, R.L.; Kennedy, J.T.; Nattell, T.C.; Weisfuse, I.B.; and Novick, L.F. HIV seroprevalence in a facility for runaway and homeless adolescents. Supplement. *Am J Public Health* 81:50-53, 1991.

U.S. Bureau of the Census. *Statistical Abstract of the United States: 1991.* 11th ed. Washington, DC: Supt. of Docs., U.S. Govt. Print. Off., 1991. p. 12.

AUTHOR

Elizabeth Steel, M.S.W.
Deputy AIDS Coordinator (Retired)
National Institute on Drug Abuse
841 Bowie Road
Rockville, MD 20852

Current Issues and Future Needs in the Assessment of Adolescent Drug Abuse

Ken C. Winters and Randy D. Stinchfield

INTRODUCTION

Assessing adolescent alcohol and other drug abuse requires careful and skillful procedures. Drug abuse among adolescents usually occurs with other problems such as school difficulties, poor family and peer functioning, psychiatric and psychological distress, medical problems, and delinquency (Jessor and Jessor 1977; Kandel 1978; Newcomb et al. 1986). Assessment strategies must be multifaceted and comprehensive to address the constellation of personal, family, and environmental liabilities. This need for complexity is not without challenges. Due to expanded early identification of high-risk and preteenage drug-abusing youths, there is a great need for accurate and user-friendly assessment strategies that can accommodate a wide range of service providers and health officials, many of whom may not have formal training in assessment.

The availability of sound and proven self-report assessment instruments offers great promise to many practitioners who are looking for aids when assessing youth. Instruments can objectively, efficiently, and meaningfully document the extent and nature of clinical phenomena and can interface with databases used in program evaluations. This chapter reviews the current status of adolescent drug abuse instrumentation within the context of the field's advancement over a decade, the current gaps in psychometric sophistication and implementations, and the assessment priorities that should be addressed by future research.

STAGES OF ASSESSMENT

This chapter distinguishes between screening and comprehensive assessment procedures. These two broad categories of assessment can be differentiated by the intensity of inquiry, the assessor's level of expertise, and the depth of commitment by the agency or organization that provides the assessment services. The essential aim of screening is to determine the need for a comprehensive assessment; establishing a diagnosis and deciding treatment needs would be inappropriate for screening procedures. The screening process is characterized by relatively short and simple strategies that should be within the expertise of a wide range of service providers.

The following is an example of a textbook screening as a function of the information source, the method employed by the assessor, and content of the information gathered.

Source: The adolescent client and one knowledgeable adult, preferably a parent.

Method: Brief self-report questionnaire and brief structured interview of the client, and a brief unstructured interview of the parent.

Content: Drug use frequency and onset and an overview of possible consequences of drug use and key psychosocial factors that may have been affected by such use (e.g., suicide potential, physical and sexual abuse, family problems).

It is likely that this screening process could be completed in less than 2 hours, especially if the questionnaire for the client is simple and short (e.g., under 50 items) and easy to score and interpret. The intensity of screening procedures can vary, however, as a function of setting, professional qualifications, and availability of resources. Although far from ideal, a simple screening procedure could involve just a single source (client), single method (self-report questionnaire), and single content area (drug use problem severity). This miniscreening may be the only practical approach in settings that are required to serve large numbers of youth and where staff are overly burdened with multiple administrative tasks. Juvenile detention centers in major metropolitan areas come to mind as settings where a 2-hour screening is probably a luxury beyond the agency's resources. There is some comfort in the fact that accurate and short screening tools exist that rely solely on the client's self-report of problem severity.

Some professionals recommend routine laboratory testing as part of drug screening. It is often overlooked that laboratory tests yield a narrow range of information. Essentially, only quite recent drug use can be detected from analysis of urine or blood (marijuana being an exception in that the detection period can stretch to up to 6 weeks in daily users). It has been documented that self-report data can generate more findings of recent drug use than laboratory assays (McLaney et al., in press). One valuable application of laboratory testing occurs when a client claims no recent drug use yet the laboratory finding is positive. Assuming the test is accurate, this is very strong evidence that the client's report is not valid. Some of the limitations of detecting drugs from body fluid assay may become a thing of the past as the hair analysis method gains credibility. Although this method cannot detect very recent drug use and, like urinalysis, cannot measure drug quantity, it provides an accurate chronological report of an individual's drug use history.

A comprehensive assessment is the next stage of the evaluation process if the screening results indicate that the adolescent may have a drug problem. The comprehensive assessment process cannot use any shortcuts. At minimum, it should include the following:

- An indepth examination of the severity and nature of the drug abuse identified by the screening process.

- A thorough assessment of additional problems flagged during the screening and additional inquiry into problems that may not have been included in the screening, such as delinquency, family environment, peer relations, the norms and values of the community, mental health status, school functioning, and physical health status.

- A concerted effort to utilize multiple methods and sources, with an emphasis towards including the youth's family in the assessment, ensuring that standardized multiscale questionnaires and structured interviews are used when appropriate, and obtaining and reviewing previous assessments and other relevant records.

Of course, the ability to include the youth's family in the comprehensive assessment is problematic when a traditional family is absent. Some youth seeking treatment may be homeless or from dysfunctional families. In some States, a minor may need an adult's signature to gain access to treatment services. In the absence of a parent or guardian, it is sometimes necessary to make the youth a temporary ward of the State. Nevertheless, when possible, it is important for assessors to attempt to form a therapeutic alliance with the family. From an assessment standpoint, parents can provide limited information about their child's possible drug problem and they are a necessary source of information when assessing the home environment and the community. Moreover, parent involvement is crucial to helping the adolescent if treatment is warranted.

The skill level of the assessor is crucial to this advanced stage of assessment. Comprehensive tools usually require advanced training in assessment. It is vital to match the skill level of the assessor with the training requirements of the test. In cases when a single professional is involved in the comprehensive assessment activities, training and accreditation must be consistent with the assessment demands. An assessor not licensed to make mental health diagnoses would have to refer a client elsewhere for diagnostic services. Likewise, some standardized tests need to be interpreted and confirmed by a licensed psychologist, psychiatrist, or other mental health worker. (Administering most objective tests is another matter; a trained unlicensed technician usually can administer such tests.)

TRENDS IN SELF-REPORT INSTRUMENT DEVELOPMENT

Prior to the mid-1980s, very few self-report standardized adolescent drug abuse instruments existed. Winters and Henly (1988) found only two alcohol screening tools that had been standardized: the Youth Diagnostic Screening Test (Alibrandi 1978) and the Adolescent Alcohol Involvement Scale (Mayer and Filstead 1979). Also, a limited number of child/adolescent diagnostic interviews (Herjanic and Reich 1982) were available that covered the criteria for abuse and dependence as defined in the "Diagnostic and Statistical Manual of Mental Disorders," 3d. edition (DSM-III) as well as a small group of survey instruments used in epidemiological studies (Block et al. 1974; Kandel 1971). A survey of 70 adolescent drug abuse treatment facilities (Owen and Nyberg 1983) indicated that most programs used either in-house nonstandardized instruments or adult tools for assessing adolescent drug abuse. The facilities expressed a high desire to use adolescent standardized instruments if they existed.

Since the mid-1980s, there has been a burst of development of self-report instruments in the adolescent drug abuse field. This growth has been accelerated by concerns about inappropriate, subjective diagnostic practices and the expansion of the adolescent drug treatment industry (Winters 1990). A wide variety of tools, ranging from very brief screening instruments to multilevel batteries, has been developed. This new attention to adolescent drug abuse instrumentation has enhanced the opportunities for clinicians to accurately, objectively, and efficiently document the severity of drug abuse and level of care. Although some of the new tools are virtual clones of a single model, the breadth of options now available is impressive. As shown in table 1, the post-1985 era is characterized by a number of new screening tools, multiscale inventories and interviews, and assessment systems. The increases are especially noteworthy for screening tools (a jump from 2 to 14) and multiscale instruments (an increase from none to 14). An overview of these instruments is provided below.

TABLE 1. *Count of adolescent drug abuse assessment tools.*

Type	Pre-1985	Post-1985	Total
Assessment systems	0	2	2
Screens	2	14	16
Comprehensive	0	14	14

ASSESSMENT SYSTEMS

Assessment systems integrate screening, diagnostic evaluation, and comprehensive assessment. Screening involves detecting both overt and subtle indicators of drug abuse to identify a high percentage of those adolescents who likely need treatment services. Initial screening is followed by a more focused evaluation of recent and past drug use, diagnostic drug abuse signs and symptoms, and other biopsychosocial problem areas that may have been affected by drug involvement or that may have contributed to initiation or maintenance of that involvement.

Assessment systems present several advantages in comparison with only screening: initial identification of large numbers of adolescents who may be in need of drug treatment and related services, more rapid referral of adolescents to comprehensive assessment and adjunctive services, standardization of the evaluation and referral process, assurance that several important content areas (e.g., child sexual abuse, family functioning, school functioning) that may affect decisions about the type and intensity of treatment required are examined, and enhancement of capabilities to provide program evaluation in identifying client needs and determining if those needs are addressed through referral for appropriate services. Possible disadvantages of using an integrated approach included additional costs of commercial assessment products and the need for staff expertise and training to ensure adequate skill levels when using comprehensive, and often statistically sophisticated, assessment instruments. Two recent examples of integrated assessment systems were located.

Adolescent Assessment and Referral System

The National Institute on Drug Abuse (NIDA) initiated the Adolescent Assessment/Referral System (AARS) (Rahdert 1991) project in April 1987 after identifying the need to develop a broader assessment approach that encompassed the wide range of problem areas presented by drug-involved youth. This project was designed to identify current assessment instruments that were reliable and valid and to develop standard procedures that would guide use of these instruments in clinical settings for adolescents aged 12 to 19. The AARS was developed with the understanding that drug-involved adolescents present a wide range of functional problems and that identification of these problem areas creates a greater likelihood of successfully resolving lifestyle difficulties that contribute to the onset and continuation of substance abuse. A panel of experts was convened to develop screening items, establish preliminary scoring rules, and nominate comprehensive tools for evaluation of the functional problems associated with substance abuse. The AARS project has yielded a screening instrument, the Problem Oriented Screening Instrument for Teenagers (POSIT), as well as a manual that lists appropriate comprehensive tools and describes a strategy for preparing a directory of adolescent services. This directory will provide the procedures and materials for developing a listing and description of available adolescent drug abuse treatment resources within a particular community. A more detailed discussion of the AARS components is provided below.

1. *POSIT.* This 139-item, yes/no self-administered instrument is designed to screen for adolescent problems in 10 functional areas: substance use/abuse, physical health, mental health, family relations, peer relations, educational status, vocational status, social skills, leisure/recreation, and aggressive behavior/delinquency.[1] A copy of

the POSIT scoring templates and administration procedures is included in the AARS Manual (Rahdert 1991). Initial data indicate that each problem area was identified as a potential problem in at least 75 percent of youth in a drug treatment sample. Convergent and discriminant evidence for the POSIT has been reported by an independent research team (McLaney et al., in press) and additional work is being conducted by NIDA to validate the instrument's cutting scores.

Also included with the POSIT is the Client Personal History Questionnaire (CPHQ). As a companion instrument to the POSIT, the CPHQ provides a structured interview format to obtain information regarding client demographics, history of juvenile justice and mental health system contacts, school performance, health care utilization, and current life stressors. Copies of the POSIT and CPHQ are available in Spanish and English.

2. *Comprehensive Assessment Battery (CAB).* The CAB elicits information for more thoroughly examining problem areas identified by the POSIT. The CAB offers a listing and brief description of appropriate assessment tools for each of the 10 functional areas addressed by the POSIT. These instruments were selected by a panel of national experts as the preferred measure for their particular content domain. Areas previously identified as potential problems for the client can be selectively assessed without administering the entire battery. In most cases, the CAB describes at least two assessment instruments per content area. Unfortunately, no particular instructions are provided as to how assessment staff would choose between the two instruments within a problem area; apparently the intention of the CAB is to allow a certain degree of discretion in choosing among instruments. Examples of recommended CAB assessment tools are Personal Experience Inventory (PEI) (Winters and Henly 1989), the Adolescent Diagnostic Interview (ADI) (Winters and Henly 1993) (drug abuse); Family Assessment Measure (FAM) (Skinner et al. 1983) (family relations); and the Diagnostic Interview Schedule for Children (DISC-2.3) (Shaffer 1992) (mental health status). The AARS Manual provides a brief description of each recommended instrument in addition to information on obtaining and administering instruments, costs to purchase instruments, and references.

3. *Treatment Planning.* Following administration of selected CAB instruments, the AARS recommends that staff develop a treatment plan. Recognizing that the treatment plan will be guided by the geographic availability of specific services, the AARS provides a plan for developing a Directory of Adolescent Services. The AARS Manual recommends that this directory include two sections: an Adolescent Services Matrix to describe available facilities or programs and the type of services provided; and a Provider Information Form used to summarize key characteristics of each provider agency, including address and phone numbers, hours of operation, eligibility requirements, types of clients served, number of staff, and contact persons. Also included in the AARS is a plan for compiling a list of adolescent service providers, conducting a survey of providers to ascertain types of services provided and other descriptive information, and developing the Adolescent Services Matrix and Provider Information Forms. Sample forms for the Adolescent Services Matrix, the Provider Information Form, and the Provider Questionnaire are included in the AARS Manual.

Minnesota Chemical Dependency Adolescent Assessment Package (MCDAAP)

This battery of assessment instruments was developed by a consortium of drug abuse treatment service providers and researchers (Winters and Henly 1988). The assessment approach used in developing the battery is similar to NIDA's approach in developing its system in that both screening and more intensive assessment are incorporated within a system. The MCDAAP differs from the AARS, however, in several ways: the MCDAAP tools are primarily geared to measure drug abuse characteristics and related problems and only screens for coexisting mental and behavioral disorders; the MCDAAP screening tool contains fewer items than the POSIT; and the MCDAAP does not include resources related to additional assessment and treatment referral. The three MCDAAP instruments are described below.

1. *Personal Experience Screening Questionnaire (PESQ).* The PESQ (Winters 1991, 1992) is a brief 40-item screening instrument designed to identify adolescents who may be abusing alcohol or other drugs. In addition to the problem severity scale, the PESQ briefly measures drug use history, select psychosocial problems, and response distortion tendencies (faking good and faking bad). Norms have been collected on normal, juvenile offender, and drug-abusing

populations. Internal consistency reliability estimates for the PESQ are high (coefficient alpha, 0.91 to 0.95) and its accuracy rate in predicting a need for a comprehensive drug abuse assessment is estimated at 87 percent.

2. *Adolescent Diagnostic Interview (ADI).* The ADI (Winters and Henly 1993) addresses the range of symptoms associated with psychoactive substance use disorders as described in DSM-III-R. The interview's structured format covers sociodemographic information, substance abuse history, and signs of abuse or dependence in all major drug categories. In addition, the ADI screens other mental health disorders as well as several domains of functioning (e.g., school performance, peer and family relationships, leisure activities, and legal difficulties). ADI research indicates high interrater agreement and stability of diagnoses over a 1-week period, evidence for concurrent validity on the basis of significant correlations with self-report measures of problem severity, and evidence for criterion validity on the basis of significant associations with independent clinical diagnostic ratings (Winters and Henly 1993; Winters et al. 1993*a*).

3. *Personal Experience Inventory (PEI).* The paper-and-pencil PEI is divided into two sections: Chemical Involvement Problem Severity and Psychosocial Risk Factors. The Chemical Involvement Problem Severity section measures 10 constructs of drug use severity, drug use frequency and onset, and response distortion tendencies. The Psychosocial Risk Factors section examines interpersonal risk factors (e.g., negative self-image, social isolation, and absence of goals) and environmental risk factors (e.g., parent and sibling drug abuse, physical and sexual abuse, and estrangement from the family). Select clinical problems are also addressed by the PEI such as eating disorders, suicide potential, other mental health symptoms, and parental history of drug abuse. Normative data are available on the PEI for adolescents 12 to 15 years of age, 16 to 18 years of age, by gender, and for adolescents identified within drug clinic and school settings. The computerized score report includes narratives and statistical scores for each scale, a summary of the client's status on level of treatment indicators, and other clinical information.

PEI scores have been found to be highly correlated with other measures of drug abuse problem severity and psychosocial risk factors, independent recommendations regarding need for drug abuse treatment, and independent clinical diagnoses (Henly and Winters 1988, 1989; Winters and Henly 1989; Winters et al. 1993*b*).

SCREENING TOOLS

In addition to the POSIT (part of the AARS) and the PESQ (part of the MCDAAP), which have screening tools within an integrated system, several other individual screening measures were located. The reader is cautioned that psychometric data are limited or nonexistent for some of these tools.

Adolescent Alcohol Involvement Scale (AAIS)

The AAIS is a 14-item self-report questionnaire that requires approximately 15 minutes to administer (Mayer and Filstead 1979). The instrument examines the type and frequency of drinking, the last drinking episode, reasons for the onset of drinking behavior, drinking context, short- and long-term effects of drinking, the adolescent's perception about drinking, and how others perceive his/her drinking. An overall score ranging from 0 to 79 is generated, describing severity of alcohol abuse problems (nonuser/normal user; misuser; abuser/dependent). Estimates of internal consistency range from 0.55 in a clinical sample (Moberg 1983) to 0.76 in a general sample. Test scores are significantly related to substance use diagnosis and ratings from other sources (e.g., parents).

Adolescent Drinking Index (ADI)

The ADI (Harrell and Wirtz 1990) is a 24-item paper-and-pencil questionnaire that examines adolescent problem drinking through assessment of four major domains: psychological symptoms, physical symptoms, social symptoms, and loss of control. Internal consistency reliability of the instrument is high (coefficient alpha, 0.93 to 0.95), and studies have confirmed the validity of this tool in measuring the severity of adolescent drinking problems.

Adolescent Drug Involvement Scale (ADIS)

Moberg (1991) modified the AAIS to address drug use problem severity. Psychometric studies on the 12-item ADIS questionnaire reveal favorable internal consistency (coefficient alpha, 0.85) and preliminary validity evidence is encouraging (e.g., significant correlations with concurrent problem severity measures).

Client Substance Index-Short (CSI-S)

The CSI-S (Thomas 1990) is being developed and evaluated as part of a larger substance abuse screening protocol through the National Center for Juvenile Justice. The complete protocol will include a user's manual and guidelines for the screening and assessment process within the juvenile justice system. The CSI-S is a 15-item, yes/no self-report instrument that was adapted from Moore's (1983) Client Substance Index (described below). The objective of this brief screen is to identify juveniles within the court system who are in need of additional drug abuse assessment. Reliability and validity evaluations are currently underway.

Drug and Alcohol Problem Quick Screen

This screening questionnaire (yes/no format) has been tested in a pediatric practice setting (Schwartz and Wirtz 1990). While no reliability or criterion validity evidence is available on this tool, the authors report that about 15 percent of the respondents in the pediatric clinic sample endorsed six or more items (judged to be a red flag cutting score).

MMPI-A Scales: Alcohol/Drug Problem Acknowledgment (ACK) and Alcohol/Drug Problem Proneness (PRO)

The adolescent version of the revised Minnesota Multiphasic Personality Inventory (MMPI, MMPI-A) includes two scales for the assessment of alcohol and other drug problems (Weed et al. 1994). The 13-item ACK scale was developed to measure open acknowledgment of problems with use of alcohol and other drugs, and the 36-item PRO scale was developed to measure the potential for developing alcohol or other drug problems. Internal consistency for ACK and PRO is 0.70 and 0.76, respectively, and test-retest reliability is fair. Both scales discriminate well between clinical and nonclinical adolescent groups.

Perceived Benefit of Drinking and Drug Use Scales

Based on the approach that one's perception of the benefits of chemical use is a gauge of actual use, this 10-item instrument was constructed to serve as a nonthreatening problem severity screen. Five perceived-benefit questions are asked regarding use of alcohol and then repeated for drug use. Research findings indicate that the scales are related to several key indicators of drug use behavior when tested in school (Petchers et al. 1988) and adolescent inpatient psychiatric samples (Petchers and Singer 1990), and estimates of internal consistency range from 0.69 to 0.74.

Rutgers Alcohol Problem Index (RAPI)

The RAPI (White and Labouvie 1989) is a 23-item questionnaire that focuses on a consequences of alcohol use pertaining to family life, social relations, psychological functioning, delinquency, physical problems, and neuropsychological functioning. The RAPI has satisfactory reliability and is highly correlated with DSM-III-R criteria.

Substance Abuse and Mental Health Preliminary Screening (SAMH-1)

The SAMH-1 (Florida Department of Health and Rehabilitative Services 1990) is designed for use by intake staff with adolescents for whom a delinquency petition is to be filed. The screening interview includes background demographic information, current legal charges, suicide risk screening, drug abuse characteristics, and mental health status. No psychometric data are available for this instrument.

Substance Abuse Potential Scale (SAP)

MacAndrew (1986) developed a 36-item MMPI-derived scale geared to older adolescent and young adult male drug abusers. The scale appears to tap behaviors relevant to delinquency and general reward-seeking behaviors that have been found to characterize young drug-abusing men. Scale scores revealed very favorable group discrimination results (e.g., drug abusers versus students versus psychiatric patients).

Substance Involvement Instrument (SII)

The SII provides a background history and drug history section in addition to a measure of drug use involvement (Aladar 1987). The self-administered instrument includes 60 items that tap 20 behavioral indicators believed to reflect a progression towards drug addiction. Limited research has been conducted investigating the validity of the instrument.

Youth Diagnostic Screening Test (YDST)

The YDST (Alibrandi 1978) is a 36-item paper-and-pencil instrument that taps three aspects of problem drinking: pathological style, problematic consumption, and consequences. No reliability data are available on the YDST. A cutting score for a diagnosis of alcoholism is provided by the author, but the validity of that decision rule has not been empirically demonstrated.

MULTISCALE INVENTORIES AND INTERVIEWS

This next section reviews comprehensive multiscale instruments and interviews. These tools address several content domains and include both paper-and-pencil and interview formats. The comprehensiveness of instruments in this group varies considerably; many of them are perhaps best described as midrange instruments.

Five tools are structured along the lines of a popular and well-researched adult drug abuse measure, the Addiction Severity Index (ASI) (McLellan et al. 1980). The ASI is an adult-oriented structured interview that provides a history of drug abuse over the past 30 days and over the lifetime, briefly reviews the type and frequency of drug abuse treatment received, and identifies the major problem drug. In addition, six other areas of psychosocial functioning are examined: psychiatric status, medical status, employment/support status, family history, family/social relationships, and legal status. Composite scores for the functioning domains have been found to be valid measures of problem severity and to correlate with other measures of substance abuse and psychosocial dysfunction. Several adolescent versions of the ASI have been developed: the Adolescent Drug Abuse Diagnosis (ADAD), the Adolescent Problem Severity Index (APSI), the Comprehensive Addiction Severity Index for Adolescents (CASI-A), the Substance Abuse and Mental Health Assessment (SAMH-2), and the Teen Addiction Severity Index (TASI).

ADAD

The ADAD is a 150-item structured therapy-evaluation interview that addresses the following content areas: medical status, drug and alcohol use, legal status, family background and problems, school/employment, social activities and peer relations, and psychological status. The interviewer rates the patient's need for additional treatment in each content area on a 10-point scale. These severity ratings translate to a problem severity dimension (no problem/slight/moderate/considerable/ extreme problem). The drug use section includes a detailed drug use frequency checklist and a brief set of items that address aspects of drug involvement (e.g., polydrug use, attempts at abstinence, withdrawal symptoms, and use in school). Psychometric studies of the ADAD provide initial evidence for its reliability and validity (Friedman and Utada 1989). A shorter form (83 items) of the ADAD for treatment outcome evaluation is available.

APSI

The APSI was developed by Metzger and colleagues (1991) at the University of Pennsylvania/VA Medical Center. The APSI includes a general information section that addresses the reason for the assessment, the referral source, and the adolescent's understanding of the reason for the interview. Additional sections of the APSI include drug/alcohol use; family relationships; education/work; medical, legal, and psychosocial adjustment; and personal relationships. Initial validity data indicate that the APSI's alcohol and drug section correlates highly with PESQ scores, and predictive validity studies are underway. Computer software for automated scoring is available.

CASI-A

The CASI-A is a structured interview instrument developed by Meyers (1991). (The CASI-A, including extensive appendices and administration manual, is available through the Carrier Foundation (NJ)). The CASI-A is similar in format to the APSI but requires significantly more time to administer due to differences in content and format. For example, multiple responses must be entered by the interviewer for most test items, and its administration requires frequent use of materials from appendices to guide questions and responses. The CASI-A incorporates results from a drug urine screen and observations from the assessor. No psychometric data on the CASI-A have been published.

SAMH-2

As a second-level instrument to the SAMH-1, the SAMH-2 (Florida Department of Health and Rehabilitative Services 1990) is a structured interview that focuses on multiple life areas. The interview's section on legal status reviews current/pending offenses and prior offenses, but does not address prior delinquency adjudications. Other sections of the SAMH-2 describe educational/vocational status, home/living situation, substance abuse history, family history, psychological/medical status, mental health symptoms, and physical/sexual abuse. In contrast to most of the other ASI clones, the SAMH-2 does not address peer relationships, social adjustment, or leisure/recreational activities. Psychometric data are not available on the SAMH-2.

TASI

Another adolescent version of the ASI was adapted by Kaminer and colleagues (1991). The TASI consists of seven content areas: chemical use, school status, employment-support status, family relationships, legal status, peer-social relationships, and psychiatric status. A medical status section was not included because it was deemed to be less relevant to adolescent drug abusers. Patient and interviewer severity ratings are elicited on a 5-point scale for each of the content areas. Interviewer confidence ratings are also generated for each area. Preliminary data indicate adequate interrater agreement for the seven scales. No validity data have been reported yet.

The next set of instruments reviewed are not organized around an ASI format but can be considered multiscale questionnaires and interviews.

Adolescent Chemical Health Inventory (ACHI)

The ACHI (Renovex 1988) consists of 128 items that address drug use problem severity and several psychosocial factors. For example, scales are included that measure family closeness, depression, alienation, family support, family chemical use, and physical/sexual abuse. The test also screens for defensiveness. The test is self-administered through use of a personal computer. Validity data collected for the ACHI indicate that the instrument is able to differentiate between adolescent drug abusers and nonabusers.

Chemical Dependency Assessment Profile (CDAP)

This 235-item self-report questionnaire assesses several dimensions of drug use, including expectations of use (e.g., drugs reduce tension), physiological symptoms, and quantity and frequency of use.

Unfortunately, normative data are available thus far on only 86 subjects (Harrell et al. 1991).

Client Substance Index (CSI)

This 113-item instrument (Moore 1983) is based on Jellinek's (1960) 28 symptoms of drug dependence. Scores on the CSI reflect the degree of drug dependence ranging from no problem, to misuse of substances and abuse of substances, to chemical dependency. CSI scores have been shown to discriminate normal from drug treatment samples.

Guided Rational Adolescent Substance Abuse Profile (GRASP)

This structured interview instrument developed by the Addiction Recovery Corporation (1986) includes information obtained from family members and other informants. The instrument provides for yes/no responses but allows for additional questioning of initial responses. The GRASP includes content areas describing alcohol/drug involvement, family relationships, adolescent behavior/personality, and the family perspective of the adolescent's substance abuse. An examination of DSM-III criteria for substance abuse disorders is provided in the alcohol/drug involvement section. The manual does not include any psychometric data.

Juvenile Automated Substance Abuse Evaluations (JASAE)

The JASAE (A.D.E., Inc. 1987) is a 102-item, true/false instrument that is based on a similar adult measure, the Substance Abuse/Life Circumstance Evaluations (SALCE). Both tools were developed by A.D.E., Inc. The JASAE produces a 5-category score, ranging from no use to drug abuse accompanied by physical or psychological symptoms of addiction. The instrument also includes a psychosocial stress index and a scale for test-taking attitude. The JASAE has been shown to discriminate clinical groups from nonclinical groups.

Prevention Management Evaluation System (PMES)

This 150-item structured interview and questionnaire is appropriate for youth already admitted into drug treatment. The content areas accommodate treatment planning by providing qualitative information on family background, school and legal problems, family relations, peer activity, and self-esteem (Barrett et al. 1988). Interrater agreement for the interview is good, but evidence for the instrument's validity is lacking.

Substance Abuse Subtle Screening Inventory-Adolescent Version (SASSI-A)

The adolescent version of the SASSI (Miller 1990) is an 81-item, paper-and-pencil questionnaire that consists of three face-valid drug abuse scales (i.e., scale items "look" like they are related to drug abuse experiences), one subtle or nonface-valid drug abuse scale, and two scales that measure faking good tendencies. Also, two experimental scales can be scored (correctional and random responding). Scoring procedures result in a dichotomous rating of chemically dependent or nonabuser. Scores on the SASSI-A highly discriminate drug treatment and normal adolescent groups.

Diagnostic Interviews

Most structured diagnostic interviews that address formal criteria for substance use disorders are designed for use with adult clients. Two prominent examples include the Diagnostic Interview Schedule (DIS) (Robins et al. 1981) and the Structured Clinical Interview for DSM-III (SCID) (Spitzer and Williams 1984). The development of the DIS led directly to the development of similar fully structured diagnostic interviews for children and adolescents. The Diagnostic Interview for Children and Adolescents (DICA) (Herjanic and Reich 1982) and the Diagnostic Interview Schedule for Children (DISC) (Shaffer 1992) are prominent examples of such interviews. Following in this tradition, Hoffmann and Harrison (1984) developed a structured interview for evaluating DSM-III substance use disorders in adults, the Abuse Modified Diagnostic Interview Schedule.

Semistructured diagnostic interviews, which require more clinical skill to administer and score, have also made a significant impact in the assessment field. The first tool in this group was the Schedule for Affective Disorders and Schizophrenia (SADDS) (Endicott and Spitzer 1978). This interview is considered one of the best for making adult psychiatric diagnoses according to DSM-III and Research Diagnostic Criteria. It was a natural progression that an adolescent/child version of the SADDS was developed. The Kiddie-SADDS (Puig-Antich 1982) has several advantages, including provisions for collecting information from parents, incorporating archival data, and clarifying answers to questions.

As already discussed, recent additions to the group of adolescent substance abuse interviews include the DSM-III-based GRASP (Addiction Recovery Corporation 1986) and the DSM-III-R-based ADI (Winters and Henly 1993). These instruments are unique in that they focus on diagnostic criteria for adolescent substance use disorders.

COMPUTERIZED TESTING

Whereas most tests are available in paper-and-pencil formats, it is becoming more common for tests to be accompanied by software for computerized administration and scoring. Computerized instruments may be costlier to purchase but real savings can occur in assessor time, the single greatest expense in the assessment process. Furthermore, computer scoring programs may provide descriptive narratives, highlight critical responses, identify factors that need to be pursued in a subsequent interview, suggest treatment modalities, and summarize the standardized scale scores. Of course, computerized score reports are only as good as the information fed into the program and the skill exhibited by the programmer. Preprogrammed computer narratives may provide descriptors that are too general and may indicate treatment recommendations or other diagnostic labels without empirical justification.

The advantages of computerized testing compared with other testing methods have been debated in the literature. There is evidence for both sides of the argument. Some studies point to increased disclosure rates of sensitive material (which may or may not indicate more validity), whereas other studies do not find any differences between computerized testing and paper-and-pencil format. While the debate remains unresolved, the popularity of computerized testing is unequivocal.

FUTURE RESEARCH DIRECTIONS

Validity of Self-Report

Because the validity of self-report has been called into question (Fuller et al. 1988; Watson et al. 1984), it is important to further examine this issue for adolescent drug abuse assessment. Validity of self-report has been minimally studied in drug use surveys of student samples and essentially ignored in the adolescent clinical literature (Winters et al. 1991). One research direction is to examine the ability of validity or response distortion scales to detect faking tendencies. Although some adolescent drug abuse instruments contain validity scales, their effectiveness in detecting denial, problem exaggeration, and random responding is not well understood.

Another area for future research is the development of validity scales specifically designed for adolescents. For example, faking good (defensiveness) scales are often based on items adapted from outdated adult social desirability scales. These items may not be appropriate for adolescents, particularly adolescents in a drug-abusing subculture.

Predictive Validity

To date, most adolescent drug abuse assessment research has focused on demonstrating convergent and discriminant validity. These data are limited because they typically do not include large samples of nonwhite adolescents. Future research needs to advance to the more difficult level of evaluating a test's ability to predict future behavior such as response to treatment, treatment completion, and treatment outcome. This research will require sensitivity to possible moderating and mediating variables including treatment setting, client demographics, and therapist variables.

Critical Comparison of Tests

The recent proliferation of adolescent substance abuse assessment instruments is a double-edged sword. Professionals and researchers have a number of different tools from which to choose. On the other hand, selecting the right one for a given client or subject in a particular situation can be a guessing game. What is needed is a critical comparison of weaknesses of each instrument. Empirically, little is known about what instruments perform the best with which adolescent populations and in what settings.

The closest effort to a systematic comparison of adolescent drug and alcohol assessment instruments was prepared by researchers at the University of Washington (Farrow et al. 1993). The purpose of their report was to identify and critically evaluate the field of standardized assessment tools for adolescent drug abuse. The authors organized their review around three broad categories of instruments: screening, midrange, and comprehensive. These categories were formed on the basis of the amount of time needed to administer the instrument and the extent to which the instrument measured referral and treatment content areas. Each tool was briefly described and their psychometric properties were critically evaluated. A final section includes a table that summarizes by letter grade the authors' ratings of each tool on a range of characteristics (e.g., ease of administration and scoring, readability, reliability and validity). The authors also nominated the best instrument for each category.

Assessment of Treatment Outcome

Another area of growing importance is the assessment of treatment effectiveness. Many funding and regulatory agencies require treatment programs to demonstrate their effectiveness. Do current assessment instruments hold promise as valid treatment outcome measures? Because clinical assessment is related, but not identical, to the purpose of treatment outcome assessment, a valid clinical tool may not be an appropriate outcome assessment tool.

One issue to consider when evaluating the appropriateness of an assessment tool for use in treatment outcome is the timeframe within which the items are organized. When a clinical tool taps only lifetime experiences, its value as an outcome measure is limited. For example, one key index of treatment effectiveness is relative change, which involves comparing the client's behavior during a specified time period prior to treatment and during an identical time period after treatment. Assessment items or scales that can be easily adapted to outcome measures should be cast in time-limited periods (e.g., past 6 months). Also, because corroborating sources are important for followup data, parent versions of outcome instruments are desirable. The authors know of several examples of outcome adaptations of clinical tools: the ADAD (Friedman and Utada 1989), the POSIT (Rahdert 1991), the PEI (Winters and Henly 1989), and the ADI (Winters and Henly 1993). Parent versions of the PEI and ADI exist as well.

From a more psychometric standpoint, effective outcome instruments need to be reliable. For example, if test-retest stability estimates are low, the tool's ability to reliably measure change is greatly hampered. Similarly, it is important for interview schedules to be associated with high interrater agreement and for paper-and-pencil questionnaires to have high internal consistency reliability.

A recent investigation (Stinchfield, submitted) raised the question of when is the best time to measure pretreatment problem severity. Identical measures of drug use were administered to an adolescent drug clinic sample at intake and again at treatment discharge (about 1 month postintake). At both data points, the clients were instructed to report drug use frequency during the 3 months prior to intake. Over one-third of the sample reported a significantly higher level of pretreatment drug use at discharge compared with their intake report. Whether one assumes that these individuals were defensive at intake but not at discharge, or whether other response style and psychometric issues influenced the intake-discharge discrepancy, the finding nevertheless has treatment outcome implications. Entering the intake data into the relative change analysis attenuates the measured change for individuals prone to the intake-discharge effect, whereas entering the discharge data into the analysis expands the measured change. Obviously, future research needs to clarify if intake-discharge discrepancies are important enough to pursue so that clinicians and researchers have a better understanding of which report is more or less valid for which clients.

CONCLUDING REMARKS

Adolescent drug abuse assessment, which has made significant advances in instrumentation during the past few years, will continue to grow. Greater use of computerized testing and more sophisticated laboratory testing (e.g., hair analyses) may be popular advances. Cross-addictions will need to receive more assessment attention because many drug-abusing youths maintain other addiction-like behaviors after sobriety. Areas of interest include eating disorders, nicotine and caffeine use, and gambling. Yet one should not lose sight of a rather simple prescription for growth in the field: A continuation of consistent and widespread use of standardized assessment instruments and routine implementation of treatment outcome evaluations by service providers.

NOTES

1. An earlier version of the POSIT has been published by Tarter (1990) and referred to as the Drug Use Screening Inventory (DUSI). The DUSI represents work completed up to 1988 by NIDA and various contractees to develop the AARS. After that date, the screening tool was named the POSIT and further revised under contract with the Pacific Institute for Research and Evaluation. Revisions include eliminating some objectionable items, rewording some items to avoid

content confusion, preparing a Spanish version, and conducting an extensive validation study. Thus, the POSIT and DUSI are essentially two different names for the same screening tool developed under contract with funds from NIDA.

REFERENCES

A.D.E., Incorporated. *Juvenile Automated Substance Abuse Evaluations* (JASAE). Clarkston, MI: A.D.E., Incorporated, 1987.

Addiction Recovery Corporation. *Guided Rational Adolescent Substance Abuse Profile.* Waltham, MA: Addiction Recovery Corporation, 1986.

Alibrandi, T. *Young Alcoholics.* Minneapolis: Comp Care Publications, 1978.

Aladar. *Substance Involvement Instrument.* Lacy, WA: Aladar, 1987.

Barrett, M.E.; Simpson, D.D.; and Lehman, W.E. Behavioral changes of adolescents in drug abuse intervention programs. *J Clin Psychol* 44:461-473, 1988.

Block, J.R.; Goodman, N.; Ambellan, F.; and Revenson, J. *A Self-Administered High School Study of Drugs.* Hempstead, NY: Institute for Research and Development, Inc.,1974.

Endicott, J., and Spitzer, R.L. A diagnostic interview: The Schedule for Affective Disorders and Schizophrenia. *Arch Gen Psychiatry* 35:773-782, 1978.

Farrow, F.A.; Smith, W.R.; and Hurst, M.D. *Adolescent Drug and Alcohol Assessment Instruments in Current Use: A Critical Comparison.* Seattle, WA: University of Washington, 1993.

Florida Department of Health and Rehabilitative Services. *Substance Abuse and Mental Health Preliminary Screening.* Tallahassee, FL: Florida Department of Health and Rehabilitative Services, 1990.

Friedman, A.S., and Utada, A. A method for diagnosing and planning the treatment of adolescent drug abusers (Adolescent Drug Abuse Diagnosis Instrument). *J Drug Educ* 19:285-312, 1989.

Fuller, R.; Lee, K.; and Gordis, E. Validity of self-report in alcoholism research: Results of a Veterans Administration cooperative study. *Alcohol Clin Exp Res* 12:201-205, 1988.

Harrell, A.H., and Wirtz, P.W. *Adolescent Drinking Index.* Odessa, FL: Psychological Assessment Resources, Inc., 1990.

Harrell, T.H.; Honaker, L.M.; and Davis, E. Cognitive and behavioral dimensions of dysfunction in alcohol and polydrug abusers. *J Subst Abuse* 3:415-426, 1991.

Henly, G.A., and Winters, K.C. Development of problem severity scales for the assessment of adolescent alcohol and drug abuse. *Int J Addict* 23:65-85, 1988.

Henly, G.A., and Winters, K.C. Development of psychosocial scales for the assessment of adolescents involved with alcohol and drugs. *Int J Addict* 24:973-1001, 1989.

Herjanic, B., and Reich, W. Development of a structured psychiatric interview for children: Agreement between child and parent on individual symptoms. *J Abnorm Child Psychol* 10:307-324, 1982.

Hoffmann, N.G., and Harrison, P.A. Substance Abuse Modified Diagnostic Interview Schedule (SAMDIS). *Psychol Documents* 14:10, 1984.

Jellinek, E.M. *The Disease Concept of Alcoholism.* New Brunswick: Rutgers Center of Alcohol Studies, 1960.

Jessor, R., and Jessor, S.L. *Problem Behavior and Psychosocial Development: A Longitudinal Study of Youth.* New York: Academic Press, 1977.

Kaminer, Y.; Bukstein, O.; and Tarter, R.E. The teen-addiction severity index: Rationale and reliability. *Int J Addict* 26:219-226, 1991.

Kandel, D.B. *Study of High School Student—Students Questionnaire, Wave 1.* New York: Biometrics Research, 1971.

Kandel, D.B., ed. *Longitudinal Research on Drug Use: Empirical Findings and Methodological Issues.* Washington, DC: Hemisphere Publishing Corporation, 1978.

MacAndrew, C. Toward the psychometric detection of substance misuse in young men: The SAP Scale. *J Alcohol Stud* 47:161-166, 1986.

Mayer, J., and Filstead, W.J. The Adolescent Alcohol Involvement Scale: An instrument for measuring adolescent use and misuse of alcohol. *J Alcohol Stud* 4:291-300, 1979.

McLaney, M.A.; DelBoca, F.K.; and Babor, T.F. A validation study of the Problem Oriented Screening Instrument For Teenagers (POSIT). *J Mental Health*, in press.

McLellan, A.T.; Luborsky, L.; Woody, G.E.; and O'Brien, C.P. An improved diagnostic evaluation instrument for substance abuse patients: The Addiction Severity Index. *J Nerv Ment Dis* 186:26-33, 1980.

Metzger, D.; Kushner, H.; and McLellan, A.T. *Adolescent Problem Severity Index.* Philadelphia: University of Pennsylvania, 1991.

Meyers, K. *Comprehensive Addiction Severity Index for Adolescents.* Philadelphia: University of Pennsylvania, 1991.

Miller, G. *The Substance Abuse Subtle Screening Inventory—Adolescent Version.* Bloomington, IN: SASSI Institute, 1990.

Moberg, D.P. Identifying adolescents with alcohol problems: A field test of the Adolescent Alcohol Involvement Scale. *J Alcohol Stud* 44:701-721, 1983.

Moberg, D.P. The Adolescent Drug Involvement Scale. *J Adolesc Chem Depend* 2:75-88, 1991.

Moore, D. *Client Substance Index.* Olympia, WA: Olympic Counseling Services, 1983.

Newcomb, M.D.; Maddahian, E.; and Bentler, P.M. Risk factors for drug use among adolescents: Concurrent and longitudinal analyses. *Am J Pub Health* 76:525-531, 1986.

Owen, P.L., and Nyberg, L.R. Assessing alcohol and drug problems among adolescents: Current practice. *J Drug Educ* 13:249-254, 1983.

Petchers, M.K., and Singer, M.I. Clinical applicability of a substance abuse screening instrument. *J Adolesc Chem Depend* 1:47-56, 1990.

Petchers, M.K.; Singer, M.I.; Angelotta, J.; and Chow, J. Revalidation and expansion of an adolescent substance abuse screening measure. *Dev Behav Pediatr* 9:25-28, 1988.

Puig-Antich, J. Major depression and conduct disorder in prepuberty. *J Am Acad Child Psychiatry* 21:118-128, 1982.

Rahdert, E., ed. *The Adolescent Assessment and Referral System Manual.* DHHS Publication No. (ADM)91-1735. Rockville, MD: National Institute on Drug Abuse, 1991.

Renovex, Inc. *Adolescent Chemical Health Inventory.* Minneapolis: Renovex, Inc., 1988.

Robins, L.N.; Helzer, J.E.; Croughan, L.; and Ratcliff, K.S. National Institute of Mental Health Diagnostic Interview Schedule: Its history characteristics and validity. *Arch Gen Psychiatry* 38:381-389, 1981.

Schwartz, R.H., and Wirtz, P.W. Potential substance abuse detection among adolescent patients. *Clin Pediatr* 29:38-43, 1990.

Shaffer, D. *The Diagnostic Interview Schedule for Children -2.3 Version.* New York: Columbia University, 1992.

Stinchfield, R.D. Validity of adolescent self report: Discrepancies between intake and discharge assessment of pretreatment alcohol and other drug use. Manuscript submitted for publication.

Skinner, H.; Steinhauer, P.; and Santa-Barbara, J. The Family Assessment Measure. *Can J Commun Ment Health* 2:91-105, 1983.

Spitzer, R.L., and Williams, J.B.W. *Structured Clinical Interview for DSM-III.* New York: New York State Psychiatric Institute, 1984.

Tarter, R.E. Evaluation and treatment of adolescent substance abuse: A decision tree method. *Am J Drug Alcohol Abuse* 16:1-46, 1990.

Thomas, D.W. *Substance Abuse Screening Protocol for the Juvenile Courts.* Pittsburgh: National Center for Juvenile Justice, 1990.

Watson, C.; Tilleskjor, C.; Hoodecheck-Schow, E.; Pucel, J.; and Jacobs, L. Do alcoholics gave valid self-reports? *J Studies Alcohol* 45:344-348, 1984.

Weed, N.C.; Butcher, J.N.; and Williams, C.L. Development of MMPI-A alcohol/drug problem scales. *J Studies Alcohol* 55:296-302, 1994.

White, H.R., and Labouvie, E.W. Towards the assessment of adolescent problem drinking. *J Stud Alcohol* 50:30-37, 1989.

Winters, K.C. Need for improved assessment of adolescent substance involvement. *J Drug Issues* 20:487-502, 1990.

Winters, K.C. *The Personal Experience Screening Questionnaire and Manual.* Los Angeles: Western Psychological Services, 1991.

Winters, K.C. Development of an adolescent alcohol and other drug abuse screening scale: Personal Experience Screening Questionnaire. *Addict Behav* 17:479-490, 1992.

Winters, K.C., and Henly, G.A. Assessing adolescents who misuse chemicals: The Chemical Dependency Adolescent Assessment Project. In: Rahdert, E.R., and Grabowski, J., eds. *Adolescent Drug Abuse: Analyses of Treatment Research.* National Institute on Drug Abuse Research Monograph No. 77. DHHS Pub. No. (ADM)88-1523. Washington, DC: Supt. of Docs., U.S. Gov. Print. Off., 1988.

Winters, K.C., and Henly, G.A. *The Personal Experience Inventory Test and User's Manual.* Los Angeles: Western Psychological Services, 1989.

Winters, K.C., and Henly, G.A. *The Adolescent Diagnostic Interview Schedule and User's Manual.* Los Angeles: Western Psychological Services, 1993.

Winters, K.C.; Stinchfield, R.D.; Fulkerson, J.; and Henly, G.A. Measuring alcohol and cannabis use disorders in an adolescent clinical sample. *Psychol Addict Behav* 7:185-196, 1993*a*.

Winters, K.C.; Stinchfield, R.D.; and Henly, G.A. Further validation of new scales measuring adolescent alcohol and other drug abuse. *J Alcohol Stud* 54:534-541, 1993*b*.

Winters, K.C.; Stinchfield, R.D.; Henly, G.A.; and Schwartz, R.H. Validity of adolescent self-report of alcohol and other drug involvement. *Int J Addict* 25:1379-1395, 1991.

AUTHORS

Ken C. Winters, Ph.D.
Director

Randy D. Stinchfield, Ph.D.
Associate Director

Center for Adolescent Substance Abuse
University of Minnesota
Box 721
420 Delaware Street, SE
Minneapolis, MN 55455

Cultural Competence in Assessing Hispanic Youths and Families: Challenges in the Assessment of Treatment Needs and Treatment Evaluation for Hispanic Drug-Abusing Adolescents

William M. Kurtines and José Szapocznik

INTRODUCTION

For more than two decades the authors' work has been dedicated to developing therapeutic interventions for working with troubled Hispanic youth and their families. This work with drug-abusing Hispanic adolescents and their families began in 1972 in an effort to provide services to the local Hispanic community in Miami. Based on the authors' early research, structural family therapy was identified as a particularly well-suited approach for this population (Szapocznik et al. 1978*b*, 1978*c*, 1986*c*, 1989*b*).

Having adopted structural family therapy as the intervention modality of choice, the authors launched a series of studies to investigate its effectiveness and to develop innovative intervention strategies within the framework of this theory. In addition, extensive work was done on developing innovative methodologies for clinical diagnosis and clinical research outcome assessment.

As described in detail elsewhere (Szapocznik et al. 1990), a complex interplay of theory, research, and application was necessary to achieve breakthroughs in therapeutic interventions with this population. This chapter focuses on some of the more critical issues and problems faced in developing measures and assessment methodologies for working with culturally diverse populations.

In testing the efficacy of the interventions developed for working with this Hispanic population, it was essential to develop measures that were—as recommended by Kazdin (1986)—theoretically appropriate, clinically relevant, and with psychometric properties adequate for use in research settings. In the process of developing measures and assessment methodology for the research program, the authors have had to confront a number of basic methodological issues common to all research on therapeutic interventions with children and adolescents. In working with Hispanic youth and their families, however, the authors were confronted with the additional task of applying the basic principles of sound methodology to the challenge of working with culturally diverse populations.

This description of the issues related to the development of clinical assessment methods for working with families within culturally diverse contexts is divided into five sections, reflecting the authors' understanding of these basic issues. This description of the issues that clinical researchers encounter in working with culturally diverse populations is not considered exhaustive, but representative of the type of issues addressed in this work. The assessment related germane issues including back translation, identification of special characteristics of the treatment population, cultural cross validation, immigrant-specific problems and measures, and assessing transcultural and culture-specific dimensions of family functioning.

BACK TRANSLATION

One basic issue that confronts all researchers who work with linguistically diverse populations is that of insuring the linguistic comparability of instruments. Brislin (1980) has described the most frequently accepted and used procedure for ensuring linguistic comparability of instruments across two languages. According to Brislin, the initial document developed in language 1 is translated by translator 1 into language 2. Then translator 2, independently and blind to the instrument in language 1, translates the instrument from language 2 to language 1.

At this point there are two versions of the instrument in language 1: the original version and the back translator version. These two versions of the document are compared and whenever the items are identical, it is accepted that the translation was successful. For those items that are not identical, a committee is brought together to address the difficulties inherent in translating constructs or expressions that may be unique to one language but not the other. This committee is typically comprised of experts in test construction, bilingual individuals with expertise in each language (for example, an expert in language 1 who is comfortable in both languages, and vice versa), and either a representative of the target population or someone who works closely with the target population. This committee examines the items in all three instruments—the original in language 1, the translation in language 2, and the back translation in language 1—and makes a decision regarding the most appropriate translation into language 2, recognizing the limitations inherent in translating certain constructs or expressions that do not translate well across cultures.

IDENTIFICATION OF SPECIAL CHARACTERISTICS OF THE TREATMENT POPULATION

A second and more complex issue that confronts researchers who work with families in culturally diverse contexts is that of identifying clinically relevant cultural characteristics as well as a theoretical/clinical framework to match these characteristics and adequately address the special problems that arise in such contexts.

In the early phases of the research program development, a major study on value orientation (Szapocznik et al. 1978*c*) was undertaken to determine the most appropriate treatment intervention for the local Cuban immigrant population. The goal was to identify core values in the treatment population with the aim of using this information to identify a treatment modality that matched or was congruent with the values of the Cuban population, and therefore more acceptable and accessible.

The authors' early clinical experiences with the treatment population and a survey of the literature on cross-cultural comparisons of value orientation suggested that the theory of value orientations developed by Kluckhohn and Strodbeck (1961) would provide a useful framework for contrasting cultural value differences between Cuban immigrants and Anglo Americans. They postulated that to compare profiles between two cultures, it is necessary to delineate common human problems and to investigate the corresponding variations or ways of responding to these problems. They described five human problems generally common to all cultures: human nature, person-nature, activity, time, and relational. The solutions provided by each culture to these problems are indicative of world views or basic value orientations within that culture.

As part of the value orientation study, the authors used Kluckhohn and Strodbeck's (1961) theory as a framework for developing a measure of value orientation. Data on Cuban and Anglo American differences on the measure collected as part of the value orientation study subsequently played a central role in selecting, developing, and refining the primary therapeutic intervention.

The Value Orientation Scale

The Value Orientation (VO) Scale (Szapocznik et al. 1978*c*) consists of 22 items (human problems situations) factorially derived from a larger set of items representative of Kluckhohn and Strodbeck's (1961) five dimensions. The 22 items on the VO Scale include 9 relational, 4 human nature, 4 person nature, 3 time, and 2 activity items.

Subjects for the value orientation study included 533 participants from various educational institutions such as high schools, junior colleges, universities, and continuing education centers; from social agencies such as senior citizens' activity centers; and from other frequently used facilities such as Cuban medical clinics. Fifty-one percent of the total sample were Cuban, 32 percent were Anglo, and 17 percent were others (mostly non-Cuban Hispanics and blacks).

The results of the analysis of the differences in value orientation between Cuban and Anglo Americans provided support for using an approach in which therapists take an active, directive, present-oriented leadership role that matched the expectations of the population. Structural family therapy has been identified as a particularly well-suited approach for this population (Szapocznik et al. 1978*b*, 1978*c*). Through extensive clinical experience and a series of pilot research studies, structural family therapy was adapted to enhance its acceptability and effectiveness by adding a number of elements, some of the most important of which include strategic and time-limited aspects. To distinguish the particular family therapy approach that emerged from this phase of the work, the authors termed it Brief Strategic Family Therapy (BSFT).

Since the authors' early work linking value orientation to counseling approaches, other investigators have explored the implications of worldview for counseling ethnically diverse populations (Carter 1991), and have developed more complete measures of worldview (Carter and Helms 1990).

CULTURAL CROSS-VALIDATION

A third basic issue that confronts all researchers who work with culturally diverse populations is that of the cultural cross-validation of measures developed for use with mainstream populations. The cultural cross-validation of measures is necessarily preceded by the cross-translation of the measures. However, this is only a first step; the translated measure can then be used to provide a database for a more extensive evaluation of the extent to which the psychological and sociocultural concepts and constructs assessed by the measures are comparable across culturally diverse populations.

There are as many methods for evaluating the cross-cultural validity of psychological and sociocultural constructs measures as there are for evaluating the validity of measures within cultures (e.g., content validity, criterion-related validity, construct validity). This section describes only one: evaluating the factor consistency of measures. The authors describe their work on cross-culturally validating the factor structure of two instruments whose original development and validation were initially conducted on mainstream populations: the Revised Behavior Problem Checklist (RBPC) and the Family Environment Scale (FES).

The Revised Behavior Problem Checklist

The RBPC (Quay and Peterson 1987) is an empirically derived measure consisting of 89 problem behaviors that assesses 6 behavior problem dimensions: conduct disorder, socialized aggression, attention problems-immaturity, anxiety-withdrawal, psychotic behavior, and motor tension-excess. Informed observers rate those problem behaviors in the adolescent as 0 = no problem; 1 = mild problem; 2 = severe problem. The Behavior Problem Checklist (BPC) provides a measure of parental perception of each adolescent's problems. The BPC was originally constructed in English and standardized on a primarily English-speaking mainstream population (Quay and Peterson 1987).

The first step in adapting the BPC for use with the Hispanic population was to translate it into Spanish using the techniques described earlier. The second step was to collect data on the Spanish translation as part of the ongoing research program. The third step was to use the collected data to evaluate the cross-cultural consistency of the BPC's factor structure with the target population (Rio et al. 1989).

Subjects for this factor study consisted of 144 Hispanic American mothers of 6- to 19-year-olds, all of whom were subjects in one of two psychotherapy research studies conducted as part of the research program. The subjects for the first study consisted of 77 problem-behavior problem male children of elementary school age who were referred to one of the authors' outpatient treatment research projects (Szapocznik et al. 1989*a*). Subjects for the second study were junior and senior high school age adolescents referred to one of the author's drug-abuse treatment research projects (Szapocznik et al. 1983, 1986*a*). Approximately 80 percent of this combined sample were Cuban and approximately 20 percent were of other Hispanic origin (primarily Colombian). Mothers of all subjects completed the Spanish language version of the RBPC at the time of intake. Directions for completing the test were the same as those proposed by Quay and Peterson (1987).

Factor analysis (principal-axis method) yielded a 6-factor solution that accounted for over 48.5 percent of the common variance. Tucker's congruence coefficients (Harman 1967) indicated a very high degree of comparability between the factor structures of the original and Spanish versions, with the exception of the psychotic behavior scale.

The Family Environment Scale

The FES (Moos 1974) provides scores based on 10 subscales: cohesion, expressiveness, conflict, independence, achievement orientation, intellectual-cultural orientation, active-recreational orientation, moral-religious emphasis, organization, and control. Scale scores are viewed as relatively independent measures of each family member's perception of family environment or climate. The FES is a 90-item, true-false questionnaire that is individually completed by each family member. The FES was originally developed by Moos and colleagues using 1,000 mainstream family members' responses to 200 items related to the construct being measured. From this initial item pool, 90 true-false statements were selected and grouped into the 10 subscales described above.

As with the BPC, the first step in adapting the FES for use with the target Hispanic population was to translate it into Spanish using the methods described above. The second step was to collect data on the Spanish translation as part of the ongoing research program. The third step was to use the data to evaluate the factor structure of the FES with the population.

Recent factor studies of FES (Oliver et al. 1988; Robertson and Hyde 1982; Waldron et al. 1990) indicate that the dimensionality of the measure appears more complex than assessed by the 10 subscales originally described by Moos (Moos 1974). The findings of the above-cited studies, for example, do not confirm the presence of the original 10 dimensions. Second, and perhaps more interesting, factor analytic studies such as these have been unable to resolve the issue of the exact number of dimensions underlying the FES or even if there is a determinate number of factors. The number of interpretable factors reported in the literature has ranged from 4 to 10, and these dimensions have been defined by a diversity of item content. Third, and perhaps most interesting, is the striking consistency with which the factor analytic studies have found a single large factor that accounts for most of the explained variance. The consistency of the content of this factor has also been striking. For example, studies have consistently found this factor to be largely defined by items from the FES cohesion subscale. This finding suggests that the FES is complex because it is defined in part by a large, coherent dimension of cohesion that is common to all populations, and in part by smaller, secondary factors that appear to be population specific.

A factor study of the Spanish translation of the FES conducted by the authors (McIntosh et al., unpublished data) provided cross-cultural validation of the finding that the structure of the FES is complex because it is defined by both a large cohesion factor and by smaller, secondary factors that appear to be population specific. Subjects for this factor study consisted of 749 family members from 4 separate family therapy studies conducted as part of the authors' program of research. The 749 subjects included 235 fathers, 257 mothers, and 257 youth. Approximately 67 percent of the total subsample of youths were male. Minimum age for youths given the FES was 12 years old, and their mean age was 15.1 years (standard deviation (SD) = 1.4 years), with the ages ranging from 12 to 21. Approximately 80 percent of this combined sample were Cuban and approximately 20 percent were of other Hispanic origin (primarily Colombian and Nicaraguan). Each of the subjects completed the FES (Form R) at the time of intake. Directions used for completing the test were those proposed by Moos (1974).

The results of factor analysis yielded a 10-factor oblique solution that accounted for over 83 percent of the common variance. This solution provided support for the existence of a large, coherent dimension of cohesion that accounted for approximately 27 percent of the variance in the rotated solution. This cohesion dimension was similar to the original FES cohesion dimension reported by Moos (1974) and similar to the cohesion dimension that emerged as the largest and most distinct factor in recent factor studies (Oliver et al. 1988; Robertson and Hyde 1982; Waldron et al. 1990). The 10-factor solution also provided support for the existence of a number of population-specific secondary factors.

IMMIGRANT-SPECIFIC PROBLEMS AND MEASURES

A fourth issue that confronts researchers working with culturally diverse populations is specific to populations who are experiencing the stress and strain of immigration. The authors recently described (Szapocznik and Kurtines 1993) their experience in working with troubled Hispanic youths and their families undergoing the trauma of immigration. The problem faced in work with this population was to develop a theoretical understanding of the effects of a culturally pluralistic environment and to develop practical measures for assessing the impact of cultural diversity on families.

Acculturation and Biculturation

The authors' earliest understanding of problems related to acculturation and biculturation was that the target Cuban families were embedded in a culturally diverse context wherein parents and children were exposed to both Hispanic and mainstream values and customs. As a result of the exposure to these two cultures, following traditional learning curves, young people acculturated far more quickly to the mainstream, whereas parents tended to remain far more attached to their traditions. As part of the authors' research, measures of acculturation and biculturalism were developed that proved instrumental in formulating a theoretical understanding of the effects of cultural diversity on immigrant youth and families.

The Behavioral Acculturation Scale. The Behavioral Acculturation Scale (Szapocznik et al. 1978*d*) is a 24-item scale consisting of self-reported behaviors characteristic of each culture (e.g., reading Spanish or English language newspapers, eating Cuban or Anglo food) in which the subject rates the relative frequency of each behavior along a five-point Likert scale ranging from Spanish/Cuban (+1) to English/Anglo (+5). Total acculturation scales may thus range from 20 to 120, and ascending scores indicate increased acculturation levels.

The Bicultural Involvement Questionnaire. The Bicultural Involvement Questionnaire (Szapocznik et al. 1980) is a 24-item scale similar to the acculturation scale and consisting of ratings of self-reported behaviors characteristics of each culture on a 5-point Likert scale. The Bicultural Involvement Questionnaire is used to measure two conceptually independent bipolar dimensions: a dimension of biculturalism which ranges from monoculturalism to biculturalism, and a dimension of overall cultural involvement that ranges from cultural marginality to cultural involvement. Scores for each of these dimensions are computed on the basis of two subscales, one measuring Americanism (items reflecting an involvement in the American culture) and the other Hispanicism (items reflecting an involvement in Hispanic culture). The biculturalism score is derived by calculating the difference between the Hispanicism and Americanism scores. Scores close to zero indicate biculturalism; scores deviating from zero indicate monoculturalism. A positive difference score reveals monoculturalism in the Hispanic direction, whereas a negative difference score reveals monoculturalism in the American direction.

The use of these instruments in the authors' clinical outcome studies with Hispanic families helps to shed some light on the complex process by which culture affects individuals and families. Research findings on acculturation (Szapocznik and Kurtines 1980; Szapocznik et al. 1978*d*) summarized in figure 1 show that, when exposed to a culturally diverse environment, young people acculturate faster than their parents.

As figure 1 shows, the acculturation measure provided the means for explaining how family dynamics evolved within a culturally diverse environment and how such changes were linked to the emergence of conduct problems in youngsters (Szapocznik et al. 1986*b*). Families exposed to a culturally diverse environment developed a classic Ericksonian challenge: a family struggle in which some family members (the youth) struggled for autonomy and others (the elders) for family connectedness. As figure 2 illustrates, this struggle usually develops in families around the time of adolescence, but in this case the magnitude of the struggle was considerably exacerbated by acculturational differences across generations. As a result of this struggle, children lost emotional and social support from their families and parents lost their positions of leadership.

The impact of a culturally diverse environment on these families resulted in the emergence of conflict-laden intergenerational acculturational

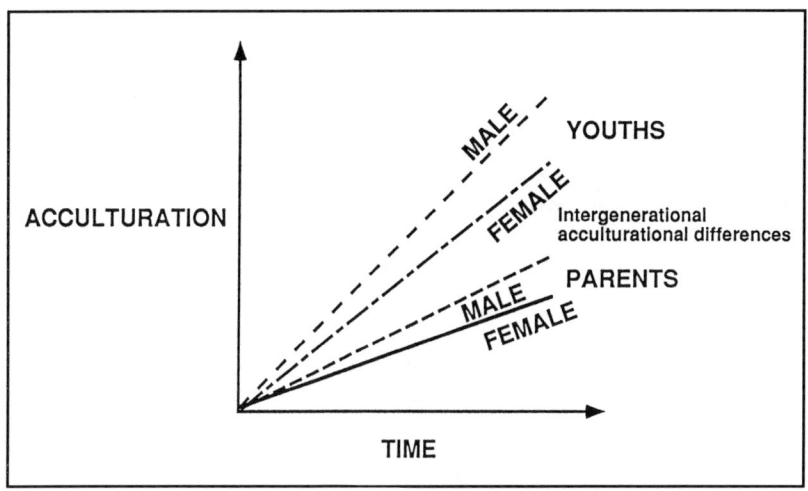

FIGURE 1. *The development of intergenerational acculturation differences in nuclear families as a function of time.*

SOURCE: Reproduced from Szapocznik, J.; Scopetta, M.A.; Kurtines, W.; and Aranalde, M.A. Theory and measurement of acculturation. *Interam J Psychol* 12:113-130, 1978.

differences in which parents and youths developed different cultural alliances (Hispanic and American, respectively). These intergenerationally related cultural differences added to the usual intergenerational conflicts that occur in families with adolescents to produce a much compounded and exacerbated intergenerational and intercultural conflict. As a consequence, parents became unable to properly manage youngsters who in turn made strong claims for autonomy and no longer accepted their parents' traditional Cuban ways, giving rise to the emergence of conduct problems in adolescents.

With development of appropriate measures and the resulting enhanced theoretical understanding of the effects of cultural diversity, the authors were able to develop an intervention that addressed the problems that arise in multicultural contexts through formulating a family-oriented intervention to enhance bicultural skills in all family members (Szapocznik et al. 1984, 1986*c*, 1989*b*). The authors' work in developing this intervention focused on enhancing the bicultural skills that parents and youngsters need to develop (i.e., greater competence in managing

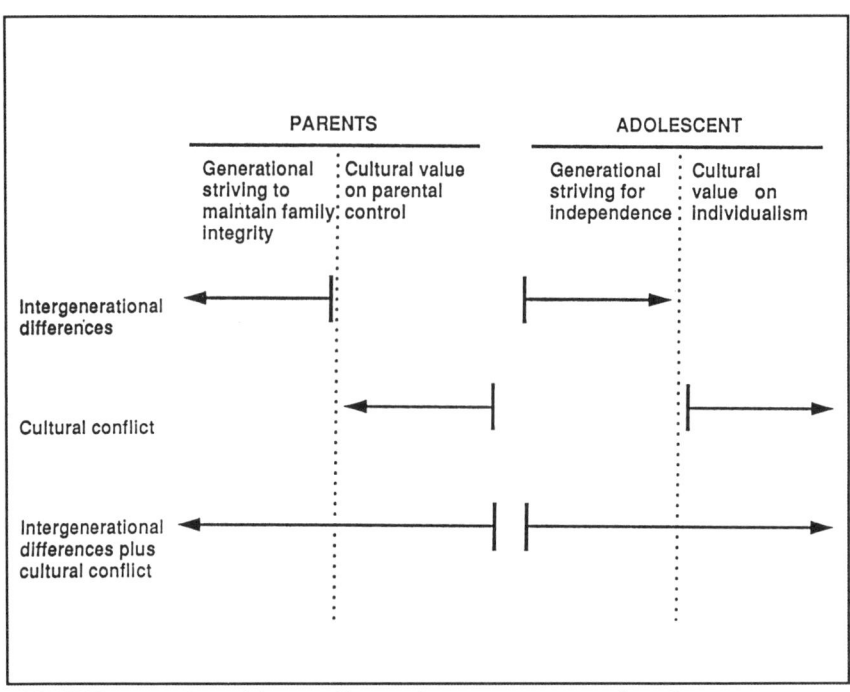

FIGURE 2. *The additive effects of intergenerational and acculturational differences in Cuban-American families.*

SOURCE: Reproduced from Szapocznik, J.; Santiseban, D.; Kurtines, W.M.; Perez-Vidal, A.; and Hervis, O. *Hispanic J Behav Sci* 6(4):317-344, 1984.

their cultural differences within the family and successfully functioning in a culturally pluralistic milieu).

ASSESSING TRANSCULTURAL AND CULTURE-SPECIFIC DIMENSIONS OF FAMILY FUNCTIONING

A final issue confronted in working with families in culturally diverse contexts is developing measures that index both transcultural and culture-specific dimensions of family functioning. To begin assessment of family functioning in the target population, the authors borrowed from the work of Minuchin and colleagues with the Wiltwick Family Tasks (Minuchin et al. 1978). The tasks were useful as standard stimuli, but the scoring of these tasks presented problems of standardization and reliability. Therefore the authors reorganized the scoring procedure into broad theoretically and clinically important dimensions of structural family functioning; standardized the administration procedure; developed a detailed manual with anchors and examples to enhance reliability and replicability of the scoring procedure; and obtained validational evidence of the measure's usefulness and nonreactivity when used in treatment outcome studies. The measure developed provided the cornerstone for extensive research that involved refining and validating the measure (Szapocznik and Kurtines 1989; Szapocznik et al. 1983, 1986*a*, 1989*a*, 1989*b*).

The Structural Family Systems Ratings Scale

The Structural Family Systems Ratings Scale (SFSR) (Szapocznik et al. 1991) developed as part of the authors' research assesses family interactions along six dimensions. Based on the theoretical work of Minuchin (Minuchin et al. 1978), six Likert scales were developed to rate: structure, flexibility, resonance (enmeshment and disengagement), developmental stage, identified patienthood, and conflict resolution. Ratings were obtained by asking the family to interact with each other on three of the Wyltwick standardized tasks: deciding on a menu for a meal, telling what pleases and displeases them about other family members, and describing the most recent family fight or argument. A trained rater observes videotapes of the family performing these tasks, recording specific categories of interaction on a rating form. These clinical ratings are then scaled (5-point Likert) for each of the six dimensions which tap both transcultural and culture-specific dimensions of family functioning (see below).

Structure. Structure refers to the organization of interactional patterns within the family system. Like all of the definitions of SFSR dimensions and identifying variables, structure has both transcultural and culture-specific validity. The structural dimension of SFSR is transcultural in that all SFSR cultural contexts are used to evaluate the subsystem organization and particularly the executive subsystem that provides leadership within the family. The patterns that define a particular family, however, must be evaluated in a culturally specific context. For example, in a conventional nuclear family model, the individuals in the parent roles (usually the biological parent or parents) are expected to provide leadership to the family. In the context of a mainstream cultural framework that adheres to the values of the nuclear family, intrusion from extended family members is viewed as dysfunctional.

However, using the SFSR to examine cross-cultural executive systems, and particularly the cultural contexts that value the extended family over the nuclear family, the authors found executive system organizations that involve the parent figure as well as an extended family member who is culturally and functionally adaptive. Examples of extended family members adaptively functioning in executive roles can be found in African-American and Hispanic families with a single mother living in the grandmother's home. In these cases, if a mother is old enough to parent, the mother and her own mother (the child's grandmother) may co-parent in a functional executive system. From a cultural perspective that values nuclear families, parenting by an extended family member might be scored as dysfunctional because it undermines parental authority. From the perspective of a culture that values involvement of the extended family, however, co-parenting by mother and grandmother might be scored as adaptive as long as the co-parenting relationship was functional.

Why this latter caveat? Clearly co-parenting relationships, whether composed of two biological parents or a parent and a grandparent, can be functional or maladaptive. In a functional co-parenting relationship there is shared decisionmaking, and the parental figures support each other with regard to rules and consequences. In a maladaptive relationship there might be a struggle for power between the parental figures and inability to reach joint decisions; as a consequence, rules and consequences are unclear and variable. In such a maladaptive case, the child may be triangulated in the executive system conflict.

From a *transcultural* perspective, the authors define adaptive executive systems in a similar way: cooperation and collaboration. From a *culture-specific* perspective, the participation of certain sets of individuals is defined as adaptive or maladaptive according to the cultural norms.

Another example of how family structure is influenced by highly culture-specific cross-generational intrusions can be found in Asian-American families. In some Asian-American families the husband's mother is highly involved in giving her daughter-in-law direction for proper behavior with her husband, her husband's parents and siblings, and with their children. From a culture-specific perspective, the husband's mother is expected to help shape her daughter-in-law's behavior since the latter will become a member of her husband's family. The husband and his mother, in turn, remain quite close as a means of securing care for the mother when her own husband dies.

Resonance. Resonance is another dimension in which it is important to be sensitive to the transcultural and culture-specific differences when using the SFSR. For example, in the resonance dimension the amount of closeness that is found in a Hispanic family is much greater than in an Anglo family. Variable markers for closeness in assessing resonance, such as interruptions, simultaneous speaking, and continuations, are all more typical of Hispanics than of white Americans from Boston, the Midwest, or California. White Americans have come to value individuation and separation more than Hispanics. As such, Hispanics are relatively more enmeshed and many white Americans are relatively more disengaged.

Are either of these situations adaptive or maladaptive? It depends upon the circumstances. If a Hispanic daughter or son is rebelling because individuation is not allowed, the tendency toward greater emotional and psychological closeness in this particular Hispanic family is related to the emergence of symptomatic behavior. As such, it needs to be addressed even though it is culturally syntonic for the parents.

The authors encountered a father in a family from a culture that encourages individuation who told his 17-year-old daughter that she was expected to go away to college. The daughter attempted suicide as a way of communicating that she was not ready to separate. Hence, culture-syntonic behavior of a parent may produce a symptom in an already troubled child.

Developmental Stage. The rate at which children are expected to take on responsibilities in a family not only varies considerably from family to family, but also from culture to culture. Thus, the use of the SFSR to assess developmentally appropriate roles varies considerably across cultures and must be sensitive to transcultural and culture-specific differences. For example, in a Hispanic immigrant family an 8-year-old girl may be expected to miss school during harvest time to work with the family in the fields. Yet in the urban context of some Latin American cities, a 16-year-old girl may not be allowed to date unchaperoned. In contrast, in some Asian cultures, children are committed to each other for marriage at an early age and marriage may occur as early as the onset of puberty.

In many Western cultures, a child acting as the emotional support of the mother might be considered developmentally inappropriate because this burdensome role is more appropriate to an adult. Yet in some Asian cultures, a son may be expected to provide emotional and material support to a mother in the long term and may show signs of growing in this direction early in life.

Conflict Resolution. Conflict resolution styles also vary considerably across cultures, and are another dimension of family functioning in which it is important to be sensitive to transcultural and culture-specific differences in using the SFSR. In the mental health culture, for example, full conflict emergence with resolution is valued. In contrast, some Hispanic groups make frequent use of conflict diffusion; in some groups (upper class, higher SES, well educated) conflict diffusion is considered an enviable art.

CONCLUSION

From the authors' earliest work, one concern has been the impact of culturally diverse contexts on immigrant youth and their families. As noted, the authors were confronted with the task of applying the basic principles of sound methodology to the challenge of working with Hispanic youth and their families. One of the outcomes of the past 20 years of the Miami effort has been an enhanced understanding of the methodological issues to be addressed in working with culturally diverse treatment populations. In this chapter the authors have sought to contribute to the wisdom of the field by sharing some of the knowledge acquired in developing assessment strategies for evaluating interventions targeted at troubled Hispanic youths and their families.

REFERENCES

Brislin, R.W. Translation and content analysis of oral and written materials. In: Triandis, H., ed. *Handbook of Cross-Cultural Psychology.* Boston: Allyn and Bacon, 1980.

Carter, R.T. Cultural values: A review of empirical research and implications for counseling. *J Couns Dev* 70:164-173, 1991.

Carter, R.T., and Helms, J.E. "The Intercultural Values Inventory (ICV)." *Tests in Microfiche Test Collection.* Princeton, NJ: Educational Testing Service, 1990.

Harman, H.H. *Modern Factor Analysis.* 2d ed. Chicago: University of Chicago Press, 1967.

Kazdin, A.E. Comparative outcome studies of psychotherapy: Methodological issues and strategies. *J Consult Clin Psychol* 54:95-105, 1986.

Kluckhohn, F.R., and Strodtbeck, F.L. *Variations in Value Orientations.* Evanston, IL: Row, Peterson, 1961.

Minuchin, S.; Rosman, B.L.; and Baker, L. *Psychosomatic Families: Anorexia Nervosa in Context.* Cambridge: Harvard University Press, 1978.

Moos, R.H. *Family Environment Scale (Form R).* Palo Alto, CA: Consulting Psychologists Press, 1974.

Oliver, J.M.; Handal, P.J.; Enos, D.M.; and May, M.J. Factor structure of the Family Environment Scale: Factors based on items and subscales. *Educ Psychol Meas* 48:469-477, 1988.

Quay, H.C., and Peterson, D.R. *Manual for the Revised Behavior Problem Checklist.* 1987. Available from H.C. Quay, University of Miami, Dept. of Psychology, PO Box 248185, Coral Gables, FL 33124.

Rio, A.T.; Quay, H.C.; Santisteban, D.A.; and Szapocznik, J. A factor analytical study of a Spanish translation of the Revised Behavior Problem Checklist. *J Clin Child Psychol* 18(4):343-350, 1989.

Robertson, D.U., and Hyde, J.S. The factorial validity of the Family Environment Scale. *Educ Psychol Meas* 42:1233-1241, 1982.

Szapocznik, J., and Kurtines, W. Acculturation, biculturalism and adjustment among Cuban Americans. In: Padilla, A., ed. *Psychological Dimensions on the Acculturation Process: Theory, Models and Some New Findings.* Boulder, CO: Westview, 1980.

Szapocznik, J., and Kurtines, W. *Breakthroughs in Family Therapy with Drug Abusing Problem Youth.* New York: Springer Co., 1989.

Szapocznik, J., and Kurtines, W.M. Family psychology and cultural diversity: Opportunities for theory, research and application. *Am Psychol* 48(4):400-407, 1993.

Szapocznik, J.; Kurtines, W.M.; and Fernandez, T. Bicultural involvement and adjustment in Hispanic American youths. *Int J Intercult Relat* 4:353-366, 1980.

Szapocznik, J.; Kurtines, W.M.; Foote, F.; Perez-Vidal, A.; and Hervis, O.E. Conjoint versus one person family therapy: Some evidence for effectiveness of conducting family therapy through one person. *J Consult Clin Psychol* 51:889-899, 1983.

Szapocznik, J.; Kurtines, W.M.; Foote, F.; Perez-Vidal, A.; and Hervis, O.E. Conjoint versus one person family therapy: Further evidence for the effectiveness of conducting family therapy through one person. *J Consult Clin Psychol* 54(3):395-397, 1986*a*.

Szapocznik, J.; Kurtines, W.M.; Santisteban, D.A.; and Rio, A.T. The interplay of advances among theory, research, and application in treatment interventions aimed at behavior problem children and adolescents. *J Consult Clin Psychol* 58(6):696-703, 1990.

Szapocznik, J.; Rio, A.T.; Hervis, O.E.; Mitrani, V.B.; Kurtines, W.M.; and Faraci, A.M. Assessing change in family functioning as a result of treatment: The Structural Family Systems Ratings Scale (SFSR). *J Marital Fam Ther* 17(3):295-310, 1991.

Szapocznik, J.; Rio, A.; Murray, E.; Cohen, R.; Scopetta, M.A.; Rivas-Vasquez, A.; Hervis, O.E.; and Posada, V. Structural family versus psychodynamic child therapy for problematic Hispanic boys. *J Consult Clin Psychol* 57(5):571-578, 1989*a*.

Szapocznik, J.; Santisteban, D.; Kurtines, W.M.; Perez-Vidal, A.; and Hervis, O.E. Bicultural effectiveness training: A treatment intervention for enhancing intercultural adjustment. *Hispanic J Behav Sci* 6(4):317-344, 1984.

Szapocznik, J.; Santisteban, D.; Rio, A.; Perez-Vidal, A.; and Kurtines, W.M. Family effectiveness training for Hispanic families: Strategic structural systems intervention for the prevention of drug abuse. In: Lefley, H.P., and Pedersen, P.B., eds. *Cross Cultural Training for Mental Health Professionals.* Springfield, IL: Charles C. Thomas, 1986*b*.

Szapocznik, J.; Santisteban, D.; Rio, A.; Perez-Vidal, A.; Kurtines, W.M.; and Hervis, O.E. Bicultural effectiveness training (BET): An intervention modality for families experiencing intergenerational/ intercultural conflict. *Hispanic J Behav Sci* 6(4):303-330, 1986*c*.

Szapocznik, J.; Santisteban, D.; Rio, A.; Perez-Vidal, A.; Santisteban, D.; and Kurtines, W.M. Family Effectiveness Training: An intervention to prevent drug abuse and problem behavior in Hispanic adolescents. *Hispanic J Behav Sci* 11(1):3-27, 1989*b*.

Szapocznik, J.; Scopetta, M.A.; Aranalde, M.A.; and Kurtines, W.M. Cuban value structure: Clinical implications. *J Consult Clin Psychol* 46(5):961-970, 1978*c*.

Szapocznik, J.; Scopetta, M.A.; and King, O.E. The effect and degree of treatment comprehensiveness with a Latino drug abusing population. In: Smith, D.E.; Anderson, S.E.; Burton, M.; Gotlieb, N.; Harvey, W.; and Chung, T., eds. *A Multicultural View of Drug Abuse.* Cambridge, MA: G.K. Hall and Co., 1978*a*.

Szapocznik, J.; Scopetta, M.A.; and King, O.E. Theory and practice in matching treatment to the special characteristics and problems of Cuban immigrants. *J Community Psychol* 6:112-122, 1978*b*.

Szapocznik, J.; Scopetta, M.A.; Kurtines, W.M.; and Aranalde, M A. Theory and measurement of acculturation. *Interam J Psychology* 12:113-130, 1978*d*.

Waldron, R.J.; Sabatelli, R.M.; and Anderson, S.A. An examination of the factor structure of the Family Environment Scale. *Am J Family Ther* 18(3):257-272, 1990.

AUTHORS

William M. Kurtines, Ph.D.
Professor of Psychology
Department of Psychology
Florida International University
University Park Campus (DM 430)
Miami, FL 33199

José Szapocznik, Ph.D.
Director, Center for Family Studies
University of Miami
School of Medicine
1425 Northwest 10th Avenue, 3rd Floor
Miami, FL 33136

Therapeutic Communities for Adolescents

Nancy Jainchill, Gauri Bhattacharya, and John Yagelka

INTRODUCTION

Adolescents who enter drug-free residential therapeutic communities (TCs) include young people with the most severe substance abuse problems for whom drug use has already precipitated serious dysfunction in their lives.

The TC views substance abuse as a disorder of the whole person, involving the possibility of impeded personality development with concomitant deficits in social, educational, and economic/survival skills (De Leon 1986). This global perspective of the problem recommends a multidimensional rehabilitative approach that occurs in a 24-hour setting. In a 1988-89 survey of membership of the national organization Therapeutic Communities of America (TCA) which, if not inclusive, is representative of TCs in the United States, approximately 20 percent of clients in TCs were youth (20 years of age and younger) (Pompi 1994).

The traditional TC model focused on the habilitation or rehabilitation of the adult (usually male) addict. Although there is a commonality to the social and psychological characteristics of TC admissions, age differences have been identified (De Leon and Deitch 1985). Adolescents entering treatment have less involvement with opioids, have shorter periods of drug abuse (in part, because of their younger age) although initiation of drug use is generally earlier than for adults, and have greater involvement with marijuana and alcohol. The need to accommodate developmental differences, facilitate maturation, and address differences in lifestyle and cultural and psychosocial circumstances has become increasingly evident as the number of adolescents entering treatment has increased. In response, TCs are establishing segregated facilities for adolescents and recognizing that the treatment structure must be adapted to deal with issues unique to young substance abusers. Modifications to treatment include shorter recommended lengths of stay for adolescents, participation by families in the therapeutic process, limited use of peer pressure focusing on positive influences since pretreatment peer influences have been generally negative, and less reliance on the use of life experiences to foster understanding about one's self and one's behaviors. Adolescent residents participate in the horizontal authority structure of the TC by sharing responsibility for daily operations. However, they do not participate in the vertical authority structure of the TC; all activities are staff supervised and staff have ultimate control over all decisions (Operation PAR, Adolescent Residential Center, unpublished data).

Until recently, there has been relatively little research describing the adolescents who enter TC treatment programs or how effective TCs are in the treatment of adolescents with substance abuse disorders and related problems. This chapter provides an overview of the research and treatment issues unique to adolescents in TCs. The initial section provides a review of the main findings and conclusions of early studies of adolescents in TC treatment. The second section discusses recent and current research of adolescents in TCs. The final section offers a discussion of client and treatment issues, with recommendations for future research initiatives.

EARLY STUDIES

Two major multimodality projects funded by the National Institute on Drug Abuse (NIDA) were the Drug Abuse Reporting Program (DARP) and Treatment Outcome Prospective Study (TOPS). The findings relevant to adolescents in TCs are summarized below. (A more detailed review of these and other studies can be found in Pompi 1994.)

DARP

The DARP sample consisted of adolescents in treatment during the late 1960s and early 1970s. Of the 34 TCs, only one was adolescent specific; the other programs were adult treatments although the client population averaged one-third adolescents. The majority were male (63 percent), white (71 percent), and abused opioids (47 percent). Approximately 25 percent of the adolescents left treatment (dropped out) within the first 30 days, and 15 percent completed treatment. Overall, posttreatment outcomes revealed a decreased use of opioids; however, marijuana use increased slightly and there was no change in alcohol consumption. There were positive changes in measures reflecting employment (increased) and criminal activity (decreased). There was a direct positive relationship between posttreatment outcome and retention in treatment;

that is, improved behaviors at followup were related to longer time in treatment (Sells and Simpson 1979).

TOPS

The TOPS sample consisted of admissions to 14 TCs from 1979 to 1981. Adolescents constituted 14 percent of the treatment population and participated in adult-oriented treatment programs. The youth were primarily male (70 percent), white (80 percent), and were abusers of non-opioids (Hubbard et al. 1985). About one-third dropped out within the first month, and approximately 10 percent completed treatment (Pompi 1994). One year posttreatment, positive behavior changes were reflected in decreased use of opioid and nonopioid drugs, lower criminal activity, and increased employment. Positive outcomes were associated with longer time in program (TIP).

TCA Consortium

Seven TCs were involved in a multisite project to establish self-evaluation capability in residential treatment programs. Data collection involved admissions to treatment during a 6-month period of 1979. Adolescents constituted 21 percent of the admissions to the programs. A majority were male (73 percent) and use of opioids was infrequent. Thirty-day dropout was relatively high (~37 percent). Program completion rates and other outcome data were not obtained (De Leon 1980; De Leon and Schwartz 1984).

Single Program Studies. Several single program studies have been completed by program-based researchers (De Leon 1984, 1988; Holland 1978, 1984; Pompi and Resnick 1987; Sansone 1980). All of the programs were age integrated, with a majority of the population being adult. Sansone (1980) reported 32 percent 30-day retention rates. Pompi and Resnsick (1987) reported notably higher retention rates for their population: 87 percent of the juvenile justice (court-referred) sample remained in treatment through 30 days, which was higher than that reported for adolescents by other investigators, but lower than the adults included in their study. Long-term retention was associated with being court referred, male, and older. Holland (1978) and De Leon (1984) reported similar completion rates of approximately 18 percent. Outcome data reported by De Leon showed overall improvements posttreatment, including reduced drug use and criminal activity.

In summary, adolescents constituted a minority of the treatment population in age-integrated TCs. There were some differences across the studies; however, overall retention rates and posttreatment outcomes were similar. At followup adolescents showed positive changes in such behavioral measures as drug use and criminal activity, and these improvements were directly related to TIP. With some exceptions (Sansone 1980), these results are similar to those obtained by adults. The notably higher retention rates reported by Pompi and Resnick (1987) probably reflect the fact that over 97 percent of their sample was court referred to treatment, compared to other programs which averaged 40 to 45 percent court referrals.

RECENT AND CURRENT STUDIES

A recently completed study of adolescent admissions to two TCs described the social and psychological profiles of the adolescents and identified factors that might contribute to retention in treatment (Jainchill and De Leon 1992). The study provided the opportunity to compare two age groups of adolescents, clients under 18 years old and those 18 to 21 years of age. Program I does not admit clients beyond 18 years of age, whereas Program II admits individuals who are 18 or older. Table 1 presents the characteristics of the two samples including demography, primary drug of abuse, selected psychological variables, TIP, and correlates of retention.

Despite differences in demography and primary drug of abuse, the two samples are psychologically more similar than dissimilar. For example, their Tennessee Self Concept (TSC) profiles (table 1, total positive scale) reveal poor self-esteem and considerable disturbance in addition to substance abuse. The profiles are characteristic of drug abusers in general and of previous adult admissions to other TCs. The pattern of dropout is similar for the two programs and is also similar to dropout/retention curves reported for adult samples in previous studies.

The Circumstance, Motivation, Readiness and Suitability Scales (CMRS) (De Leon 1986) were administered to all admissions. Circumstances refer to external conditions that drive people to seek treatment; motivation refers to the individual's inner reasons for personal change; readiness relates to a person's need for any treatment to assist in personal change compared with alternative options (e.g., nontreatment alternatives); and suitability refers to the appropriate match between a particular

TABLE 1. *Profiles of younger versus older adolescent admissions to therapeutic community treatment.*

	Program I N	Program I %	Program II N	Program II %	p[a]	Totals N	Totals %
Totals	70	50.7	68	49.3		138	100.0
Males	51	72.9	59	86.8	n.s.	110	79.7
Females	19	27.1	9	13.2		28	20.3
White	47	67.1	6	8.8	0.000	53	38.4
Black	9	12.9	40	58.8		49	35.5
Hispanic	14	20.0	22	32.3		36	26.1
Primary Drug							
Marijuana	16	22.9	5	7.4	0.000	21	15.2
Crack	17	24.3	45	66.2		62	44.9
Cocaine	14	20.0	11	16.2		25	18.1
Alcohol	21	30.0	1	1.5		22	15.9
Heroin	2	92.9	6	8.8		8	5.8
Age at Entry							
Mean	15.74		20.00		0.000	17.84	
Standard Deviation	1.37		0.96			2.44	
Psychological status at admission:							
Serious depression							
Ever	32	51.6	41	60.3	n.s.	73	56.2
Past 30 days	18	29.0	21	30.9	n.s.	39	30.0
Serious Anxiety							
Ever	27	43.5	45	66.2	0.016	72	55.4
Past 30 days	16	25.8	31	45.6	0.031	47	36.2
TSC Total Positive Scale[b]	63	(mean score) 292.3	66	(mean score) 291.6	n.s.	129	(mean score) 292.0
Retention[c]							
Time in program							
≥ 30 days	51	72.9	56	82.4	n.s.	107	77.5

a = The chi square was used to assess differences between groups on the categorized variables. A t-test for independent samples was used to evaluate the age difference between the programs.
b = Normative sample; mean = 336.6.
c = The relationship between demography, primary drug, psychological status, behavioral measures (e.g., criminal activity), and CMRS scale scores was examined. Only correlation coefficients significant at p <0.05 level or smaller are shown. There were only two significant correleates of retention and these were for Program II: CMRS Suitability Scale: 0.250; Drug Use Severity: -0.235.

treatment and the individual (De Leon and Jainchill 1986; De Leon et al. 1993). The results revealed that older clients felt more motivated and ready for treatment and also perceived treatment to be more suitable for them. However, the relationship between these factors and retention was less clear. There was only one significant correlation between retention and any of the CMRS scales. Older clients (Program II) who perceived the treatment setting as more suitable had a greater likelihood of remaining in treatment beyond 30 days. Discriminant analyses revealed that the most consistent predictor of 30-day retention was age. In summary, an association between the separate CMRS scale scores, the CMRS total score, and 30-day dropout/retention is suggested. Age emerges as a strong factor influencing or mediating the association between retention and the CMRS dimensions.

Drug Abuse Treatment Outcome Study (DATOS)

The DATOS project (Tims et al. 1991) is a major national followup study sampling long-term residential TC, drug-free outpatient, and short-term inpatient programs. The goal of the DATOS-Adolescent (DATOS-A) project is to increase understanding of adolescent drug abuse treatment, including factors that influence its effectiveness. The major elements of the project are a study of client characteristics, an assessment of treatment structure and process, and an outcome evaluation.

The DATOS-A project seeks to address the following questions: What are the client characteristics and pretreatment behaviors of adolescent drug users entering various types of treatment? Are there client "types" that can be identified considering pretreatment behaviors, patterns of drug use, prosocial activities (e.g., school and employment), and mental health? What factors predict the types of clients served by different adolescent treatment? How do the characteristics of adolescent drug users entering treatment from 1993 to 1995 compare with those who entered in 1979 to 1981 and 1969 to 1974?

Questions about the nature of the treatment programs and the treatment process will address the following issues: the nature and structure of treatment and the services received by the adolescents; the correlates of retention and progress through treatment; the behaviors and cognitions of adolescents and their families during treatment, and the factors that influence change; and the evolution of treatments and services across more than 10 years.

The followup study will examine behavioral measures including levels of drug use, delinquent behavior, and psychosocial functioning, reviewing their change from pretreatment and identifying factors associated with any observed changes. Clients will be interviewed 1 year after separation from the treatment program (Hubbard, unpublished data). Data collection for DATOS-A was scheduled to begin in fall 1993.

Center for Therapeutic Community Research (CTCR)

A major project of the NIDA-funded CTCR is a study of adolescents in TC treatment. Six treatment programs at nine sites that are self-described TCs and that vary on a number of dimensions including size, planned duration of stay, and demographic composition of clients are participating in the study. The programs are located throughout the U.S. East Coast and Canada. Data collection was phased in beginning April 1992, with all programs collecting data by October 1992.

The aims of the study are to profile adolescent substance abusers in residential TC treatment, to evaluate the effectiveness of the TC for treatment of adolescents with substance abuse problems and accompanying disorders, and to clarify the relationship between initial admission status, progress in treatment, and retention. The remainder of this chapter presents findings from this study, which is the most recent research conducted on adolescents in TCs.

Sample and Instrumentation. The study sample includes all clients who are admitted to the six participating programs during the period of data collection. Clients are excluded from the study if they refuse to participate or if parents refuse to give permission for their child's participation in those programs that require parental consent. Refusal rates (clients and parents) have varied considerably across programs, but average less than 5 percent.

Interviewing of new admissions occurs during the first 10 days of treatment over several sessions, and takes approximately 7 hours to complete. The interview battery includes an extensive baseline questionnaire that obtains information on personal background, social relations, education, family, drug use, and criminal activity. Other measures assess the adolescent's motivation, readiness for treatment, and psychological status. A structured interview is administered to obtain psychiatric diagnoses as defined in the "Diagnostic and Statistical Manual of Mental Disorders," 3d ed. revised (DSM-III-R). To assess client progress, adolescents who are still in treatment at the program midpoint complete selected psychological measures from the baseline battery and a midpoint questionnaire. To evaluate the effectiveness of the TC, followup interviews are being conducted with clients 12 months posttreatment, whether they have left prematurely or completed the program. Outcomes on behavioral measures of drug use, criminal activity, social relations, and psychological/psychiatric status are obtained. There is also extensive questioning about the client's treatment experience.

Findings are presented based upon a sample of 938 adolescents admitted to the six programs between April 1992 and April 1994. Followup data are not presented since sample sizes as yet are too small for meaningful analyses. The results are reported for the full sample when the sample size is too small to permit presentation of findings for individual programs.

Programs are identified in the tables by the numbers 1 through 6. Letters indicate facilities except for "1A" and "1D," which refer to two different treatment tracks at one facility. At this facility all of the admissions are court referrals; "1A" clients are designated drug abusers, while "1D" clients are individuals who have been mandated to treatment because of dealing drugs, though they also use substances.

The demographic characteristics and primary drug of abuse of the sample are shown in table 2. As can be seen, there is considerable variability among the programs in terms of ethnic and gender distribution. Two of the programs do not admit females, and those programs that are mixed gender have a large proportion of males. (Although Program 1 admits females, they are housed in a separate facility (1W) and treatment is completely segregated.) Program 2 was established and is staffed by Hispanics for the treatment of Hispanics. The staff and residents of the other programs are of mixed ethnic composition. The clients at Programs 2 and 3 are somewhat older than the adolescents in the other TCs.

There were interesting differences in the distribution of primary drug among the programs. The percentage of adolescents who report that crack or other cocaine is their primary drug of abuse is relatively low. Although over 40 percent had used crack/cocaine in their lifetime (not shown), only 9 percent stated it was their main drug. Also of note is the high proportion of primary heroin abusers in Program 2. Program 3 also had a considerable number of primary heroin abusers. Both programs are

TABLE 2. Demography, primary drug of abuse, source of referral, and totals for six programs.

Program	1D	1A	1W	2	3	4B	4R	5	6M	6T	Totals
N =	100	100	82	83	81	91	76	103	123	99	938
					PERCENT						
Gender											
Males	100.0	100.0	0.0	100.0	100.0	60.4	63.2	76.7	71.5	84.8	76.5
Females	0.0	0.0	100.0	0.0	0.0	39.6	36.8	23.3	28.5	15.2	23.5
Ethnicity											
White	5.0	48.0	40.2	0.0	21.3	63.7	27.6	73.8	91.9	90.9	49.4
Black	75.0	43.0	46.3	0.0	50.7	13.2	22.6	22.3	0.8	3.0	27.3
Hispanic	20.0	9.0	13.4	100.0	28.0	13.6	38.2	2.9	0.0	0.0	20.6
Other	0.0	0.0	0.0	0.0	0.0	5.5	6.6	1.0	7.3	6.1	2.8
Age at Entry											
< 16	26.0	23.0	56.1	30.1	18.5	48.4	63.1	35.0	31.7	6.1	32.8
16-17	68.0	72.0	42.7	42.2	39.5	50.5	30.3	63.1	61.8	73.7	56.0
≥ 18	6.0	5.0	1.2	27.7	42.0	1.1	6.6	1.9	6.5	20.2	11.2
Primary Drug											
Alcohol	20.2	23.5	31.9	6.5	10.7	33.3	29.3	8.7	8.1	33.3	20.0
Marijuana	70.2	65.3	47.8	45.5	48.0	55.6	64.0	80.6	38.2	40.0	55.6
Crack/Cocaine	3.2	3.1	13.0	9.1	14.7	3.3	4.0	7.8	17.9	12.1	9.0
Herion/Opiates/Other	1.1	1.0	0.0	33.8	22.7	1.1	0.0	0.0	1.6	0.0	5.3
No primary drug	5.3	7.1	7.2	5.2	4.0	6.7	2.7	2.9	34.1	14.1	10.1

TABLE 2 (continued). *Demography, primary drug of abuse, source of referral, and totals for six programs.*

Program	1D	1A	1W	2	3	4B	4R	5	6M	6T	Totals
N =	100	100	82	83	81	91	76	103	123	99	938
Source of Referral											
Self	0.0	0.0	0.0	21.7	13.6	19.8	10.5	12.6	8.1	2.0	8.5
Legal/Court/	100.0	100.0	91.5	73.5	82.7	33.0	26.3	82.5	2.4	92.9	67.5
Probation/Parole	0.0	0.0	1.2	0.0	0.0	35.9	38.5	1.0	13.8	1.0	8.3
Other Family	0.0	0.0	1.2	3.6	2.4	1.1	10.5	0.0	4.1	0.0	1.8
Medical/Other Treatment	0.0	0.0	4.9	1.2	1.2	8.8	9.2	2.9	49.6	4.0	9.5
Treatment/Friend/Other	0.0	0.0	1.2	1.2	2.5	6.6	3.9	1.0	22.0	0.0	4.4

located in the same city and serve older adolescents. All of Program 2 clients are Hispanic, and the heroin abusers in Program 3 are probably also Hispanic.

Table 2 also shows the percentage of clients who are referred to treatment by the criminal justice system. In the current study 70 to 100 percent of admissions are legal referrals for all but two of the programs. With the exception of Pompi and Resnick's work (1987), earlier studies (De Leon and Schwartz 1984; Hubbard et al. 1985) reported a range of 40 to 50 percent legal referrals. In general, proportionately more adolescents than adults are referred to treatment through the criminal justice system. Although most of the earlier studies involved adult-oriented programs that included adolescents, it appears that increasing numbers of adolescents are entering treatment because of legal pressure.

Psychological Status. A psychological history was obtained, incorporating selected questions from the Addiction Severity Index and the Adolescent Problem Severity Index into the CTCR baseline interview. As shown in table 3, the adolescents entering TCs for treatment of substance abuse problems also have experienced a wide range of other problems in their lifetime. For example, over half the sample reported that they had experienced a serious depression at some time in their life, 40 percent had experienced serious anxiety, and more than one-quarter of the sample had had serious thoughts of suicide in their lifetime. Of note, over 40 percent of the sample stated that they had experienced trouble controlling violent behavior. Nonetheless, only a minority indicated that treatment for any of these problems was important to them.

The psychological status of the clients at admission to treatment was assessed with selected self-administered paper-and-pencil measures. Table 4.1 shows the results for the full sample and for the individual programs/facilities. There is variability across the programs on all of the measures of psychopathology. The adolescents at the facilities with a greater proportion of whites (4B, 6M, 6T) revealed the highest levels of depression and anxiety (highest scores) and the poorest self-esteem (lowest total positive score). They also obtained the highest score on the number of deviant signs TSC scale, the single best indicator of overall disturbance. This finding corroborates earlier research on adults concerning degree of psychological disturbance at admission to TC treatment (De Leon and Jainchill 1981-82). In general, the least deviant

TABLE 3. *Psychological history.*

	N	Lifetime %
Experienced serious depression	498	54.5
Experienced serious anxiety	369	40.4
Experienced hallucinations	151	16.5
Had problems concentrating	386	42.2
Trouble controlling violent behavior	384	42.0
Serious thoughts of suicide	276	30.3
Attempted suicide	214	23.5
Took medication for psychological problems	124	13.6
Trouble making/keeping friends	128	14.0
Serious problems with boy/girlfriend	298	32.6
Got into trouble because of friends	573	62.7
Felt no one really cared about you	410	44.9
How important is treatment for any of these problems?		
Not important	409	47.6
Fairly important	194	22.6
Very important	256	29.8
Past treatment for psychological problems	341	37.4

N ~914

TABLE 4.1. *Psychological characteristics of adolescent admissions to six programs.*

Program	1A	1D	1W	2	3	4B	4R	5	6M	6T	Totals
N =	100	100	80	74	70	78	69	113	113	92	874
Psychological Scale											
Beck Depression Inventory	8.2	8.7	15.4	13.1	13.4	16.8	15.4	14.3	17.2	16.5	13.7
Taylor Manifest Anxiety	7.1	7.4	9.8	4.8	6.1	11.5	9.4	9.4	12.7	11.8	9.2
Tennessee Self-Concept Scale											
Total Positive	320.2	322.7	312.3	325.7	320.3	292.1	307.2	298.7	286.5	288.0	306.6
Personality Disorder	62.6	63.8	62.1	62.0	61.5	53.9	57.2	54.6	54.7	53.7	58.9
Personality Integration	11.9	11.1	6.2	9.4	10.6	5.8	6.3	7.1	6.0	6.1	8.1
Number Deviant Signs	32.9	33.1	39.0	25.3	20.0	40.9	38.1	33.7	41.1	41.2	35.0

scores were obtained by admissions to Program 1 (A and D). Table 4.2 summarizes the significant differences among the programs.

Motivation and Expectations of Treatment. Previous research has indicated that there is a direct relationship between age and a client's motivation and readiness for treatment (Jainchill and De Leon 1992). Younger clients are less motivated to be in treatment, and do not perceive treatment as being suitable for them. As discussed, the large majority of the adolescents in the present study are court mandated to treatment so that intrinsic pressures (motivation) versus extrinsic pressures (circumstances such as court referral) may exert more influence on whether a client leaves or remains than on the decision to enter treatment. Although at admission clients state that they expect to be helped to reduce their drug and/or alcohol use, when asked about their expectations for the future, only half state that they think they will eventually quit drugs forever.

The CMRS scales (De Leon 1986) were completed as part of the admissions interview battery. This instrument is being used by a number of programs, and the prediction of retention for adolescents has been poor. A variety of different methods have been used to maximize the predictability of the instrument, including the derivation of total scale scores and the use of subsets of items that have the highest zero-order correlations with retention. Recently, using the data collected in the current study, the CMRS items that had a zero-order correlation of 0.10 or better on 2 of 3 retention variables were submitted to a components analysis with oblique rotation to ascertain the degree of dimensional coverage of the items. A transformed index score was created for each client. Higher scores reflect more external as well as internal pressure to be in treatment, and perceptions that the program is suitable for the client.

This score yielded a zero-order correlation of 0.29 with days in treatment, indicating a robust positive relationship between level of motivation and retention. Table 5 lists the items that entered into this index. Table 6 shows the scores for each of the programs and/or facilities. Higher scores suggest that the clients at a particular setting are self-reported to be more motivated and ready for treatment. Clients at 1A and 1D had significantly higher scores than the majority of the other programs. As will be seen, dropout is also extremely low at 1A and 1B.

TABLE 4.2. *Summary of significant differences of psychological characteristics among programs/facilities.*

Beck Depression Inventory	1A, 1D > A5, 4B, 4R, 5, 6M, 6T
Taylor Manifest Anxiety	2, 3 > 4B, 4R, 5, 6M, 6T 1A, 1D > 4B, 6M, 6T 1W, 4R, 5 > 6M
Tennessee Self-Concept Scale	
Total positive	6M, 6T < 1A, 1D, 1W, 2, 3 4B < 1A, 1D, 2, 3 5 < 1A, 1D, 2
Personality disorder	4B, 5, 6M, 6T < 1A, 1D, 1W, 2, 3 4R < 1D
Personality integration	1A, 1D, 2, 3, > 1W, 4B, 4R, 6M, 6T 1A, 1D, 3 > 5 1A > 2
Number of deviant signs	3 > 1A, 1D, 1W, 4B, 4R, 5, 6M, 6T 2 > 1W, 4B, 6M, 6T

NOTE: The Scheffe Multiple Comparison test was used to assess differences among groups. Differences significant at $p < 0.05$ or better are reported.

KEY: < = worse than; > = better than.

Retention in Treatment. A number of investigators have documented the positive relationship between retention in TCs and client outcomes posttreatment. TIP is the largest and most consistent predictor of treatment outcomes (De Leon 1988). Positive outcomes (e.g., no drug use, no criminal activity, employment, and improvement on psychological measures) are associated with longer TIP (De Leon 1984; Hubbard et al. 1985; Simpson and Sells 1982). Nonetheless, dropout is the rule, and the largest percentage of clients who leave treatment do so within the first 30 days.

TABLE 5. *CRMS 18-item index.*

Circumstances

I am sure that I would be in treatment without the pressure of my legal involvement.

I am worried that I will have serious money problems if I stay in residential treatment.

Basically, I feel I have too many outside problems that will prevent me from completing treatment (parents, spouse/relationship, children, loss of job, income, education, family problems, loss of home/place to live. etc.).

Speaking honestly, I really do not need treatment. I am here because of pressure on me (family, legal).

Motivation

I am sure that I will stay in treatment even if my family/relationship wants me to leave.

Lately, I feel like I really can't control my life, things are too much to handle.

I am afraid that I will end up dead if I don't stop using drugs.

Readiness

I am in this program because I really feel that I am ready to deal with myself in treatment.

Basically, I don't see any other choice for help at this time except some kind of treatment.

Suitability

Overall, this treatment seems to be the right approach to my problems.

Overall, I don't think I can adjust well to the demands of this program.

I really believe that some other kind of treatment would be more helpful to me.

I know that it will mean a lot of sacrifice to stay in this program.

I'll stay in this program as long as I have to in order to change my life for the better.

Basically, I do feel that drug use is only a part of my problem and that I have to change a lot about myself in order to make a new start in life.

Basically, I have to stay away from the people who use drugs and the places where drugs are used in order to change my life for the better.

In the current study there is large variability in the dropout/retention rates and in the pattern of dropout for the different programs. Table 7 shows the retention profiles for the different programs and facilities. The N is slightly reduced to include only those clients with 90-day retention potential at the time of analysis. As shown in table 7, 30-day retention ranges between 65 percent (35 percent dropout) in program 3 and 98 percent (2 percent dropout) in program 1, treatment D. Different

TABLE 6. *Index of adolescent CMRS scores by program site.*

Program Site	N	Score	Program Differences p < 0.005
1A	94	60.9	1A > 1W, 2, 3, 4B, 5, 6M, 6T
1D	81	60.2	1D > 2, 3, 4B, 6M, 6T
1W	61	56.7	
2	68	54.2	
3	73	54.8	
4B	77	56.2	
4R	67	57.2	
5	88	57.2	
6M	72	55.9	
6T	83	56.4	
Totals	764	57.1	

N = 764; F = 10.6322; p = 0.0000

facilities within a single program also yield different retention rates. For example, 4B has 83 percent retention (17 percent dropout) at 30 days compared with 4R, which has 68 percent retention (32 percent dropout). The dropout pattern also differs in that readmission to treatment is much more frequent for 1W and 4B admissions than for other programs/facilities. This trend is seen as a clinical issue by the 1W program staff, and readmission is tolerated more than at other settings.

Predicting Retention. Previous research has demonstrated the positive relationship between posttreatment improvement and length of time in treatment. However, investigators have been generally unsuccessful at identifying factors that correlate with retention, particularly for adolescents (Jainchill and De Leon 1992). The current study examined a range of variables reflecting sociocultural and personal background,

TABLE 7. Dropout/retention profile of adolescent admissions to six therapeutic communities through 90 days.

Program	1D	1A	1W	2	3	4B	4R	5	6M	6T	Totals
N =	100	100	82	82	81	86	69	100	122	98	920
					PERCENT						
"Split" Status											
Did not split	97.0	96.0	63.4	39.0	38.3	40.7	39.1	42.0	48.4	40.8	55.5
Split-did not return	3.0	4.0	11.0	52.4	50.6	30.2	46.4	56.0	41.8	38.8	32.9
Split-returned (single or multiple times)	0.0	0.0	25.7	8.6	11.1	29.1	14.4	2.0	9.8	20.4	11.5
# Days in Tx (Max. = 90)											
≤ 5 days	0.0	0.0	1.2	7.3	6.2	5.8	2.9	3.0	1.6	1.0	2.7
6-10 days	0.0	0.0	3.7	7.3	9.9	2.3	7.2	1.0	5.7	0.0	3.5
11-15 days	0.0	0.0	2.4	4.9	7.4	3.5	8.7	4.0	4.9	7.1	4.1
16-29 days	2.0	0.0	1.2	13.4	11.1	5.8	13.0	19.0	9.0	5.1	7.8

TABLE 7 (continued). Dropout/retention profile of adolescent admissions to six therapeutic communities through 90 days.

Program	1D	1A	1W	2	3	4B	4R	5	6M	6T	Totals
N =	100	100	82	82	81	86	69	100	122	98	920
					PERCENT						
Cumulative											
30 days	2.0	0.0	8.5	32.9	34.6	17.4	31.8	27.8	21.2	13.2	18.1
30-60 days	0.0	4.0	9.8	14.6	13.6	14.0	13.0	13.0	15.6	20.4	11.7
61-89 days	1.0	0.0	15.9	13.4	13.6	26.7	14.5	18.0	13.9	24.5	13.9
≥ 90 days	97.0	96.0	65.9	39.0	38.3	41.9	40.6	42.0	49.2	41.8	56.2

antisocial behavior, psychological status, and motivation and readiness for treatment in relation to retention.

A treatment setting index was created that reflects the perceived environmental risk of leaving a particular program/facility. The index is a preliminary attempt to assess the program environment in terms of its atmosphere for "splitting." The index is based on factors such as location of the program/facility, stringency and application of rules and regulations, and staff characteristics including perceived cohesiveness, caring, and accessibility. Each program/facility was given a score on the index, reflecting the degree of risk for leaving perceived to be inherent in the treatment setting. Continued work to refine the index will require ethnographic study of the individual settings and further identification of distinguishing program characteristics.

The variables that correlated significantly with retention through 90 days are shown in table 8. The data suggest that an antisocial lifestyle may predict early dropout: more criminal involvement, more problems with fighting or controlling violent behavior, and friends who are more involved with drugs and crime. Poorer psychological status was also associated with early dropout. Other significant predictors of dropout/retention are the CMRS Index, the Environmental Risk Index, and interviewer impressions. The latter variable is a judgment provided by the research assistant at the end of the admissions interview, as to whether the client will stay long enough to be helped.

Table 9 shows the results of a regression analysis to predict 90-day retention. A stepwise hierarchical approach was used. The order of entry was as follows: static client factors, previous behaviors and psychiatric disturbance, program factors, client's motivation, and interviewer impressions. Twenty percent of the variance is explained. The significant predictors are: gender being male, TSC self-esteem, the CMRS Index score, interviewer impressions, and the Environmental Risk Index.

The Environmental Risk Index and interviewer impressions were large predictors even though they entered the equation last. It will be important to identify the client characteristics that influence the interviewers' response, as they may have important implications for interventions early in the treatment process. A caveat is in order regarding the findings for the Environmental Risk Index: It will be necessary to remove Program 1(A and D) (same score assigned to both) from the index to ascertain the

TABLE 8. *Adolescents in TCs: Client correlates of 90-day retention.*

Motivation/readiness
   CMRS index score (+)
   Most important reason for entering Tx/legal pressure (+)
   Troubled by drug problems during month pretreatment (-)

Previous behaviors
- Alcohol/drug use
    - Earlier use of marijuana (-)
    - Drug/alcohol use instead of school (-)
    - Less use of crack/cocaine in lifetime (+)
- Antisocial behaviors
    - Weapons offenses (-)
    - Trouble controlling violent behavior (-)
    - School behavior problems: fighting, trouble with teachers (-)
- Peers
    - Friends drank to get high (-)
    - Friends used street drugs (-)
    - Friends dealt drugs (-)
    - Friends did other things against the law (-)

Psychological status/attitudes
   Beck Depression—higher scores (-)
   Manifest Anxiety—higher scores (-)
   Tennessee Self Concept—selected scales-better scores (+)
   Suicidal thoughts/attempts during lifetime (-)
   Felt no one cared about you (-)

Interviewer impressions
- Client is socially well adjusted (+)
- Client will stay long enough to be helped (+)

Program factors
- Treatment setting index (+)

N ~850

KEY: (+) = Positive correlation with retention in treatment.
         (-) = Negative correlation with retention in treatment.

TABLE 9. *Regression predicting 90-day retention.*

Predictor	r	Beta
Gender (males)	0.103	0.091
Age at entry	0.003	-0.054
Minority status in program	0.047	0.031
Primary drug—marijuana	-0.010	-0.034
Primary drug—alcohol	0.050	-0.019
School grades	0.077*	0.039
School problems	-0.098**	-0.051
Social adjustment	0.021	0.028
Age first used alcohol to intoxication	0.038	-0.021
Peers' deviancy	-0.176***	-0.056
Age first involved in criminal activity	-0.026	-0.043
Total number of psychiatric diagnoses	-0.029	0.039
Interviewer impressions:		
Client will stay long enough to be helped	0.337***	0.282**
Client motivation (CMRS score)	0.237***	0.106**
Enviromental risk index	-0.326***	-0.252***

N = 533

Multiple R	0.48	
R^2	0.23	
Adjusted R^2	0.20	F = 10.130***

KEY: * = $p < 0.05$; ** = $p < 0.01$; *** = $p < 0.001$.

efficacy of the index in excluding a program with retention at the extreme end of the continuum. The size of the multiple R and the amount of variance explained is relatively large for this kind of research and this population. These findings suggest approaches to research and treatment and are discussed in more detail below.

CONCLUSIONS AND RECOMMENDATIONS

Summary

There is variability among admissions to the programs in terms of gender, ethnicity, and primary drug of abuse. However, the large majority of clients are males who enter treatment with marijuana and/or alcohol abuse problems. The exception is seen among Hispanic admissions to treatment, who report significant abuse of heroin.

The large majority enter treatment because of pressure from the criminal justice system. Psychologically, they reveal mild to moderate levels of disturbance (e.g., depression, anxiety, poor self-esteem), and females appear more disturbed than males. The dropout/retention rates differ considerably across the six programs. Predictors of retention for the full sample include measures of self-esteem, the CMRS Index, the Environmental Risk Index, and interviewer impressions of the client's likelihood of staying to be helped.

Comparisons with Adults

Although there are disproportionately more males than females among adult admissions to TCs, the difference is even larger among adolescents. The distribution of primary drug of abuse by adolescents also differs from that of adults; most notably, there is less crack/cocaine use. A much larger proportion of adolescents enter treatment through the criminal justice system, whereas most adult clients seek treatment for other more personal reasons (e.g., disgusted with lifestyle).

Psychologically, the profiles of adolescents are similar to those of adult admissions to TCs: Both reveal moderate levels of depression, anxiety, and low self-esteem. The variability in retention rates among the six adolescent programs precludes comparisons with previous research on adult samples. In general, however, early dropout is the rule for both adolescents and adults.

Methodological Issues in Evaluation

Instrumentation. Until recently, few measures had been developed to assess adolescent behaviors, pathology, and life circumstances. It is critical that investigators who engage in research on adolescents use the newly available instruments, such as the Diagnostic Interview for

Children and Adolescents (DICA) or the Diagnostic Interview Schedule for Children (DISC) for psychiatric assessment, the Problem Oriented Screening Instrument for Teens (POSIT) for problem assessment, and the Personal Experience Inventory (PEI) for personal profile. Measures developed with adult samples should be used with caution, and comparisons with norms based on adolescents' samples are recommended for meaningful interpretation of findings.

Definition of Adolescent. The definition of adolescence may be guided by chronological years, by societal status (e.g., emancipation, voting rights, legal definition of juvenile), or by sources of funding. The parameters of adolescence are also influenced by factors such as gender and culture. It may be helpful for both researchers and clinicians to view adolescence as a continuum and to distinguish among age groups and their interaction with other factors along the continuum.

Interpretation of Findings. The criteria used to define success based on previous outcome studies of adult populations may not be relevant for adolescents. For example, successful outcomes among adolescents should be viewed in the context of developmental stages. Absolute abstinence might be a criterion for success for one subgroup of youth, while for others reduction in use might be indicative of positive treatment impact and success. Concommitment indicators of positive outcomes that need to be assessed are appropriate changes in attitudes and values which are captured in verbal report and are also reflected in constructive behaviors.

Implementation Issues in Research on Adolescents. Briefly, these include issues of consent, confidentiality, interviewing techniques, and followup. Problems with consent arise because some States require parental consent for minors to participate in research studies. Often the parents are unavailable or unwilling to sign consent forms. Other problems occur when adolescents are under the jurisidiction of the legal system. Confidentiality issues occur when clients reveal that they have been abused and the possibility of future abuse exists. A possible solution is to include delimiting statements in consent forms, although this often inhibits disclosure. Both problems—consent and confidentiality—could be alleviated by the development of standard regulations and guidelines.

Interviewers must be trained to work with adolescents. Problems that may arise include short attention spans, client neediness, and recency of physical or sexual abuse incidents. Adolescents are often emotionally hungry and needy, which can introduce transference or countertransference issues into the interview session. Interviewers must respect personal boundaries, but they can also be empathic to facilitate a successful interview experience. Interviewers should be comfortable discussing physical and sexual abuse histories, and be trained to recognize signs of serious upset or disturbance. Procedures should be established for program clinical staff to be available, as needed, to provide postinterview support to the client.

Followup of adolescents requires a technology that addresses the mobility of adolescents and the fact that their contacts are often dysfunctional and/or uncooperative families. One option is development of alternative liaisons with schools and community programs that might have contact with these clients. The very real need to "work the streets" to locate individuals requires development of procedures that are safe as well as effective.

Future Research Initiatives

Treatment Factors. The relationship between the client, treatment, and outcome is interactive, complex, and poorly understood. As discussed above, the traditional TC model has been modified for adolescents in terms of the services delivered (e.g., greater emphasis on family and education), the structure of the community, and the recommended length of treatment. However, there is considerable variability among programs and the impact of these modifications on client retention and outcomes is not known. Studies are needed to assess the relative efficacy of mixed-age versus age-segregated treatment environments and gender-segregated versus heterosexual programs. The role of the family in the therapeutic process needs to be more clearly defined and evaluated. Existing aftercare/continual care programs need to be enhanced and assessed.

The preliminary Environmental Risk Index developed by Jainchill and colleagues (this volume) highlights the importance of carefully describing individual settings and delineating the tangible (e.g., rules) and intangible (e.g., staff cohesiveness) elements of treatment. The use of ethnographic investigation is planned. The relationship between environmental factors and client retention and outcome is an important focus of study.

Client Factors. The relationship between age, legal referral status, and retention needs to be clarified. For example, the effect of mandatory retention is not understood. Clients who remain in treatment because of legal pressure may or may not be positively impacted by the therapeutic process. The fact that a client remains in treatment does not ensure that benefits accrue from the experience.

Motivational issues and their role in retention and recovery are a focus of continuing study. Compared with adults, adolescents are less motivated to change, do not perceive treatment as suitable for them, and are more likely to be in treatment because of external pressures. Nonetheless, there are differences in levels of motivation among young people entering TCs. Client characteristics that may be associated with higher levels of motivation or readiness for treatment need to be identified. Clarification of the interaction of client and treatment factors in impacting motivation may be useful in guiding the clinical process.

REFERENCES

De Leon, G. "Therapeutic Communities: Training Self-Evaluation." Final report of project activities under National Institute on Drug Abuse Grant No. H81-DA 01976, 1980.

De Leon, G. *The Therapeutic Community: Study of Effectiveness.* DHHS Pub. No. (ADM)84-1286. Washington, DC: Supt. of Docs., U.S. Govt. Print. Off., 1984.

De Leon, G. The therapeutic community for substance abuse: Perspective and approach. In: De Leon, G., and Ziegenfuss, J.T., eds. *Therapeutic Communities for Addictions: Readings in Theory, Research and Practice.* Springfield, IL: Charles C. Thomas, 1986. pp. 8-18.

De Leon, G. Legal pressure in therapeutic communities. In: Leukefeld, C.G., and Tims, F., eds. *Compulsory Treatment of Drug Abuse: Research and Clinical Practice.* National Institute on Drug Abuse Research Monograph No. 86. DHHS Pub. No. (ADM) 88-158. Washington, DC: Supt. of Docs., U.S. Govt. Print. Off., 1988. pp. 160-177.

DeLeon, G., and Deitch, O. Treatment of the adolescent substance abuser in a therapeutic community. In: Friedman, A., and Beschner, G., eds. *Treatment Services for Adolescent Substance Abusers.* DHHS Pub. No. (ADM)85-1342. Rockville, MD: National Institute on Drug Abuse, 1985. pp. 216-230.

De Leon, G., and Jainchill, N. Male and female drug abusers: Social and psychological status 2 years after treatment in a therapeutic community. *Am J Drug Alcohol Abuse* 8(4):465-497, 1981-82.

De Leon, G., and Jainchill, N. Circumstances, motivation, readiness and suitability as correlates of tenure in treatment. *J Psychoactive Drugs* 18:203-208, 1986.

De Leon, G., and Schwartz, S. Therapeutic communities: What are the retention rates? *Am J Drug Alcohol Abuse* 10(2):267-284, 1984.

De Leon, G.; Melnick, G.; Schoket, D.; and Jainchill, N. Is the therapeutic community culturally relevant? Some findings on race/ethnic differences in retention in treatment. *J Psychoactive Drugs* 25(1):77-86, 1993.

Holland, S. Gateway houses: Effectiveness of treatment on criminal behavior. *Int J Addict* 13:369-381, 1978.

Holland, S. Adolescent and adult drug treatment clients: Patterns and consequences of use. *J Psychoactive Drugs* 16:79-89, 1984.

Hubbard, R.L.; Cavanaugh, E.A.; Craddock, S.F.; and Rachal, J.V. Characteristics, behaviors and outcomes for youth in the TOPS. In: Friedman, A.S., and Beschner, G.M., eds. *Treatment Services for Adolescent Substance Abusers.* Rockville, MD: National Institute on Drug Abuse, 1985.

Jainchill, N., and DeLeon, G. "Adolescent Drug Abusers in TCs: A Preliminary Study." Final report of project activities under National Institute on Drug Abuse grant no. RD1-0A0512, 1992.

Pompi, R.F. Adolescents in therapeutic communities: Retention and post-treatment outcome. In: Tims, F.M.; DeLeon, G; and Jainchill, N., eds. *Therapeutic Community: Advances in Research and Application.* National Institute on Drug Abuse Research Monograph No. 144. NIH Pub. No. 94-3633. Washington, DC: Supt. of Docs., U.S. Govt. Print. Off., 1994.

Pompi, R.F., and Resnick, J. Retention in a therapeutic community for court referred adolescents and young adults. *Am J Drug Alcohol Abuse* 13(3):309-325, 1987.

Sansone, J. Retention patterns in a therapeutic community for the treatment of drug abuse. *Int J Addict* 15:711-736, 1980.

Sells, S., and Simpson, D.D. Evaluation of treatment outcome for youths in the drug abuse reporting program (DARP): A follow-up study. In: Beschner, G., and Friedman, A.S., eds. *Youth Drug Abuse.* Lexington, MA: Lexington Books, 1979. pp. 571-628.

Simpson, D.D., and Sells, S.B. Effectiveness of treatment for drug abuse: An overview of the DARP research program. *Adv Alcohol Substance Abuse* 2(1):7-29, 1982.

Tims, F.M.; Fletcher, B.W.; and Hubbard, R.L. Treatment outcomes for drug abuse clients. In: Pickens, R.W.; Leukefeld, C.G.; and Schuster, C.R., eds. *Improving Drug Abuse Treatment.* National Institute on Drug Abuse Research Monograph No. 106. DHHS Pub. No. (ADM)91-1754. Washington, DC: Supt. of Docs., U.S. Govt. Print. Off., 1991. pp. 93-113.

ACKNOWLEDGMENT

Preparation of this chapter was supported by the National Institute on Drug Abuse grant P50 DA07700.

AUTHORS

Nancy Jainchill, Ph.D.
Principal Investigator

Gauri Bhattacharya, D.S.W.
Project Director

John Yagelka, Ph.D.
Project Director, Research Systems

Center for Therapeutic Community Research
National Development & Research Institutes
11 Beach Street
New York, NY 10013

Family-Based Treatment for Adolescent Drug Use: State of the Science

Howard A. Liddle and Gayle A. Dakof

Adolescent drug abuse continues to be a public health problem with serious personal and societal consequences (Institute of Medicine 1990; National Research Council 1993). In the latest University of Michigan High School Survey, researchers discovered that substance abuse is increasing in the early adolescent population (Johnston et al. 1992). Significant proportional increases in the number of early adolescent substance users prompted the following warning: "This newest wave of adolescents entering the teen years may be at the vanguard of a reversal of previously improving conditions" (Johnston 1993, p. 3).

Given the immediate and long-term consequences of adolescent drug abuse (Halikas et al. 1983; Kandel et al. 1986; Newcomb and Bentler 1988; Shedler and Block 1990), as well as the startling conclusion that within the field of adolescent drug abuse, treatment is the least understood and researched topic (Newcomb and Bentler 1988), the need for additional knowledge about effective interventions is clear.

Four areas are covered in this chapter. First the historical context of family-based treatments for adolescent drug use is reviewed. In a conceptual vein, the chapter then presents a brief overview of the family's role in adolescent drug use. Key findings are summarized from studies on family-based treatments for adolescent drug use, and the contributions made by these approaches are highlighted. Last, the authors offer treatment research recommendations.

HISTORICAL CONTEXT OF FAMILY-BASED TREATMENTS FOR ADOLESCENT DRUG USE

In over four decades of existence, family therapy has focused on some important clinical problems including schizophrenia, sexual and physical abuse, delinquency, and conduct disorder. In the drug abuse field, however, family-oriented approaches are more recent arrivals. In the mid-1970s, one study revealed that 69 percent of the drug treatment programs surveyed provided family therapy for the addicts and their families, and 74 percent of the programs considered family treatment "highly important" for the addict's recovery (Coleman and Davis 1978). The Addicts and Families Project (Stanton et al. 1982) conducted at the Veterans Administration Hospital in Philadelphia in the late 1970s was a landmark study for both the family therapy and drug abuse fields (Gurman et al. 1986; Kaufman 1985). This project developed and tested an integrative family therapy approach in collaboration with two of family therapy's pioneers, Minuchin and Haley.

The Addicts and Families Project was the first study to test family therapy in the treatment of heroin addiction in a scientifically rigorous manner. Results of this study were impressive. Stanton and colleagues (1982) reported that two-thirds of the cases using the family therapy approach experienced what was considered a good outcome. Adult male opiate addicts showed dramatic changes in their drug-taking behaviors as a result of a 10-session family therapy. This project marked a high point in the beginning era of research on the family therapy of drug abuse.

In the last decade there has been significant progress in the family therapy treatment of drug abuse generally (Heath and Stanton 1991; Liddle 1994*b*), and (as this chapter documents) in family therapy for adolescent drug abuse in particular. As family therapy became more acceptable and defined, several research projects attempted to test family-based interventions with adolescent drug use. Previously most treatment research consisted of large-scale evaluation studies that, while useful, could characterize outcome only in broad-based ways (Hubbard et al. 1985; Sells and Simpson 1979).

A tradition of family therapy research with conduct disorder and delinquent youth was established in the 1970s and 1980s (Alexander and Parsons 1973; Henggeler et al. 1986; Patterson 1986; Szapocznik et al. 1990; Tolan and Loeber 1993). In 1983, the National Institute on Drug Abuse (NIDA) Request for Applications titled "Family Therapy Approaches for Adolescent Drug Abuse" signaled a new era for family therapy as well as a new phase of the drug abuse therapy involvement with family-based models of intervention. As Selekman and Todd (1990) have chronicled, three research projects began as a result of the 1983 NIDA initiative: the Purdue Brief Therapy Project (Lewis et al. 1991), the Adolescent Drug Treatment Program at Texas Tech University

(Joanning et al. 1992), and the Adolescents and Families Project at the University of California, San Francisco (Liddle and Dakof 1992).

NIDA's programmatic interest in family therapy for adolescent drug abuse and simultaneous support of these three projects followed a series of meetings with consultants who urged increased endorsement of family-based treatments for adolescent drug use, as well as the success of an earlier project (Szapocznik et al. 1983). Considering the history of funded research on adolescent treatment generally, this initiative was significant. In a review covering a 25-year period, Davidge and Forman (1988) concluded that too few studies had focused on the effectiveness of any form of psychological treatment methods with adolescent drug users. Another review, a literature analysis covering 20 years of treatment research on child and adolescent problems, found that family therapy was evaluated in only 4.1 percent of studies (Kazdin et al. 1990).

Despite the prevalence of family therapy as a treatment modality in the mental health and drug abuse fields (Coleman and Davis 1978), there has been comparatively little evaluation of its efficacy in treating drug abuse among adolescents as well as among adults (Liddle 1994*b*). Even with this less than voluminous record, the studies that have been conducted on family-based interventions on drug use and related problem areas such as delinquency and child behavior problems (Alexander and Parsons 1973; Patterson 1986) prompted various sources to term family-based treatments promising (Catalano et al. 1990-1991; De Leon 1993; Haverkos 1993; Kazdin 1987).

ROLE OF THE FAMILY IN ADOLESCENT DRUG USE

The family has been included in the therapeutic concept of adolescent drug abuse for some time (Blum 1972; Hirsch 1961). Family-oriented interventions for adolescent drug use also have a long history (Hirsch 1961; Kaufman 1985). These interventions rest upon two fundamental assumptions: the family plays an important role in the creation of conditions related to adolescent drug use, and certain family environments and parent-adolescent relationships can both protect adolescents against drug use and offer an antidote for drug use that has already begun.

What evidence exists for these beliefs? Before answering this question, a caveat is in order. Given the current preference for multidimensional frameworks of adolescent drug use (Brook et al. 1989; Newcomb and

Bentler 1988), the question, "What are the family-based factors related to adolescent drug abuse?" does not quite work. The contemporary perspective, which is comprised of factors such as clinical practice patterns, prevailing clinical models, and empirical data, demands changes in view of the problem of adolescent drug abuse. Today the emphasis is on simultaneous and interacting influences, many of which only indirectly include the family (e.g., intrapersonal and extrafamilial risk factors), on the presence and perpetuation of adolescent drug use (Hawkins et al. 1992; Newcomb and Felix-Ortiz 1992).

These influences usually are divided into social, intrapersonal, interpersonal, and contextual categories. For example, the diverse realms of neighborhood disorganization, association with a deviant peer subculture, age at first use, and school failure are individually powerful predictors of adolescent drug use and abuse.

The isolation or contextual consideration of family or any other variables pose conceptual, empirical, and treatment difficulties (see Shedler and Block 1990 for their critique of the "peer centered" theories of adolescent drug abuse). Researchers have established empirical justification for a reconceptualization of adolescent problems such as drug use (Donovan and Jessor 1985; Donovan et al. 1988; Newcomb and McGee 1991). Consider the contemporary conceptual framework known as the problem behavior syndrome (Jessor and Jessor 1977) or the general deviance syndrome (Newcomb and McGee 1991). These frameworks show how adolescent problem behaviors are highly correlated. Newcomb and Bentler (1989, p. 243) summarized this matter as follows:

> Substance use and abuse during adolescence are strongly associated with other problem behaviors such as delinquency, precocious sexual behavior, deviant attitudes, or school dropout. Any focus on drug use or abuse to the exclusion of such correlates, whether antecedent, contemporaneous, or consequent, distorts the phenomenon by focusing on only one aspect or component of a general pattern or syndrome.

Treatment providers have been warned about the dangers of not sufficiently appreciating the interlinked nature of these behaviors in youth (Kazdin 1987). Current family treatment models define themselves as conceptually comprehensive and multicomponent in terms of interventions (Henggeler and Borduin 1990; Liddle 1991*a*). Current conceptualizations and available data from epidemiological and longitudinal studies urge consideration of drug abuse within the context of other problem behaviors, thus necessitating new frameworks of diagnosis and assessment (Bukstein et al. 1989). These factors have transformed how adolescent drug abuse treatment and research are conceived. (Refer to Beschner 1987 for a characterization of this specialty (i.e., family treatment definition, research base) during the late 1970s and early 1980s.)

Given this background, several family-related factors replicated across studies and sites have been associated with the development of adolescent drug use (Brook et al. 1990). Familial attitudes and behavior, family emotional environment, and parenting practices are dimensions consistently targeted by family-based interventions. Familial alcohol and drug behavior and attitudes predict adolescent drug use, but parental attitudes toward a teenager's use are an even more powerful predictor of adolescent drug use (McDermott 1984). Family environment is a strong predictor of adolescent drug use (Baumrind 1991; Block et al. 1988; Brook et al. 1990). Chronic parent-child conflict and marital conflict, pervasive expression of negative emotion, and the quality of parent-adolescent relationships (e.g., low bonding, emotional disengagement) are related to drug use as well as development of other problem behaviors. Third, parenting and family management practices are critically related to the development of drug use in youth. Several factors such as parental monitoring, a parenting style characterized by the ability to make developmentally appropriate demands and responses, consistent and authoritative versus authoritarian discipline techniques, and supportive parenting behaviors have been found to buffer against drug use (Patterson et al. 1992; Wills 1990).

Family-Based Treatments for Adolescent Drug Use: Conceptual Frameworks and Major Features

The term "family based" has replaced "family therapy" for reasons explained below. Briefly, these interventions now encompass more than the family unit per se. Family-based approaches go beyond intrafamilial or intraindividual factors; they view drug abuse by one person as a problem across entire ecosystems (Stanton et al. 1982). "Even though child or teenage drug use is an individual behavior, it is embedded in a sociocultural context that strongly determines its character and manifestations" (Newcomb and Bentler 1988, p. 242). This perspective permits "a comprehensive analysis of direct and indirect influences among levels and subsystems inside and outside the family domain" (Miller and Prinz 1990, p. 299). There is variation within the family-based perspective since these models represent different traditions. Some models have behavioral roots (Bry 1988) and emphasize contingency contracting, family management and parenting skills, or communication training. Other models such as Alexander's functional family therapy developed from a social learning theory framework. Another approach could be characterized as having developed primarily from two family therapy perspectives, with one subgroup having structural family therapy as the most prominent influence (Stanton and Todd 1979; Szapocznik et al. 1990), and the other having strong strategic therapy connections (Joanning et al. 1992; Piercy and Frankel 1989).

Before discussing the integrative approaches, clarification of the aforementioned family therapy perspectives is necessary. "Structural" and "strategic" refer to treatments that involve the whole family since symptoms are understood as being related to family functioning, present and past; conceptualize problems in terms of problematic family structures (inverted hierarchy, overinvolvement, underinvolvement) and interactional patterns (triangulation, conflict detouring); and define the therapist's role in active and directive terms (Stanton et al. 1982). The primary goal in classic family treatment is to alter the interactional patterns—the behavioral redundancies—that characterize family relationships. The assumption is that the interactions seen in family sessions are representative of, or actually are, the behavioral patterns that are related to problem formation, continuation, or both. Family therapy aims to change these interactions.

A third set of contemporary family-based approaches, part of a growing trend, focuses on what has been termed "integrative models" (Coyne and Liddle 1992; Gurman and Kniskern 1992). In the adolescent treatment area, this group of approaches, in accord with developments in psychotherapy that emphasize construction of systematic and prescriptive treatment packages, have been characterized as "multisystemic" (Henggeler and Borduin 1990) and "multidimensional" (Liddle et al. 1991). With their focus on the entire ecology of the adolescent drug abuser, these models assess and intervene in (or at least systematically take into account) the network of influences (Brook et al. 1989) that constitute adolescent drug use. In addition, these approaches tend to draw not only from family therapy for theory and technique, but also from other intervention approaches within mainstream psychotherapy. Interventions are based on the knowledge that adolescents and their families are embedded in a variety of natural ecologies. The clinical focus includes the various subsystems within the family, but interventions in subsystems are important as well (e.g., adolescent in relation to peer culture, school, and juvenile justice system).

Empirical Support for Family-Based Treatment of Adolescent Drug Use

Given evidence of the powerful roles of parent and family in the genesis of adolescent drug use and other forms of antisocial behavior (Baumrind 1991; Brook et al. 1988; Coombs et al. 1988; Hawkins et al. 1992; Kandel 1990; Kellam et al. 1983; Patterson 1986; Shedler and Block 1990) and the developmental level of available family therapy models, it follows that a variety of family-based psychosocial interventions for adolescent drug abuse have been developed and tested.

The efficacy of certain types of family-based approaches in the treatment of delinquency and conduct disorder has been established (Alexander et al. 1976; Henggeler et al. 1986; Mann et al. 1990; Patterson et al. 1992; also see reviews by Alexander et al. 1994; Gurman et al. 1986; Hazelrigg et al. 1987; Henggeler et al. 1993; Shadish et al. 1993; Tolan and Loeber 1993). These findings have important implications for adolescent drug use given its strong relationship to other serious problem behaviors (Bukstein et al. 1989; Dembo et al. 1990; Farrell et al. 1992; Kazdin 1982; Loeber 1990).

The work of two research groups (Alexander and colleagues; Patterson and colleagues) stand out as particularly noteworthy and relevant to the treatment of adolescent drug use. Alexander's functional family therapy approach has been identified as one of the three most effective approaches with conduct disorder youth (Kazdin 1987). This approach has accumulated considerable evidence of its efficacy with delinquents (primary criterion of rearrest and incarceration). For over two decades, the research conducted by the Oregon Social Learning Center has articulated the parent-child interactional patterns that contribute to and exacerbate problem behaviors (Patterson et al. 1992). Family management strategies and parenting practices have been found to be important and alterable concomitants of a variety of antisocial behaviors including drug use.

Bry (1988) revealed the field had more to say about theory and therapeutic techniques than about research findings on treatment effectiveness. This researcher was able to identify only two controlled studies that assessed the efficacy of a family-based approach on directly reducing adolescent drug use (Szapocznik et al. 1983, 1986). Most studies reviewed focused on adolescent and family behaviors known to be related to adolescent drug use such as academic performance, delinquency, and adolescent-parent conflict, instead of drug use per se. The situation is much improved since those findings were published.

In the late 1980s clinical research programs began investigating the effectiveness of family-based approaches in treating adolescent drug use. Several conducted randomized clinical trials (Friedman 1989; Henggeler et al. 1991; Joanning et al. 1992; Lewis et al. 1991; Liddle and Dakof 1992; Szapocznik et al. 1988). Although some of these studies contained methodological flaws frequently found in psychotherapy research (e.g., small and investigator-recruited versus regular clinic samples; lack of minority representation; minimal symptom severity (experimenters versus regular users); focus on middle-class families; insufficiently defined treatments; lack of detail on the therapists and on their training for the project; measurement ambiguities; weak or incomplete statistical analyses), others had few or only minimal methodological problems, and all significantly advance the knowledge about how to best treat adolescent drug use. These studies demonstrated the efficacy of family-based approaches for adolescent drug use, asked more sophisticated research questions (e.g., identification of the active ingredients in family-based models), and offered suggestions for improving the scientific conduct of clinical trials targeting adolescent drug use. Given the practical difficulties of conducting drug abuse intervention research (Ashery and McAuliffe 1992; McAuliffe and Ashery 1993; Parker 1991), succeeding rounds of studies on treating adolescent drug use will no doubt build upon these foundational studies.

Whereas the considerable contributions of Patterson and colleagues and Alexander and colleagues remain unquestioned, they did not specifically focus on adolescent drug use. The presenting problem of the children and adolescents treated and evaluated in these studies was conduct disorder or delinquency, which may or may not include drug use. Thus, the scientific evaluation of family-based psychological treatments specifically designed to treat adolescent drug use must begin with Szapocznik and colleagues (see Szapocznik et al. 1990 for background). They were the first to establish the effectiveness of family therapy in treating adolescent drug use (Szapocznik et al. 1983, 1986). Their first publication reported that two different time-limited (12 sessions) family-based approaches (conjoint family therapy (CFT) and one-person family therapy (OPFT)) significantly reduced adolescent drug use and behavior problems and improved family functioning in Hispanic families with drug-using adolescents. These results were demonstrated at termination and maintained at followup, 6 to 12 months later. The followup analysis revealed that, while improvements from both treatments were maintained, the one-person family therapy approach continued to improve the adolescent symptomatology in several areas of functioning including drug use.

It is important to note certain limitations of these landmark studies. Like many psychotherapy studies, Szapocznik and colleagues (1983, 1986) were plagued by a small sample (19 were posted in OPFT and 18 in CFT), and only 24 families (65 percent) returned for followup assessment. The small sample size limits the statistical power to detect differences between treatments; with a larger sample size there might have been more consistent differences in outcome between the two groups. The small sample at posttest and the even smaller sample at followup limits generalizability of these findings beyond the current study. The study also failed to have an appropriate control/comparison group. Whereas different types of control or comparison groups would yield different results, a design of this nature would greatly enhance interpretation of the findings and yield information about how these models (OPFT and CFT) compare with treatment that drug-using youth typically receive. Perhaps both OPFT and CFT would yield significantly more improvement in both family functioning and adolescent symptomatology in these circumstances. Another possibility would be to select a well-established mode of treatment such as peer group therapy or individual adolescent therapy. Given the success of OPFT, it would seem useful to conduct this study with individual adolescent therapy (e.g., cognitive-behavioral therapy) as the comparison group. Because both OPFT and CFT are family-based models, the study findings do not provide information about whether family-based treatments are more effective than peer or individual treatments in reducing adolescent drug use.

The next series of studies conducted by this research group focused on engagement and retention. This work was motivated by the well-known fact that recruiting, engaging, and retaining both adult (Kleinman et al. 1990; Stanton et al. 1982) and adolescent drug users in treatment is notoriously difficult (Feigelman 1987; Stark and Campbell 1988). The help-seeking behavior of adolescents indicates that teenagers pose unique and difficult challenges to those who offer them counseling (Kellam et al. 1983; Riggs and Cheng 1988). Strategic-Structural Systems Engagement (SSSE) was designed to improve this unfortunate clinical reality. Two studies (Santisteban et al., in press; Szapocznik et al. 1988) tested the efficacy of an enhanced engagement program versus traditional engagement strategies (engagement as usual (EAU)) to engage and then retain adolescents and their families in treatment. The findings from the initial (Szapocznik et al. 1988) and subsequent study (Santisteban et al., in press) are stunning. In the original study, 57.7 percent of the families in the EAU group refused to attend the intake session, whereas only 7.1 percent in the SSSE group failed to attend the intake session. After intake, an equivalent number of cases dropped from each group and results indicated no differences in treatment effectiveness between the two engagement conditions. After engagement, both groups received the same family-based treatment protocol.

A second study on engagement conducted with more strict controls, a larger and more diverse sample, and two control groups (family therapy without SSSE and group therapy without SSSE) replicated the results of the first study and extended it to an analysis of factors which influence engagement success and failure. Santisteban and colleagues (in press) found that 81 percent of the families assigned to an SSSE group versus 60 percent of the families assigned to an EAU group were successfully engaged in treatment. Moreover, SSSE was more successful with non-Cuban Hispanic families than with Cuban Hispanic families (97 percent of the non-Cuban families versus 64 percent of the Cuban families were successfully engaged in the SSSE group). Data indicated that 89 percent of the engagement failures were families with resistant parents. More detailed analyses revealed that all of the engagement failures with parental resistance were Cuban Hispanic families. They concluded that SSSE was effective with all families except Cuban families in which there was parental resistance.

The interpretation of these results has relevance beyond the Cuban community. Santisteban and colleagues suggested that the Cuban families in their study were more fully acculturated than the non-Cuban Hispanics. One result of such acculturation may be the incorporation of an "individualistic orientation of the mainstream culture" and adeptness "at maneuvering within the mental health system." A large number of the engagement failures "insisted on hospitalization or individual therapy for their adolescent...[and] were willing to work the mental health system to obtain it." They concluded by suggesting that engagement could be improved with these families by early problem identification and acknowledgement of parents' preference for individual adolescent therapy prior to attempting to change this view through restructuring techniques. These two studies on engagement were well designed and executed and represent a significant contribution to the field.

At this time, Szapocznik and colleagues are the only research group with published programmatic research on family-based approaches to treating adolescent drug use (Szapocznik et al. 1991). This comprehensive research has resulted in significant contributions to the treatment of adolescent drug use by demonstrating not only the effectiveness of family therapy, but also by articulating how cultural variables can be synthesized within a model to enhance treatment engagement and outcome. Szapocznik and colleagues used cultural knowledge in their treatment conceptualizations of specific clinical problems and implemented that knowledge in the form of specific interventions in therapy. The result has been a problem-specific and culturally sensitive model of treatment that has demonstrated excellent results with Hispanic populations. It is important to recognize, however, that none of these studies compared family-based approaches to other approaches (i.e., individual or group). This body of work, albeit impressive, disallows conclusions about whether family-based treatments are more effective than other forms of adolescent treatment.

Other research groups have recently published results of randomized clinical trials assessing the comparative effectiveness of family-based treatments for adolescent substance use. Although these studies vary in methodological rigor and clinical sophistication, they significantly advance the field. All were randomized clinical trials that used well-articulated family therapy models and demonstrated the effectiveness of family-based approaches in retaining adolescents in drug treatment and in reducing drug use. A few of the trials demonstrated the superiority of family therapy over other treatments in the areas of individual counseling (Henggeler et al. 1991), parent education and skill-building groups (Joanning et al 1992; Lewis et al. 1990; Liddle and Dakof 1992), and peer group therapy (Joanning et al. 1992; Liddle and Dakof 1992).

All five studies demonstrated that family-based models can engage and retain cases in drug treatment. The dropout rates ranged from a low of 11 percent (Henggeler et al. 1991) to a high of 30 percent (Liddle and Dakof 1992). Studies that compared family-based models to peer group therapy found that retention rates in the family-based models (family therapy as well as family education) were significantly better than those in peer group therapy (Joanning et al. 1992; Liddle and Dakof 1992). Peer group treatment dropout rates ranged from 56 percent (Joanning et al. 1992) to 49 percent (Liddle and Dakof 1992). These findings, coupled with the results of Szapocznik and colleagues, clearly demonstrate that family therapy models of intervention can engage and retain youth and their families in treatment. The relatively low dropout rates in the family-based models are especially important given the intractable nature of substance abuse and the difficulty of retaining clients in treatment (De Leon and Jainchill 1986; Kazdin et al. 1993; Weidman 1985).

All of these studies clearly demonstrate the efficacy of family-based models in ameliorating drug use in youth. For instance, Szapocznik and colleagues (1988) found that 7 percent of youth were drug free at the beginning of a family-based treatment and 80 percent were drug free at termination. These youth were not extremely heavy drug users: 41 percent used primarily marijuana 1 or 2 times a week, and 47 percent used marijuana as the primary drug several times per week. Joanning and colleagues (1992) found that 54 percent of adolescents receiving family treatment were not using drugs at termination. Lewis and colleagues (1990) found that 44 percent of hard drug users reported no drug use at posttest. Friedman (1989) reported that family-based treatments reduced drug use by more than 50 percent approximately 1 year after termination.

Liddle and colleagues (submitted) found that 53 percent of youth receiving family therapy were hard drug users at pretreatment. At termination, only 9 percent used hard drugs, and at 1-year followup only 3 percent were using hard drugs. Taken as a group these results compare favorably with other studies of non-family-based interventions which show relapse rates, defined in a variety of ways, of between 35 percent and 85 percent (Catalano et al. 1990-1991).

The superiority of family-based adolescent drug treatment over other approaches has been demonstrated in several studies (Joanning et al. 1992; Lewis et al. 1991; Liddle and Dakof 1992). Youth receiving family therapy showed significantly less drug use at termination than youth receiving peer group therapy (Joanning et al. 1992; Liddle and Dakof 1992), parent education (Joanning et al. 1992; Lewis et al. 1990) or multifamily intervention (Liddle and Dakof 1992).

Each of the three family models that showed superiority over more traditional adolescent drug treatment (family systems therapy, Purdue Brief Family Therapy, and Multidimensional Family Therapy (MDFT)) are integrative models designed specifically to treat adolescent substance use. Family therapy has shown superiority over other approaches at followup as well as at termination. Henggeler and colleagues (1991) found that youth who completed multisystemic therapy (MST) had significantly fewer substance use-related offenses 4 years after termination than those who received individual counseling. Liddle and colleagues (submitted) found that reductions in drug use at termination were maintained 1 year later. Furthermore, youth receiving MDFT had significantly lower drug use at 1-year followup than youth who received a family-based education and communication intervention. At the 1-year followup, there was no difference in adolescent substance use among those receiving MDFT or peer group therapy; both had relatively low usage.

Study Limitations. While methods of inquiry and research findings about family-based treatment of adolescent drug use have advanced significantly since Bry's 1988 review, this body of work, as a whole, is not without its limitations and flaws. Studies reviewed in this chapter were limited by lack of sufficient data on comorbid conditions and failure to report (or perhaps assess) substance use and other conditions along the dimensions defined by the American Psychiatric Association (1981) in the "Diagnostic and Statistical Manual of Mental Disorders," 3d. ed. (DSM-III). Many also failed to adequately or clearly measure, scale, and describe the substance use of the sample (Henggeler et al. 1991; Joanning et al. 1992; Lewis et al. 1990). The lack of details and appropriate measurement about comorbidity, DSM-III status, and type and frequency of substances used greatly impedes researchers' ability to generalize these results beyond a given study and to transfer these clinical models to community treatment of adolescent drug use (Weisz et al. 1992).

Study samples were typically male (60 percent or greater), European-American, or were not sufficiently large to conduct analyses by gender and ethnicity. Such restrictions on the study populations precludes any exploration or development of gender and culturally sensitive models of intervention. One study (Friedman 1989) did not assess change immediately after treatment; the first postintervention assessment was done 9 months after termination. Two studies (Joanning et al. 1992; Lewis et al. 1990) only reported pretest-posttest data and failed to report results at followup. Clearly, it is important to analyze the impact of treatment at termination and some specified followup period (preferably 9 to 12 months posttermination). It is vital to know whether or not the symptom reduction achieved at termination is maintained beyond this period.

While all of the studies reviewed here have certain limitations, one is more serious than the others and as such needs to be highlighted. One study (Joanning et al. 1992) reported that youth receiving group therapy and families receiving family education participated in a set number of sessions, but those receiving family therapy did not. Moreover, the average number of sessions received by the family therapy group was not reported. Did these families receive more or less therapy than participants in the other two treatments? If adolescents assigned to family therapy received significantly more hours of treatment than those assigned to the other two treatments, the reported superiority of family therapy in reducing substance use may be due to length of treatment and not its ingredients. Treatment evaluation studies with drug users (Stark 1992) and others (Orlinsky and Howard 1986) consistently demonstrate that length of treatment is related to outcome.

Limitations and flaws notwithstanding, the scientific work carried out since Szapocznik's groundbreaking work in the early and mid-1980s has further established that family intervention is an effective treatment of adolescent drug use. Family therapy can retain families in treatment and significantly reduce drug use in youth. Importantly, the most recent work has gone beyond the Szapocnik findings to demonstrate that various integrative family therapy models are more effective than peer group therapy, individual counseling, and other family-based treatments (parent groups, multifamily therapy) in eliminating or reducing drug use at termination (Henggeler et al. 1991; Joanning et al. 1992; Lewis et al. 1990; Liddle and Dakof 1992) and followup (Henggeler et al. 1991; Liddle and Dakof 1992).

NEW AND PROMISING DEVELOPMENTS IN UNDERSTANDING AND TREATING ADOLESCENT DRUG USE

Federal Funding Support and Availability of Studies

Several new research projects have been launched in recent years, some of which have been continuations of research programs testing family-based interventions for adolescent drug use. Although not uncommon in the treatment of adult drug abuse, treatment evaluation research centers have not previously focused on adolescents. In 1991, NIDA funded a multisite treatment evaluation research center to study family-based treatments for adolescent drug use (Liddle et al. 1991), and another one of its research centers (De Leon 1991) conducts a major project that is assessing the efficacy of a therapeutic community approach for adolescent drug abusers (Jainchill 1991).

Treatment Specificity

Many of today's family-based approaches are now highly evolved, with treatment manuals, corresponding therapist adherence and competence scales, therapist training protocols, and videotape training materials. While the specification of the treatment variable or the active ingredients of what constitutes intervention sounds straightforward, to accomplish this takes a team, a facilitative context, deep clinical knowledge, and above all, time and opportunity. Today's family-based interventions combine or draw upon diverse bodies of knowledge and evidence an ability to establish relationships and intervene with a number of people rather than a single adolescent.

This multivariate focus requires a high level of professional functioning and training and ongoing supervision at the early stages of a therapist's development. While the specification of family treatment strategies at the level of detail required to implement a model in a research project has begun, this area still has much progress to make. To gain perspective on this matter, it may be helpful to remember that the first randomized clinical trial with drug abusers, the Addicts and Families Project, did not have a treatment manual established a priori. It had a clearly stated set of therapeutic principles that were crafted, through extensive case conferences and supervision, into a comprehensive treatment manual that could be articulated at the project's conclusion (Stanton et al. 1982).

Treatment Informed by Developmental Sensibilities

Consensus exists on the premise that adolescents cannot be treated with models developed for adults. Just as the longitudinal perspective of investigators such as Kandel, Kellam, Brook, Newcomb, Rutter, and Baumrind guided their search for causative factors of adolescent drug use, the developmental perspective can guide clinical work. This viewpoint asserts that treatment and therapy model constructions are enhanced by knowledge about development and the lifespan perspective

(Kazdin 1993; Liddle 1988). Although this framework remains to be fully realized and the exact features of developmentally informed models are still unclear, recommendations have been made for how this work might be done (Kendall et al. 1984) and prototypes have been put forth (Liddle 1994*b*). For example, knowledge about the effects of normative and nonnormative transitions from the family studies literature can help clinicians make decisions about interventions (Liddle et al., in press). Knowing how the effects of divorce, stepfamily formation, or single parent status can impact development informs a therapist about potentially fruitful areas of intervention.

Research-Informed Treatments

Three areas of work have particular relevance for adolescent drug use treatment. First, the adolescent development literature, including areas such as the dimensions of autonomy-connectedness and the intrapersonal and interpersonal aspects of identity development have been used to inform adolescent drug abuse treatment. A deep knowledge of the normative and nonnormative aspects of core developmental markers such as adolescent ego development and identity can guide interventions.

On the basis of this knowledge, some family therapy models no longer see the family together for the whole course of treatment. Individual sessions with parent and teenager, within the context of what is still a family-based treatment, are conducted concurrently. Sometimes these individual sessions focus on the relationship aspects of symptomatic behavior (e.g., communication skills, perspectives on the behavior of the parent or adolescent). At other times, the individual sessions are more focused on the teenager or parent.

Cognizance of intrapersonal and interpersonal or social domains of development informs interventions. Family-based treatments no longer overemphasize interpersonal conceptualizations of problems or interventions designed to alter family interaction. While still critical, these interventions are complemented by approaches that focus on the self of the adolescent and parent, as well as other aspects of the adolescent's ecology.

Literature on parenting beliefs, parenting styles, and parental cognitions is instrumental to planning and the focus obtained in these sessions, as well as in the overall case formulation (Liddle and Schmidt 1994). The emerging risk and protective factor literature (Hawkins et al. 1992;

Newcomb and McGee 1991) also promises to be a source of guidance for prevention and treatment interventions.

Comprehensiveness

Accompanying a more complex conceptualization of the circumstances that form and maintain adolescent drug use is a parallel notion about the interventions necessary to change this multiply-embedded problem. Current concepts of what constitutes effective interventions include assumptions about the need for comprehensiveness—the necessity of targeting drug-using behavior as well as other correlated problem behaviors (Kazdin 1987). These target areas might include school failure; family conflict and disorganization; parental drug abuse or psychopathology; the involvement of extrafamilial sources of influence or control, such as the juvenile justice system; and skills deficits in various realms (interpersonal, problem solving, communication). The "big bang" that was family therapy announced an appreciation of family relationships as a primary context of human development, problem formation, and change. Later, the family therapy movement began to understand how a variety of other systems also influence development and dysfunction (i.e., intrapersonal and extrafamilial systems of influence). In accord with these changes, adolescent drug use is understood as being connected to, influencing, and being influenced by many systems simultaneously.

"Family therapy" may be an unnecessarily limited term to describe what some clinical model developers and researchers do; hence the preferred term "family-based interventions." Conceptual progress may outpace the capacity to deliver models that correspond to the new, more complex frameworks. Interventions that flow from an expanded, multivariate framework may be easier to describe than to carry out. Whereas therapy effectiveness is one critical area of exploration, the advent of these more bulky intervention packages brings challenges in treatment feasibility or viability. Questions need to be asked about the capacity to implement these comprehensive interventions. The costs and benefits of enlisting family members in extensive and intensive treatments will be an important future area of research (Pike and Piercy 1990). Given the importance of therapist variables in clinical research (Crits-Cristoph 1991), training issues must be discussed in this regard as well (Henry et al. 1993*a*; 1993*b*). What will it take to train clinicians to implement complex interventions that would have several modules, each of which would presumably require some discrete knowledge and skills? Will funders accept the cost-benefit bottom line, once such factors are determined? Comprehensive treatments may conflict with the cost-conscious tenor of the times.

Design Issues in Multicomponent Intervention Models

With comprehensiveness comes the realization that single interventions, even those with many facets such as family therapy, cannot impact all of the realms that influence problem formation or continuation. Regarding comprehensiveness, questions about how much comprehensiveness is needed for what kind of problem remain unanswered. The same situation exists when considering multicomponent interventions. Of necessity, given the field's development, clinical wisdom and judgment, along with developmental knowledge, must be used to specify the combination of interventions that might cohere to form an effective hybrid intervention package. For example, if one considers it important to assess and intervene into the social world of an adolescent's peer culture, how might one gain access to this world? The usual method, to add group treatment to individual or family counseling, is not necessarily a thoughtful, coherent strategy. Rules remain to be formulated for multicomponent treatments based upon presently undefined assessment schema for deciding what to include, when to use each module, and how each module should be used in relation to the other components.

The risk factor literature provides, by analogy, insight on an important dilemma in this realm of theory- and research-informed clinical model construction. While the variety of factors that predict problem behaviors such as drug use in adolescence are known, the most problematical risk factors—those most likely to lead to drug use—are still unidentified. Knowledge of a specific risk factor's relative destructive potential vis-a-vis other risk factors is weak. While there is knowledge of a variety of promising, empirically tested family-based treatments, efficacy data are lacking on these interventions used in particular (theory-informed) sequences and combinations. However, the growing literature on treatment acceptability (Miller and Prinz 1990) and help-seeking behavior of adolescents (Kellam et al. 1981) may be useful in this regard.

Rethinking the Treatment Delivery System

A prerequisite for revising the comprehensiveness of treatments may be to reenvision the treatment delivery context (General Accounting Office 1992). Engagement strategies can be defined according to the characteristics of a treatment model, the skills and training of the model's practitioners, and how a treatment model is delivered.

Increasingly, the field is aware of the challenges of service delivery to particular populations. Two advances illustrate the kind of work needed in this area. Both relate to the ecology of the development, maintenance, and treatment of drug abuse. The first development, case management, has a long tradition in fields such as social work. Recently, it has received attention in the drug abuse and mental health fields as well. The ecological view of problem formation and continuation gives an understanding of how practical problems in living hinder access to or full utilization of treatment (Ridgely and Wellbring 1992). Case management services seem to be an important component to intervention with disadvantaged populations, and although some pilot study findings are available (Comfort et al. 1990), research on the use of case management in drug abuse treatment is still in the early stages (Thompson et al. 1984). (See Ridgely and Wellbring 1992 for a review of case management research dilemmas in drug abuse.)

Home-based services, a defining feature of the family preservation movement, is the second development pertaining to service delivery. The family treatment and family preservation movements have pursued mostly unrelated tracks of development and thus have failed to explore the enriching possibilities of increased interaction. This is unfortunate since family preservation approaches understand something vital—that service delivery concerns and attention to basic material needs are critical to engagement and, according to some initial results (Haapala and Kinney 1988), to treatment success as well. The home-based family intervention approach of Henggeler and colleagues (1992) shows how standard family therapy interventions can be adapted to fit the contextual realities of some families. Although appreciation of the multiple ecologies in which an individual and family exist has been present for some time (Friedman 1974), it is only in recent years that powerful ideas such as this one have been sufficiently articulated or researched. Henggeler's research also shows how a treatment model can be adapted to become more ecologically valid without sacrificing scientific ideals.

Culture, Race, Class, and Gender as Definers of Treatment Focus and Characteristics

Family-based treatments for adolescent drug use, most notably the work of Szapocznik and colleagues, evidence the increased complexity of this area (Szapocznik and Kurtines 1993). Various programs in the drug abuse field tailor treatments to fit different cultural or ethnic groups, and seek to understand sensitive issues of this nature (Malgady et al. 1990; Szapocznik et al. 1990). As an understanding of the differences between ethnic factors and those that are more related to poverty has developed, issues of class become increasingly important in defining therapy and therapy research (American Psychological Association 1993).

Gender-sensitive model development and evaluation are conspicuously absent in adolescent drug treatment. Whereas it is true that adult males are more likely than adult females to use alcohol or drugs (e.g., marijuana, cocaine, hallucinogens), this is not the case for youth between the ages of 12 and 17. There are no significant gender differences in rates of lifetime, past year, and past month use of alcohol and marijuana, no significant gender differences in lifetime and past month use of cocaine, and no significant gender differences in lifetime hallucinogen use among youth (NIDA 1991). Yet none of the adolescent treatment evaluation studies conducted statistical analyses by gender, and none has addressed the issues involved in developing gender-sensitive therapeutic models.

Multiproblem Youth: Moving to Multivariate Conceptual Models

Sometimes known as treatment of comorbid conditions, this important area opens new possibilities and poses many significant challenges. While it is one thing to say that individual symptoms are connected and should be treated in the context of correlated problem behaviors, implementation is complex and as of yet, not fully realized. While many in the field consider positive the field's movement away from overspecialization or focusing on one disorder or another (and thereby miss other areas of dysfunction or possibilities for accessing these youth in treatment), the challenges that come with this expanded vision must also be recognized. (See Dryfoos 1991 for a comprehensive summary.)

New Assessment Frameworks

Formal assessment devices can help plan treatment and pinpoint interventions. In the adolescent drug abuse area, many psychometrically sound instruments are available for screening and diagnosis purposes. The Problem Oriented Screening Instrument (Rahdert 1990), Personal Experience Inventory (Winters 1990), and the Adolescent Problem Severity Index (Metzger 1990) are three of these instruments. In the quest to make clinical interventions more theory- and research-informed, exemplars are needed to guide this work. In making standardized instruments clinician-friendly, models need to demonstrate the everyday utility of formal assessment devices.

Connection with Advances in Psychotherapy Intervention Literature

Various developing traditions are informing the area of family-based treatments for adolescent drug abuse (Henggeler 1993) and the drug abuse treatment area generally (Moras 1993; Onken and Blaine 1990; Onken et al. 1993). Process research—studies that attempt to understand the mechanisms of treatment while taking into account individual and family level characteristics—has the potential to change the way clinicians think about research (Beutler 1990; Liddle et al. 1991; Pinsof 1989). This work includes attempts to build models that can empirically establish the kind of client-therapist interactions related to retention in treatment or dropout (Alexander et al. 1994; Shoham-Salomon 1991), show changes in specific treatment dimensions over the course of therapy, or define in-session change events and build performance models about previously elusive change processes (Diamond and Liddle, submitted; Greenberg 1986). Other methodological and statistical advances such as component analysis, clinical significance, aptitude-treatment interaction research, matching studies, latent growth modeling, structural equation modeling, meta-analyses, and survival analyses offer promise (De Leon 1984; Gottman and Rushe 1993; Jacobson and Revenstorf 1988; Leukefeld and Bukowski 1991; McLellan et al. 1983; Newman and Howard 1991; Snow 1991).

RECOMMENDATIONS FOR RESEARCH PRIORITIES

Support for Multicomponent, Comprehensive, Community-Based, Multisystems Approaches

Consensus exists regarding the complexity of adolescent drug abuse. However, movement from a position of increased complexity in the conceptualization of a treatment model to one in which the model is viable in community settings is slow, requiring focus and opportunity. Progress may be achieved through a variety of interventions on this front (i.e., different study designs). Enough promise seems to have been evidenced with this new generation of treatment models to warrant their further development. These advances promise to make clinical research more clinically relevant—an oft-cited criticism of clinicians (Morrow-Bradley and Elliott 1986).

Treatment Development Studies

Randomized clinical trials are critical to answering questions of comparative treatment effectiveness. This research tradition has not been without its critics; however, impressive developments have recently occurred. First, there is an increased frankness in the articulation of normative pragmatic difficulties associated with the conduct of clinical trials research (Ashery and McAuliffe 1992; McAuliffe and Ashery 1993). Solutions have been offered to improve the quality of this research (Bentler 1991; Howard et al. 1990, 1993; Moncher and Prinz 1991; Waltz et al. 1993). In tandem with these advances is a new wave of studies that, at least indirectly, challenge the inclusion of insufficiently developed or articulated treatments in previous clinical trials. Treatment development studies, currently receiving widespread Federal funding, are an important milestone for the treatment research field. Continued support for this kind of work should be encouraged. These initiatives should be considered basic research in the psychosocial treatment research area that creates opportunities for fundamental work in model and intervention specifications as well as for tests of the enhanced model's effectiveness and ecological validity.

Alternative Research Strategies

Qualitative studies can be valuable, especially when they result in new or enhanced interventions. The field must remain open to new methodological and statistical procedures. The psychotherapy research field, for instance, is interested in developing the possibilities for model development and efficacy testing from case study research, a tradition once thought be of limited scientific value (Jones 1993).

Tailoring Standardized Treatments to Individual Cases

While standardized treatments surely will be seen as a benchmark of progress in the treatment research specialty, perhaps there is another aspect of these therapies that is yet to be realized. When treatment manuals and treatment studies that use manuals can be further adapted to the realities of practice by a clinically flexible application of standard principles and methods (Jacobson et al. 1989), then a new stage of development will have been reached. Proving that treatment manuals do not foster a "one size fits all" treatment philosophy remains a major challenge in this area. There are methodological problems with research of this type, but studies in which a basic treatment model is tailored to the specifics of a case are likely to yield significant gains (Persons 1991).

Prototypes for Research-Practice Interaction

Treatment development research initiatives typically emphasize technical aspects of treatment model development. A foundation for these contemporary models can be basic research. The treatment development initiatives currently being supported by at least two Federal institutes offer a viable funding source for activities that would contribute to the integration of research and practice, in addition to creating opportunities for model specification and testing in community settings.

Clinical and Research Training Issues

The enhanced models that are being proposed necessitate a population of providers who are knowledgeable about adolescent development, the parent development literature, and family therapy methods. Given these ambitious goals, how will this next generation of clinicians be trained? What tools will be used to evaluate this training? Training researchers to carry out the intervention studies is another area in need of support.

Redefinition of Family-Based Intervention

The field needs to broaden the base of what constitutes interventions and how they are delivered. The serious educational problems of drug-abusing youth should not be minimized. Tutoring and mentoring programs might be useful in combination with other forms of treatment. Home-based services are also an attractive alternative for certain clients, particularly those for whom coming in to a central clinical locale presents difficulties.

Research Funding

The increased appreciation of context delineated in this chapter represents a major shift in the family-based treatment of adolescent drug abuse. The macrolevel context of much of drug abuse treatment and research is the Federal Government's leadership and commitment to eliminating drug use among youth. According to a General Accounting Office report to

Congress, research for treatment accounts for 5 percent of money spent on drug abuse (General Accounting Office 1992). Given the public health need to develop effective treatments and the failure of a drug control policy that has emphasized interdiction over treatment services (Dryfoos 1991), this level of funding seems inequitable if not misguided.

CONCLUSION

While there have been family therapy interventions that focused nearly exclusively on the family variables that pertain to adolescent drug involvement, future interventions will be more complex, multicomponent approaches that target more dimensions in and outside of the family. This conceptual shift has many implications in model development and research on adolescent drug use treatment. Although at an early stage of development in the articulation and evaluation of these models, their scope and appreciation of the ecology of the adolescent's drug problem are signs of progress—progress that will be judged by the robustness of the findings that are achieved.

Findings on family-based treatments of adolescent drug use are also encouraging. Studies consistently report that family involvement in the treatment of adolescent drug use is critical to engaging and retaining adolescents in treatment, as well as to successful treatment as defined by reduction of drug use, decrease of behavior problems, and affiliation with the family and with prosocial peers.

Finally, the authors believe that because of several factors—decreased reliance on the dogma and ideology that was family therapy, increased complexity of conceptualization, greater specificity of treatments, a gradual increase in the number of research programs that test and refine these treatments, and participation in the community of clinical research—family-based treatment for adolescent drug abuse is coming of age. Family therapy has faced some formidable challenges over the years (Bednar et al. 1988; Garfield 1982; Markman 1990). With respect to treating adolescent drug abuse, these challenges are being met.

REFERENCES

Alexander, J.F., and Parsons, B.V. Short-term behavioral intervention with delinquent families: Impact on family process and relativist. *J Abnorm Psychol* 81:219-225, 1973.

Alexander, J.F.; Barton, C.; Schiavo, R.S.; and Parsons, B.V. Behavioral intervention with families of delinquents: Therapist characteristics and outcome. *J Consult Clin Psychol* 44:656-664, 1976.

Alexander, J.F.; Holtzworth-Munroe, A.; and Jameson, P.C. Research on the process and outcome of marriage and family therapy. In: Begin, A.E., and Garfield, S.L., eds. *Handbook of Psychotherapy and Behavior Change*. 4th ed. New York: John Wiley and Sons, 1994.

American Psychiatric Association. *Diagnostic and Statistical Manual of Mental Disorders*. 3d ed. Washington, DC: American Psychiatric Association, 1981.

American Psychological Association. *Youth and Violence*. Vol. 1. Washington, DC: American Psychological Association, 1993.

Ashery, R.S., and McAuliffe, W.E. Implementation issues and techniques in randomized trials of outpatient psychosocial treatments for drug abusers: Recruitment of subjects. *Am J Drug Alcohol Abuse* 18:305-329, 1992.

Baumrind, D. The influence of parenting style on adolescent competence and substance abuse. *J Early Adolesc* 11:56-95, 1991.

Bednar, R.L.; Burlingame, G.M.; and Masters, K.S. Systems of family treatment: Substance or semantics? *Ann Rev Psychol* 39:401-434, 1988.

Bentler, P.M. Modeling of intervention effects. In: Leukefeld, C.G., and Bukoski, W.J., eds. *Drug Abuse Prevention Intervention Research: Methodological Issues*. National Institute on Drug Abuse Research Monograph No. 107. DHHS Pub. No. (ADM)91-1761. Washington, DC: Supt. of Docs., U.S. Govt. Print. Off., 1991. pp. 159-179.

Beschner, G. The problem of adolescent drug abuse: An introduction to intervention strategies. In: Friedman, A.S., and Beschner, G.M., eds. *Treatment Services for Adolescent Substance Abusers*. DHHS Pub. No. (ADM)89-1341. Washington, DC: Supt. of Docs., U.S. Govt. Print. Off., 1987.

Beutler, L.E. Introduction to the special series on advances in psychotherapy process research. *J Consult Clin Psychol* 58:263-264, 1990.

Block, J.; Block, J.H.; and Keyes, S. Longitudinally foretelling drug usage in adolescence: Early childhood personality and environmental precursors. *Child Dev* 59:336-355, 1988.

Blum, R.H. *Horatio Alger's Children*. San Francisco, CA: Jossey-Bass, 1972.

Brook, J.S.; Brook, D.W.; Gordon, A.S.; Whiteman, M.; and Cohen, P. The psychosocial etiology of adolescent drug use: A family interactional approach. *Genet Soc Gen Psychol Monogr* 116:2, 1990.

Brook, J.S.; Nomura, C.; and Cohen, P. A network on influences on adolescent drug involvement: Neighborhood, school, peer, and family. *Genet Soc Gen Psychol Monogr* 115:123-145, 1989.

Brook, J.S.; Whiteman, M.; Nomura, C.; Gordon, A.S.; and Cohen, P. Personality, family and ecological influences on adolescent drug use: A developmental analysis. In: Coombs, R.H., ed. *The Family Context of Adolescent Drug Use*. New York: Haworth Press, 1988.

Bry, B.H. Family-based approaches to reducing adolescent substance use: Theories, techniques and findings. In: Rahdert, E.R., and Grabowski, J., eds. *Adolescent Drug Abuse: Analyses of Treatment Research*. NIDA Research Monograph No. 77. NIH Pub. No. 94-3712. Washington, DC: Supt. of Docs., U.S. Govt. Print. Off., 1988. pp. 39-68.

Bukstein, O.G.; Brent, D.A.; and Kaminer, Y. Comorbidity of substance abuse and other psychiatric disorders in adolescents. *Am J Psychiatry* 146:1131-1141, 1989.

Catalano, R.F.; Hawkins, J.D.; Wells, E.A.; Miller, J. and Brewer, D. Evaluation of the effectiveness of adolescent drug abuse treatment, assessment of risks for relapse, and promising approaches for relapse prevention. *Int J Addict* 25:1085-1140, 1990-1991.

Coleman, S.B., and Davis, D.I. Family therapy and drug abuse: A national survey. *Fam Process* 17:21-29, 1978.

Comfort, M.; Shipley, T.E.; White, K.; Griffith, E.M.; and Shandler, T. Family treatment for homeless alcohol/drug-addicted women and their preschool children. *Alcohol Treat Q* 7:129-147, 1990.

Coombs, R.H.; Paulson, M.J.; and Palley, R. The institutionalization of drug use in America: Hazardous adolescence, challenging parenthood. In: Coombs, R.H., ed. *The Family Context of Adolescent Drug Use*. New York: Haworth Press, 1988. pp. 9-38.

Coyne, J., and Liddle, H.A. The future of systems therapy: Shedding myths and facing opportunities. *Psychother Theory Res Pract* 29:44-50, 1992.

Crits-Christoph, P. Implications of therapist effects for the design and analysis of comparative studies of psychotherapies. *J Consult Clin Psychol* 59:20-26, 1991.

Davidge, A.M., and Forman, S.G. Psychological treatment of adolescent substance abusers: A review. *Child Youth Services Rev* 10:45-55, 1988.

De Leon, G. Program-based evaluation research in therapeutic communities. In: Tims, F.M., and Ludford, J.P., eds. *Drug Abuse Treatment Evaluation: Strategies, Progress, and Prospects.* National Institute on Drug Abuse Research Monograph No. 51. DHHS Pub. No. (ADM)88-1329. Washington, DC: Supt. of Docs., U.S. Govt. Print. Off., 1984. pp. 69-87.

De Leon, G."Treatment Evaluation Research Center for Therapeutic Communities." Report of activities under National Institute on Drug Abuse grant number P50DA07700, 1991.

De Leon, G., ed. Report of the Psychosocial Subcommittee of the Scientific Advisory Council, National Institute on Drug Abuse. Rockville, MD: National Institute on Drug Abuse, 1993.

De Leon, G., and Jainchill, N. Circumstance, motivation, readiness and suitability as correlates of treatment tenure. *J Psychoactive Drugs* 18:203-208, 1986.

Dembo, R.; Williams, L.; La Voie, L.; Schmeidler, J.; Kern, J.; Getreu, A.; Berry, E.; Genung, L.; and Wish, E.D. A longitudinal study of the relationships among alcohol use, marijuana/hashish use, cocaine use, and emotional/psychological functioning problems in a cohort of high-risk youths. *Int J Addict* 25:1341-1382, 1990.

Diamond, G.S., and Liddle, H.A. Resolving therapeutic impasses between parents and adolescents: A process study of Multidimensional Family Therapy. *J Fam Psychol,* manuscript submitted for publication.

Donovan, J.E., and Jessor, R. Structure of problem behavior in adolescence and young adulthood. *J Consult Clin Psychol* 53:890-904, 1985.

Donovan, J.E.; Jessor, R.; and Costa, F.M. Syndrome of problem behavior in adolescence: A replication. *J Consult Clin Psychol* 56:762-765, 1988.

Dryfoos, J.G. Preventing high risk behavior. *Am J Public Health* 81:157-158, 1991.

Farrell, M.; Danish, S.J.; and Howard, C.W. Relationship between drug use and other problem behaviors in urban adolescents. *J Consult Clin Psychol* 60:705-712, 1992.

Feigelman, W. Day-care treatment for multiple-drug-abusing adolescents: Social factors linked with completing treatment. *J Psychoactive Drugs* 19:335-343, 1987.

Friedman, A.S. Family therapy vs. parent groups: Effects on adolescent drug abusers. *Am J Fam Ther* 17:335-347, 1989.

Friedman, P.H. Family system and ecological approach to youthful drug abuse. *Fam Ther* 1:63-78, 1974.

Garfield, S.L. Yes, I have heard of family psychology—But opinions are no substitute for data. [Comment]. *Am Psychol* 37:99-100, 1982.

General Accounting Office. Promising programs in adolescent drug use prevention. Report prepared for the National Institute on Drug Abuse. Washington, DC: Supt. of Docs., U.S. Govt. Print. Off., 1992.

Gottman, J.M., and Rushe, R.H. The analysis of change: Issues, fallacies, and new ideas. *J Consult Clin Psychol* 61:907-910, 1993.

Greenberg, L. Change process research. *J Consult Clin Psychol* 54:4-9, 1986.

Gurman, A.S., and Kniskern, D.P. The future of marital and family therapy. *Psychotherapy* 29:65-71, 1992.

Gurman, A.S.; Kniskern, D.P.; and Pinsof, W.M. Research on the process and outcome of marital and family therapy. In: Garfield, S.L., and Begin, A.E., eds. *Handbook of Psychotherapy and Behavior Change.* 2d ed. New York: John Wiley and Sons, 1986. pp. 565-624.

Haapala, D.A., and Kinney, J.M. Avoiding out-of-home placement of high risk offenders through the use of intensive home-bound family preservation services. *Crim Just Behav* 15:334-338, 1988.

Halikas, J.A.; Weller, R.A.; Morse, C.L.; and Hoffman, R.G. Regular marijuana use and its effect on psychosocial variables: A longitudinal study. *Compr Psychiatry* 24:229-235, 1983.

Haverkos, H. "Treatment Research Branch - 5 Year Report." Report prepared for the National Institute on Drug Abuse, 1993.

Hawkins, J.D.; Catalano, R.F.; and Miller, J.Y. Risk and protective factors for alcohol and other drug problems in adolescence and early adulthood: Implications for substance abuse prevention. *Psychol Bull* 112:64-105, 1992.

Hazelrigg, M.D.; Cooper, H.M.; and Borduin, C.M. Evaluating the effectiveness of family therapies: An integrative review and analysis. *Psychol Bull* 101:428-442, 1987.

Heath, A.W., and Stanton, M.D. Family therapy. In: Frances, R.J., and Miller, S.I., eds. *Clinical Textbook of Addictive Disorders.* New York: Guilford Press, 1991. pp. 406-430.

Henggeler, S.W. Multisystemic treatment of serious juvenile offenders: Implications for the treatment of substance-abusing youths. In: Onken, L.S.; Blaine, J.D.; and Boren, J.J., eds. *Behavioral Treatments for Drug Abuse and Dependence.* National Institute on Drug Abuse Research Monograph No. 137. NIH Pub. No. 93-3684. Washington, DC: Supt. of Docs., U.S. Govt. Print. Off., 1993. pp. 181-199.

Henggeler, S.W.; Bourdin, C.M.; Melton, G.B.; Mann, B.J.; Smith, L.A.; Hall, J.A.; Cone, L.; and Fucci, B.R. Effects of multisystemic therapy on drug use and abuse in serious juvenile offenders: A progress report from two outcome studies. *Fam Dynamics Addict Q* 1:40-51, 1991.

Henggeler, S.W., and Bourdin, C.M. *Family Therapy and Beyond: A Multisystemic Approach to Treating the Behavior Problems of Children and Adolescents.* Pacific Grove, CA: Brooks Cole, 1990.

Henggeler, S.W.; Bourdin, C.M.; and Mann, B.J. Advances in family therapy: Empirical foundations. In: Ollendick, T.H., and Prinz, R.J., eds. *Advances in Clinical Child Psychology.* New York: Plenum Press, 1993.

Henggeler, W.W.; Melton, G.B.; and Smith, L.A. Family preservation using multisystemic therapy: An effective alternative to incarcerating serious juvenile offenders. *J Consult Clin Psychol* 60:953-961, 1992.

Henggeler, S.W.; Rodick, J.D.; Bourdin, C.M.; Hanson, C.L.; Watson, S.M.; and Urey, J.R. Multisystemic treatment of juvenile offenders: Effects on adolescent behavior and family interaction. *Dev Psychol* 22:132-141, 1986.

Henry, W.P.; Schacht, T.E.; Strupp, H.H.; Butler, S.F.; and Binder, J.L. Effects of training in time-limited dynamic psychotherapy: Mediators of therapists' responses to training. *J Consult Clin Psychol* 61:441-447, 1993*a*.

Henry, W.P.; Strupp, H.H.; Butler, S.F.; Schacht, T.E.; and Binder, J.L. Effects of training in time-limited dynamic psychotherapy: Changes in therapist behavior. *J Consult Clin Psychol* 61:434-440, 1993*b*.

Hirsch, R. Group therapy with parents of adolescent drug addicts. *Psychiatric Q* 35:702-710, 1961.

Howard, K.I.; Cox, W.M.; and Saunders, S.M. Attrition in substance abuse comparative treatment research: The illusion of randomization. In: Onken, L.S., and Blaine, J.D., eds. *Psychotherapy and Counseling in the Treatment of Drug Abuse.* National Institute on Drug Abuse Research Monograph No. 104. DHHS Pub. No. (ADM)91-1722. Washington, DC: Supt. of Docs., U.S. Govt. Print. Off., 1990.

Howard, K.I.; Merton, S.K.; and Lyons, J.S. When clinical trials fail: A guide to disaggregation. In: Onken, L.S.; Blaine, J.D.; and Boren, J.J., eds. *Behavioral Treatments for Drug Abuse and Dependence.* National Institute on Drug Abuse Research Monograph No. 137. NIH Pub. No. 93-3684. Washington, DC: Supt. of Docs., U.S. Govt. Print. Off., 1993. pp. 291-302.

Hubbard, R.L.; Cavanaugh, E.R.; Craddock, S.G.; Bray, R.M.; and Rachal, J.V. Characteristics, behaviors, and outcomes for youth in the TOPS study. In: Friedman, A.S., and Beschner, G.M., eds. *Treatment Services for Adolescent Substance Abusers.* DHHS Pub. No. (ADM)85-1342. Washington, DC: Supt. of Docs., U.S. Govt. Print. Off., 1985. pp. 49-65.

Institute of Medicine. "Treating Drug Problems: A Study of the Evolution, Effectiveness, and Financing of Public and Private Drug Treatment Systems." Report prepared by the Institute of Medicine, Committee for the Substance Abuse Coverage Study, Division of Health Care Services. Washington, DC: National Academy Press, 1990.

Jacobson, N.S., and Revenstorf, D. Statistics for assessing the clinical significance of psychotherapy techniques: Issues, problems, and new developments. *Behav Assessment* 10:133-146, 1988.

Jacobson, N.S.; Schmaling, K.B.; Holtzworth-Monroe, A.; Katt, J.L.; Wood, L.F.; and Follette, V.M. Research structured vs. clinically flexible versions of social learning based marital therapy. *Behav Res Ther* 27:173-180, 1989.

Jainchill, N. "Therapeutic Communities for Adolescents." Report of activities under National Institute on Drug Abuse grant no. P50DA07700, 1991.

Jessor, R., and Jessor, S.L. The social-psychological framework. In: Jessor, R., and Jessor, S.L., eds. *Problem Behavior and Psychosocial Development: A Longitudinal Study of Youth.* New York: Academic Press, 1977. pp. 17-42.

Joanning, H.; Quinn, W.; Thomas, F.; and Mullen, R. Treating adolescent drug abuse: A comparison of family systems therapy, group therapy, and family drug education. *J Marital Fam Ther* 18:345-356, 1992.

Johnston, L. "Drug Use Rises among the Nation's Eighth Grade Students." Press release. Ann Arbor, MI: University of Michigan, 1993.

Johnston, L.D.; O'Malley, P.M.; and Bachman, J.G. *National Survey Results on Drug Use from the Monitoring the Future Study, 1975-1992.* Vol. I. *Secondary School Students.* Rockville, MD: National Institute on Drug Abuse, 1992.

Jones, E., ed. Special section: Single-case research in psychotherapy. *J Consult Clin Psychol* 61:371-430, 1993.

Kandel, D.B. Parenting styles, drug use, and children's adjustment in families of young adults. *J Marriage Fam Ther* 52:183-196, 1990.

Kandel, D.B.; Davies, M.; Karus, D.; and Yamaguchi, K. The consequences in young adulthood of adolescent drug involvement. *Arch Gen Psychiatry* 43:746-754, 1986.

Kaufman, E. Family systems and family therapy of substance abuse: An overview of two decades of research and clinical experience. *Int J Addict* 20:897-916, 1985.

Kazdin, A.E. Symptom substitution, generalization, and response covariation: Implications for psychotherapy outcome. *Psychol Bull* 91:349-365, 1982.

Kazdin, A.E. Treatment of antisocial behavior in children: Current status and future directions. *Psychol Bull* 102:187-203, 1987.

Kazdin, A.E. Psychotherapy for children and adolescents: Current progress and future research directions. *Am Psychol* 48:644-657, 1993.

Kazdin, A.E.; Bass, D.; Ayers, W.A.; and Rodgers, A. Empirical and clinical focus of child and adolescent psychotherapy research. *J Consult Clin Psychol* 58:729-740, 1990.

Kazdin, A.E.; Mazurick, J.L.; and Bass, D. Risk for attention in treatment of antisocial children and families. *J Clin Child Psychol* 22:2-16, 1993.

Kellam, S.G.; Branch, J.D.; Brown, C.H.; and Russell, G. Why teenagers come for treatment: A ten-year prospective epidemiological study in Woodlawn. *J Am Acad Child Adolesc Psychiatry* 20:477-495, 1981.

Kellam, S.G.; Brown, C.H.; Rubin, B.R.; and Ensminger, M.E. Paths leading to teenage psychiatric symptoms and substance use: Developmental epidemiological studies in Woodlawn. In: Guze, S.; Earls, F.; and Barrett, J., eds. *Childhood Psychopathology and Development.* New York: Raven Press, 1983.

Kendall, P.C.; Lerner, R.M.; and Craighead, W.E. Human development and intervention in childhood psychopathology. *Child Dev* 55:71-82, 1984.

Kleinman, P.H.; Woody, G.E.; Todd, T.C.; Millman, R.B.; Kang, S.; Kemp, J.; and Lipton, D.S. Crack and cocaine abusers in outpatient psychotherapy. In: Onken, L.S., and Blaine, J.D., eds. *Psychotherapy and Counseling in the Treatment of Drug Abuse.* National Institute on Drug Abuse Research Monograph No. 104. Washington, DC: Supt. of Docs., U.S. Govt. Print. Off., 1990. pp. 24-35.

Leukefeld, C.G., and Bukowski, W.J. Drug abuse prevention evaluation methodology: A bright future. *J Drug Educ* 21:191-201, 1991.

Lewis, R.A.; Piercy, F.P.; Sprenkle, D.H.; and Trepper, T.S. Family-based interventions for helping drug-abusing adolescents. *J Adolesc Res* 50:82-95, 1990.

Lewis, R.A.; Piercy, F.P.; Sprenkle, D.H.; and Trepper, T.S. The Purdue brief family therapy model for adolescent substance abusers. In: Todd, T., and Selekman, M., eds. *Family Therapy with Adolescent Substance Abusers.* New York: Allyn and Bacon, 1991.

Liddle, H.A. Developmental thinking and the family life cycle: Implications for training family therapists. In: Falicov, C., ed. *Family Transitions: Continuity and Change over the Life Cycle.* New York: Guilford Press, 1988.

Liddle, H.A. A multidimensional model for treating the adolescent drug abuser. In: Snyder, W., and Doms, T. *Empowering Families: Family Centered Treatment of Adolescents in Mental Health and Substance Abuse Problems.* Washington, DC: Supt. of Docs., U.S. Govt. Print. Off., 1991*a*.

Liddle, H.A. Report of project activities under National Institute on Drug Abuse grant no. 1P50DA07697, 1991*b*.

Liddle, H.A. The anatomy of emotions in family therapy with adolescents. *J Adolesc Res* 9:120-157, 1994*a*.

Liddle, H.A. "Family Therapy for Adult and Adolescent Drug Abuse: State of the Science." Report prepared for the Treatment Research Branch, National Institute on Drug Abuse. Available from Center for Research on Adolescent Drug Abuse, Temple University, Philadelphia, PA 19122. 1994*b*.

Liddle, H.A., and Dakof, G.A. "Family-Based Intervention for Adolescent Drug Abuse." Paper presented at the meeting of the Society for Psychotherapy Research, Pittsburgh, PA, June 24, 1992.

Liddle, H.A., and Schmidt, S. Using the research literature on parenting to guide clinical practice. *Fam Psychol* 10:25-29, 1994.

Liddle, H.A.; Dakof, G.A.; Parker, K.; Diamond, G.S.; Barrett, K.; Garcia, R.G.; and Hurwitz, S. "Treating Adolescent Substance Use: Results from a Comparative Clinical Trial." Manuscript submitted for publication.

Liddle, H.A.; Dakof, G.A.; and Diamond, G. Adolescent substance abuse: Multidimensional family therapy in action. In: Kaufman, E., and Kaufman, P., eds. *Family Therapy of Drug and Alcohol Abuse.* Boston: Allyn and Bacon, 1991. pp. 120-171.

Liddle, H.A.; Schmidt, S.; and Ettinger, D. Adolescent development research: Guidelines for clinicians. *J Marital Fam Ther,* in press.

Loeber, R. Development and risk factors of juvenile antisocial behavior and delinquency. *Clin Psychol Rev* 10:1-41, 1990.

Malgady, R.G.; Rogler, L.H.; and Costantino, G. Culturally sensitive psychotherapy for Puerto Rican children and adolescents: A program of treatment outcome research. *J Consult Clin Psychol* 58:704-712, 1990.

Mann, B.J.; Bourdin, C.M.; Henggeler, S.W.; and Blaske, D.M. An investigation of systematic conceptualizations of parent-child coalitions and symptom change. *J Consult Clin Psychol* 58:336-344, 1990.

Markman, H. Review of "Handbook of Family Therapy Training and Supervision." *Contemp Psychol* 35:821, 1990.

McAuliffe, W.E., and Ashery, R.S. Implementation issues and techniques in randomized trials of outpatient psychosocial treatments for drug abusers. II. Clinical and administrative issues. *Am J Drug Alcohol Abuse* 19:35-50, 1993.

McDermott, D. The relationship of parental drug use and parents' attitude concerning adolescent drug use to adolescent drug use. *Adolescence* 14:89-97, 1984.

McLellan, A.T.; Woody, G.E.; Luborsky, L.; O'Brien, C.P.; and Druley, K.A. Increased effectiveness of substance abuse treatment: Prospective study of patient-treatment "matching." *J Nerv Ment Dis* 171:597-605, 1983.

Metzger, D. *Adolescent Problem Severity Index.* Philadelphia: Addiction Research Center, University of Pennsylvania, 1990.

Miller, G.E., and Prinz, R.J. Enhancement of social learning family interventions for childhood conduct disorder. *Psychol Bull* 108:291-307, 1990.

Moncher, F.J., and Prinz, R.J. Treatment fidelity in outcome studies. *Clin Psychol Rev* 11:247-266, 1991.

Moras, K. Substance abuse research: Outcome measurement conundrums. In: Onken, L.S.; Blaine, J.D.; and Boren, J.J., eds. *Behavioral Treatments for Drug Abuse and Dependence.* National Institute on Drug Abuse Research Monograph No. 137. NIH Pub. No. 93-3684. Washington, DC: Supt. of Docs., U.S. Govt. Print. Off., 1993. pp. 217-248.

Morrow-Bradley, C., and Elliott, R. Utilization of psychotherapy research by practicing psychotherapists. *Am Psychol* 41:188-197, 1986.

National Institute on Drug Abuse. *National Household Survey on Drug Abuse: Main Findings 1990.* National Institute on Drug Abuse, Rockville, MD, 1991.

National Research Council. *Violence: Understanding and Preventing.* Washington, DC: National Academy Press, 1993.

Newcomb, M.D., and Bentler, P.M. *Consequences of Adolescent Drug Use.* Newbury Park, CA: Sage Publications, Inc., 1988.

Newcomb, M.D., and Bentler, P.M. Substance use and abuse among children and teenagers. *Am Psychol* 44:242-248, 1989.

Newcomb, M.D., and Felix-Ortiz, M. Multiple protective and risk factors for drug use and abuse: Cross-sectional and prospective findings. *J Pers Soc Psychol* 63:280-296, 1992.

Newcomb, M.D., and McGee, L. The influence of sensation seeking on general deviance and specific problem behaviors from adolescence to young adulthood. *J Pers Soc Psychol* 61:614-628, 1991.

Newman, F.L., and Howard, K.I. Introduction to the special section on seeking new clinical research methods. *J Consult Clin Psychol* 59:8-11, 1991.

Onken, L.S., and Blaine, J.D. *Psychotherapy and Counseling in the Treatment of Drug Abuse.* National Institute on Drug Abuse Research Monograph 104. NIH Pub. No. 94-3716. Washington, DC: Supt. of Docs., U.S. Govt. Print. Off., 1990.

Onken, L.S.; Blaine, J.D.; and Boren, J.J., eds. *Behavioral Treatments for Drug Abuse and Dependence.* National Institute on Drug Abuse Research Monograph 137. NIH Pub. No. 93-3684. Washington, DC: Supt. of Docs., U.S. Govt. Print. Off., 1993.

Orlinsky, D.E., and Howard, K.I. Process and outcome in psychotherapy. In: Garfield, S.L., and Begin, A.E., eds. *Handbook of Psychotherapy and Behavior Change.* 3d ed. New York: Wiley, 1986. pp. 311-384.

Parker, K.P. "Administrative and Recruitment Challenges in Conducting a Randomized Clinical Trial." Paper presented at the American Psychological Association Meeting, San Francisco, CA, August 26, 1991.

Patterson, G.R. Performance models for antisocial boys. *Am Psychol* 41:432-444, 1986.

Patterson, G.R.; Reid, J.B.; and Dishion, T.J. *A Social Learning Approach. IV. Antisocial Boys.* Eugene, OR: Castalia, 1992.

Persons, J.B. Psychotherapy outcome studies do not accurately represent current models of psychotherapy: A proposed remedy. *Am Psychol* 46:99-106, 1991.

Piercy, F.P., and Frankel, B.R. The evolution of an integrative family therapy for substance abusing adolescents: Toward the mutual enhancement of research and practice. *J Fam Psychol* 3:5-28, 1989.

Pike, C.L., and Piercy, F.P. Cost effectiveness of family therapy. *J Marriage Fam Ther* 16:375-388, 1990.

Pinsof, W. A conceptual framework and methodological criteria for family therapy process research. *J Consult Clin Psychol* 57:53-59, 1989.

Rahdert, E. The Problem Oriented Screening Instrument (POSIT). Rockville, MD: National Institute on Drug Abuse, 1990.

Ridgely, M.S., and Wellbring, M.L. Application of case management to drug abuse treatment: Overview of models and research issues. In: Ashery, R.S., ed. *Progress and Issues in Case Management.* National Institute on Drug Abuse Research Monograph No. 127. DHHS Pub. No. (ADM)92-1946. Washington, DC: Supt. of Docs., U.S. Govt. Print. Off., 1992. pp. 12-33.

Riggs, S., and Cheng, T. Adolescents' willingness to use a school-based clinic in view of expressed health concerns. *J Adolesc Health Care* 9:208-213, 1988.

Santisteban, D.A.; Szapocznik, J.; Perez-Vidal, A.; Kurtines, W.M.; Murray, E.J.; and LaPerriere, A. Efficacy of interventions for engaging youth/families into treatment and the factors that contribute to differential effectiveness. *J Fam Psychol*, in press.

Selekman, M.D., and Todd, T.C. Major issues from family therapy research and theory. In: Todd, T.C., and Selekman, M.D., eds. *Family Therapy Approaches with Adolescent Substance Abusers.* Needham Heights, MA: Allyn and Bacon, 1990. pp. 311-325.

Sells, S.B., and Simpson, D.D. Evaluation of treatment outcome for youths in the Drug Abuse Reporting Program (DARP): A follow-up study. In: Beschner, G.M., and Friedman, A.S., eds. *Youth Drug Abuse: Problems, Issues, and Treatment.* Lexington, MA: Lexington Books, 1979.

Shadish, W.R.; Montgomery, L.M.; Wilson, P.; Wilson, M.R.; Bright, I.; and Okwumabua, T. Effects of family and marital psychotherapies: A meta-analysis. *J Consult Clin Psychol* 61:992-1002, 1993.

Shedler, J., and Block, J. Adolescent drug use and psychological health: A longitudinal inquiry. *Am Psychol* 45:612-630, 1990.

Shoham-Salomon, V. Introduction to special section on client-therapy interaction research. *J Consult Clin Psychol* 59:203-204, 1991.

Snow, R.E. Aptitude-treatment interaction as a framework for research on individual differences in psychotherapy. *J Consult Clin Psychol* 59:205-216, 1991.

Stanton, M.D., and Todd, T.C. Structural family therapy with drug addicts. In: Kaufman, E., and Kaufman, P., eds. *The Family Therapy of Drug and Alcohol Abuse.* New York: Gardner Press, 1979.

Stanton, M.D.; Todd, T.C.; and Associates. *The Family Therapy of Drug Abuse and Addiction.* New York: Guilford Press, 1982.

Stark, M.J. Dropping out of substance abuse treatment: A clinically oriented review. *Clin Psychol Rev* 12:93-116, 1992.

Stark, M.J., and Campbell, B.K. Personality, drug use, and early attrition from substance abuse treatment. *Am J Drug Alcohol Abuse* 14:475-487, 1988.

Szapocznik, J., and Kurtines, W. Family psychology and cultural diversity: Opportunities for theory, research, and application. *Am Psychol* 48:400-408, 1993.

Szapocznik, J.; Rio, A.; and Kurtines, W. University of Miami School of Medicine: Brief strategic family therapy for Hispanic youth. In: Beutler, L.E., and Crago, M., eds. *Psychotherapy Research: An International Review of Programmatic Studies.* Washington, DC: American Psychological Association, 1991. pp. 123-132.

Szapocznik, J.; Kurtines, W.M.; Foote, F.H.; Perez-Vidal, A.; and Hervis, O. Conjoint versus one-person family therapy: Some evidence for the effectiveness of conducting family therapy through one person. *J Consult Clin Psychol* 51:881-889, 1983.

Szapocznik, J.; Kurtines, W.M.; Foote, F.H.; Perez-Vidal, A.; and Hervis, O. Conjoint versus one-person family therapy: Further evidence for the effectiveness of conducting family therapy through one person with drug-abusing adolescents. *J Consult Clin Psychol* 54:395-397, 1986.

Szapocznik, J.; Kurtines, W.; Santisteban, D.A.; and Rio, A.T. Interplay of advances between theory, research, and application in treatment interventions aimed at behavior problem children and adolescents. *J Consult Clin Psychol* 58:696-703, 1990.

Szapocznik, J.; Perez-Vidal, A.; Brickman, A.L.; Foote, F.H.; Santisteban, D.; Hervis, O.; and Kurtines, W. Engaging adolescent drug abusers and their families in treatment: A strategic structural systems approach. *J Consult Clin Psychol* 56:552-557, 1988.

Thompson, T.; Koerner, J.; and Grabowski, J. Brokerage model rehabilitation system for opiate dependence: A behavioral analysis. In: Grabowski, J.; Stitzer, M.; and Henningfield, J., eds. *Behavioral Interventions in Drug Abuse Treatment.* National Institute on Drug Abuse Research Monograph No. 46. DHHS Pub. No. (ADM)84-1282. Washington, DC: Supt. of Docs., U.S. Govt. Print. Off., 1984. pp. 131-146.

Tolan, P.H., and Loeber, R. Antisocial behavior. In: Tolan, P.H., and Cohler, B.J., eds. *Handbook of Clinical Research and Practice with Adolescents.* New York: John Wiley and Sons, Inc., 1993. pp. 307-332.

Waltz, J.; Addis, M.E.; Koerner, K.; and Jacobson, N.S. Testing the integrity of a psychotherapy protocol: Assessment of adherence and competence. *J Consult Clin Psychol* 61:620-630, 1993.

Weidman, A.A. Engaging the families of substance abusing adolescents in family therapy. *J Subst Abuse Treat* 2:97-105, 1985.

Weisz, J.R.; Weiss, B.; and Donenberg, G.R. The lab versus the clinic: Effects of child and adolescent psychotherapy. *Am Psychol* 47:1578-1585, 1992.

Wills, T.A. Social support and the family. In: Breenman, E., ed. *Emotions and the Family: For Better or for Worse*. Hillsdale, NJ: Erlbaum, 1990.

Winters, K. The need for improved assessment of adolescent substance involvement. *J Drug Issues* 20:487-502, 1990.

ACKNOWLEDGMENT

Support for the completion of this paper was provided by grants from the National Institute on Drug Abuse, United States Department of Education, Pennsylvania Office of Drug Abuse Prevention, and the Temple University Research Fund.

AUTHORS

Howard A. Liddle, Ed.D.
Professor of Counseling Psychology
and
Director of the Center for Research on Adolescent Drug Abuse

Gayle A. Dakof, Ph.D.
Senior Research Associate
Center for Research on Adolescent Drug Abuse
Temple University
TU 265-66
Philadelphia, PA 19122

Skills Training for Pregnant and Parenting Adolescents

James A. Hall

INTRODUCTION

Skills training for drug-using and at-risk adolescents has been studied in a variety of ways since more investigation of this topic was proposed in a National Institute on Drug Abuse (NIDA) Research Monograph (Krasnegor 1988, pp. 132-133):

> Finally, research on how to teach children basic decision-making skills and an understanding of the relationship between behavior and consequences needs to be expanded (Botvin and Wills 1985). This domain includes developing educational packages on assertiveness to be taught to at-risk children. Also needed are effective training packages to teach children how to differentiate between the immediate and long-range consequences of their behavior, particularly as such consequences affect their health. Research should be targeted on developing materials that can be used by health educators and health care providers.

Although the focus of this recommendation was on decisionmaking skills, the statement also includes assertiveness, which has been typically defined as a behavioral rather than cognitive skill. This differentiation, however, has not been consistently made by researchers and is a topic of discussion in the present chapter.

The definition of a skill varies across studies and program reports. A skill can be defined as "the exact words to say, the way to say them, and the hand movements needed to convey a message." Or a skill can be defined much more broadly as "to listen." Unfortunately, the impact of the definition on skills training effectiveness has not been studied. The targets of intervention vary by study purpose and by specific need.

Since Krasnegor's statement, much has been written about skills training as a treatment approach for various cognitive and behavioral problems with various populations including adolescents. In addition to a treatment approach, skills training has been proposed and evaluated as a prevention intervention for adolescent drug abuse (Schinke et al. 1988). Also, the "active ingredients" of both prevention interventions and treatment programs need further review; some studies refer to the treatment as working on skills in a group, and other studies describe specific techniques for skills improvement.

The relationship of adolescent drug abuse to skills of any type must be questioned as well. Some argument has been made that a deficit in skills is related to the etiology of drug use and abuse by teens (Hawkins et al. 1985). Does this then mean that improvement in those deficient skills will reduce or eliminate drug use? Unfortunately, that question has not been adequately studied. Further, the definitions of these target skills vary extensively among investigators and range from "be assertive" to saying "no" when asked to get high on cocaine. A standard level of specificity for skills does not exist at this time, but may help both researchers and clinicians to focus on the same problem. Basic problems must be resolved before common definitions can be formulated for skills training and the actual skills targeted by an intervention.

Finally, Krasnegor's reference to children rather than adolescents or teens reflects much of the confusion providers and researchers have with individuals between 12 and 18 years old. Should these individuals be considered children or adults? Should skills be taught to them using a mediator model (such as parent training) or a couples communication model that assumes equivalent power between partners? Adolescents cannot be considered a homogeneous group due to differences in age, development, gender, and ethnic background. Due to these differences, researchers should also study the problems of these specific groups rather than adolescents in general.

This chapter addresses these issues by examining the literature related to skills training and drug treatment for adolescents, and by describing a current research demonstration project funded by NIDA. At the end of the chapter, recommendations are given for future research.

RECOMMENDATIONS FOR SKILLS TRAINING

Skills training has been recommended as treatment for a variety of problems including adolescent drug abuse. Hawkins and colleagues

(1985) identified several factors that lead to adolescent drug abuse, including parental influences, peer influences, beliefs and values, and involvement in certain activities. Their social development model proposed that "youths who have not become socially bonded to family and school as a result of family conflict, school failure, and aggressive behaviors, will be easily influenced by drug prone peers and will find little reason to resist pressures to initiate drug use early in adolescence" (p. 36). One of their recommendations was to improve interpersonal skills as a way of improving bonding with family members and conventional peers and decreasing the attractiveness of drug-using peers.

Botvin and Wills (1985) also argued for the use of skills training as a prevention intervention with adolescents. Their support of skills training among adolescents to prevent drug use and abuse rests on the assumption that improved skills help reduce or eliminate drug use. Researchers still do not know, however, whether the same skills training programs can be used for both preventive and interventive needs.

Davidge and Forman (1988) concluded that although behavior therapy, skills training, and family therapy have limited effectiveness with adolescent drug abusers, other psychotherapeutic approaches have not been found to be effective. In a less positive evaluation, Kumpfer (1989) recommended that no one method will work with all drug-using or -abusing youths and that the behavioral skills programs might be too simplistic a preventive strategy for high-risk youth.

Inderbitzen-Pisaruk and Foster (1990) justified the use of skills training if related to peer acceptance and friendship. After reviewing the empirical literature related to peer acceptance and friendship, they concluded that important behaviors are anchored in specific relationships and that skills trainers need to help teens judge the qualitative aspects of a skill rather than just the frequency of occurrence. Group approaches were recommended as most appropriate for teens, and both negative and positive behaviors were targeted so that teens learn how to decrease their aversive qualities.

As further support for skills training, Miller (1992) identified several reasons for being optimistic about treatment for substance abuse. Support was cited for treatment strategies that either suppress use (e.g., behavioral self-control training, covert sensitization, and medications) or improve coping skills (including social skills training). Rather than concluding that treatment does not work for drug abuse (with any age population),

Miller proposed more study of the mechanisms of change for treatment programs even if that change is short term.

Support for skills training has been most obvious from the many descriptions of clinical programs and prevention models, but very few have been evaluation studies. As concluded in most drug treatment evaluation, methodological flaws have undermined many of the claims made for this approach. Skills training is widely supported for both drug treatment and prevention, but the myriad definitions of both the target skills and the intervention programs make conclusions difficult. Skills training has seemingly become like family treatment—everyone knows what it is in general, but many models exist. Specification of both the skills and interventions is necessary for review to be beneficial.

VARIATIONS IN SKILLS TRAINING

Even though skills training has received considerable support as both a treatment and a prevention intervention for adolescent drug abuse, how can the active ingredients (if a standard set exists) be described? In addition, what skills are being targeted as necessary for treatment of drug abuse? Skills training interventions have been included in many prevention and treatment effectiveness studies. In order to compare and contrast these interventive strategies, certain labels are necessary. Before these classifications are made, a caveat must be given. Classification labels can be used if enough information is given in the study report. As will be seen, many interventions are briefly and vaguely described, and the reader must decide if enough data are present to classify. Also, most skills training has been conducted in groups, so this approach may be assumed in almost all cases. When a nongroup approach is used (e.g., individual, couple, or family), this variation is noted.

Training Style

The first classification domain is training style, which can be further classified into three major approaches: support groups, psychoeducational groups, and behavioral groups. Support-style skills training groups focus on the primary treatment goals of self-disclosure and discussion. The trainer is more like a facilitator who asks questions at times, provides information as necessary, and lets the group work together to talk about the target skills. Typically, the agenda is loosely structured but does highlight a skill for each session. Psychoeducational-style skills training groups focus primarily on the provision of information. These groups are more like didactic classes, which assume that the improvement of knowledge is the primary goal of treatment and that discussion is necessary in order to clarify the information being provided. Finally, behavioral-style skills training groups focus on the improvement of behavioral skills—that is, what is said and how it is said. These groups tend to have highly structured agendas. The leaders model desired skills and provide positive feedback to the teens who practice the skills to learn them.

Training Organization

The second classification domain is training organization. The basic question is whether the skills training program is the same as the drug treatment program or if the skills training is just a component of the treatment. Very rarely is skills training considered the primary treatment. Most often, skills training is considered a component of the overall treatment program. The possibilities for evaluating the impact of skills training are somewhat limited depending on how many other components are present.

Training Setting

Another classification domain is training setting, the location where the skills training occurs. Some programs, mainly prevention interventions, are conducted in the schools or educational system with students ranging in age from 10 to 18. Other programs are conducted by community agencies as outpatient groups or family therapy approaches. A third set of programs are conducted by the legal system as part of a probation department or under contract to the juvenile court system. Finally, drug treatment agencies conduct skills training programs either as programs by themselves or as components of their usual approaches.

Training Specificity

Finally, the specificity of the skills training intervention package also varies. In some studies, skills training is loosely defined whether or not it is part of an overall treatment package. In other studies, the skills training program is specifically defined and includes one or more training techniques (e.g., provision of information, modeling, role playing, structured feedback, and homework assignments). As with the definition of skills, training specificity has also not been evaluated for effectiveness.

THEORETICAL LINKAGES: SKILLS TRAINING AND TEEN DRUG ABUSE

As mentioned, skills training has been advocated for a variety of problems ranging from family conflict (Lewis et al. 1990) to adolescent drug abuse (Hawkins et al. 1991). The main assumption has been that improvement of skills—however defined—will lead to better personal and interpersonal functioning and to decreases in problems (e.g., drug use, criminal activity). Skills training has also been advocated as an effective prevention strategy.

In general, the term "skills training" has been cited extensively in the psychological literature. A general review of the psychological literature since 1986 found over 1,000 articles that mentioned skills training as a descriptive label. Even when the search was limited to adolescents, 125 articles were identified—too many to be reviewed effectively in a chapter of this size. Several of these adolescent studies focused on employment and job skills, which could be considered life skills. This area is not included in this chapter.

Other investigators have studied the efficacy of skills training for use with the mentally ill (Fine 1991; Foxx et al. 1989); physically or developmentally disabled (Duran 1986; Gerstein 1988; Hardoff and Chigier 1991; Hinderscheit and Reichle 1987; Hostler et al. 1989; Oswald et al. 1990); children diagnosed with attention deficit-hyperactivity disorder (ADHD) (Abikoff et al. 1988); adolescent offenders (Becker et al. 1988; Guerra and Slaby 1990; Shorts 1989; Walker 1989); pregnant and parenting teens (Balassone 1988; Bennett and Morgan 1988; Kissman 1991; Ladner 1987); teens and their parents (Anderson and Nuttall 1987; Brown and Mann 1991; Mittl and Robin 1987; Noble et al. 1989); juvenile delinquent, troubled, behavior-disordered, conduct-disordered, or antisocial teens (Baum et al. 1987; Epstein and Cullinan 1987; Hains and Herman 1989; Serna et al. 1986; Svec and Bechard 1988; Tannehill 1987; Tisdelle and St. Lawrence 1988); hospitalized, inpatient, mentally ill, or cognitively impaired teens (Dryfoos 1991; Jackson 1987; Jamison et al. 1986; Lichstein et al. 1987); acquired immunodeficiency syndrome (AIDS)-risk adolescents (Boyer and Kegeles 1991); female sexual abuse victims (Davis 1990); Native Americans (LaFromboise and Bigfoot 1988); and even sports-injured teens (Smith and Johnson 1990).

In all of these studies, skills training has been defined in a variety of ways depending on the type of skill targeted. Across the training style domain, the main approaches have been support groups and psychoeducational groups. Across the training organization domain, most of these skills training programs have been a component of a larger treatment program. Across the training setting domain, these mainly descriptive studies have been located in a variety of settings ranging from inpatient hospitals to community agencies to schools. Most of the studies across the training specificity domain defined their interventions in rather broad terms and by session topics, rather than with the actual treatment techniques used to change the clients. Due to vagueness about the skills training interventions and the targeted skills, closer examination of most of these studies will not be helpful. Only those studies that focus on skills training with drug-abusing teens are thoroughly reviewed in this chapter.

IMPLEMENTATION OF SKILLS TRAINING

Although data do not support the effectiveness of a skills training-only program, some research suggests that skills training may be used effectively as part of a drug treatment or prevention program (Hawkins et al. 1991; Schinke et al. 1988). In order to use skills training as part of drug treatment, it is necessary to diagnose a skills deficit with either a standardized assessment instrument or through a clinical interview. When skills training is used as part of drug treatment, a professional counselor, teacher, or probation officer usually refers teens based on interactions with the teen and on feedback concerning other areas of the teen's life. To facilitate the diagnosis of skills deficits, a severity instrument such as the Problem Oriented Screening Instrument for Teens (POSIT) (Rahdert 1991) can be used. The POSIT assesses 10 drug use-related domains including social skills and would improve the ability to make standardized comparisons of skills deficits. The POSIT has been used extensively in various settings. The main drawback of the POSIT is that it relies on self-report by the teens. Once a standardized social skills deficit has been identified, however, skills training can focus on the improvement of the deficit skill.

Skills training may also be able to be used as part of a preventative program to deter substance use and abuse. Skills training has been evaluated as a prevention technique (Forman and Linney 1988; Hansen 1992). When using skills training in a prevention program, initial diagnosis of a problem is unnecessary. Even though a client has not been formally diagnosed with a specific skills deficit, training in one or more skills may improve the client's ability to resist drug use or related problems. Thus learning skills such as how to handle criticism is hypothesized to reduce or eliminate drug use.

When skills training is used in a substance use treatment or prevention program, efforts should be made to accurately define social skills and to assess skills before and after training procedures. Through careful investigation of innovative intervention, researchers may be able to provide the data necessary to support skills training as a significant means of treating and preventing substance use.

Skills Training as Prevention Interventions

Skills training has been extensively evaluated as a prevention intervention technique with teens. Forman and Linney (1988) and Hansen (1992) reviewed the prevention literature and advocated using social influence and social skills interventions to prevent drug use and abuse among teens. In addition, the work of Botvin and colleagues (Botvin and Botvin 1992; Dusenbury and Botvin 1992; Dusenbury et al. 1990) has been based on the version of skills training called life skills training (LST). Unfortunately, LST also has several definitions ranging from activities of daily living (ADLs) for developmentally disabled or dual-diagnosed individuals to general skills of living for welfare recipients (e.g., budgeting, planning).

Two prevention approaches that have also been used for treatment bear mention. Goldstein (1989) has published extensively about the Skillstreaming approach to skills training and has even identified a set of these skills as refusal skills for saying "no" to drug and/or alcohol use. Sprunger and Pellaux (1989) reported on the development of the Quest Program for skills training. The Quest Program is cosponsored by the Lions Clubs International, has been extensively documented, and has received celebrity endorsements. Entire school systems have adopted the Quest Program, and Skillstreaming materials have been used by school counselors and others around the country. Unfortunately, evaluations of those studies could not be found for inclusion in this review.

Skills Training as a Family Intervention

As noted above, skills training has been used with parents and teens to improve communication and problem solving. The work of Lewis and colleagues (1990) involving Purdue Brief Family Therapy (PBFT) is reported below as a key study. Mittl and Robin (1987) investigated the acceptability of alternative interventions for parent-adolescent conflict and found that problem solving communication skills training was significantly more acceptable than behavioral contracting, medication, and paradox interventions, in that order. Kifer and colleagues (1974) were among those who investigated the efficacy of training parents and their adolescents to communicate more effectively. Serna and colleagues (1991) later evaluated the effectiveness of reciprocal social communication skills training in a clinic setting. Even with homework assignments, skills learned in the clinic did not generalize to the home until the therapists began to practice with the families in their homes.

Anderson and Nuttall (1987) evaluated another approach to skills training—parent training—for three age groups of children: preschool, elementary school, and early teens. Although parent training (that is, teaching only the parents to communicate more effectively with their children) led to positive outcomes across all ages of children, the teens showed the least response to treatment and were still judged to be less cooperative and less demanding than their younger counterparts. This coincides with the research of Hall and Rose (1987), who also found that training parents in groups to communicate more effectively with their teens did indeed result in better communication than if no training was given.

Skills Training for Delinquent Teens

Several investigators (see above) have studied the effectiveness of skills training with teens who were involved with the legal system (Hudson 1989; Tannehill 1987). Guerra and Slaby (1990) used a cognitive mediation model of skills training to improve the thinking skills of adolescent offenders. After 12 sessions, those in the experimental group showed increased skills in solving social problems, decreased endorsement of beliefs supporting aggression, and decreased aggressive behavior. Their focus on cognitive skills was developmentally more in line with the operationalization stage for middle years teens, but not consistent with the more behaviorally oriented skills training used with other delinquent teens (see Hawkins et al. 1991).

In a combined family approach with parents and their delinquent adolescents, Serna and colleagues (1986) tested the efficacy of training both the teens and their parents in communication skills. Although both experimental and control teens were taught the reciprocal skills, teens whose parents were also trained in these skills maintained a much higher level of skills at the 10-month followup evaluation. Thus, even with a difficult population, these investigators found that skills training did have an impact.

SKILLS TRAINING AND ADOLESCENT DRUG ABUSE

In a review of the literature related to skills training as a treatment for adolescent drug abuse, only seven studies could be identified. Although many descriptions of prevention programs and case studies were found, only these seven studies identified skills training as either the sole treatment approach or a major component of treatment. However, the variations between studies make comparisons difficult.

In table 1, the seven identified studies are presented for comparison across targeted skills, interventions used, and reported results. Only the study by Hawkins and colleagues (1991) evaluated skills training as the primary treatment with incarcerated adolescents to increase resistance to drug use. The obvious limitation of this study for the purposes of this chapter is that these teens did not have a primary diagnosis of drug abuse. The investigators did find strong evidence that the teens in the experimental group improved their skills in avoidance of drug use, self-control, social interaction, and problem solving from pretreatment to posttreatment and were significantly better at posttest than the control teens. Their results in skills improvement are stronger than most studies due to the use of a situational role play test in which the teens were asked to respond to a series of problem situations. Although the authors caution about generalizing beyond the posttest differences, this behavioral measure lends more support to their results than many of the self-report questionnaires or general observation inventories by staff described in other studies of social skills.

In an earlier study, Hawkins and colleagues (1986) reported the results of a study with residents of therapeutic communities (TCs). Some of the study participants were adolescents, but most were not. Those who received the skills training program (called Project Skills) improved their skill levels as compared with the control group in avoiding drug use, coping with relapse, social interaction, problem solving, and coping with stress. Although this study included only a few adolescents, the specificity of the skills training program, the targeted skills, and the

TABLE 1. *Comparison of studies evaluating skills training with adolescent drug abuse and delinquency.*

	Targeted Skills of Study			Intervention Characteristics		
Authors (year)	Skills	Measures	Type	Techniques		Results
Gross and McCaul 1992	Drug resistance (several mentioned)	Youth Self-Report (Achenbach and Edelbrock 1981)	LST (Botvin 1983) adapted	13 1-hour sessions: didactic and exercises		Limited; no report of skills improvement
Friedman and Utada 1992	Drug resistance (several mentioned)	Botvin LST q. ADAD int. sch. Staff ratings	LST or value clarification + Anti-violence	Not specified		Mixed; no report of skills improvement
Hawkins et al. 1991	7 specific cognitive-behavioral skills	Audiotaped role play test: APSI	Behavioral skills training with social support	7 specific techniques in group setting		Signif. results for trained and untrained situations
Lewis et al. 1990	Several parent-teen communication skills	Videotapes of dyads performing tasks	Lewis' PBFT or Payne's TIPS program	Both approaches described in general		Both helped lower drug use; no report of skills
Yen et al. 1989	Drug and alcohol resistance (in general)	Self-report q. by staff and teen delinquents	Substance abuse program including skills training	Didactic lessons and group discussions		Staff and teens reported better knowledge, etc.
Schinke et al. 1988	Communication, coping, and decisionmaking	Interactive behavior test: written responses	Culturally sensitive group treatment	Verbal and nonverbal skills; very specific		Signif. for knowledge, skills, and attitudes
Hawkins et al. 1986	Social and network; several specific skills	Audiotaped role play test (PSI): 5 overall skills	Project Skills: 2 phases with TC clients	7 specific techniques in group setting		Signif. for all skills; no drug results reported

KEY: q = questionnaire; int. sch. = interview schedule; TC = Therapeutic Community; LST = Life Skills Training; ADAD = Adolescent Drug Abuse Diagnosis instrument; APSI = Adolescent Problem Situation Inventory; PBFT = Purdue Brief Family Therapy; TIPS = Training in Parenting Skills; PSI = Problem Situation Inventory.

reliability of skills measurement make this study easier to describe and interpret than other less specific study reports. These same investigators (Hawkins et al. 1989) reported the results of their followup evaluations and found that the trained subjects still had higher skill levels at 6 and 12 months after the end of the program than the controls, even though skill levels had decreased from posttest. The impact on drug use, however, was mixed; only the use of marijuana and amphetamines were affected by skills training. Although their data do not support the use of skills training to treat drug abuse, skills training was a component of larger treatment programs such as TCs and thus cannot be totally negated as an approach.

Gross and McCaul (1992) reported on the effectiveness of a psychoeducational group approach for children of substance abusers. They administered a 13-week intervention that included education about drugs and related topics and drug resistance skills training using the Botvin LST curriculum (Botvin 1983). Since this was a prevention intervention study, no participant could be denied treatment. Teens who had a parent who abused drugs were compared with those teens who did not report such a parent. Unfortunately, the investigators did not find any significant results between the groups at posttest or at followup. Due to the scheduling differences between treatment sites, the modifications to the skills training program, and the lack of a specific measure of social skills, extreme caution must be used when interpreting these results. Unless an experimental design was used and random assignment made to experimental and true control conditions, detected differences between groups might be due to factors other than the intervention.

Also using the Botvin LST model of skills training, Friedman and Utada (1992) reported an evaluation of skills training as compared with a second treatment of values clarification and antiviolence. Although teens were randomly assigned to treatment, the nonskills-training model resulted in more positive results on several items according to these authors. These investigators made over 100 comparisons between groups and over time (within groups analyses), but tended to use an alpha level of 0.05, thus allowing for the detection of differences or changes over time by chance. Since study measures were mainly self-report or staff ratings (although with high reliability), the results were quite mixed, and the intervention (if implemented according to Botvin) was not supported as a treatment for drug use with adjudicated teens.

In a family-based skills training study, Lewis and associates (1990) evaluated the PBFT program with drug-using adolescents and their parents. Although the approach is called family therapy, the client participants were the teens and parents rather than families. Since some measures used did include the subject's perceptions of the family, the family was used as a unit of measure as well as the individual and the parent-teen dyad. As in the Friedman and Utada study, the PBFT approach was compared with another treatment—this time the Training in Parenting Skills (TIPS) (Lewis et al. 1990). By comparing two good treatments, the investigators lessened their chances of detecting a difference at posttest; both groups were likely to improve without the experimental subjects improving significantly more than the treated controls. A greater percentage of PBFT teens reported decreased drug use than the TIPS teens, but these differences were not described in detail by the authors (e.g., by the 14 drug classes indicated on the main interview schedule).

Gilchrist and colleagues (1987) and Schinke and colleagues (1988) described another prevention intervention that included skills training as the primary intervention model. Using behavioral measures that asked the teens to write in their responses to problem situations, they adapted skills training procedures for Native American teens. At 6-month followup evaluations, teens who had received the intervention showed better knowledge and skills than control teens (tested only). This study is one of few that addresses the ethnic differences between teens.

SKILLS TRAINING WITH PREGNANT AND PARENTING TEENS

An extensive literature about pregnant teens exists with many of the recommendations emphasizing education, job training, improved opportunities for jobs, peer support, inclusion of teen fathers, sex education, and family life education (Ladner 1987). An LST program was described by Ladner (1987) as one way of helping pregnant teens to improve their lives. Little information was given about the specificity of the targeted skills or the intervention procedures used.

Kerson (1990) advocated using the behavioral skills training model developed by Hawkins and colleagues (1991), which has been titled Project ADAPT. The skills training model was integrated with other interventions appropriate for pregnant teens (e.g., case management, prenatal care) so that evaluation as a separate approach would be difficult. The Targeted Adolescent Pregnancy Substance Abuse Project provided these interventions through the obstetrical clinic of a large medical center in Seattle. Evaluation data were not reported in this brief program note.

THE CURRENT STUDY: PROJECT PALS AND SKILLS TRAINING

Skills training has not been adequately justified or evaluated for pregnant, parenting, and nonpregnant teens who are at risk for drug abuse and pregnancy. Currently, this type of study (supported by NIDA) is being conducted at the University of California, San Diego (UCSD) Medical Center. The Positive Adolescent Life Skills Project (Project PALS) was funded as one of the second group of NIDA Perinatal-20 research demonstration projects in 1990.

The purpose of Project PALS is to evaluate the effectiveness of two treatment approaches with drug-using and at-risk pregnant and nonpregnant teens. The primary treatment approach is called PALS training and focuses on two sets of skills: cognitive-behavioral (or social) skills and network skills. The secondary treatment approach is case management (sometimes called casework), originally developed to keep teens attending program activities and medical appointments. The overall goal of Project PALS is to eliminate or significantly reduce drug use and criminal activity by teens who qualify for the study.

Research Design

The PALS treatment approaches are evaluated using a two-factor randomized research design. Teens are randomly assigned by pregnancy status (pregnant/parenting or nonpregnant) to one of four conditions: PALS training and case management, PALS training only, case management only, and no treatment control group. In actuality, all teens who qualify for Project PALS and who volunteer to participate receive at least a psychoeducational class called "Facts of Life."

Potential participants are initially screened for possible participation in Project PALS using the POSIT (Rahdert 1991). Pregnant and drug-dependent teens qualify automatically due to their at-risk and addiction diagnoses, respectively. A nonpregnant, nondrug-dependent teen can qualify to participate in Project PALS in several ways. First, a nonpregnant teen can qualify by receiving a "red flag" for drug use, a score indicating possible problems, or by receiving "red flags" in two out of three key domains of the POSIT (i.e., mental health, aggressive behavior/delinquency, family relations). In addition, the teen can qualify for the study by being referred by a professional clinician or counselor who can evaluate the severity of the teen's problems. At the time of the writing of this chapter, over 475 teens had been screened for Project PALS using the POSIT. The initial data are presented in table 2. As can be seen, some small differences exist between the participants and the nonparticipants. For example, participants scored on the average about one point higher than the nonparticipants in the POSIT domains of mental health, vocational status (i.e., work involvement), and aggressive behavior/delinquency. Although these differences might be statistically significant, the concurrent validity of the POSIT has not yet been adequately supported; testing was concluded to be inappropriate for such small differences. Future analyses will be directed toward this issue.

The effectiveness of the treatments will be estimated by assessing several key variables derived from primary, secondary, and treatment concepts. The primary concepts of interest are drug use, delinquency, pregnancy, and involvement with work or school. Secondary concepts of interest are mental health, family relations, peer relations, physical health, and leisure and recreation activities. The treatment concepts are cognitive-behavioral skills and network skills. These domains correspond directly to those in the POSIT.

After both parent and teen have consented to participate, key variables are assessed before teens are randomly assigned to a treatment condition. Teens are assessed at five points during the project: pretreatment, mid-treatment (after the first 8 weeks of treatment), posttreatment (after the second 8 weeks of treatment), 3 months following treatment, and 12 months following treatment. Parents are assessed at three points: pretreatment, posttreatment, and at 12 months following treatment.

Recruitment efforts usually result in 40 to 45 teen participants every 6 months. The project is organized into waves or samples of teens who are then randomly assigned to one of the four conditions. Over time, Project PALS should have seven waves with about 300 teens who have agreed to participate. Although various recruitment strategies have been attempted, only one out of every three or four teens screened actually qualifies for the project *and* formally agrees to participate. Unless the

TABLE 2. *POSIT mean scores (SDs) and ranges for Project PALS participants versus those who did not participate.*

	Participants (N = 170)			Nonparticipants (N = 315)		
POSIT Domains (Total items/red flag)	Means (SDs)	Ranges Lo	Hi	Means (SDs)	Ranges Lo	Hi
Substance use/abuse (18/01)	1.14 (2.34)	0	16	1.23 (2.23)	0	14
Physical health (10/03)	3.29 (1.78)	0	8	3.16 (1.94)	0	10
Mental health (22/04)	8.31 (4.68)	0	19	7.39 (4.73)	0	21
Family relations (14/04)	5.98 (3.17)	0	14	5.55 (3.27)	0	14
Peer relations (14/04)	5.76 (2.24)	0	9	2.90 (2.23)	0	9
Educational status (27/06)	9.47 (3.94)	0	19	8.68 (4.03)	0	18
Vocational status (18/05)	6.73 (2.75)	0	13	5.73 (3.09)	0	13
Social skills (11/03)	3.54 (1.90)	0	10	3.29 (2.01)	0	10
Leisure/recreation (12/05)	5.52 (2.08)	0	11	4.82 (2.45)	0	11
Aggressive behavior delinquency (16/06)	5.65 (3.72)	0	15	4.74 (3.43)	0	14

teen is at least 18 years old or has legal, written proof of emancipation, parental permission is required. Even for members of an at-risk population who do not have transportation and usually lead relatively disorganized lives, parental permission has been obtained in all but a few cases. Many of the pregnant teens are recruited through the Adolescent Medicine Teen OB Clinic at the UCSD Medical Center. Others are recruited through a variety of community programs for pregnant teens. The nonpregnant teens come from numerous sources as well: school counselors, UCSD adolescent medicine clinics, juvenile probation, and previous participants. Detailed records are kept about recruitment efforts; these will be described in an upcoming study.

Through five waves, 202 teens have participated in Project PALS. Of those, 37.7 percent were African American, 13.4 percent were white, 44.1 percent were Mexican American, and the remainder (4.8 percent) were of other ethnic groups (e.g., Native American and Asian). Most were not married (96.5 percent) and most were students and/or unemployed. (Note: Although table 2 was based on the first four waves of Project PALS, the differences between participants and nonparticipants are not expected to change as the sampling frame has remained relatively constant.)

Skills Training Procedures

As with previously cited studies (Hawkins et al. 1991; Schinke et al. 1988), five specific treatment techniques are used to teach social skills: providing information, demonstrating desired behaviors by appropriate models, role playing desired behaviors by teens, giving structured and supportive feedback, and assigning homework to practice skills in the teen's natural environment. One or two adult leaders conduct the structured sessions with small groups of teens. Due to the availability of teens to participate, one skills training group is typically conducted within each of the waves.

The senior leader has been with Project PALS since the beginning and has been thoroughly trained in the skills training approach. The main goal of this type of treatment is to improve the social and network skills of the teens so that they can accomplish the five basic goals of Project PALS.

1. Assertively refuse requests to engage in high-risk behavior such as using gateway drugs (alcohol, tobacco, marijuana), using or abusing all other illegal drugs or medications, or engaging in unwanted and unprotected sexual activity.

2. Assertively handle fair and aggressive criticisms from parents, stepparents, and guardians; teachers, principals, and other school personnel; and friends, best friends, significant others, and acquaintances.

3. Increase positive support in the social network by describing who is in the social network by domain, increasing the number of positive people in the network, spending more time with positive people in positive activities, and improving social conversation skills.

4. Decrease negative support in the social network by describing negative people and negative support in the network, decreasing the number of negative people in the network, and using avoidance and coping skills to spend very little time with those who engage in high-risk behaviors.

5. Develop assertive responses using structured problem solving for difficult situations such as handling uncomfortable feelings (e.g., anger, depression) and handling new and difficult problems through preparation and reanalysis.

These goals have been operationalized into 16 90-minute sessions split between social and network skills.

A total of 14 skills corresponding to the basic 5 goals are included in the treatment program.

1. Assertive speaking (versus passive or aggressive)
2. Assertive listening (what I hear you saying is...)
3. Giving positive feedback (praise)
4. Receiving positive feedback (accepting compliments)
5. Giving negative feedback (criticizing)
6. Receiving negative feedback (handling criticism from others)
7. Social conversation with peers and adults (small talk and asking questions)
8. Handling questions for information, help, or support
9. Refusing requests to engage in high-risk behaviors (drinking alcohol, using drugs, stealing, having unprotected or unwanted sex)
10. Assertive self-talk (what you say to yourself)
11. Handling uncomfortable feelings
12. Assertive problem solving before, during, and after problems
13. Describing and assessing one's social network
14. Modifying one's network to increase positive support and decrease negative support

Each lesson focuses on a new skill and reviews previous skills that are relevant to the session topic.

The session agenda remains fairly constant throughout the 16 weeks of PALS training. Initially, the group leaders welcome all teens to the session and introduce everyone in attendance. The agenda and goals for the session are described and teens are asked for their reactions to the session topic. For social skills lessons, specific situations are the focus of training; for network skills lessons, specific domains (e.g., households, school friends) are the focus of training. PALS points are awarded for attendance and homework completion (each teen has his or her own point chart) and the leaders encourage the efforts of every teen in the group no matter how many points have been earned. After the point awards, the leaders review the homework from the previous session using a variety of procedures (e.g., dyadic preparation, role playing, demonstrations). The emphasis is on the positive (i.e., what has been accomplished) rather than what has not been accomplished.

Eventually the teens question the positive orientation of the skills training (e.g., "Why don't you ever tell us when we do bad?"). In response, the leaders review the overall philosophy of the treatment approach. Group leaders do give negative feedback to the teens, but since the criticism is based on the assertion training paradigm (Rose 1977) they often do not define the feedback as negative (e.g., "You know, Celia, if I were you, I think I would speak with a louder voice and make sure I said the words, "No, I do not do drugs" somewhere in my initial statement. What do you think?").

The session continues with the topic of the day such as situations for social skills and domains or tasks for network skills. Leaders describe the skill and ask questions to engage the teens in the topic. When the teens understand the skill, leaders model the skill either in a demonstration role play or with a completed worksheet based on their own life. Teens then practice the skills in dyads to help them prepare for practice in front of the entire group. After guided practice in dyads, the leaders practice with the teens in the large group either by working with dyads in front of the group or by building assertive components across group members. Dyads cannot return to their chairs until they can demonstrate the desired set of assertive components (parts of a social skill). After each role play, leaders and group members give the protagonist role player (who is practicing the assertive components) positive feedback and suggestions for improvement.

Following the skill lesson, homework assignments are given to extend the day's learning into the teen's natural environment. Typical assignments include daily journal entries of positive uses of skills or difficult problems encountered, feedback from social skills practice, reports from interviews with network members, or information about possible additions to their social networks (e.g., how to join an after-school club or lists of groups meeting at a local church). Each teen contracts with the group leaders to accomplish these assignments by the next session, typically in 1 week.

The final session activity is evaluation of that session by both the teens and the group leaders. Teens complete 1-page evaluation forms that ask for what they liked, what they didn't like, points for further clarification, suggestions for session improvement, and an overall rating of the usefulness of that session (from 0 for worthless to 10 for fantastic). Group leaders rate each of the teens on participation (absent, low, moderate, high) and role-playing effectiveness. Using a program catalog, teens can redeem vouchers they receive for their PALS points to purchase prize items such as school notebooks, mirrors, hair dryers, athletic gear, and so on. Prizes are distributed at the next session.

At the end of a session, teens are either taken home by program drivers or have a short break before going to a "Facts of Life" class. Snacks are available during the skills training sessions, and more food (e.g., pizza, taquitos, burritos) is available between sessions. PALS points, food, and transportation have proven to be very powerful incentives in keeping teens involved with PALS. Although the staff is experienced with teens and families, basic incentives are necessary for this population to keep coming to the sessions. Some community agencies have pointed out that this arrangement is not typical; however, for research purposes the teens are exposed to treatment so that the skills training program can be properly evaluated.

Social Skills Training

As mentioned above, group leaders focus many of the sessions on acquisition of social or cognitive-behavioral skills. To "build assertive components across group members," the leader plays the antagonist (e.g., critical parent, police officer, bothersome peer) and asks each teen in the group to respond by role playing the first component. The leader systematically role plays with each teen, giving positive feedback to every appropriate response. After each teen can demonstrate the first assertive component, the teens role play the first two components, then the first three, and so on. The idea is to build the desired social skill by teaching the components first and then asking the teen to incorporate the entire skill into his or her personal arsenal of skills.

As an example, the situation used to teach the skill of handling aggressive criticism from a parent is described.

> It is Saturday night and your parents are staying home. You ask your mother for the car so you can drive to your friend's house on the other side of town. Your mother says, "No, your friend can come here to pick you up. You think you can do just what you want when you want! You always want the car whenever you want, but never on Sunday when your father washes it! You don't take any responsibility around here for anything! You're just a lazy, selfish kid! You always want things given to you. You have never had to work for anything!"
>
> WHAT DO YOU SAY OR DO NOW?

In the session introduction, the teens are asked what they would normally do in this situation. In the skills training exercise, leaders focus on the desired behaviors and specifically on the assertive components developed based on the assertion training paradigm (Alberti and Emmons 1978) and on feedback from professionals who work with teens in a variety of settings. For this situation, the assertive components are:

1. *Seek more information* (e.g., ask a question, "Can we talk about this, Mom?");
2. *Agree with speaker* (e.g., defuse the anger, "You're right, Mom, I haven't done too well with taking care of the car.");
3. *Self-assertion* (e.g., apologize and/or state a positive goal for yourself, "I sure would like to figure out a way to do better, so I can use the car in the future."); and
4. *Describe plan* (e.g., propose a compromise through negotiation, "I'll change my plans for tonight and stay here with my friend, OK?").

Overall, 10 assertive components have been identified and grouped with the various problem situations presented in group sessions: (1) agree with speaker, (2) seek more information, (3) self-assertion, (4) describe plan, (5) self-question (cognitive), (6) describe problem, (7) evaluate consequences, (8) disagree with speaker/say no, (9) provide a reason, and

(10) cope with a mistake. Obviously, from a strictly behavioral standpoint, each of these components can also be broken into smaller units, which is sometimes done in these groups so that the teen can learn the overall skill.

This social skills training program is based on two paradigms of antecedents, behavior, and consequences (ABC). First, skills are improved using ABC operant theory in which social skills are learned through modeling, practice, and corrective feedback (positive and negative). Antecedents are defined as personal (feelings, thinking, and physical health) and social (network members and social support). Behaviors are defined as visual (e.g., gestures, body language), verbal (i.e., what one says), or vocal (e.g., intonation, loudness). Consequences are either reinforcing (usually praise statements, PALS points, etc.) or aversive (feared or actually experienced).

The other ABC paradigm is focused on the individual teen to help describe internal states—affect (feelings) or cognitions (self-talk and imagery)—and communication with the surrounding environment—behavior. To be socially skilled not only means acquisition of a behavioral skill, but also reduction of uncomfortable feelings (anxiety, depression, etc.) and self-defeating thinking. For the most part, group leaders have reported the greatest improvement in behavioral skills.

The teen group members are taught how to be aware of their affect, behavior, and cognitions and how to see their behavior in a social context (i.e., social networks and social support). When teens are taught a behavioral social skill, role play demonstrations and practice are interpersonal—that is, communication between the teen and one other person. When the teens are taught a cognitive social skill, they practice using the steps of problem solving and develop plans that may include interpersonal communication.

Network Skills

To teach teens how to improve positive social support, group leaders first teach them to describe their social networks by domain. The teens are somewhat familiar with this process, having completed a rather extensive network analysis during the pretreatment assessment (Social Network Inventory). Their initial tasks are to complete domain-specific worksheets describing network members and rating the types of support—positive and negative—given by each member. As a way of increasing positive support, homework assignments are given to interview one or two positive members in each domain about their definitions of social support. Despite concerns that teens would have difficulty with the abstract nature of network analysis, there has been continuous feedback at the end of treatment about how helpful this analysis has been (e.g., "Gee, I never even knew I had a social network!" or "I didn't realize how many losers I had in my network").

After describing their network membership and support, teens make some decisions based on PALS principles about whether or not they need to modify their networks. This network change plan is integrated with their goals for improvement of social skills and includes specific outcomes for both types of skills. Later PALS training sessions focus on network change procedures including increasing positive support by working on current relationships, increasing positive support by finding new positive people (joining school-based clubs or community organizations), decreasing negative support by reducing the frequency and intensity of contacts with negative people, and decreasing negative support by avoiding negative people. Even with this last procedure or skill (avoidance), teens initially do not think that this is possible. After some brainstorming, options are generated and integrated with the PALS suggestions on how to avoid negative people. Teens are also reminded that they can use their social skills to cope with those negative people they cannot totally avoid.

When homework assignments are reviewed for either social or network skills, all levels of completion are praised and noncompletion is used as an opportunity to solve a problem. When teens give excuses for noncompletion, the group leaders follow the PALS principle that allows the teens to participate at their own pace. Teens are encouraged to be truthful so that program staff can help them to solve their own problems and take control of their lives. The PALS model is based on individual empowerment rather than partners or family systems. For some teens, another approach may be preferable; outcome data should help to resolve this question.

ASSESSMENT OF SKILLS

Teen participants in Project PALS are assessed at five points during the project: pretreatment, midtreatment, posttreatment, 3 months following treatment, and 12 months following treatment. The first, third, and fifth sessions are defined as major assessments and all assessment instruments are administered. The second and fourth sessions were developed as minor assessments and only a subset of instruments are given. Parents are asked to participate in the three major assessment sessions and complete a smaller set of instruments than the teens. (For a list of instruments given to teens and parents, please contact the author.)

SOCIAL SKILLS ASSESSMENT

The targeted skills in PALS training are assessed with two major instruments and one minor instrument. Social skills are assessed using the Problem Situation Inventory for Teens (PSIT), a situation-based role play test. Problem situations were derived from the work of Freedman (1974) and Rosenthal (1978). Their original lists of situations were reviewed by drug treatment staff and counselors who were experienced with adolescents. Each situation was rated on relevancy to adolescents and on the perceived association with drug use. If a staff person felt that the situation was common to many adolescents—based on their professional experiences—and connected to drug use (a lack of this skill might lead to drug use), the situation was rated high on the significance scales (0 to 10). Mean scores for these situations were compared and the skill demand noted. Situations with the highest significance scores were included in the original PSIT as long as duplication of previous skills was minimized.

The final PSIT includes 20 situations and assesses skills in handling aggressive criticism; saying "no" to requests to engage in high-risk behaviors (e.g., use drugs or drink alcohol, steal, or have unprotected or unwanted sex); solving problems using assertive thinking; and coping with mistakes, failures, and negative emotions. The first two skills are mainly behavioral while the second two skills are mainly cognitive.

PSIT Administration

The PSIT is given individually to teens by a staff person who has been thoroughly trained in the proper procedures. After describing the purpose and procedures for the PSIT, the teen is given two practice situations in order to learn how to role play responses and to become accustomed to the overall process.

After each of the practice situations, the staff person asks the teen to rate the response using three questions:

1. How realistic was your response?
2. How many times has this, or something similar, happened to you before?
3. How satisfied were you with how you just handled this situation?

Once the staff person is convinced that the teen understands how to role play responses, the PSIT is administered one situation at a time and the teen's responses recorded on an audiotape player-recorder.

The recording audiotape is turned on for the duration of the session. The stimulus audiotape is played so that the teen hears problem situation #1. After the situation is played, the stimulus audiotape is turned off while the teen responds as if personally in that situation. For behavioral situations, the teen is instructed to imagine that the staff person is the antagonist while role playing the response. For cognitive situations, the teen is asked to describe how the teen would handle the situation.

After all 20 situations have been played and the teen's responses have been recorded, the teen is asked for feedback about the role play test. The staff person is asked to evaluate the validity of these responses based on the teen's responses and pre- and postrecording comments. So far, the program's staff feels that the role play test assesses skills as accurately as possible in the testing offices.

Rating Procedures

Teen responses are recorded on audiotape for later rating on three domains: assertive components (i.e., verbal content of response); response type (assertive, passive, or aggressive); and social competence (from 00 for very low to 10 for best possible response). Raters are trained to rate these social skills by listening to sample tapes recorded for training purposes. These training tapes range in difficulty so that the raters have experiences with all types of possible responses.

After 20 to 40 hours of training, raters begin listening to audiotapes randomly assigned across raters. To assess reliability of ratings, a 20 percent sample of tapes are rated again by a second rater (interrater reliability). In order to begin rating tapes, the raters must attain at least

85 percent agreement and then must average 90 percent or better as they rate the actual Project PALS audiotapes. As this chapter is being written, trained raters have completed over 500 tapes and have averaged about 93 percent agreement over the 15 weeks of ratings. The results of these ratings will be reported in an upcoming study.

Besides interrater reliability, a 10 percent sample of tapes were rerated by the same rater in order to assess intrarater reliability (rater drift). The mean scores for all raters for intrarater reliability has averaged over 90 percent during the 15 weeks of rating.

Desired Responses

For each situation, a set of desired responses was developed based on the studies and feedback from professionals. Four sets of desired assertive components were developed for the four general social skills identified earlier and labeled response codes.

For the second rating domain (response type) the teen's response was rated as passive, aggressive, or assertive (Alberti and Emmons 1978). Although the assertive rating was selected as most appropriate for most situations, the passive response was designated as most appropriate for those situations in which the teen was asked to handle aggressive criticism from an authority figure such as a parent or a teacher. Thus, in the analysis of this domain, appropriateness of response type was the primary variable of interest and the actual response classification (passive, aggressive, or assertive) was secondary.

For response competency, the raters gave a global rating from 00 to 10 to each response. Each even number and 00 were anchored with definitions that allowed a high rating of competence even if the response did not fit the previous domain classifications:

>   00 = Aggressive behavior or least acceptable
>   02 = Passive behavior or less acceptable than 04
>   04 = Ineffectual behavior, difficult to judge
>   06 = Assertive behavior, minimally acceptable
>   08 = Assertive behavior, but not the best
>   10 = Assertive behavior, seems to be the best possible

Although raters were asked to rate the response using an even number, they could use an odd number if they could not choose between two adjacent even numbers.

Data Analysis

For the initial study of PSIT results, each domain will be analyzed separately. For each global social skill (e.g., handling aggressive criticism), sets of desired response codes have been developed. For handling aggressive criticism, the ideal responses were:

01 Agree with speaker
02 Seek more information (ask a question)
03 Self-assertion
04 Describe plan

For saying "no" to requests to engage in high-risk behaviors or disagree with speaker, the ideal responses were:

02 Seek more information
08 Disagree with speaker
04 Describe plan
09 Provide a reason

For the cognitive skill of problem solving, the ideal responses were:

05 Self-question
06 Describe problem
07 Evaluate consequences
04 Describe plan

For the cognitive skill of coping with a mistake or failure, the ideal responses were:

05 Self-question
06 Describe problem
03 Self-assertion or 10 Relapse principle
04 Describe plan

The numbers to the left of each response code correspond to the numbers used in rating each teen's response.

Social Skills Checklist

As a secondary measure, the teen's parent was asked to rate the teen's social skills using the social skills checklist developed from the work of Goldstein (1989) and associates. Goldstein lists 50 social skills and groups them by level of difficulty (i.e., basic skills to advanced problem-solving skills). The parent rates the general competency of each of these 50 skills using this scale:

> N = Never good at using this skill
> R = Rarely good at using this skill
> S = Sometimes good at using this skill
> O = Often good at using this skill
> A = Always good at using this skill

Responses from the parent are compared with the teen's performance on the PSIT and used as a separate measure of change over time in the teen's social skills. The parent completes this questionnaire at pretreatment, posttreatment, and 12 months following treatment.

Social Network Inventory

The Social Network Inventory (SNI) (Hall et al. 1992) was developed to assess both the number of members in the teen's social network and the quality of relationships with these people. Initially, teens are interviewed by one of the project social workers who enters the list of network members into the computer. The interviewer organizes the list by domain to help the teen remember all those who are true network members (i.e., the teen communicates with this person at least once each month and this person makes a significant impact on the teen based on the teen's subjective judgment).

This list is retrieved into a computer program that assists the teen to rate each network member across several variables. This program can be adjusted to limit the possible responses input by the teen (e.g., only M for male and F for female are accepted as responses for gender), thus reducing error through data entry.

Demographic Ratings. The teen describes each network member according to demographic variables such as gender, age, ethnicity, and so on. Although first names and initials are used to help keep the teen focused on the correct person in their network, the names are later stripped from the program in favor of code numbers.

Negative Support Ratings. The teen next rates each network member on negative support. This includes the network member's individual drug and alcohol use, problems related to substance use, illegal activities, and activities with the teen completing the SNI.

Positive Support Ratings. The teen rates each network member on positive support, both as an individual and in relation to the teen. Positive support includes helping with personal problems, homework, or child care (if needed). Also included are meals together and conventional activities together (e.g., after school clubs, church attendance).

Overall Support Ratings. Finally, each teen is asked to rate each network member globally on positive support and negative support using a 7-point scale. Taking these first two ratings into account, the teen then rates each network member on overall support using a different rating scale that goes from -3 for most negative, to 0 for a midpoint, to +3 for most positive. The teen is instructed to assume that every network member offers both positive and negative support, but that each person can usually be classified as more positive or negative.

Data Analysis. Since the SNI was developed for this specific project, a detailed data analysis plan does not exist but is being developed. Key variables of interest have been identified in previous research as number of members overall, number of members per domain, number of peers, number of adults, number of drug or alcohol users, and so on. More complex arrangements of these variables will be developed based upon network and support theories. Data from the PSIT and the SNI are currently being rated and entered. Results will be reported by this author and other Project PALS researchers.

RECOMMENDATIONS FOR FUTURE RESEARCH

Based on the literature reviewed and on the questions still unanswered by Project PALS, the following four recommendations are made.

Validation of the Need for Skills Training

The theoretical linkage between skills training and reduced drug use has not been firmly established and needs further review. Data will be available through Project PALS to continue this process.

Development of Assessment Procedures

Unfortunately, no standardized measure exists for skills assessment. Although Hawkins (Hawkins et al. 1989), Schinke (Schinke et al. 1988), and Project PALS used a situational role play test or written response test, the arena of skills assessment has not been developed as much as skills training.

Identification of Specific Treatment Techniques

As mentioned above, skills training programs come with a variety of specific or nonspecific techniques. More work is needed to identify intervention programs labeled as skills training and possibly using the three-option system proposed.

Identification of Predictors of Success

As with any evaluation of treatment, within-groups analyses should be conducted to identify who does best with which type of approach. Treatment programs (if they are described in sufficient detail) can then be matched with clients based on their characteristics.

In conclusion, skills training—and most specifically, behavioral skills training—has shown a great deal of promise for treatment of adolescent drug abuse. Further research in this area should help to identify specifically needed skills and the most effective treatment techniques.

REFERENCES

Abikoff, H.; Ganeles, D.; Reiter, G.; Blum, C.; Foley, D.; and Klein, R.G. Cognitive training in academically deficient ADHD boys receiving stimulant medication. *J Abnorm Child Psychol* 16(4):411-432, 1988.

Alberti, R.E., and Emmons, M.L. *Your Perfect Right: A Guide to Assertive Behavior*. San Luis Obispo, CA: Impact Publishers, 1978.

Anderson, S.A., and Nuttall, P.E. Parent communications ranging across three stages of childrearing. *Fam Relat* 36:40-44, 1987.

Balassone, M.L. Multiple pregnancies among adolescents: Incidents and correlates. *Health Soc Work* 13(4):266-276, 1988.

Baum, J.G.; Clark, H.B.; McCarthy, W.; Sandler, J.; and Carpenter, R. An analysis of the acquisition and generalization of social skills in troubled youths: Combining social skills training, cognitive self-talk, and relaxation procedures. *Child Fam Behav Ther* 8(4):1-27, 1987.

Becker, J.V.; Kaplan, M.S.; and Kavoussi, R. Measuring the effectiveness of treatment for the aggressive adolescent sexual offender. *Ann N Y Acad Sci* 528:215-222, 1988.

Bennett, T., and Morgan, R.L. Teaching interaction skills to adolescent mothers. *Soc Work Educ* 10(3):143-151, 1988.

Botvin, G.J. *Life Skills Training: Teachers' Manual.* New York: Smithfield Press, 1983.

Botvin, G.J. Prevention of adolescent substance abuse through the development of personal and social competence. In: Glynn, T.J.; Leukefeld, C.G.; and Ludford, J.P., eds. *Preventing Adolescent Drug Abuse: Intervention Strategies.* National Institute on Drug Abuse Research Monograph No. 47. DHHS Pub. No. (ADM)83-1280. Washington, DC: Supt. of Docs.,U.S. Govt. Print. Off., 1985.

Botvin, G.J., and Botvin, E.M. Adolescent tobacco, alcohol, and drug abuse: Prevention strategies, empirical findings, and assessment issues. *Dev Behav Pediatr* 13(4):290-301, 1992.

Botvin, G.J., and Wills, T.A. Personal and social skills training: Cognitive-behavioral approaches to substance abuse prevention. In: Ball, C., and Battjes, R., eds. *Prevention Research: Deterring Drug Abuse Among Children and Adolescents.* National Institute on Drug Abuse Research Monograph No. 63. DHHS Pub. No. (ADM)87-1334. Washington, DC: Supt. of Docs., U.S. Govt. Print. Off., 1985.

Boyer, C.B., and Kegeles, S.M. AIDS risk and prevention among adolescents. *Soc Sci Med* 33(1):11-23, 1991.

Brown, J.E., and Mann, L. Decision-making, competence and self-esteem: A comparison of parents and adolescents. *J Adolesc* 14:363-371, 1991.

Davidge, A.M., and Forman, S.G. Psychological treatment of adolescent substance abusers: A review. *Child Youth Serv Rev* 10:43-55, 1988.

Davis, S. Helping young girls come to terms with sexual abuse. *Brit J Occup Ther* 53(3):109-111, 1990.

Dryfoos, J.G. Adolescents at risk: A summation of work in the field-programs and policies. *J Adolesc Health* 12:630-637, 1991.

Duran, E. Developing social skills in autistic adolescents with severe handicaps and limited English competencies. *Education* 107(2):203-207, 1986.

Dusenbury, L., and Botvin, G.J. Substance abuse prevention: Competence enhancement and the development of positive life options. *J Addict Dis* 11(3):29-45, 1992.

Dusenbury, L.; Botvin, G.J.; and James-Ortiz, S. The primary prevention of adolescent substance abuse through the promotion of personal and social competence. *Prev Hum Serv* 7(1):201-224, 1990.

Epstein, M.H., and Cullinan, D. Effective social skills curricula for behaviorally disordered students. *Pointer* 31(2):21-24, 1987.

Fine, S.; Forth, A.; Gilbert, M.; and Haley, G. Group therapy for adolescent depressive disorder: A comparison of social skills and therapeutic support. *J Am Acad Child Adolesc Psychiatry* 30(1):79-85, 1991.

Forman, S.G., and Linney, J.A. School-based prevention of adolescent substance abuse: Programs, implementation and future directions. *Sch Psychol Rev* 17(4):550-558, 1988.

Foxx, R.M.; Kyle, M.S.; Faw, G.D.; and Bittle, R.G. Teaching a problem solving strategy to inpatient adolescents: Social validation, maintenance, and generalization. *Child Fam Behav Ther* 11(3/4):71-88, 1989.

Freedman, B. "An Analysis of Social Behavioral Skill Deficits in Delinquent and Non Delinquent Boys." Ph.D. diss., University of Wisconsin, 1974.

Friedman, A.S., and Utada, A.T. Effects of two group interaction models on substance-using adjudicated adolescent males. *J Community Psychol* 106-117, 1992.

Gerstein, A.I. A psychiatric program for deaf patients. *Psychiatr Hosp* 19(3):125-128, 1988.

Gilchrist, L.D.; Schinke, S.P.; Timble, J.E.; and Cvetkovich, G.T. Skills enhancement to prevent substance abuse among American Indian adolescents. *Int J Addict* 22(9):869-879, 1987.

Goldstein, A.P. Refusal skills: Learning to be positively negative. *J Drug Educ* 19(3):271-283, 1989.

Gross, J., and McCaul, M.E. An evaluation of a psychoeducational and substance abuse risk reduction intervention for children of substance abusers. *J Community Psychol* 21:75-87, 1992.

Guerra, N.G., and Slaby, R.G. Cognitive mediators of aggression in adolescent offenders: 2. Intervention. *Dev Psychol* 26(2):269-277, 1990.

Hains, A.A., and Herman, L.P. Social cognitive skills and behavioral adjustment of delinquent adolescents in treatment. *J Adolesc* 12:323-328, 1989.

Hall, J.A.; Palinkas, L.A.; and Noel, P.J. Social network inventory. Unpublished instrument description. San Diego: University of California, 1992.

Hall, J.A., and Rose, S.D. Evaluation of parent training in groups for parent-adolescent conflict. *Soc Work Res Abs* 23(2):3-8, 1987.

Hansen, W.B. School-based substance abuse prevention: A review of the state of the art in curriculum, 1980-1990. *Health Educ Res* 7(3):403-430, 1992.

Hardoff, D., and Chigier, E. Developing community-based services for youth with disabilities. *Pediatrician* 18(2):157-162, 1991.

Hawkins, J.D.; Catalano, R.F.; Gillmore, M.R.; and Wells, E.A. Skills training for drug abusers: Generalization, maintenance, and effects on drug use. *J Consult Clin Psychol* 57(4):559-563, 1989.

Hawkins, J.D.; Catalano, R.F.; and Wells, E.A. Measuring effects of a skills training intervention for drug abusers. *J Consult Clin Psychol* 54(5):661-664, 1986.

Hawkins, J.D.; Jenson, J.M.; Catalano, R.F.; and Wells, E.A. Effects of a skills training intervention with juvenile delinquents. *Res Soc Work Pract* 1(2):107-121, 1991.

Hawkins, J.D.; Lishner, D.M.; Catalano, R.F.; and Howard, M.O. Childhood predictors of adolescent substance abuse: Toward an empirically grounded theory. In: Jones, C.L., and Battjes, R.J., eds. *Etiology of Drug Abuse: Implications for Prevention*. National Institutes on Drug Abuse Research Monograph No. 56. DHHS Pub. No.(ADM)85-1335. Washington, DC: Supt. of Docs., U.S. Govt. Print. Off., 1985. pp.75-126.

Hinderscheit, L.R., and Reichle, J. Teaching direct select color encoding to an adolescent with multiple handicaps. *Augmentative Alternative Commun* 3(3):137-142, 1987.

Hostler, S.L.; Gressard, R.P.; Hassler, C.R.; and Linden, P.G. Adolescent Autonomy Project: Transition skills for adolescents with physical disabilities. *Child Health Care* 18(1):12-18, 1989.

Hudson, B.L. Social skills training in the probation service. *Issues Crim Legal Psychol* 14:58-68, 1989.

Inderbitzen-Pisaruk, H., and Foster, S.L. Adolescent friendships and peer acceptance: Implications for social skills training. *Clin Psychol Rev* 10:425-439, 1990.

Jackson, M.A. The LD adolescent at risk: Developmental tasks, social competence, and communication effectiveness. *J Read Writ Learn Disabil Inter* 3(3):241-257, 1987.

Jamison, R.N.; Lambert, E.W.; and McCloud, D.J. Social skills training with hospitalized adolescents: An evaluative experiment. *Adolescence* 21(81):55-65, 1986.

Kerson, T.S. Targeted adolescent pregnancy substance abuse project. *Health Soc Work* 15:73-74, 1990.

Kifer, R.E.; Lewis, M.A.; Green, D.R.; and Phillips, E.L. Training predelinquent youths and their parents to negotiate conflict situations. *J Appl Behav Anal* 7:357-364, 1974.

Kissman, K. Parent skills training: Expanding school-based services for adolescent mothers. *Res Soc Work Prac* 2(2):161-171, 1991.

Krasnegor, N.A. Adolescent drug use: Suggestions for future research. In: Rahdert, E.R., and Grabowski, J., eds. *Adolescent Drug Abuse: Analyses of Treatment Research*. National Institute on Drug Abuse Research Monograph No. 77. NIH Pub. No. 94-3712. Washington, DC: Supt. of Docs., U.S. Govt. Print. Off., 1988.

Kumpfer, K.L. Prevention of alcohol and drug abuse: A critical review of risk factors and prevention strategies. In: Shaffer, D.; Philips, I.; and Enzer, N.B., eds. *Prevention of Mental Disorders, Alcohol and Other Drug Use in Children and Adolescents*. OSAP Prevention Monograph 2. Rockville, MD: Department of Health and Human Services, 1989. pp. 309-371.

Ladner, J.A. Black teenage pregnancy: A challenge for educators. *J Negro Educ* 56(1):53-63, 1987.

LaFromboise, T.D., and Bigfoot, D.S. Cultural and cognitive considerations in prevention of American Indian adolescent suicide. *J Adolesc* 11(2):139-153, 1988.

Lewis, R.A.; Piercy, F.P.; Spenkle, D.H.; and Trepper, T.S. Family-based interventions for helping drug-abusing adolescents. *J Adolesc Res* 5(1):82-95, 1990.

Lichstein, K.L.; Wagner, M.T.; Krisak, J.; and Steinberg, F. Stress management for acting-out, inpatient adolescents. *J Child Adolesc Psychother* 4(1):19-31, 1987.

Miller, W.R. The effectiveness of treatment for substance abuse: Reasons for optimism. *J Subst Abuse Treat* 9:93-102, 1992.

Mittl, V.F., and Robin, A. Acceptability of alternative interventions for parent-adolescent conflict. *Behav Asses* 9:417-428, 1987.

Noble, P.S.; Adams, G.R.; and Openshaw, D.K. Interpersonal communication in parent-adolescent dyads: A brief report on the effects of a social skills training program. *J Fam Psychol* 2(4):483-494, 1989.

Oswald, L.K.; Lingnugaris-Kraft, B.; and West, R. The effects of incidental teaching on the generalized use of social amenities at school by a mildly handicapped adolescent. *Educ Treat Child* 13(2):142-152, 1990.

Rahdert, E.R., ed. *The Adolescent Assessment/Referral System Manual*. DHHS Pub. No. (ADM)91-1735. Rockville, MD: National Institute on Drug Abuse, 1991.

Rose, S.D. *Group Therapy: A Behavioral Approach*. Englewood Cliffs, NJ: Prentice-Hall, Inc., 1977.

Rosenthal, L. "The Development and Evaluation of the Problem Inventory for Adolescent Girls." Ph.D. diss., The University of Wisconsin, 1978.

Schinke, S.P.; Orlandi, M.A.; Botvin, G.J.; Gilchrist, L.D.; Trimble, J.E.; and Locklear, V.S. Preventing substance abuse among American-Indian adolescents: A bicultural competence skills approach. *J Counsel Psychol* 35(1):87-90, 1988.

Serna, L.A.; Schumaker, J.B.; Hazel, J.S.; and Sheldon, J.B. Teaching reciprocal social skills to parents and their delinquent adolescents. *J Clin Child Psychol* 15(1):64-77, 1986.

Serna, L.A.; Schumaker, J.B.; Sherman, J.A.; and Sheldon, J.B. In-home generalization of social interactions in families of adolescents with behavior problems. *J Appl Behav Anal* 24:733-746, 1991.

Shorts, I.D. Community-based training programmes for young offenders: Perceptions of programme impact. *Ir J Psychol Med* 6(1):26-29, 1989.

Smith, R.E., and Johnson, J. An organizational empowerment approach to consultation in professional baseball. *Sport Psychol* 4(4):347-357, 1990.

Sprunger, B., and Pellaux, D. Skills for adolescence: Experience with the International Lions-Quest Program. *Crisis* 10(1):88-104, 1989.

Svec, H., and Bechard, J. An introduction to metabehavioral model with implications for social skills training for aggressive adolescents. *Psychol Rep* 62:19-22, 1988.

Tannehill, R.L. Employing a modified positive peer culture treatment approach in a state youth center. *J Offender Consel Serv Rehab* 12(1):113-129, 1987.

Tisdelle, D.A., and St. Lawrence, J.S. Adolescent interpersonal problem-solving training: Social validation and generalization. *Behav Ther* 19:171-182, 1988.

Walker, E.N. The Community Intensive Treatment for Youth program: A specialized community-based program for high risk youth in Alabama. *Law Psychol Rev* 13:175-199, 1989.

ACKNOWLEDGMENTS

This chapter was prepared with support from National Institute on Drug Abuse grant DA-06911-03. Owen Groze and Mark Fortney assisted with compilation and analysis of literature. Christopher Carswell provided editorial suggestions and advice. Christopher Miller assisted with data analysis.

AUTHOR

James A. Hall, Ph.D., LCSW
Associate Professor
School of Social Work

and

Director of Practice Research
UIHC Department of Social Service
University of Iowa
North Hall, Room 308
Iowa City, IA 52242

Pharmacotherapy for Adolescents with Psychoactive Substance Use Disorders

Yifrah Kaminer

Adolescence is a crucial developmental phase for the onset and diagnosis of psychiatric disorders including psychoactive substance use disorders (PSUD) (American Psychiatric Association 1987). The co-occurrence of PSUD with other psychiatric disorders has been termed "dual diagnosis."

Psychiatric comorbidity is highly prevalent among children and adolescents in the general population (Anderson et al. 1987). Dual-diagnosed adolescents constitute the largest subgroup of adolescents with PSUD in clinical settings (Bukstein et al. 1992; Kaminer 1991).

The literature on treatments of adolescents diagnosed with PSUD is replete with descriptions of treatment philosophies, modalities, and programs. Very little empirical research on treatment outcome has been reported, and virtually no studies have yet documented the differential efficacy of various therapies or packages of treatment components (Kaminer 1994*a*). Pharmacotherapy for PSUD in this age group appears to be the most neglected therapeutic modality.

In this chapter, relevant literature on adult-oriented psychopharmacotherapy is used and relied on whenever necessary. These publications serve as a basis for generalization; however, these generalizations are made cautiously and their limitations noted whenever possible. Although this chapter deals exclusively with pharmacological treatment, it should be noted that a comprehensive treatment plan using a variety of individualized therapeutic interventions (e.g., behavioral-cognitive therapy, self-help groups) must be designed to meet the needs of the adolescent in order to achieve a beyond-threshold treatment dosage effect (a descriptive term encompassing frequency, quality, quantity, type, and specificity of intervention) (Kaminer et al. 1992*a*).

The objectives of this chapter are fourfold: to improve understanding of the reasons for the scarcity of publications on and research of pharmacological interventions of PSUD in adolescents; to review the present knowledge concerning treatment outcome and its relationship with pharmacotherapy of adolescents with PSUD; to provide an update on the pharmacotherapy for PSUD and dual diagnosis in adolescents; and to outline suggestions for future directions for the development of pharmacotherapies for this age group.

DIFFICULTIES IN THE DEVELOPMENT OF PHARMACOTHERAPY FOR ADOLESCENTS WITH PSUD

In contrast to the increased acceptance of pharmacotherapy in adults with PSUD, there has been no systemic research evaluating the efficacy and safety of psychotropic medications in the treatment of adolescents with PSUD.

Pharmacotherapy in this population may be viewed as a new subset of pediatric psychopharmacology (PP) and has met with similar difficulties in developing and achieving recognition. Most of the dissimilarities between pharmacotherapy of adolescents with PSUD (with or without psychiatric comorbidity) and PP stem from the adult-targeted, disease model-oriented treatment approach. This approach has dominated the addiction research field for almost 60 years and lacks the age-appropriate developmental perspective needed to meet the needs of adolescents.

Several factors contribute to the present limited scope of PP clinical research and treatment. Biderman (1992) noted the problematic controversy regarding the use of psychotropic agents in the treatment of individuals who have not completed their physical and psychosocial development. Furthermore, most parents of adolescents with PSUD face a dilemma: Is their offspring's potential to outgrow early onset disorder without pharmacological intervention a realistic expectation, or merely a form of denial and rationalization that may permit the disorder to take a chronic and debilitating course across age groups? Unfavorable public perceptions of PP are related to concerns about the inappropriate use of medications, especially in institutional patients (Biderman 1992). Criticism by the media or religious groups, which promote the myth that psychopharmacological treatment is an experimental approach or at best a means of last resort (e.g., stimulants for attention deficit-hyperactivity disorder (ADHD)), has created a significant public image problem.

Lack of clarity in parents and children's understanding of the efficacy and risks of pharmacotherapy has led to the emergence of ethical issues that include the rights of minors to refuse treatment (e.g., medications) at certain treatment modalities and the use of inactive placebos in adolescents in need of pharmacotherapy while participating in research trials.

There is a relatively incomplete knowledge of pediatric pharmacokinetics and a lack of clear approvals or guidelines from the Food and Drug Administration (FDA) for the use of most psychotropics in minors (Biderman 1992). A continuing decrease in the number of adolescents hospitalized and a shortened length of stay leading to closure of inpatient units, combined with a reduction in research support, have had a negative impact on efforts to provide precise monitoring of adolescents in treatment based on lengthy delivery of psychopharmacological treatment. Moreover, the number of pediatric psychopharmacologists is too small to meet the needs of the field and to continuously advocate for its national recognition.

As noted above, the unique factors of pharmacological treatment of adolescents with PSUD that differentiate this subset from PP at large are embedded in philosophical, conceptual, and economical aspects that create a special environment and politics of treatment (Hoffmann et al. 1987). Hoffmann and colleagues (1987) referred to the difficulty of self-help groups such as Alcoholics Anonymous (AA) to recognize and accept the importance of accurate medical and psychiatric differential diagnoses and the need for pharmacotherapy that may accompany PSUD with or without psychiatric comorbidity. Sponsors of dual-diagnosed adolescents in self-help groups may have a strong objection to any medication, even those without known abuse potential (e.g., lithium, neuroleptics), thus exposing the adolescent to increased risk for relapse of both disorders (Kaminer 1994*a*).

PHARMACOTHERAPY AND TREATMENT OUTCOME

A study on treatment outcome of adolescents with PSUD was conducted in a unit for the dual diagnosed (Kaminer et al. 1992*a*). Staff, treatment graduates, and dropouts' perceptions of the value of treatment components in the recovery process were examined. Kaminer and colleagues (1992*a*) hypothesized that the smaller the discrepancy between staff and patient's perception of the value of treatment variables, the higher the likelihood the patient would complete treatment. Ten therapeutic modalities including pharmacotherapy were employed in the program. Psychotropic medications were administered to patients as necessary based on strict medical criteria and usually only after a medication-free evaluation phase. Comparison was made using a standard rank-ordering system. The data were analyzed using the binomial theorem to investigate group differences.

Staff ranked psychotropic medications and substance abuse education equally as the most important therapeutic components (Kaminer et al. 1992*a*). In contrast, the two groups of patients ranked medications at the bottom of the list. The sharp disagreement in perceptions of the value of medications for treatment outcome, particularly between staff and treatment graduates, is intriguing because even the inactive treatment effect (i.e., placebo effect) is accepted as a beneficial intervention, especially in short-term treatment, when recommended by a trusted therapist. Also, treatment experiences and patients' perception of the treatment environment are strong predictors of outcome (Miller 1985). Conversely, patients' misconception of treatment (i.e., the level of discrepancy in treatment expectations) is negatively correlated with treatment retention (Zweben and Li 1981).

Thus, regardless of the disagreement about the role of medications in the therapeutic process, other therapeutic interventions in the treatment program contributed to create a beyond-threshold treatment dosage effect. This effect is critical in achieving patient-treatment matching and completion of planned treatment. In this study, a contract-based individual treatment plan, therapeutic group meetings (modified psychotherapeutic process focusing on the "here and now"), and educational counseling were perceived by staff and graduates to be significantly important (clinically and statistically) for completion of the treatment program.

Kaminer and colleagues (1992*b*) reported another study that prospectively assessed treatment attrition in the same cohort of patients previously assessed. The authors found that mood and adjustment disorders as defined in the "Diagnostic and Statistical Manual of Mental Disorders," 3d. ed., rev. (DSM-III-R) were more prevalent among graduates, whereas dropouts were more likely to be assigned a conduct disorder diagnosis (American Psychiatric Association 1987). A higher percentage of treatment graduates than dropouts received psychotropic medications (28 percent versus 7 percent). Kaminer and colleagues (1992*b*) suggested that a mood or adjustment disorder protects the adolescent with or without a comorbid conduct disorder from terminating treatment, either because of the nature of the disorder or the patient's perception of symptoms of these disorders. Use of psychotropic medications for the treatment of these disorders in adolescents is supported by observations that administering medications has improved the likelihood of treatment completion in adult alcoholics (Gerard and Saenger 1966; Smart and Gray 1978).

DRUG-SPECIFIC PHARMACOTHERAPY

To consider pharmacological intervention in the presence of drug-specific pathopsychophysiological symptoms, it is imperative to comprehend what is known about the specific origin of these symptoms including the body organs, brain structures, and behavioral mechanisms involved. It is also of great importance to define the goals of treatment (e.g., complete abstinence only, psychosocial adaptation) and to recognize the fact that polysubstance abuse is common and may hamper any treatment focusing only on the abused drugs.

Detoxification from opioids, alcohol, barbiturates, benzodiazepines, and other psychoactive agents needs to follow rigorous procedures in a timely fashion. There have been no empirical studies on detoxification of adolescents with PSUD; however, clinical experience suggests that there is no reason to assume that this therapeutic process should be any different from that of adults with PSUD as long as legal consent is obtained (Kaminer 1994*a*). Therefore, detoxification procedures are not reviewed in this chapter.

There are four drug-specific pharmacological strategies that are commonly used for the treatment of PSUD (Kaminer 1992*a*): make psychoactive substance administration aversive (e.g., disulfiram for alcohol dependence); substitute for the psychoactive substance (e.g., methadone for heroin dependence); block the reinforcing effects of the psychoactive substance (e.g., naltrexone for opioids abuse); and relieve craving/withdrawal (e.g., clonidine for heroin dependence, desipramine for cocaine dependence). To employ any one of these approaches, an appropriate agent must be identified and its appeal increased by promoting a feeling of well-being that encourages the patient to comply with the assigned treatment.

This chapter reviews pharmacotherapy for the abuse and dependence of nicotine, alcohol, cocaine, and opioids, with special emphasis on adolescents' needs.

Cigarette Smoking (Nicotine)

The Annual National High School Senior Survey (Johnston et al. 1992) provides epidemiological data regarding psychoactive substance use. No clinical implications can be directly drawn from this study. However, based on the relative stability of 30-day prevalence in the daily use of half a pack or more of cigarettes over the last 5 years and the high addictive potential of nicotine, it appears that nicotine dependence among adolescents is common.

Pharmacotherapy of nicotine dependence uses the strategy of finding a substitute for the psychoactive substance. The invention of nicotine gum and its successor, the nicotine transdermal patch, as self-administering agents was a breakthrough in the treatment of cigarette dependence. The efficacy of these agents doubled success rates of treatment programs from about 15 percent (validated long-term abstinence) to about 30 percent (West 1992). Furthermore, their success in reducing nicotine craving improved even more when behavioral or cognitive therapy sessions were also part of a comprehensive treatment plan (Lichtenstein and Glasgow 1992). Only one study of 612 subjects who had received a prescription for nicotine gum included an unknown number of 15- to 18-year-old adolescents (Johnson et al. 1992). No special reference was made regarding the characteristics and treatment outcome of these adolescents in the outpatient clinic sample studied.

Side effects of nicotine gum include bad taste and sore mouth and jaws because it is hard to chew. The transdermal patch may increase nicotine toxicity, particularly if the person continues to smoke. It can irritate the user's skin and disrupt sleep if left on for 24 hours. Also, some people find it difficult to wean themselves off it (Lichtenstein and Glasgow 1992). Neither treatment should be used by an active smoker. Unfortunately, pharmaceutical companies advertised these agents as recommended for decrease as well as discontinuation of smoking. Smoking during nicotine replacement therapy may induce nicotine intoxication.

No specific contraindications for the use of the nicotine gum or patch by adolescents with nicotine dependence are known. It appears that any therapeutic trial should start as a carefully designed case study on an individual basis for consenting adolescents with severe dependence.

New developments in the nicotine substitute field include nicotine inhalers and nicotine sprays (Tonnesen et al. 1993). These devices will offer the person the choice of when and where to use them (similar to cigarette smoking). A potential concern could be that it would be difficult to quit using the device.

Alcohol

Alcohol dependence has been characterized as a set of disorders known as the alcoholisms (Jacobson 1976), a term that reflects its phenomenologic and etiologic heterogeneity (Gilligan et al. 1987). The presumed heterogeneity of patients' typologies led to the development of research attempting to subtype alcoholics. This effort resulted in two classifications: type 1 and, more importantly for adolescents, type 2 (male-limited) alcoholism (Cloninger 1987). Type 2 alcoholism may be first diagnosed in adolescence. It is characterized by an early onset of spontaneous alcohol-seeking behavior, fighting, and arrests when drinking. Three personality traits characterize type 2 patients: high novelty seeking, low harm avoidance, and low reward dependence. Buydens-Branchey and colleagues (1989*a*) reported that patients with early-onset alcoholism were incarcerated more frequently for violent crimes, were three times as likely to be depressed, and were four times more likely to have attempted suicide as patients with late-onset alcoholism (type 1-milieu limited) according to Cloninger (1987). The typologic distinction drawn by these investigators resembles the typology identified by Babor and colleagues (1992) in the areas of familial alcoholism, antisocial behavior, and comorbid mood disorder. Furthermore, Buydens-Branchey and colleagues (1989*b*) reported an inverse relationship between a measure of central nervous system (CNS) serotonergic activity and measures of depression and aggression in the early-onset group. Based on the dichotomous typology of alcoholism supported by these data, treatment planning and objectives need to take into consideration the heterogeneity of patient populations.

The most common unidimensional pharmacotherapy to prevent alcohol consumption is aversive therapy with disulfiram. This antidipsotropic agent produces a reaction with ethanol by inhibiting the liver enzyme aldehyde dehydrogenase, which catalyzes the oxidation of aldehyde (the major metabolic product of ethanol) to acetate. The resulting accumulation of acetaldehyde is responsible for the aversive symptoms. These symptoms are expected to be cognitively paired with ethanol consumption and create negative reinforcement for alcohol drinking behavior. The success of this debatable pharmacotherapy has been mediocre at best (Alterman et al. 1991).

Aversive therapy in children and adolescents has always been controversial and has been used only in extreme cases of violent behavior or severe self-injurious behavior among the mentally retarded (Council on Scientific Affairs 1987). Due to ethical and legal reasons, it appears unlikely that aversive pharmacotherapy will be used in alcohol-dependent adolescents.

Recent findings in the pharmacotherapy of alcoholism generated interest in the effect of alcohol consumption on opioid receptors and the potential use of an opioid antagonist such as naltrexone to block the reinforcing properties of alcohol (O'Malley et al. 1992). The serotonergic system also appears to play a role in the pathophysiology of alcohol dependence. Fluoxetine, a selective antagonist, was found to significantly reduce alcohol consumption (Naranjo et al. 1990). According to the results of a study by Buydens-Branchey and colleagues (1989*b*), it could be of heuristic value to determine whether adolescent males with type 2 active alcoholism would benefit from pharmacotherapy with serotonin uptake antagonists because serotonin is the neuromodulator affecting behavioral inhibition (Cloninger 1987).

Cocaine

Despite encouraging reports that adolescents continued for the sixth consecutive year to move away from the use of cocaine (Johnston et al. 1992), there is still a need for efficacious interventions to address psychophysiological changes secondary to cocaine dependence and withdrawal symptoms resulting from cessation after chronic use.

The neurotransmitter dopamine (DA) emerged as the leading catecholamine responsible for the specific reinforcing effects of cocaine and the suggested mechanisms for craving/withdrawal (Kosten 1990). Neuroleptics were hypothesized to block the cocaine-induced euphoria initiated by mesolimbic and mesocortical neuroanatomic reward pathways, leading to attenuation of cocaine self-administration by animals (Gawin et al. 1989*a*). However, neuroleptics are known to produce anhedonia and extrapyramidal side effects in humans, and compliance has been problematic. Flufenthixol decanoate is a neuroleptic agent that was reported in an open-label trial to rapidly decrease cocaine craving and use and increase the average time retained in treatment (Gawin et al. 1989*a*). It has been postulated that compliance with this medication would be satisfactory due to the lack of anhedonic effect.

Sporadic case reports about the capacity of lithium to block cocaine-induced euphoria were not confirmed even in cocaine abusers with bipolar spectrum disorders (Nunes et al. 1990). The pharmacological treatment strategy for cocaine abuse has been focused mainly on the reduction/elimination of cocaine abstinence-related craving. This is essential to improve relapse prevention rates by reducing treatment attrition and enabling the introduction of additional therapeutic interventions.

Based on the theory that chronic stimulant use results in depletion of DA and reduction in dopaminergic activity, it was hypothesized that cocaine craving would be reduced by increasing dopaminergic stimulation. There is sparse evidence to support this depletion therapy. However, the following direct and indirect dopamimetic agents have shown some efficacy in open-label trials: levodopa, carbidopa, bromocriptine, amantadine, methylphenidate, and mazindol (Meyer 1992). Another theory that appears to have superior neurobiological support suggests that craving is mediated by supersensitivity of presynaptic inhibiting dopaminergic autoreceptors. The tricyclic antidepressant desipramine was found to desensitize these receptors and facilitate cocaine abstinence by attenuating craving for 7 to 14 days from the onset of therapy. Gawin and colleagues (1989*b*) reported a 6-week double-blind random assignment study of desipramine treatment for cocaine craving. The treated outpatient cocaine abusers were more frequently abstinent, were abstinent for longer periods, and had less craving for cocaine compared with lithium- and placebo-treated patients. Kosten and colleagues (1992) presented 6-month followup data on 43 of the 72 patients originally reported by Gawin and colleagues (1989*b*). It was found that self-reported cocaine abstinence during the 6-month period was significantly greater in patients treated with desipramine (44 percent) than in those treated with lithium (19 percent) or placebo (27 percent).

There has been only one reported case of facilitation of cocaine abstinence in an adolescent by desipramine (Kaminer 1992*a*). A 6-month followup utilizing the Teen Addiction Severity Index (T-ASI) (Kaminer et al. 1991) confirmed continued abstinence and progress in other life domains. In this case desipramine treatment was instituted for the treatment of three psychiatric disorders simultaneously: cocaine dependence, major depressive disorder (MDD), and ADHD, thus preventing polypharmacy. The intensity of cocaine craving was reported to be independent of depression during the first week in newly abstinent chronic cocaine abusers (Ho et al. 1991). This finding suggests that withdrawal-related dysphoria during the first week of abstinence will not respond to the antidepressant properties of desipramine and may be alleviated earlier than the depressive symptoms of a patient diagnosed as cocaine-dependent with MDD. The response to desipramine may also differentiate a cocaine-dependent adolescent from a dual-diagnosed individual. It is recommended that the conclusions drawn from a single case study be generalized with caution.

Two cocaine-dependent adolescents were recently treated by the author (Kaminer 1994*b*). One patient's clinical symptoms responded favorably to desipramine for about 30 days whereupon the patient dropped out of treatment. The second patient developed postural hypotension and the medication was discontinued. Additional side effects of desipramine are reviewed later in this chapter.

The author's case study did not confirm the three-stage model of cocaine abstinence (i.e., crash, withdrawal, extinction) as suggested by Gawin and Kleber (1986). A two-stage process of cocaine craving response to treatment by desipramine characterized this case. Weddington and colleagues (1990) described similar findings in a study of 12 adult cocaine addicts.

A recent development in the pharmacological treatment of cocaine dependence is the use of carbamazepine in open-label trials (Halikas et al. 1990). The theoretical rationale for this intervention is that the agent blocks cocaine-induced kindling and increases DA concentration. The pattern of continued cocaine use despite decreased craving and dysphoria may suggest inherent limitations of the DA agonist approach to cocaine pharmacotherapy. Furthermore, DA system dysregulation is probably not the only mechanism underlying cocaine addiction. Many cocaine abusers are polysubstance abusers (heroin and methadone included). Buprenorphine, an opioid used for the treatment of cocaine and opioid abuse (Kosten et al. 1989), is discussed below.

Stimulants have proven to be useful for the treatment of children and adolescents diagnosed with ADHD. The pharmacokinetic similarities between an illegal stimulant such as cocaine and therapeutic stimulants such as methylphenidate, magnesium pemoline, and dextroamphetamine led to the assumption that they might be useful for the treatment of cocaine abuse. Also, it was suggested that adult abuse of cocaine could be attributed to a residual type of ADD (Weiss et al. 1985). Neither assumption was confirmed (Kaminer 1992*b*). The abuse potential of therapeutic stimulants deserves comment. Regardless of the common perception that these agents may be abused by children and adolescents, only two cases of methylphenidate abuse by patients diagnosed with ADHD were reported (Kaminer 1992*b*).

It is noteworthy that cocaine addicts show more conditioned responses than any other drug addicts. It is hypothesized that many repetitions cause release of the neurotransmitter DA that may be responsible for both the reinforcing effects of cocaine and for craving and withdrawal phenomenology. The memory of the experience alone, even with no cocaine present, may initiate DA release equal to the cocaine effect and may lead to subsequent craving and withdrawal (O'Brien, personal communication, December 1992). A combination of pharmacologic intervention and behavioral and cognitive therapy should be further explored for the treatment of cocaine abuse in adolescents.

Finally, as an alternative to therapeutic approaches based on the pharmacology of the cocaine receptor, the delivery process of cocaine could be interrupted. Antibodies that may catalyze degradation of cocaine to an inactive form followed by release of the inactive products and continued ability for further binding could provide a treatment for cocaine dependence by blunting reinforcement (Landry et al. 1993). This form of passive immunization by an artificial enzyme could provide a new method of treatment.

Opioids

Methadone maintenance (MM) is a common form of opioid substitution therapy and is usually reserved for the treatment of adult heroin addicts. The desired result of MM is threefold: to prevent the onset of opioid abstinence syndrome, to eliminate drug hunger or craving, and to block the euphoric effects of any illicitly self-administered opioids. As a general rule, patients who have been dependent on opioids for less than 1 year or who have not previously made any attempt at withdrawal are not appropriate candidates for prolonged opioid maintenance (Jaffe 1986). MM should not rely on methadone administration alone, even in adequate daily dosage, to be a magic bullet for heroin addiction. McLellan and colleagues (1993) reported that patients in an MM program who also received a psychosocial services package fared better than two other groups of patients who received counseling in addition to MM, or MM only.

MM, not opioid detoxification, is the treatment of choice for pregnant adolescents who abuse heroin. This pharmacotherapy given daily eliminates the danger of contracting AIDS from a contaminated needle. It also ensures a relatively stable plasma level of the drug as compared with heroin, which reduces the fetus' risk of developing intrauterine distress. Heroin also has a short half-life that causes abrupt changes in plasma level (Finnegan and Kandall 1992).

No person under 18 years of age may be admitted to an MM treatment program unless an authorized adult signs an official consent form (Parrino 1992). Treatment programs for patients under 18 years of age need to comply with FDA regulations, which require that patients under age 18 make two documented attempts at short-term detoxification or drug-free treatment to be eligible for MM. A 1-week waiting period is required after a detoxification attempt. However, before an attempt is repeated, the program physician has to document in the minor's record that the patient continues to be or is again physiologically dependent on narcotic drugs (Parrino 1992).

Two additional oral pharmacotherapies in therapeutic trials are expected to expand the arsenal of opioids available for maintenance treatment. Levo-alpha-acetyl-methadol (LAAM) is an opioid that is quite similar to methadone in its pharmacological actions. It is converted into active metabolites that have longer biological half-lives than methadone. Opioid withdrawal symptoms are not experienced for 72 to 96 hours after the last oral dose; therefore, LAAM is given only three times a week as compared with daily administration of methadone. LAAM has been shown to have effects equivalent to methadone in suppressing illicit opioid abuse and encouraging a more productive lifestyle (Jaffe 1986).

Buprenorphine is a partial opioid agonist-antagonist that is also used as an analgesic due to its ability to produce morphine-like effects at low doses. This agent relieves opioid withdrawal, diminishes craving, and does not produce euphoria. It is more difficult to overdose on buprenorphine than methadone because of its antagonist effects in high doses (Rosen and Kosten 1991).

Many heroin addicts also abuse cocaine, which heightens the rush from heroin injected alone (i.e., a "speed ball"). MM treatment does not reduce cocaine abuse for many patients. Based on preliminary data, buprenorphine may reduce cocaine use in opioid addicts (Kosten et al. 1989). The mechanism of action in combination with cocaine remains to be clarified.

PHARMACOLOGY OF COMORBID PSYCHIATRIC DISORDERS

Psychiatric comorbidity in the form of dual and triple diagnoses has been found to be common among adolescents with PSUD (Bukstein et al. 1989; Kaminer 1991). The most common psychiatric diagnoses are mood disorders and conduct disorders. Other diagnoses reported include anxiety disorders, eating disorders, ADHD, and schizophrenia. Personality disorders, especially DSM-III-R cluster B which includes antisocial, borderline, histrionic, and narcissistic personality disorders (American Psychiatric Association 1987), have been identified among these adolescents with or without additional comorbid psychiatric disorders (Kaminer 1994*a*).

It is often unclear whether a patient's symptoms are a sequence of substance abuse or indicate a comorbid psychiatric disorder. Moreover, the sequelae of psychoactive substance intoxication and withdrawal in such patients are often difficult to distinguish from the signs and symptoms of a concurrent psychiatric disorder. It is important to reemphasize that dual diagnoses is a term limited to the relationship between disorders *only* and not symptoms associated with PSUD. These symptoms may serve as indications of the severity of PSUD.

The diagnostic process in comorbid psychiatric disorders and the reliability and stability of dual diagnoses are of great significance from a treatment perspective. An incorrect diagnosis of comorbidity and a precocious introduction of medications may lead to errors in treatment. A washout period of at least 2 weeks and sometimes longer is recommended before initiating pharmacotherapy. This delay in pharmacotherapy is especially important with antidepressant medications, because even in children and adolescents with major depressive disorder (MDD) without a comorbid PSUD, approximately 25 percent of those initially diagnosed as depressed have a spontaneous syndromatic recovery within 2 weeks (Ambrosini et al. 1993*a*). The authors noted that treatments initiated in this period could produce inflated recovery rates. There also appear to be both biological and depressive severity differences between those who recover and those who remain syndromatically ill after a 2-week followup phase.

MAJOR DEPRESSIVE DISORDER

Conceptual difficulties regarding the validity of depression as a distinct diagnostic entity in children and adolescents are still debated. Substantial uncertainty still exists regarding what factors to rate in depressed children and adolescents: individual symptoms, regularly occurring syndromes, or constitutionally based disorders. It is also unclear which mental status variables should be examined in depressed youth when evaluating treatment effects (Kaminer et al. 1992*c*). Empirical data do not support antidepressants' efficacy in child and adolescent MDD, although these medications have been proven for the treatment of adult MDD. Geller and coworkers (1990) and Ryan and colleagues (1986) tried to replicate studies with adult MDD, which reported that tricyclic antidepressants steady-state plasma levels of more than 125 micrograms per liter (μg/L) predict response (Nelson et al. 1984). No relation was found between plasma levels of imipramine or desipramine and clinical response in adolescents with MDD.

Lithium augmentation in refractory adolescent MDD and monoamine oxidaze inhibitor (MAOI) treatment of adolescent atypical depression were reported in open-design studies (Ryan et al. 1988*a*, 1988*b*; Strober et al. 1992). These reports suggest the potential use of these agents in the management of refractory MDD in adolescents, and await further confirmation by controlled studies.

Clinical experience suggests that many patients with PSUD are diagnosed as depressed, especially on admission to inpatient treatment programs. This diagnosis could be attributed to various factors other than primary depression such as the mood-altering effects of the drug or withdrawal symptoms; loss of the availability of psychoactive substances and related lifestyle; or a reaction to the loss of freedom, friends, and family following the admission. Most of the patients experience a gradual and spontaneous lifting of the depressive symptomatology within 2 weeks. Regardless of the results of empirical studies, adolescents who are diagnosed with MDD are commonly treated with tricyclic antidepressants such as imipramine and amitriptyline or by the new selective serotonin reuptake inhibitors (SRIs) such as fluoxetine, sertraline, and paroxetine.

Clinical improvement following tricyclic medications is usually expected after 3 to 4 weeks of pharmacotherapy, as reported by Kaminer and colleagues (1992c) who employed the Emotional Disorders Rating Scale (EDRS) as a measure of response to treatment of MDD. This result confirmed findings in the adult literature (Nelson et al. 1984). Clinical response to SRIs usually occurs after a shorter period of treatment than tricyclic antidepressant treatment.

Ambrosini and colleagues (1993a) recently reviewed treatment studies of children and adolescents that focused on tricyclic antidepressants. The authors concluded that these medications' superiority to placebo has not been proven. However, they pointed out that this finding does not preclude their routine clinical use in MDD because, on the average, more than half of the subjects treated openly do respond. Ambrosini and colleagues (1993a) suggested that the maximal benefits from antidepressants most likely emerge after 8 to 10 weeks of treatment when plasma levels of tricyclics are maintained in the 200 nanograms per milliliter (ng/mL) range. Maintenance treatment should be continued for 5 to 6 months after remission.

In summary, it is of enormous importance to elucidate conceptual and clinical implications of the response of MDD symptomatology to antidepressants across age groups. The Maudsley study carried out by Harrington and colleagues (1990) indicated that depression in children and adolescents shows substantial specific continuity into adulthood, although the majority of adults with MDD had not experienced a depressive disorder in their preadulthood years. However, according to Ambrosini and colleagues (1993a), the implications of the Maudsley data are that the 30 to 35 percent of adults who do not respond to antidepressants have a history of child and adolescent MDD.

It appears that this group of adults may represent a distinct biological subpopulation characterized by age of MDD onset as a possible biological marker with specificity to different pharmacotherapeutic response patterns. This pattern has significant similarities to Cloninger's (1987) alcohol typologies and to recent findings regarding the pharmacotherapy of alcoholism reviewed earlier in this chapter.

Side Effects

Antidepressants generate side effects in adolescents similar to those reported in adults. The tricyclics may be lethal in overdose primarily because of cardiovascular toxicity (Ambrosini et al. 1993*b*). Four cases of sudden death related to the use of desipramine in children ages 8 to 12 years old were reported (Riddle et al. 1993). The suspected pathophysiological mechanism is that desipramine may increase noradrenergic neurotransmission, which leads to increased cardiac sympathetic tone and could predispose vulnerable persons to ventricular tachyarrhythmias, syncope, and sudden death.

Neurotoxic effects of antidepressants include seizures, behavioral changes, and delirium. Data concerning tricyclic neurotoxicity in adolescents is limited to sporadic case reports. Anticholinergic effects of tricyclic antidepressants are usually correlated with plasma levels and most commonly include dry mouth, drowsiness, nausea, constipation, urinary retention, tremor, flushed face, and excessive sweating. Tricyclic antidepressants can induce behavioral toxicity, primarily precipitation, induction, or rapid cycling of manic symptoms (Strober and Carlson 1982). A recent study reported on mania associated with treatment of five adolescents for depression with the SRI fluoxetine (Venkataraman et al. 1992).

Abrupt discontinuation of tricyclic antidepressants may produce withdrawal symptoms. The most common symptoms are cholinergic effects. Coadministration of SRIs with tricyclic antidepressants or within a few weeks following tricyclic discontinuation is contraindicated because it may raise the plasma level of these agents to a toxic level, most likely due to interference with their hepatic oxidative metabolism. Side effects of SRIs in adolescents have been reported in case studies and in preliminary studies. Ambrosini and colleagues (1993*b*) reviewed and classified these side effects as gastrointestinal, neuropsychiatric, and behavioral.

It is noteworthy that abuse of amitriptyline for its sedative effects was reported by an adolescent and adults with PSUD (Kaminer 1994*b*).

The risk of suicide among adolescents with PSUD is high (Kaminer 1992*c*). SRIs are less cardiotoxic with overdoses, and they lack sedative potentiation with alcohol as compared with tricyclic antidepressants; therefore their use is preferable for MDD in impulsive or suicidal adolescents.

Current experience suggests that before initiating tricyclic antidepressant treatment of any psychopathology in adolescents, a baseline electrocardiogram (EKG) needs to be done. The physical examination and medical history should emphasize the cardiovascular system of the patient and family members in order to detect any cardiac vulnerability. Resting pulse should not exceed 130 beats per minute, and blood pressure should not exceed 140/90 mm Hg. Prolongation of the P-R interval on the EKG should not exceed 0.21 seconds, the QRS complex should not be prolonged by more than 30 percent over baseline, and the QTc interval in particular should be within normal limits.[1]

BIPOLAR DISORDERS

The core phenomenology of bipolar disorder is similar regardless of age. However, as in the treatment of MDD and alcoholism type 1 versus type 2, it is not clear whether age of onset influences treatment response.

Lithium is the pharmacotherapy of choice although there are no large-scale, systematic studies in children and adolescents (Carlson 1990). Anticonvulsants such as carbamazepine and valproic acid serve as a second tier. Combinations of these medications have been reported to have a synergistic effect in adult patients resistant to lithium monotherapy. The following indications for the initiation of lithium treatment for adolescents were noted by Carlson (1990, p. 32): presence or history of disabling episodes of mania and depression; episode(s) of severe depression with a possible history of hypomania; presence of an acute severe depression characterized by psychomotor retardation, hypersomnia, and psychosis; positive family history for a bipolar disorder (these adolescents are at risk for developing a manic episode when treated with antidepressants and may develop a rapid cycling course); an acute psychotic disorder with affective features; and behavior disorders characterized by severe emotional lability and aggression when there is a positive family history of major mood or bipolar disorder or lithium responsiveness. DeLong and Aldershof (1987) reported that of 59 bipolar child and adolescent patients studied, two-thirds were considered favorable responders to lithium therapy. Poor responders consisted of subjects with ADHD, conduct disorder, or both. Indeed, children misdiagnosed with ADHD have been shown to actually suffer from bipolar mood disorder (Isaac 1991). Lithium's efficacy in treatment of acute symptomatology and long-term management of bipolar disorder in adults is well established and extensively documented in the literature; however, the failure rate for lithium in prevention of bipolar disorder is approximately 33 percent (Prien and Gelenberg 1989).

Side effects of lithium in adolescents are similar to those manifested in adults; tremor, urinary frequency, nausea, and diarrhea are the most common. Contraindications for the use of lithium include heart and kidney disease, diuretic use, chronic diarrhea, and electrolyte imbalance. Baseline assessments before initiating lithium therapy include blood electrolytes, urea and nitrogen levels, blood count with differential, thyroid function tests, and pregnancy test due to the potential teratogenic effects of lithium. The recommended therapeutic blood level is within the therapeutic range of 0.7 to 1.2 millequivalents per liter (mEq/L). A level of more than 1.4 mEq/L should not be exceeded due to a risk of toxicity. Signs of toxicity include severe neurobehavioral and gastrointestinal symptoms.

Anticonvulsants' recommended blood levels, contraindications, and side effects are similar along age groups. Compared to lithium, monitoring of fluid and electrolyte intake is not required, and the risk of toxicity is lower should serum levels exceed the recommended therapeutic range. In some cases, bipolar disorder may be refractory to all of these agents. One alternative, verapamil (a calcium channel antagonist), has been used without consistently proving a clear effectiveness in the treatment of adults with a bipolar disorder. In addition, verapamil is associated with depression (Barton and Gitlin 1987). However, successful use of verapamil and valproic acid in the treatment of prolonged mania in an adolescent was reported (Kastner and Friedman 1992). Another alternative based on a single case report of an adolescent with a rapid cycling bipolar disorder was described by Berman and Wolpert (1987). The authors noted that the disorder, which was precipitated by a tricyclic antidepressant, responded to electrocurrent therapy. An adolescent with PSUD and a comorbid bipolar disorder is at very high risk for suicide and aggressive behavior and should be followed carefully. The need for blood level monitoring of lithium is a special challenge particularly at the outpatient level.

ANXIETY DISORDER

Panic and obsessive-compulsive disorders (OCD) in youth share phenomenological similarities with the adult patterns. However, avoidant disorder, overanxious disorder, separation anxiety, and school phobia are unique to children and adolescents as delineated in DSM-III-R (American Psychiatric Association 1987). The use of medications with addictive properties for the pharmacotherapy of anxiety disorders in adolescents with PSUD is not recommended. Furthermore, benzodiazepines such as alprazolam, which are commonly used among adults with anxiety disorders, have not been unequivocally proven to be more efficacious than tricyclic antidepressants.

Panic disorder and OCD among adolescents with PSUD are rare. The median age for the onset of anxiety disorders is 15 years of age (Christie et al. 1988). No studies regarding the pharmacological treatment of panic disorder in adolescents have been reported. A recent study of adults with panic disorder reported that both the benzodiazepine alprazolam and the antidepressant imipramine demonstrated efficacy during acute treatment of panic disorder on most measures of panic and nonpanic anxiety, as well as measures of phobic avoidance and panic-related social disability (Schweizer et al. 1993). These clinical benefits were achieved without any concomitant behavioral therapy or psychotherapy and were sustained throughout an 8-month course of maintenance therapy without any dose escalation. The same research group studied short- and long-term outcome after drug taper (Rickels et al. 1993). The authors concluded that "over the long term, patients originally treated with imipramine or placebo did as well at follow-up as patients treated with alprazolam, without the problems of physical dependence and discontinuation that any long-term alprazolam therapy entails" (Rickels et al. 1993, p. 67).

The psychopharmacological treatment of OCD has been extensively studied and reviewed (Rapoport 1987). Antianxiety agents appear to be ineffective, but the tricyclic antidepressant clomipramine was reported to have significant superiority over placebo in lessening OCD symptoms in children and adolescents (DeVeaugh-Geiss et al. 1992). Clomipramine appears to have better results than desipramine, but this conclusion remains to be tested in future studies. Open-label studies with SRIs such as fluoxetine (Ambrosini et al. 1993*b*) suggest it may be effective in adolescent OCD with or without clomipramine.

Separation anxiety and school phobia have been studied for more than 20 years. In contrast to the early report regarding a positive response to imipramine compared to placebo (Gittelman-Klein and Klein 1971) recent studies have failed to show superiority of tricyclic antidepressants (e.g., imipramine, clomipramine) to placebo (Bernstein 1990; Klein et al. 1992). It is noteworthy that these disorders were found to be associated with adult forms of panic and depressive disorders (Gittelman and Klein 1984; Weissman et al. 1984).

A study of the effects of alprazolam on children and adolescents with overanxious and avoidant disorders was reported (Simeon et al. 1992). The authors' findings failed to show efficacy of the medication in comparison to placebo. This finding stands in marked contrast to the favorable effects reported in studies with adults. Simeon and colleagues (1992) intend to increase the dosage of alprazolam and the length of pharmacotherapy in a future study. The authors did not discuss the implications of the addictive potential of alprazolam in this study. It is important to note that the DSM-III-R overanxious and avoidant disorders diagnoses have been dropped from the most recent edition's section titled "Anxiety Disorders of Childhood or Adolescence" (American Psychiatric Association 1994). Avoidant disorder is now included in the modified social phobia diagnosis, and overanxious disorder has been subsumed by generalized anxiety disorder.

Buspirone hydrochloride is a relatively new anxiolytic drug, pharmacologically different from the benzodiazepines. This agent has been marketed as a less sedative anxiolytic that does not potentiate alcohol effects and has a low, if any, abuse potential. Buspirone has been used to successfully treat an adolescent with overanxious disorder who did not tolerate treatment with desipramine (Kranzler 1988), and may be particularly useful in clinical treatment of teens with PSUD and anxiety symptoms.

The studies reviewed above have significant importance for the treatment of adolescents with PSUD and anxiety disorders. Moreover, they have unequivocal implications for the treatment and detoxification of benzodiazepine abuse and dependence. Tricyclic antidepressants are useful substitutes for benzodiazepines, which are abused for their sedative properties.

EATING DISORDERS

Anorexia and bulimia nervosa are psychiatric disorders predominantly diagnosed in females. There are striking similarities between these disorders and PSUD. Biopsychosocial factors are responsible for shaping the individual's anorexic or bulimic behavior and neurophysiological adaptation. Strober and Katz (1987) questioned the traditional linkage between anorexia and bulimia, which has been based on the common denominator of eating disorders.

One of the criteria for bulimia nervosa according to DSM-III-R (American Psychiatric Association 1987) has included the use of laxatives or diuretics in order to prevent weight gain. The misuse of medications without an addictive potential and in the "service of the disorder" does not meet the criteria for PSUD. However, females in general and bulimic patients in particular tend to use diet pills. Indeed, Johnston and colleagues (1992) reported that stimulant use among female high school seniors equals males' rate of use, and diet pill use was higher among females. The abuse of medications with addictive potential (e.g., stimulants sold over the counter) and the fashionable use of cocaine in order to lose weight create a nosological dilemma in determining whether the patient qualifies for the diagnosis of PSUD, particularly when the person is bulimic. However, discussion of this issue is beyond the scope of this chapter.

Since the mid-1980s, pharmacological trials in adult patients have demonstrated the short-term efficacy of several antidepressants in diminishing bingeing frequencies in bulimic patients. These include imipramine, desipramine, and phenelzine (an MAOI) as well as several new-generation antidepressants including trazodone, bupropion, and fluoxetine (Kennedy and Garfinkel 1992). The bulimic symptomatology improved even in the absence of coexistent depression and was not correlated with pretreatment severity or plasma medication levels. These findings do not support early studies linking the etiology of mood disorders and eating disorders based on epidemiological and family studies (Hudson et al. 1983). Lithium carbonate was reported to reduce bulimic episodes in open-label studies (Hsu 1984).

Anorexia nervosa and PSUD is a rare dual diagnosis. No effective pharmacotherapy for anorexia nervosa has been reported in a double-blind, placebo-controlled trial. Only a limited number of open-label trials with fluoxetine noted some short-term improvement.

SCHIZOPHRENIA

No studies on the comorbidity of PSUD and schizophrenia have been reported among adolescents. However, there are no data from adult patients to suggest that there should be any difference between the pharmacotherapy of schizophrenic patients with or without accompanying PSUD. Therefore, neuroleptics remain the category of medications of choice.

DISRUPTIVE BEHAVIOR DISORDERS

Conduct disorder (CD), ADHD, and oppositional defiant disorder (ODD) represent the largest group of psychiatric referrals. Comorbidity among these disorders is very common, and ODD is most probably a mild variant or precursor of CD and not a discrete disorder (Abikoff and Klein 1992).

ATTENTION DEFICIT-HYPERACTIVITY DISORDER

The effectiveness of stimulant therapy for ADHD in childhood has been extensively documented (Greenhill 1990). Methylphenidate and magnesium pemoline are the most commonly used medications. Antidepressants have also been found to be effective in the treatment of the aggression, inattention, and hyperactivity that characterize the heterogenous population of children diagnosed with the disorder (Ambrosini et al. 1993*b*). Desipramine, clomipramine, and MAOIs should be considered alternate therapy to stimulants, which have less severe side effects and produce a more consistent response from patients (Pliszka 1987). However, these antidepressants should be used when an ADHD patient is manifesting a comorbid anxiety or depressive disorder. Side effects of stimulants include weight loss, decreased appetite, possible mood lability, and a potentially reversible growth suppression once the medication is discontinued. This issue (growth suppression) still generates debate. Abuse of therapeutic stimulants by patients with ADHD is rare; however, peers and relatives may abuse the medication either due to its availability or because they have PSUD (Kaminer 1992*b*).

Neuroleptics and carbamazepine and clonidine (including a transdermal form) have been tested as treatments for childhood ADHD. However, only equivocal reports of efficacy were noted in uncontrolled studies of neuroleptics and carbamazepine and in controlled studies of clonidine, especially in patients with comorbid tic disorders (Steingard et al. 1993). Serious side-effects that characterize these medications limit their use in ADHD.

Stimulant therapy for adolescents with ADHD has also been found to be effective (Klorman et al. 1990). Methylphenidate and dextroamphetamine appear to be more effective than magnesium pemoline. The author has treated adolescents with PSUD and comorbid ADHD with methylphenidate, producing a positive response. Adults with the disorder also respond to this treatment (Wender et al. 1985).

CONDUCT DISORDER

In child and adolescent psychiatry, aggression is most commonly associated with a diagnosis of CD. Pharmacological treatment of aggression in CD is part of a comprehensive treatment plan that also includes psychosocial and behavioral interventions (Stewart et al. 1990). Neuroleptics have been used for aggressive behavior with and without CD in adolescents since the 1960s (Campbell et al. 1984; Werry and Aman 1975). Campbell and colleagues (1984) reported that lithium was superior to placebo for the treatment of aggression in subjects with CD.

Stimulants and anticonvulsants were also used in early studies, but the results were ambiguous mostly due to lack of differentiation between aggressive subjects with and without ADHD (Conners et al. 1971; Hechtman 1985). Beta blockers have shown some usefulness in a small group of subjects with aggressive behavior and additional disruptive or organic disorders (Kuperman and Stewart 1987). Treatment of violent children and adolescents aged 5 to 15 years with clonidine was reported in an open-label study (Kemph et al. 1993). Aggression decreased with minimal side-effects in most children, and plasma gamma aminobutyric acid (GABA) increased in 5 of the 17 cases.

A high percentage of adolescents diagnosed with CD will be diagnosed with antisocial personality disorder, which is highly correlated with PSUD. No specific pharmacological treatment for personality disorders has been developed. However, symptomatic relief of depressive or anxiety disorders that may accompany CD or a personality disorder could be achieved by selective pharmacotherapy (Kaminer et al. 1992*b*).

THE LEGAL ANGLE

It is important to be aware of the legal aspects of adolescent and family consent for treatment of PSUD including psychopharmacotherapy. Facilities that treat minors have to follow some basic common rules and protect confidentiality. Consent for admission to an inpatient unit needs to be given by the caretaker and adolescent (unless the adolescent has been committed). Any patient under 18 years of age who is married, a parent, or emancipated has the right to consent on his/her behalf.

Before rendering any care without parental consent, the facility must obtain a written acknowledgment from the minor stating that he or she was advised of the purpose and nature of such treatment services, told that he or she may withdraw the signed acknowledgment at any time, aware that the facility will make attempts to convince the minor of the need for involvement of other family members in treatment and the facility's preference for parental consent for the rendering of treatment services, and advised that a medical/clinical record of treatment services will be made and maintained by the facility. Various laws and regulations have established that parental consent is usually, but not always, required to deliver PSUD treatment for minors. Patients with PSUD must be notified of the protection afforded by Federal rules upon admission (Kaminer 1994*a*).

THE FUTURE OF PHARMACOTHERAPY FOR ADOLESCENTS WITH PSUD AND COMORBID DISORDERS

Eichelman (1988) described four important principles for the pharmacologic treatment of adults: treat the primary illness, use the most benign interventions when treating empirically, have some quantifiable means of assessing efficacy, and institute drug trials systematically. These principles are even more important with younger subjects.

Ethical principles must govern research and treatment in adolescent PSUD and comorbid psychiatric disorders (Munir and Earls 1992). Improved communication with and education of the public is necessary, especially parents of patients, regarding the nature of PSUD and the efficacy of pharmacotherapy. Knowledge of the process whereby a medication's therapeutic efficacy and dosage levels are established will improve public perception and acceptance of treatment programs. Biderman (1992) suggested a careful and systematic study of new therapeutic agents. Case reports and case series should be followed by open studies that will lead to controlled, double-blind studies. Collaboration between centers will increase the number of subjects studied and improve the significance of the results.

The study by McLellan and colleagues (1993) reviewed in this chapter empirically confirmed that the cumulative effect of more treatment modalities is better than just a single pharmacological intervention. Pharmacotherapy alone cannot deal with polysubstance abuse and the various domains that the adult or adolescent with PSUD struggles with in the recovery process. Patients who would like to maintain their motivation to comply with the medication regime may be encouraged to join or establish self-help groups. Parents and therapists in the treatment facility may be instrumental in helping them succeed in this effort.

However, no single strategy appears to be superior to others in dealing with adolescent PSUD. It would be helpful to have a measurement of units of treatment and dosage regardless of the modality of treatment intervention used (i.e., net effect of change). The Treatment Services Review (TSR) (McLellan et al. 1992) is such an assessment instrument designed to quantify different treatment modalities in adults with PSUD as delineated in the Addiction Severity Index (McLellan et al. 1980). A modification of this instrument for adolescents could prove to be beneficial using an approach similar to the T-ASI (Kaminer et al. 1991).

Finally, the age of onset of a disorder (i.e., mood disorder, PSUD) and the age-specific response to medications may represent a biological marker. This marker may facilitate and improve identification of heterogeneous clinical subpopulations, course of disorders, and long-term morbidity, and may potentiate future research for specific treatments tailored to the groups identified.

NOTE

1. QT interval represents the time required for ventricular electrical systole. It varies with heart rate, and one can estimate QTc (corrected QT) interval normally less than 0.42 second in males and 0.43 second in females by the formula QTc = QT/R-R interval.

REFERENCES

Abikoff, H., and Klein, R.G. Attention-deficit hyperactivity and conduct disorder: Comorbidity and implications for treatment. *J Consult Clin Psychol* 60:881-892, 1992.

Alterman, A.I.; O'Brien, C.P.; and McLellan, A.T. Differential therapeutics for substance abuse. In: Frances, R.J., and Miller, S.I., eds. *Clinical Textbook of Addictive Disorders.* New York: Guilford Press, 1991. pp. 369-390.

Ambrosini, P.J.; Bianchi, M.D.; Rabinovich, H.; and Elia, J. Antidepressant treatments in children and adolescents: I. Affective disorders. *J Am Acad Child Adolesc Psychiatry* 32:1-6, 1993*a.*

Ambrosini, P.J.; Bianchi, M.D.; Rabinovich, H.; and Elia, J. Antidepressant treatments in children and adolescents: II. Anxiety, physical, and behavioral disorders. *J Am Acad Child Adolesc Psychiatry* 32:483-492, 1993*b.*

American Psychiatric Association. *Diagnostic and Statistical Manual of Mental Disorders.* 3d ed. rev. Washington, DC: American Psychiatric Association, 1987.

American Psychiatric Association. *Diagnostic and Statistical Manual of Mental Disorders.* 4th ed. Washington, DC: American Psychiatric Association, 1994.

Anderson, J.C.; Williams, S.; McGee, R.; and Silva, P.A. DSM-III disorders in preadolescent children. *Arch Gen Psychiatry* 44:69-76, 1987.

Babor, T.F.; Hofmann, M.; DelBoca, F.K.; Hesselbrock, V.; Meyer, R.E.; Dolinsky, Z.S.; and Rounsaville, B. Types of alcoholics: II. Evidence for an empirically-derived typology based on indicators of vulnerability and severity. *Arch Gen Psychiatry* 49:599-608, 1992.

Barton, B., and Gitlin, M.J. Verapamil in treatment-resistant mania: An open-label. *J Clin Psychopharmacol* 7:101-103, 1987.

Berman, E., and Wolpert, E.A. Intractable manic-depressive psychosis with rapid cycling in an 18-year-old depressed adolescent successfully treated with electroconvulsive therapy. *J Nerv Ment Dis* 175:236-239, 1987.

Bernstein, G.A. Anxiety disorders. In: Garfinkel, B.D.; Carlson, G.A.; and Weller, E.B., eds. *Psychiatric Disorders in Children and Adolescents.* Philadelphia: W.B. Saunders, 1990. pp. 64-83.

Biderman, J. New developments in pediatric psychopharmacology. *J Am Acad Child Adolesc Psychiatry* 31:14-15, 1992.

Bukstein, O.G.; Brent, D.; and Kaminer, Y. Comorbidity of substance abuse and other psychiatric disorders in adolescents. *Am J Psychiatry* 146:1131-1141, 1989.

Bukstein, O.G.; Glancy, L.J.; and Kaminer, Y. Patterns of affective comorbidity in a clinical population of dual-diagnosed substance-abusing adolescents. *J Am Acad Child Adolesc Psychiatry* 31:1041-1046, 1992.

Buydens-Branchey, L.; Branchey, M.H.; and Noumair, D. Age of alcoholism onset: I. Relationship to psychopathology. *Arch Gen Psychiatry* 46:225-230, 1989*a*.

Buydens-Branchey, L.; Branchey, M.H.; Noumair, D.; and Lieber, C.S. Age of alcoholism onset: II. Relationship to susceptibility to serotonin precursor availability. *Arch Gen Psychiatry* 46:231-236, 1989*b*.

Campbell, M.; Small, A.M.; Green, W.H.; Jennings, S.J.; Perry, R.; Bennett, W.G.; and Anderson, L. A comparison of haloperidol and lithium in hospitalized aggressive conduct disordered children. *Arch Gen Psychiatry* 41:650-656, 1984.

Carlson, G.A. Bipolar disorders in children and adolescents. In: Garfinkel, B.D.; Carlson, G.A.; and Weller, E.B., eds. *Psychiatric Disorders in Children and Adolescents.* Philadelphia: W.B. Saunders, 1990. pp. 21-36.

Christie, K.A.; Burke, J.D.; Regier, D.A.; Rae, D.S.; Boyd, J.H.; and Locke, B.Z. Epidemiologic evidence for early onset of mental disorders and higher risk of drug abuse in young adults. *Am J Psychiatry* 145:971-975, 1988.

Cloninger, C.R. Neurogenetic adaptive mechanisms in alcoholism. *Science* 236:410-416, 1987.

Conners, C.K.; Kramer, R.; Rothchild, G.H.; Schwartz, L.; and Stone, A. Treatment of young delinquent boys with diphenylhydantoin sodium and methylphenidate. *Arch Gen Psychiatry* 24:156-160, 1971.

Council on Scientific Affairs. Aversion therapy. *JAMA* 258:2562-2566, 1987.

DeLong, G.R., and Aldershof, A.L. Long-term experience with lithium treatment in childhood: Correlation with clinical diagnoses. *J Am Acad Child Adolesc Psychiatry* 26:389-394, 1987.

DeVeaugh-Geiss, J.; Moroz, G.; Biederman, J.; Cantwell, D.; Fontaine, R.; Griest, J.H.; Reichler, R.; Katz, R.; and Landau, P. Clomipramine hydrochloride in childhood and adolescent obsessive-compulsive disorder: A multicenter trial. *J Am Acad Child Adolesc Psychiatry* 31:45-49, 1992.

Eichelman, B. Toward a rational pharmacotherapy for aggressive and violent behavior. *Hosp Comm Psychiatry* 39:31-39, 1988.

Finnegan, L.P., and Kandall, S.R. Maternal and neonatal effects of alcohol and drugs. In: Lowinson, J.H.; Ruiz, P.; Millman, R.B.; and Langrod, J.G., eds. *Substance Abuse, A Comprehensive Textbook.* Baltimore: Williams and Wilkins, 1992. pp. 628-656.

Gawin, F.H., and Kleber, H.D. Abstinence symptomatology and psychiatric diagnosis in cocaine abusers. *Arch Gen Psychiatry* 43:107-113, 1986.

Gawin, F.H.; Allen, D.; and Humblestone, B. Outpatient treatment of crack cocaine smoking with flupenthixol decanoate. *Arch Gen Psychiatry* 46:322-325, 1989*a*.

Gawin, F.H.; Kleber, H.D.; Byck, R.; Rounsaville, B.J.; Kosten, T.R.; Jatlow, P.J.; and Morgan, C. Desipramine facilitation of initial cocaine abstinence. *Arch Gen Psychiatry* 46:117-121, 1989*b*.

Geller, B.; Cooper, T.B.; Graham, D.L.; Marsteller, F.A.; and Bryant, D.M. Double-blind placebo controlled study of nortriptyline in depressed adolescents using a "fixed plasma level" design. *Psychopharmacol Bull* 26:85-90, 1990.

Gerard, D.L., and Saenger, G. *Outpatient Treatment of Alcoholism.* Toronto: University of Toronto Press, 1966.

Gilligan, S.; Reich, T.; and Cloninger, C.R. Etiologic heterogeneity in alcoholism. *Genet Epidemiol* 4:395-414, 1987.

Gittelman-Klein, R., and Klein, D.F. Controlled imipramine treatment of school phobia. *Arch Gen Psychiatry* 25:204-207, 1971.

Gittelman, R., and Klein, D.F. Relationship between separation anxiety and panic and agoraphobic disorders. Supplement. *Psychopathology* 17(1):56-65, 1984.

Greenhill, L.L. Attention deficit hyperactivity disorder in children. In: Garfinkel, B.D.; Carlson, G.A.; and Weller, E.B., eds. *Psychiatric Disorders in Children and Adolescents.* Philadelphia: W.B. Saunders, 1990. pp. 149-182.

Halikas, J.A.; Kuhn, K.L.; and Madduz, T.L. Reduction of cocaine use among methadone maintenance patients using concurrent carbamazepine maintenance. *Am J Clin Psychiatry* 2:3-6, 1990.

Harrington, R.; Fudge, H.; Rutter, M.; Pickles, A.; and Hill, J. Adult outcomes of childhood and adolescent depression. *Arch Gen Psychiatry* 47:465-473, 1990.

Hechtman, L. Adolescent outcome of hyperactive children treated with stimulants in childhood: A review. *Psychopharmacol Bull* 21:178-191, 1985.

Ho, A.; Cambor, R.; Bodner, G.; and Kreek, M.J. Intensity of craving is independent of depression in newly abstinent chronic cocaine abusers. In: Harris, L., ed. *Problems of Drug Dependence 1991.* National Institute on Drug Abuse Research Monograph No. 119. DHHS Pub. No. (ADM)92-1888. Washington, DC: Supt. of Docs., U.S. Govt. Print. Off., 1992. p. 441.

Hoffmann, N.G.; Sonis, W.A.; and Halikas, J.A. Issues in the evaluation of chemical dependency treatment programs for adolescents. *Pediatr Clin North Am* 34:449-459, 1987.

Hsu, L.K.G. Treatment of bulimia with lithium. *Am J Psychiatry* 141:1260-1262, 1984.

Hudson, J.I.; Pope, H.G.; Jonas, J.M.; and Yurgelum-Todd, D. Phenomenologic relationship of eating disorders to major affective disorder. *Psychol Res* 9:345-354, 1983.

Isaac, G. Bipolar disorder in prepubertal children in a special education setting: Is it rare? *J Clin Psychiatry* 52:165-168, 1991.

Jacobson, G.R. *The Alcoholisms: Detection, Diagnosis, and Assessment.* New York: Human Sciences Press, 1976.

Jaffe, J.H. Opioids. In: Frances, A.I., and Hales, R.E., eds. *Annual Review.* Vol. 5. Washington, DC: American Psychiatric Press, 1986. pp. 137-159.

Johnson, R.E.; Stevens, V.J.; Hollis, J.F.; and Woodson, G.T. Nicotine chewing gum use in the outpatient care setting. *J Fam Pract* 34:61-65, 1992.

Johnston, L.; Bachman, J.G.; and O'Malley, R.M. *Details of Annual Drug Survey.* Ann Arbor, MI: University of Michigan News and Information Services, 1992.

Kaminer, Y. Desipramine facilitation of cocaine abstinence in an adolescent. *J Am Acad Child Adolesc Psychiatry* 31:312-317, 1992*a*.

Kaminer, Y. Clinical implications of the relationship between attention-deficit hyperactivity disorder and psychoactive substance use disorders. *Am J Addict* 1:257-264, 1992*b*.

Kaminer, Y. Psychoactive substance abuse and dependence as a risk factor in adolescent attempted and completed suicide. *Am J Addict* 1:21-29, 1992*c*.

Kaminer, Y. The magnitude of concurrent psychiatric disorders in hospitalized substance abusing adolescents. *Child Psychiatry Human Devel* 22:89-95, 1991.

Kaminer, Y. *Understanding and Treating Adolescent Substance Abuse.* New York: Plenum Press, 1994*a*.

Kaminer, Y. Cocaine craving. [Letter to the editor] *J Am Acad Child Adolesc Psychiatry* 33:592, 1994*b*.

Kaminer, Y.; Bukstein, O.G.; and Tarter, R.E. The Teen Addiction Severity Index (T-ASI): Rationale and reliability. *Int J Addict* 26:219-226, 1991.

Kaminer, Y.; Tarter, R.E.; Bukstein, O.G.; and Kabene, M. Staff, treatment completers', and noncompleters' perceptions of the value of treatment variables. *Am J Addict* 1:115-120, 1992*a*.

Kaminer, Y.; Tarter, R.E.; Bukstein, O.G.; and Kabene, M. Comparison between treatment completers and noncompleters among dual-diagnosed substance-abusing adolescents. *J Am Acad Child Adolesc Psychiatry* 31:1046-1049, 1992*b*.

Kaminer, Y.; Seifer, R.; and Mastrian, A. Observational measurement of symptoms responsive to treatment of major depressive disorder in children and adolescents. *J Nerv Ment Dis* 180:639-643, 1992*c*.

Kastner, T., and Friedman, D.L. Verapamil and valproic acid treatment of prolonged mania. *J Am Acad Child Adolesc Psychiatry* 31:271-275, 1992.

Kemph, J.P.; DeVane, C.L.; Levin, G.M.; Jarecke, R.; and Miller, R.L. Treatment of aggressive children with clonidine: Results of an open pilot study. *J Am Acad Child Adolesc Psychiatry* 32:577-581, 1993.

Kennedy, S.H., and Garfinkel, P. Advances in diagnosis and treatment of anorexia nervosa and bulimia nervosa. *Can J Psychiatry* 37:309-315, 1992.

Klein, R.G.; Koplewicz, H.S.; and Kanner, A. Imipramine treatment of children with separation anxiety disorder. *J Am Acad Child Adolesc Psychiatry* 31:21-28, 1992.

Klorman, R.; Brumaghin, J.T.; Fitzpatrick, P.A.; and Borgstedt, A.D. Clinical effects of a controlled trial of methylphenidate on adolescents with attention deficit disorder. *J Am Acad Child Adolesc Psychiatry* 29:702-709, 1990.

Kosten, T.R. Neurobiology of abused drugs: Opioids and stimulants. *J Nerv Ment Dis* 178:217-227, 1990.

Kosten, T.R.; Gawin, F.H.; Kosten, T.A.; Morgan, A.; Rounsaville, B.J.; Schottenfeld, R.; and Kleber, H.D. Six month follow-up of short-term pharmacotherapy for cocaine dependence. *Am J Addict* 1:40-49, 1992.

Kosten, T.R.; Kleber, H.D.; and Morgan, C. Treatment of cocaine abuse with buprenorphine. *Biol Psychiatry* 26:637-639, 1989.

Kranzler, H.R. Use of buspirone in an adolescent with overanxious disorder. *J Am Acad Child Adolesc Psychiatry* 27:789-790, 1988.

Kuperman, S., and Stewart, M.A. Use of propranolol to decrease aggressive outbursts in younger patients. *Psychosomatics* 28:315-319, 1987.

Landry, D.W.; Zhao, K.; Yang, X.Q.; Glickman, M.; and Georgiadis, T.M. Antibody-catalyzed degradation of cocaine. *Science* 259:1899-1901, 1993.

Lichtenstein, E., and Glasgow, R.E. Smoking cessation: What have we learned over the past decade? *J Consult Clin Psychol* 60:518-527, 1992.

McLellan, A.T.; Alterman, A.I.; Cacciola, J.S.; Metzger, D.; and O'Brien, C.P. A new measure of substance abuse treatment: Initial studies of the Treatment Survey Review. *J Nerv Ment Dis* 180:101-110, 1992.

McLellan, A.T.; Arndt, I.O.; Metzger, D.S.; Woody, G.E.; and O'Brien, C.P. The effects of psychosocial services in substance abuse treatment. *JAMA* 269:1953-1959, 1993.

McLellan, A.T.; Luborsky, L.; Woody, G.E.; and O'Brien, C.P. An improved diagnostic evaluation instrument for substance abuse patients: The Addiction Severity Index. *J Nerv Ment Dis* 168:26-33, 1980.

Meyer, R.E. New pharmacotherapies for cocaine dependence revisited. *Arch Gen Psychiatry* 49:900-904, 1992.

Miller, W.R. Motivation for treatment: A review with special emphasis on alcoholism. *Psychol Bull* 98:84-107, 1985.

Munir, K., and Earls, F. Ethical principles governing research in child and adolescent psychiatry. *J Am Acad Child Adolesc Psychiatry* 31:408-414, 1992.

Naranjo, C.A.; Kadlec, K.E.; Sanhueza, P.; Woodley-Remus, D.; and Sellers, E.M. Fluoxetine differentially alters alcohol intake and other consummatory behaviors in problem drinkers. *Clin Pharmacol Ther* 47:490-498, 1990.

Nelson, C.; Mazure, C.; Quinlan, P.M.; and Jatlow, P.I. Drug responsive symptoms in melancholia. *Arch Gen Psychiatry* 41:663-668, 1984.

Nunes, E.V.; McGrath, P.J.; Steven, W.; and Quitkin, F.M. Lithium treatment for cocaine abusers with bipolar spectrum disorders. *Am J Psychiatry* 147:655-657, 1990.

O'Malley, S.S.; Jaffe, A.J.; Chang, G.; Schottenfeld, R.S.; Meyer, R.E.; and Rounsaville, B. Naltrexone and coping skills therapy for alcohol dependence. *Arch Gen Psychiatry* 49:881-887, 1992.

Parrino, M.W., ed. "State Methadone Maintenance Treatment Guidelines." Report prepared for the Department of Health and Human Services, 1992.

Pliszka, S.R. Tricyclics antidepressants in the treatment of children with attention deficit disorder. *J Am Acad Child Adolesc Psychiatry* 26:127-132, 1987.

Prien, R.E., and Gelenberg, A.J. Alternative to lithium for preventive treatment of bipolar disorder. *Am J Psychiatry* 146:840-848, 1989.

Rapoport, J.L. Pediatric psychopharmacology: The last decade. In: Meltzer, H.Y., ed. *Psychopharmacology: The Third Generation of Progress.* New York: Raven, 1987. pp. 1211-1214.

Rickels, K.; Schweizer, E.; Weiss, S.; and Zavodnick, S. Maintenance drug treatment for panic disorder. II. Short- and long-term outcome after drug taper. *Arch Gen Psychiatry* 50:61-68, 1993.

Riddle, M.A.; Geller, B.; and Ryan, N. Another sudden death in a child treated with desipramine. *J Am Acad Child Adolesc Psychiatry* 32:792-797, 1993.

Rosen, M.I., and Kosten, T.R. Buprenorphine: Beyond methadone. *Hosp Comm Psychiatry* 42:347-349, 1991.

Ryan, N.; Puig-Antich, J.; Cooper, T.; Rabinovich, H.; Ambrosini, P.; Davies, M.; King, J.; Torres, D.; and Fried, J. Imipramine in adolescent major depression: Plasma level and clinical response. *Acta Psychiatr Scand* 73:275-288, 1986.

Ryan, N.; Meyer, V.; Dachille, S.; Mazzie, D.; and Puig-Antich, J. Lithium antidepressant augmentation in TCA-refractory depression in adolescents. *J Am Acad Child Adolesc Psychiatry* 27:371-376, 1988a.

Ryan, N.; Puig-Antich, J.; Rabinovich, H.; Fried, J.; Ambrosini, P.; Meyer, V.; Torres, D.; Dachille, S.; and Mazzie, D. MAOI in adolescent major depression unresponsive to tricyclic antidepressants. *J Am Acad Child Adolesc Psychiatry* 27:755-758, 1988b.

Schweizer, E.; Rickels, K.; Weiss, S.; and Zavodnick, S. Maintenance drug treatment of panic disorder. I. Results of a prospective, placebo controlled comparison of alprazolam and imipramine. *Arch Gen Psychiatry* 50:51-60, 1993.

Simeon, J.G.; Ferguson, H.B.; Knott, V.; Roberts, N.; Gauthier, B.; Dubois, C.; and Wiggins, D. Clinical, cognitive, and neurophysiological effects of alprazolam in children and adolescents with overanxious and avoidant disorders. *J Am Acad Child Adolesc Psychiatry* 31:29-33, 1992.

Smart, R.G., and Gray, G. Multiple predictors of dropout from alcoholism treatment. *Arch Gen Psychiatry* 35:363-367, 1978.

Steingard, R.; Biderman, J.; Spencer, T.; Wilens, T.; and Gonzalez, A. Comparison of clonidine response in the treatment of attention-deficit hyperactivity disorder with and without comorbid tic disorders. *J Am Acad Child Adolesc Psychiatry* 32:350-353, 1993.

Stewart, J.T.; Myers, W.C.; Burket, R.C.; and Lyle, W.B. A review of the pharmacotherapy of aggression in children and adolescents. *J Am Acad Child Adolesc Psychiatry* 29:269-277, 1990.

Strober, M., and Carlson, G. Bipolar illness in adolescents with major depression, clinical, genetic, and psychopharmacologic predictions in a three-to-four perspective follow-up investigation. *Arch Gen Psychiatry* 39:549-555, 1982.

Strober, M.; Freedman, R.; Rigali, J.; Schmidt, S.; and Diamond, R. The pharmacotherapy of depressive illness in adolescence: II. Effects of lithium augmentation in nonresponders to imipramine. *J Am Acad Child Adolesc Psychiatry* 31:16-20, 1992.

Strober, M., and Katz, J.L. Do eating disorders and affective disorders share a common etiology? A dissenting opinion. *Int J Eating Disorders* 6:171-180, 1987.

Strober, M.; Morrell, W.; Burroughs, J.; Lampert, C.; Danforth, H.; and Freeman, R. A family study of bipolar I disorder in adolescence: Early onset of symptoms linked to increased familial loading and lithium resistance. *J Affect Disord* 15:255-268, 1988.

Tonnesen, P.; Norregaard, J.; Mikkelsen, K.; Jorgensen, S.; and Nilsson, F. A double-blind trial of a nicotine inhaler for smoking cessation. *JAMA* 269:1268-1271, 1993.

Venkataraman, S.; Naylor, M.W.; and King, C.A. Mania associated with fluoxetine treatment in adolescents. *J Am Acad Child Adolesc Psychiatry* 31:276-281, 1992.

Weddington, W.W.; Brown, B.S.; Haertzen, C.A.; Cone, E.J.; Dax, E.M.; Herning, R.I.; and Michaelson, B.S. Changes in mood, craving and sleep during short-term abstinence reported by male cocaine addicts: A controlled residential study. *Arch Gen Psychiatry* 47:861-868, 1990.

Weiss, R.D.; Pope, H.G.; and Mirin, S.M. Treatment of chronic cocaine abuse and attention deficit disorder residual type, with magnesium pemoline. *Drug Alcohol Depend* 15:69-72, 1985.

Weissman, M.M.; Leckman, J.F.; Merikangas, K.R.; Gammon, G.D.; and Prusoff, B.A. Depression and anxiety disorders in parents and children. Results from the Yale family study. *Arch Gen Psychiatry* 41:845-852, 1984.

Wender, P.H.; Wood, D.R.; and Reimherr, F.W. Pharmacological treatment of attention deficit disorder, residual type (ADD, RT, minimal brain dysfunction, hyperactivity) in adults. *Psychopharmacol Bull* 21:222-231, 1985.

Werry, J.S., and Aman, M.G. Methylphenidate and haloperidol in children. *Arch Gen Psychiatry* 32:790-795, 1975.

West, R. The "nicotine replacement paradox" in smoking cessation: How does nicotine gum really work? *Brit J Addict* 87:165-167, 1992.

Zweben, A., and Li, S. The efficacy of role induction in preventing early dropout from outpatient treatment of drug dependency. *Am J Drug Alcohol Abuse* 8:171-183, 1981.

AUTHOR

Yifrah Kaminer, M.D.
Associate Professor of Psychiatry
University of Connecticut
　School of Medicine
263 Farmington Avenue
Farmington, CT 06030

Youth Evaluation Services (YES): Assessment, Systems of Referral, and Treatment Effects

Frances K. Del Boca, Thomas F. Babor, and Margaret Anne McLaney

INTRODUCTION

This chapter describes Youth Evaluation Services (YES), an innovative assessment and case management program that serves substance-involved youth in Connecticut, and presents preliminary data gathered from YES clients, their parents, and treatment providers. The YES Program, which does not offer any treatment services itself, was developed by the Regional Youth/Adult Substance Abuse Project (RY/ASAP), a community action initiative to coordinate services for youth with substance abuse problems. The program was supported for 4 years as a demonstration project by the Robert Wood Johnson Foundation. Investigators from the University of Connecticut Alcohol Research Center (UConn ARC) were funded under a separate grant to conduct research and evaluation activities.

In addition to offering assessment and case management services, a major goal of the program was to generate information for planners in the region. Through its comprehensive assessment battery, the program was designed to produce data about the characteristics and treatment needs of substance-involved adolescents. As a major funnel into the regional treatment network, the program was expected to yield information about gaps in service and barriers to treatment. Further, the program was created to collect data regarding treatment utilization, service costs, and outcome partly to ensure that standards of care were maintained and that the rising costs of treatment were contained. Related to this objective, program administrators were instructed to develop the means through which YES could become self-supporting, both to assure continued operation after grant funds were expended and to test the economic viability of such a service within the treatment system.

During the first 4 years of YES Program operation, UConn investigators conducted an intensive process evaluation of the program. Followup interviews with clients and their parents were conducted 6 months after initial contact with the program to obtain independent evaluation of satisfaction with YES and to assess client status relative to intake. An extensive research database was developed that included intake assessment data, treatment planning information, followup results, case management reviews, service utilization data, and cost estimates.

The results of preliminary analyses of the YES data are reported below. The characteristics and treatment needs of the initial client cohort are summarized in this chapter, and data on the program's success in achieving its aims are presented. The ability of the program to satisfy its constituencies (clients and providers), to match clients to appropriate levels of care, to access services, and to contain costs are examined. Finally, preliminary data bearing on adolescent treatment utilization and service costs are presented.

THE YES PROCESS: DESIGN AND OPERATION

As described more fully elsewhere (Babor et al. 1991; McLaney et al. 1994), the YES assessment and case management system was designed with several complementary components. The first consists of initial identification procedures to screen and involve adolescent substance users and their families in the assessment and case management program. The next stage involves a core assessment battery that focuses on substance abuse, psychosocial functioning, and family relations. Additional information is gathered through structured diagnostic interviews and from external sources (e.g., family members, school records, treatment discharge summaries) in a sequential assessment process that ends with a comprehensive diagnostic evaluation of the client's treatment needs.

Following the assessment phase, a treatment plan is developed to address the client's alcohol and other drug abuse as well as any related problems. Referral is based on a systematic set of treatment-matching criteria specifically developed for this program. Because the program does not provide treatment, there are no conflicts of interest in the assessment and placement process; referral is a rational process based on client needs. The case management component connects clients and their families with recommended providers, coordinates service, and monitors client progress through regular consultations with the client, the client's family, service providers, and school personnel. The rationale and procedures used to guide the client assessment, treatment planning, and case management components of this program were developed in collaboration with investigators from UConn ARC, who also established the comprehensive research and evaluation component.

Referral into the Program

YES was originally intended to serve as a centralized funnel for a wide variety of referral sources including schools, community agencies, physicians, and the legal system. Relatively small numbers of clients were referred to the program during its initial months of operation. In part, this was because the program concept was foreign to most potential referral sources, and contacts between the program and other agencies were not adequately established prior to the start of operation. Most of those who did make referrals, however, evaluated the program positively (Babor et al. 1991). The one continuing complaint, and a point worth underscoring for the sake of future replications, concerned the speed with which clients were assessed. Frequent delays in scheduling appointments caused the assessment process to be spread over many days and sometimes weeks. Nevertheless, close to 1,000 youths received services during the first 4 years of program operation. These youth came from a wide variety of sources: Schools were the major source of client recruitment (46 percent), followed by community service providers (e.g., physicians, clinics) (23 percent), the judicial system (18 percent), State agencies (4 percent), and family or self-referrals (4 percent).

Assessment

Based in part on the recommendations of two expert committee reports (Institute of Medicine 1990; Tarter 1990), a standardized, sequential assessment battery was developed for the YES Program. At the core of the assessment system was a 3- to 5-hour test battery that combined an initial screening questionnaire with selected diagnostic procedures for problem areas in need of more intensive evaluation.

The client's evaluation began with a lengthy intake telephone interview with a parent or guardian. Following a general orientation to the YES Program, a semistructured Personal Interview Form was completed to record the presenting problem, treatment history, and relevant demographic, medical, and psychosocial information. At the end of the interview, the client and one or both parents were scheduled for the first assessment session which typically (although not always) took place at the YES Program offices. During this first visit, the client completes the

Problem Oriented Screening Instrument for Teens (POSIT) (Rahdert 1991), a 139-item screening questionnaire designed to measure problem severity in 10 functional areas: substance use/abuse, mental health status, physical health status, aggressive behavior/delinquency, social skills, family relations, educational status, vocational status, peer relations, and leisure and recreation. A quick scoring procedure provided an estimate of the severity of each problem area, and a global severity score can be created by summing responses to all items in the instrument. While the POSIT was administered to the client, the parent was asked to complete the Problem Oriented Screening Instrument for Parents (POSIP), a parallel instrument developed by YES Program staff.

The second, diagnostic stage of the assessment procedure consisted of further evaluation in those areas identified as problematic in the screening stage. The Personal Experience Inventory (PEI) is an essential component of the diagnostic battery (Henly and Winters 1988). The PEI is a 300-item, paper-and-pencil questionnaire that assesses two broad content areas: chemical involvement problem severity and psychosocial risk factors. The problem severity section of the PEI measures the symptoms, consequences, and patterns of substance use. The second part of the PEI assesses psychosocial risk factors for substance abuse. These predisposing factors include genetic, sociodemographic, intrapersonal, social, and environmental influences.

When individuals screened positive for psychopathology on the POSIT or the PEI, selected sections of two structured psychiatric interviews were used to determine diagnoses according to the criteria in the "Diagnostic and Statistical Manual of Mental Disorders," 3d. ed., rev. (DSM-III-R). The Diagnostic Interview for Children and Adolescents (DICA) (Welner et al. 1987) provides diagnostic information about the following disorders: depression, dysthymia, conduct disorder, mania, anxiety disorder, phobia, obsessive-compulsive disorder, oppositional defiant disorder, and attention deficit-hyperactivity disorder (ADHD). The Adolescent Diagnostic Interview, revised (ADI-R) (Winters and Henly 1987) was used to diagnose substance use disorders according to DSM-III-R criteria. When necessary, further evaluation was performed by a staff psychiatrist.

The information generated by the client assessment battery was supplemented with data gathered from parents, the assesor/case manager, and schools. Parents were queried about the client's alcohol use, drug involvement, problem behavior, social adjustment, family relations, and need for treatment services. Assessors completed a brief rating form indicating the need for treatment in a variety of domains, including substance abuse, psychological adjustment, family relations, and school involvement. Data collected from schools included current and past academic performance, involvement in student activities, attendance records, and conduct reports. Finally, all clients were asked to provide a urine specimen to objectively verify self-reports regarding recent substance use.

The assessment battery was designed to provide a comprehensive profile of the characteristics, substance use patterns, related problems, and service needs of clients referred for evaluation. Preliminary findings are based on information gathered from a YES cohort comprising approximately 650 clients. In terms of demographic characteristics, the sample is comprised primarily of male youth (70 percent versus 30 percent female). The average male client was 15.6 years of age; females were slightly younger, averaging 15 years of age. Although the majority of referrals were high school students (63 percent of males and 61 percent of females), a sizable minority were in the primary grades (25 percent of males, 29 percent of females). Slightly more than half were white (51 percent), with roughly equal proportions of African Americans (29 percent) and Hispanics (22 percent). Although a majority of clients resided in Bridgeport (58 percent), a substantial minority were referred from suburban communities (42 percent). Almost half of all clients (47 percent) had received some form of psychiatric or substance abuse treatment prior to YES, with outpatient psychiatric treatment being the most common (32 percent). In terms of insurance coverage, approximately a third of the YES clients in the cohort had private insurance (34 percent), and about a fifth had coverage through a health maintenance organization (HMO) (20 percent). Public assistance covered an additional 33 percent of clients; only a minority had no form of third-party reimbursement (12 percent). In summary, client profiles indicate that initial referrals to the program represented a diverse group in terms of sex, age, grade level, race/ethnicity, community type, source of referral, treatment history, and type of insurance coverage.

Table 1, which contains mean scores for the POSIT domains for male and female clients, provides a summary of the types of problems experienced by these youth. As shown in the table, youths referred for evaluation presented with an array of problems in addition to substance use. In general, the problems of female clients equaled or exceeded those of males. A high proportion of adolescents in this sample screened positive

TABLE 1. *POSIT summary data.*

Domain	Males Mean*	(SD)	Percent Positive**	Females Mean*	(SD)	Percent Positive**
Substance abuse	2.41	(3.02)	69.3	2.25	(3.03)	60.7
Mental health status	7.27	(4.34)	50.2	8.85	(4.83)	71.3
Family relationships	3.40	(2.38)	59.2	4.31	(2.61)	69.1
Peer relations	3.41	(1.94)	92.9	3.18	(2.16)	89.9
Aggressive behavior/ delinquency	6.37	(3.00)	82.8	6.45	(3.12)	75.0

KEY: * = Mean scale scores computed by adding total number of positive items.
** = Percent scoring positive on one or more "red flag" items that strongly indicate the need for further diagnostic evaluation.
SD = standard deviation.

in the substance abuse domain (66 percent), and a significant proportion showed evidence of problems or deficits in other areas of adolescent function. Almost all clients reported difficulties with peer relations (92 percent) and school performance (85 percent). Other problem areas differed as a function of gender. For example, males were more likely to screen positive for aggressive or delinquent behavior (83 percent versus 75 percent for females), whereas female clients were more likely to be "red flagged" in the areas of mental health (71 percent versus 50 percent for males) and family relationships (69 percent versus 59 percent for males).

In addition to substance abuse, YES clients in this sample screened positive on the PEI for one or more of an array of psychological, family, and psychiatric problems. Almost half reported family histories of alcohol or drug abuse (45 percent of males, 51 percent of females). Severe family problems were common for both male and female clients (46 percent and 56 percent, respectively), and high proportions of females screened positive for psychiatric problems (32 percent) and physical (38 percent) or sexual (34 percent) abuse. It is important to note that these added problems may not have been recognized without a comprehensive assessment, and that the problems appear to be sufficiently severe to be systematically addressed in the treatment planning process.

PEI results are computed as T-scores based on normative data from two criterion samples (Henley and Winters 1988). One criterion sample was drawn from drug clinic clients and the other from a high school population. Male and female adolescents in the YES sample scored on average somewhat lower than the drug clinic normative sample, but slightly higher than the high school normative sample on the chemical involvement problem severity scales. Scores for the psychosocial scales were close to the middle of the distribution for the drug clinic sample, and considerably higher than those for the high school sample in the areas of deviant behavior, goal orientation, and family pathology.

Another important diagnostic area covered by the PEI is alcohol and other drug use. Although the validity of self-report data is suspect under certain circumstances (Babor et al. 1990), the PEI data indicate that 19 percent of this YES client sample used alcohol on a weekly basis, 18 percent used marijuana weekly, and over 6 percent used marijuana daily or almost daily. Over two-fifths of the clients of both sexes (41 percent of males, 46 percent females) reported getting high or drunk on the majority of drinking occasions. These data, supported by urine toxicology tests, suggest that many referrals did not have regular or serious substance abuse patterns, which is consistent with the early identification goals of YES. Few clients manifested sufficient dependence signs and symptoms to warrant medical detoxification. Finally, the data show that for most of the moderate and serious cases of drug use, alcohol abuse was an important part of the clinical picture.

The assessment data underscore two major points with respect to adolescent substance abuse. First, there appear to be important gender differences in problem identification and treatment referral. Problems were either more likely to go unnoticed in females because they were less visible, or there was reluctance to refer females in the early stages of use. Further, the different problem profiles for the two sexes suggest that, on average, male and female adolescents may have differing treatment needs that require different therapeutic approaches. Second, substance use alone was generally not sufficient for referral. Rather, it was when substance use was part of a larger configuration of problems that adolescents were referred for evaluation. By implication, then, intervention and treatment programs should be equipped to address the broad range of problems typically present in substance-involved youth.

Treatment Planning: The YES Criteria

An underlying assumption of the YES approach is that treatment should be tailored to the nature and severity of the medical, psychological, and social problems identified in the screening and diagnostic stages of assessment. Following the procedures suggested by the Adolescent Assessment Referral System (AARS) protocol (Rahdert 1991), YES personnel formulated a treatment plan based on the results of the assessment process. Specific recommendations for intervention were made for each problem domain according to the client's identified needs and based on the YES Treatment Matching Criteria.

In developing the YES Program, researchers reviewed the available literature dealing with treatment matching, treatment services, and other interventions for teenagers who experience substance abuse problems (see Institute of Medicine 1990 for a review). This literature, together with the collective experience of YES and RY/ASAP staff, was used to develop a set of matching guidelines to inform the treatment planning process. These guidelines were inspired in part by Skinner's (1981) problem-oriented approach and by the Cleveland Criteria (Hoffman et al. 1991). Over time the guidelines were refined and modified to incorporate ASAM guidelines. Treatment referral guidelines were also altered to consider the costs of service in addition to client needs.

Referral to Services

Despite the minimal financial resources of many YES clients, staff succeeded in finding placements for virtually all clients recommended for treatment. Most referrals appear appropriate; that is, the majority of initial treatment recommendations were in accord with the treatment matching guidelines. For example, clients referred to inpatient care scored significantly higher on all measures of problem severity on the POSIT and the PEI.

It is important to note that the inpatient versus outpatient distinction is quite general. Inpatient treatments included inpatient hospital and residential programs, short-term hospital programs, and group homes or halfway houses; outpatient treatment includes an even wider array of services. In addition, initial treatment plans were often modified during the referral process. Whether and where a client was actually placed depends on a variety of factors including client and parental attitudes and resources and the availability of services at the time of referral. In fact, roughly one-third of the cases were "mismatched" according to treatment matching guidelines due to unavailability of services, parental objections to the YES treatment recommendations, or lack of insurance coverage.

A major YES Program goal was to contain service costs while assuring that treatment was appropriate and standards of care were maintained. In practice, program staff were slow to implement explicit cost containment procedures, fearing that client treatment would be shortchanged; however, several procedures were developed during the last 2 years of the program's operation to contain and monitor costs. These included guidelines instructing assessors to attempt low-intensity interventions prior to placing clients in higher intensity treatments, referrals to the least costly provider at the appropriate level of care, administrative review of all treatment plans recommending inpatient or residential care, and regular case manager review of inpatient client progress to determine the need for further treatment.

Over time, the proportion of inpatient and residential treatment recommendations declined, with a concomitant increase in emphasis on outpatient care and low- or no-cost services. These trends are presented graphically in figure 1, which plots changes in treatment recommendations over 6-month intervals. As shown in the figure, the proportion of clients referred for inpatient care was reduced by more than half during the 4 years of YES operation: 50 percent of clients were referred for inpatient treatment during the first 6 months of operation compared with only 22 percent in the most recent 6-month interval. Although explicit cost containment guidelines probably contributed to these trends, two other factors were also important: third-party payers became increasingly unwilling to reimburse for lengthy inpatient stays; and YES clients' problem profiles suggested less severity over time, particularly in terms of substance involvement.

Case Management. Following acceptance of the treatment plan by the client and client's parents, the case management phase of the YES Program began. Case management was viewed as a process of interaction within a service network which assures that a client receives needed services in a supportive, efficient, and cost-effective manner. The YES case manager performed a variety of client-specific functions including assessment of service need, treatment planning, linking clients and families with appropriate treatment resources, monitoring client progress, coordinating aftercare services, and providing client advocacy. Formal monitoring of treatment and progress toward recovery occurred at

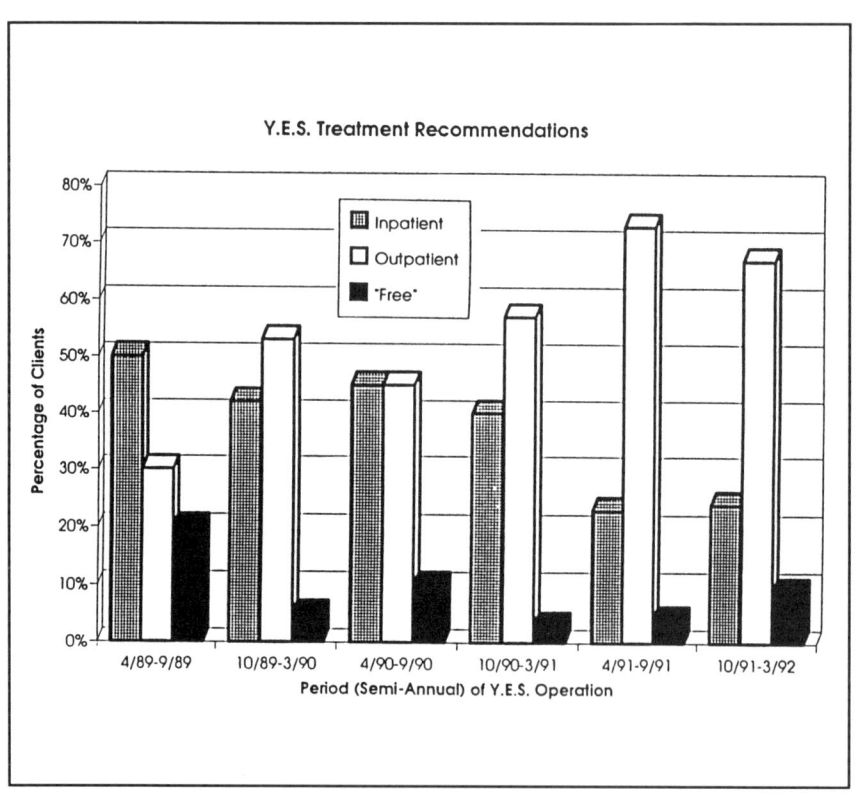

FIGURE 1. *YES treatment recommendations: Trends over a 2-year period.*

regular intervals for up to 18 months. Contact could be in person, by telephone, or through any other means that the case manager deemed appropriate. The frequency and duration of contact between client and case manager was determined by several factors including the client's needs, interest in the program, and progress in treatment.

THE YES PROGRAM: HOW WELL DID IT WORK?

As the foregoing review of program components suggests, YES was successful in achieving many of its objectives. In terms of assessment, the data indicate that the instruments that comprise the battery and the sequential evaluation process produced a comprehensive profile of treatment needs. Providers consistently reported that the summaries of assessment results received from YES were highly informative, and many elected not to conduct their own intake evaluation as a consequence

(Babor et al. 1991). Psychometric studies of the POSIT based on YES data indicate that this relatively new instrument is reliable, valid, and quite sensitive in its ability to detect youth with problems relating to substance use (McLaney et al. 1994).

The program also performed well in terms of treatment planning and referral. In general, treatment plans were in accord with matching guidelines. Program staff successfully brokered access to service for clients with limited financial resources. Nevertheless, many clients (approximately one third) elected not to follow the recommended course of treatment. The identification of gaps in service played a role in the stimulation of some new programs in the region, and YES staff facilitated collaborative arrangements among providers that resulted in better coordination and integration of regional services.

However, the program was somewhat less successful in other areas. Although YES has provided services to a large number of clients, the program did not develop into the central funnel to the regional treatment network that was originally envisioned. Partly because the program was funded by grants, YES did not implement policies that would have served to make it competitive. Outreach was minimal, marketing efforts were sporadic, and complaints regarding the speed and cost of service were not adequately addressed. The case management component of the program was diffuse, and there were significant gaps in knowledge regarding client status at different points in time. In addition, the program was slow to implement explicit cost containment procedures. Perhaps most important, program administrators were unable to negotiate the kinds of agreements with referral sources, providers, and third-party payers that would assure continued operation. Although additional funding may be secured, as of this writing the future of YES as an economically viable, freestanding assessment and case management program is uncertain.

Followup Evaluation

In combination with case records, discharge summaries, and other provider information, the independent 6-month followup evaluation conducted by UConn research assistants provided a wealth of information regarding treatment utilization, service costs, and short-term client outcomes.

Followup evaluations for eligible clients occurred approximately 6 to 8 months after their initial assessment interview at YES. Followup interviews were used to gather information about service utilization, satisfaction with services, changes in substance use, and current psychosocial adjustment. Each followup evaluation was comprised of three components: a short telephone interview with the client's parent or guardian; an extensive face-to-face client interview at the client's home or other convenient location, during which selected assessments from the intake battery were repeated; and collection of supplemental information from YES client records, school personnel, and service providers to corroborate client self-reports, verify the utilization of case management services, and validate cost estimates.

All followup evaluations were conducted by a member of the UConn staff, preferably one who had earlier contacts with the client. Participants were assured that all information gathered was strictly confidential, and obtained for program evaluation only (not for clinical purposes). Clients were paid $25 for participating in the 6-month followup session. Approximately 4 percent of the clients approached at intake refused to participate in the research component of the program; similarly, about 4 percent of research participants contacted for followup evaluation have declined to participate. Despite the low refusal rate, many clients living in poor urban areas were not able to be reached for followup evaluations and the sample obtained thus far is disproportionately white and of higher socioeconomic status.

Cost Estimation Procedures

Service utilization was determined from facility discharge summaries, clients followup reports, case notes (e.g., checklists, progress notes), YES personnel, and treatment plan projections. These sources were consulted in the order listed to ensure maximum accuracy. If a facility provided more than one treatment service, each treatment was recorded as a separate listing except in the case of inpatient treatment, which generally includes group and/or individual counseling as part of its program. Units of treatment were coded in terms of the increments in which the services were delivered and billed. Outpatient individual, family, and group therapy, as well as self-help and insight groups, were primarily measured in sessions. Partial hospital and inpatient treatment were measured in days.

Algorithms were developed to calculate total costs of inpatient and partial hospital treatment when full facility cost information was available. The formulas for inpatient and partial hospital treatment take into account the additional costs that exist above and beyond facilities' fixed or average daily rates. Such additional costs include schooling and diagnostic assessment fees as well as miscellaneous therapy sessions not included in the daily rate. Total costs were estimated for 6-month periods (6, 12, and 18 months postintake) calculated from the date of the client's initial interview. The total cost for the period was determined by counting the number of days from the admission date to the end of the treatment and multiplying the resulting figure by the unit cost for that treatment facility.

Treatment Utilization and Costs

Initial analyses in this area have focused on relating service costs to demographic characteristics, intake problem severity, types of third-party reimbursement, and short-term (6-month) client outcomes. Because the program database is updated continually, and client characteristics and referral patterns changed over time, the initial results should be regarded as preliminary.

The first analysis compared demographic information for YES clients according to three types of third-party reimbursement: private insurance companies and employee or union health insurance coverage; HMOs and prepaid health plans; and public sector funding including State assistance, Social Security, and the probation department. The groups were comparable in terms of age and gender, but differed with respect to race and ethnicity. Clients who received public sector reimbursement were more likely to be African American or Hispanic than those covered by HMOs or private insurance. Differences in problem severity between groups at intake were negligible.

In general, the analysis found that 20 percent of the clients accounted for more than 90 percent of the treatment costs, primarily because of the unit costs and length of stay associated with inpatient treatment. There was little difference in the average costs of inpatient and outpatient treatment charged to the three types of payers during the 6-month period. A review of the unit costs associated with different programs and facilities, along with the proportions of clients referred to those facilities, indicated that there was considerable price variation among providers, and that clients were not necessarily placed in the least expensive treatment alternatives.

In addition to these descriptive analyses, intake data were examined to identify predictors of service utilization and costs. Only four assessment scales (from a total of more than 30 possible measures taken from the objective assessment instruments) correlated significantly with units of treatment or service costs. In general, higher costs and longer lengths of stay were incurred by clients with high scores on substance involvement, family dysfunction, mental health problems, and physical health conditions. Although the predictors did not account for substantial portions of the variance, the results suggest that clients with higher levels of personal and social dysfunction as well as substance abuse were more likely to receive more intensive and more costly treatment.

CONCLUSION

Evaluation data from the YES Program suggest several conclusions regarding adolescent substance abuse treatment. First, client assessment profiles indicate that a systematic and comprehensive evaluation is necessary to fully ascertain the treatment needs of individuals in this population. Second, treatment needs vary as a function of gender. Moreover, the findings suggest that more attention needs to be paid to identifying females in the early stages of substance involvement. Third, although intake results predicted treatment utilization, there was a significant proportion of clients who failed to utilize appropriate services as a result of individual factors (e.g., failure to accept a treatment plan) and/or external barriers (e.g., lack of insurance coverage). These factors need to be addressed in treatment planning and referral.

The preliminary findings are also suggestive with respect to cost containment. The process evaluation of the YES Program indicated that there was considerable initial resistance to the inclusion of cost containment guidelines in the treatment planning process. At the same time, it was clear that a relatively small proportion of clients consumed a high proportion of treatment resources.

Despite the problems encountered in implementing the YES Program and in securing financial support for its continued operation, the program concept offers considerable promise as a mechanism for containing costs and maintaining standards of case in a reformed health care system. The program succeeded in developing rational procedures for screening and diagnostic assessment, appropriate treatment referral, and independent followup evaluation. In addition, a data system was established that would permit the evaluation of treatment-matching guidelines in terms of service utilization and outcome. Thus, the YES Program concept provides a model system for collecting client data, tracking the services needs of different subgroups in the population, and monitoring treatment outcomes. Future analyses of the YES dataset will address these issues with an emphasis on examining how client characteristics and treatment variables influence service utilization and costs, as well as short-term client outcomes.

REFERENCES

Babor, T.F.; Brown, J.; and Del Boca, F.K. Validity of self-reports in applied research on addictive behaviors: Fact or fiction? *Behav Assess* 12:5-31, 1990.

Babor, T.F.; Del Boca, F.K.; McLaney, M.A.; Jacobi, B.; Higgins-Biddle, J.; and Hass, W. Just say YES: Matching adolescents to appropriate interventions for alcohol and drug-related problems. *Alcohol Health Res World* 25:77-86, 1991.

Henly, G.A., and Winters, K.C. Development of problem severity scales for the assessment of adolescent alcohol and drug abuse. *Int J Addict* 23:65-85, 1988.

Hoffman, N.G.; Halikas, J.A.; Mee-Lee, D.; and Weedman, R.D. *Patient Placement Criteria for the Treatment of Psychoactive Substance Use Disorders.* Washington, DC: American Society of Addiction Medicine, 1991.

Institute of Medicine. *Broadening the Base of Treatment for Alcohol Problems.* Washington, DC: National Academy Press, 1990.

McLaney, M.A.; Del Boca, F.K.; and Babor, T.F. A validation study of the Problem-Oriented Screening Instrument for Teenagers (POSIT). *J Mental Health* 3:363-376, 1994.

Rahdert, E.R., ed. *The Adolescent Assessment/Referral System Manual.* U.S. Dept. of Health and Human Services, Public Health Service; Alcohol, Drug Abuse, and Mental Health Administration, 1991.

Skinner, H.A. Different strokes for different folks: Differential treatment for alcohol abuse. NIAAA Research Monograph No. 5. *Evaluation of the Alcoholic: Implications for Research Theory and Treatment.* Washington, DC: Supt. of Docs., U.S. Govt. Print. Off., 1981.

Tarter, R.E. Evaluation and treatment of adolescent substance abuse: A decision tree method. *Am J Drug Alcohol Abuse* 16:1-46, 1990.

Welner, Z.; Reich, W.; Herjanic, B.; Jung, K.; and Amado, H. Reliability, validity, and parent-child agreement studies of the diagnostic interview for children and adolescents (DICA). *J Am Acad Child Adolesc Psychiatry* 26:649-653, 1987.

Winters, K.C., and Henly, G.A. Advances in the assessment of adolescent chemical dependency: Development of a chemical use problems severity scale. *Psychology Addict Behav* 1:146-153, 1987.

ACKNOWLEDGMENT

This research was supported by grants from the Robert Wood Johnson Foundation (#13455), the National Institute on Alcohol Abuse and Alcoholism (T32AAD7290), and the National Institute on Drug Abuse (2R01-DA08727).

AUTHORS

Frances K. Del Boca, Ph.D.
Assistant Professor

Thomas F. Babor, Ph.D.
Professor

and

Margaret Anne McLaney, Ph.D.
Assistant Professor
Department of Psychiatry
University of Connecticut Health Center
263 Farmington Avenue
Farmington, CT 06030-1410

Posttreatment Services for Chemically Dependent Adolescents

Sherilynn F. Spear and Sharon Y. Skala

INTRODUCTION

Both clinical and research observations suggest that chemically dependent adolescents tend to become chemically dependent adults (De Leon and Deitch 1985; Gerstein and Harwood 1990; Kandel et al. 1986; McAuliffe and Gordon 1974). Even for those adolescents who successfully complete a primary treatment program, the recovery process is complex and its dimensions are not clearly understood. Recovery is almost never a linear process of sustaining abstinence and increasing successful functioning in a drug-free lifestyle (Gerstein and Harwood 1990; Marlatt and Gordon 1980; Rounsaville 1986). Relapse rates for adolescents are high. Longstanding habits associated with drug use are difficult to change and often continue to be reinforced within the individual's environment (Hall et al. 1991; McAuliffe 1989; O'Brien et al. 1991; Thompson et al. 1984). In addition, drug use by the adolescent may be enmeshed with other problem conditions such as histories of physical and/or sexual abuse, delinquency, homelessness, and co-occurring psychological disorders (Crowley, this volume; Dembo et al. 1990; Farrow, this volume; Harrison et al. 1989; Hart et al. 1989). Consequently, successful treatment is rarely a single intervention that leads to an absolute cure. Rather, treatment must be seen as a continuum of care that seeks to initiate recovery by establishing a period of abstinence and sustaining the recovery process. This continuum of care includes identifying adolescents with substance abuse problems, facilitating their entry into treatment, providing primary treatment to initiate the recovery process, and continuing posttreatment services to maintain recovery. This chapter focuses on posttreatment services for adolescents.

Unfortunately, the body of scientific literature in the area of substance abuse tends to reflect research that has focused on chemically dependent adults and primary treatment. Scientifically sound research on posttreatment services for adolescents is particularly sparse. Marlatt and

George (1984) suggested that high relapse rates among persons who complete treatment for chemical dependency underscore the need to design services that take into account the real differences in the roles of primary treatment and posttreatment services. They argued that the response to high relapse rates in the addictions field has been one of increasing the type and intensity of primary treatment services rather than directing attention to posttreatment services. The 1990 Institute on Medicine report (Gerstein and Harwood 1990) suggests posttreatment services have been neglected from both a clinical and a research perspective despite evidence of their importance.

Given the scarcity of the research, it is necessary to draw on a wide range of adult and adolescent literature to focus on some very basic issues concerning posttreatment services for chemically dependent adolescents. These issues include:

- the role of posttreatment services in the overall continuum of care,
- relapse and recovery rates and patterns among chemically dependent adolescents, and
- promising posttreatment service modalities for adolescents.

ROLE OF POSTTREATMENT SERVICES

Posttreatment Objectives

Although the literature is quite limited, there is some consensus concerning the objectives of posttreatment services. It is generally agreed that the purpose of posttreatment services is to facilitate the transition from primary treatment to maintaining a drug-free lifestyle within the larger community (Brown and Ashery 1979; De Leon 1990-1991; Hawkins and Catalano 1985; Leukefeld and Tims 1989). Various studies contrast the objectives of primary treatment with those of posttreatment services. These studies suggest that primary treatment is directed toward ending drug use and creating a period of abstinence. Part of the process of beginning abstinence involves reducing triggers associated with drug use, reducing denial of problems associated with drug use, and increasing commitment to recovery (De Leon 1990-1991; Marlatt and George 1984; McAuliffe 1989; Zackon et al. 1985). In contrast, posttreatment services are seen as focusing on maintaining recovery as the individual returns to the larger community. In general, the literature on posttreatment services for adults suggests that maintaining recovery involves two basic tasks: increasing the client's ability to function effectively in the larger community, and helping the client build a social network that supports a drug-free lifestyle (De Leon 1990-1991; Hawkins and Catalano 1985; Marlatt and George 1984; McAuliffe 1989).

Of course, it is recognized that primary treatment and posttreatment are not totally distinct in purpose (De Leon 1990-1991). Often, the posttreatment recovery process involves periods of relapse; therefore, there is a need to deal with issues related to drug use addressed in primary treatment (Marlatt and George 1984; Marlatt and Gordon 1980). Likewise, primary treatment initiates not only the abstinence process, but other aspects of the recovery process related to the successful transition to the larger community. Nevertheless, remaining drug free involves major behavioral changes for chemically dependent adolescents. The likelihood is minimal that most individuals can sustain behavioral change within the environment where the original drug-using behaviors were established without the support of posttreatment services.

Posttreatment Environment

Perhaps as important as clarifying the different though overlapping purposes of primary care and posttreatment services is the recognition of the distinct contexts wherein the two sets of objectives are pursued. During primary care, the individual is often isolated from the larger community. The interventions are intense and the adolescent lives in an environment that clearly supports and perhaps demands that the individual remain drug free. In contrast, posttreatment services usually target the chemically dependent person upon return to the larger community (Hawkins and Catalano 1985; Kanfer and Goldstein 1979). Consequently, posttreatment services need to take into account both the objectives of these interventions as well as the context within which the individual is struggling to remain drug free (McAuliffe 1989).

There is some evidence that posttreatment services need to be more responsive than primary treatment to individual differences (De Leon 1990-1991; Hawkins and Catalano 1985). This focus may be needed to accommodate the needs of individuals returning to the larger community where the environment is unique, as opposed to the shared environment that often characterizes primary treatment. The concept of tailoring posttreatment services to the individual raises another issue. The chronic nature of chemical dependency suggests the need to create a continuity of treatment for the individual. In their review of the literature on aftercare, Hawkins and Catalano (1985) discussed the potential gains of creating a continuity of care responsive to the individual when posttreatment services are offered by the same organization that provided primary treatment. They also suggested that when clinicians fail to recognize the purpose and importance of posttreatment services, there is less participation in posttreatment services by clients.

Although most of the above discussion is based on research that focused on posttreatment services for adults, the findings have clear implications for chemically dependent adolescents. Nevertheless, it is not likely that research findings for adults can be generalized indiscriminately to adolescents. Posttreatment services for adolescents, as well as adults, must focus on helping the individual maintain a drug-free lifestyle within the larger community. Basic to clarifying the nature of posttreatment services for adolescents is the need to examine what is known about relapse and recovery among adolescents who have completed primary treatment.

RELAPSE AND RECOVERY

Relapse

Two large-scale studies, the Drug Abuse Reporting Program (DARP) (Sells and Simpson 1979) and the Treatment Outcome Prospective Study (TOPS) (Hubbard et al. 1985), provide some general information on posttreatment relapse by adolescents. These studies indicate that posttreatment relapse rates are high among adolescents and adults. The greatest risk of relapse appears to be during the first 6 to 12 months following treatment. Overall, recovery is more likely among adolescents who have received treatment than among those who have not.

Brown and colleagues (1989) assessed relapse rates of adolescents and compared those rates with relapse data for adults (Hunt et al. 1971; Leukefeld and Tims 1989). The study by Brown and colleagues (1989) suggests that relapse rates and the timing of relapse for adolescents are similar to those for adults; 56 percent of the adolescents returned to regular use in the first 6 months following treatment. When relapse is defined as isolated use incidents, 64 percent of the adolescents used at least once during the first 3 months following completion of primary treatment, and 70 percent used at least once during the first 6 months following completion of primary treatment.

Preliminary analysis of findings from a study by Spear and Skala (unpublished data) suggests similar results in greater detail than the results reported by Brown and colleagues (1989). The data depict different levels of drug use after residential treatment: isolated use incidents, drug use at least once per month, and use on a weekly or more frequent basis. The data indicate that 91.9 percent of the subjects in the study had at least one isolated use incident during the first year after completion of residential treatment, with 42 percent using drugs at least once within the first month.

Approximately 75.7 percent of the clients used at least monthly by the end of the first year, and 62.2 percent had returned to weekly or multi-weekly use. It would also appear that, for adolescents, the greatest time of risk for each level of relapse is during the first 2 months. In addition, nearly all of the adolescents returning to drug use at any level do so during the first 6 months following residential treatment with approximately a 10 percent increase for each level of use during the 7 to 12 months following completion of primary treatment. Finally, although the data indicate an overall relapse rate of 62.2 percent returning to weekly or more frequent level of drug use, the rate does vary by type of drug(s) of dependence. First-year relapse (weekly/more often) rates by type of pretreatment drug of dependence are as follows: alcohol, 48.6 percent; marijuana, 76.9 percent; alcohol and marijuana, 72.0 percent; other drugs, 53.8 percent. As found in other studies, alcohol and marijuana are the drugs most frequently used by this age group, with a large percentage of the adolescents using both alcohol and marijuana.

Implications for Posttreatment Services

Posttreatment relapse rates raise important questions for the design of posttreatment services. Most programs for adolescents see total abstinence of the objective of treatment. Nevertheless, the relapse data suggest that nearly all adolescents have some level of drug use following primary treatment. The relapse rates indicate that total abstinence may be an unrealistic objective and from a research perspective may lead to treatment outcome measures that are insensitive to real though not absolute changes in drug use behaviors. Such measures may also mask the fact that adolescents in this population are at risk for significantly different levels of relapse (drug use) during the first year following completion of primary treatment.

The data suggest the need to design posttreatment services whose intensity and duration reflect differential relapse levels. In addition, the timing of such interventions is crucial (Gerstein and Harwood 1990). Thus, results from the above-reported studies indicate that posttreatment services are particularly important during the first 6 months following treatment if recovery is to be sustained during the transition to a larger community. The highest risk period is the first 2 months following treatment, suggesting the need for intense posttreatment services during this time. The findings of various studies also indicate the need to examine different levels of posttreatment drug use and when possible design interventions whose timing, intensity, and duration reflect the differential relapse patterns within the adolescent population. A key dimension of designing various posttreatment services becomes how to identify clients at risk for the different relapse patterns.

Client Characteristics Associated with Relapse

Most studies that examine the relationship between adolescent characteristics and drug use focus on those factors associated with the risk of becoming chemically dependent. Very little research has examined pretreatment and during-treatment factors associated with posttreatment drug use. The studies that have examined that relationship suggest that being male (Catalano et al. 1989; Dembo et al. 1991; Shoemaker and Sherry 1991), having higher levels of pretreatment drug use, greater family pathology, less parental involvement in treatment, and a diagnosis of psychological disorders are associated with the increased likelihood of relapse (Filstead and Anderson 1983; McLellan et al. 1986; Shoemaker and Sherry 1991).

Some findings suggest that less time in primary treatment may be associated with increased risk of relapse (Booth 1981; De Leon and Jainchill 1986; Finney et al. 1980; Friedman et al. 1987; Gerstein and Harwood 1990; Sells and Simpson 1979). In addition, there is increasing evidence that a significant proportion of adolescents who present for treatment for chemical dependence have a higher likelihood of being victims of physical/sexual abuse (Dembo et al. 1989; Harrison et al. 1989; Hart et al. 1989; Spear and Skala 1992), have a history of delinquency (Dembo et al. 1989; Harrison and Hoffman 1987), and/or coexisting psychological disorders (Crowley, this volume). Although the consequences for relapse of these coexisting conditions are unclear at present, concern for the potential impact of these characteristics on posttreatment relapse is widespread.

Work in progress by Spear and Skala suggests it might be possible to move from using individual correlates to using pretreatment characteristics to construct profiles that identify adolescents likely to return to the pretreatment level of use. Such profiles have the potential of identifying early in the treatment process adolescents at different levels of risk for returning to their pretreatment level of drug use during the first year following primary treatment. Data indicating significantly different relapse rates and intake characteristics for males and females (Spear and Skala 1991) suggest the importance of constructing distinct risk profiles for males and females. Spear and Skala (unpublished data) used discriminant analysis to construct the profiles.

Discriminant analysis of males' pretreatment characteristics correctly classified 84 percent of those likely to return to the pretreatment level of use and explained 64 percent of the variance. Overall, the model was stronger in identifying those not likely to relapse (86 percent) versus those likely to relapse (82 percent). For males, pretreatment characteristics associated with relapse during the first year following treatment included number of drug-related arrests, mother's educational level (high school or less), higher pretreatment use levels, mother defining herself as unemployed (versus working at home or employed), and identification of the first drug used as cocaine.

Discriminant analysis of pretreatment characteristics correctly classified 79 percent of females and explained 66 percent of the variance. Again, the model was more effective in identifying those not likely to return to the pretreatment level of use (86 percent) than those likely to do so. For females, the characteristics associated with risk of relapse during the first year following treatment included a history of probation, higher number of situations of pretreatment use, chemically dependent maternal grandparent, and a higher number of household moves.

Implications for Posttreatment Services

Identifying variables or sets of variables associated with relapse has significant implication for posttreatment services for adolescents. Early identification of adolescents at high risk for relapse can provide a basis for building continuity into treatment planning. Secondly, the correlates and/or profiles can serve as a basis for matching the clients to posttreatment services of different levels of duration and intensity. Lastly, measures of posttreatment services outcomes, which take into account different levels of risk of relapse, can provide a better understanding of posttreatment service effectiveness.

Posttreatment Factors Associated with Relapse and Recovery

Another area of research that is potentially important to designing effective posttreatment services focuses on posttreatment factors associated with relapse or recovery. The implication of these factors for relapse is quite different from the client characteristics discussed above. Client characteristics have the potential to identify those adolescents early in the treatment process who are at elevated risk for posttreatment relapse. Those characteristics are usually "givens" and are not susceptible to change through intervention. In contrast, the posttreatment factors associated with relapse and recovery are behaviors that are susceptible to influence and may serve as intermediate indicators of the impact of interventions on variables associated with continuing drug use or recovery.

Studies of posttreatment correlates of relapse for adults and the much sparser literature for adolescents provide some indications of behaviors associated with relapse patterns. Three studies of adolescent posttreatment correlates of treatment outcome were identified (Brown et al. 1989; DeJong and Henrich 1980; Shoemaker and Sherry 1991). While these studies examine a variety of factors and used varying definitions of relapse, they found that posttreatment factors similar to those impacting adults are associated with treatment outcome among adolescents (Catalano and Hawkins 1985; Catalano et al. 1990-1991; De Leon 1991; Hawkins and Catalano 1985; Mummé 1991; Vaillant 1988). Maintaining recovery appears to be related to greater use of behavioral and cognitive coping strategies, and more effective functioning in school (Shoemaker and Sherry 1991).

Recent work by Jenson and colleagues (1993) examined the relationship between reported intentions to use drugs in the future and actual posttreatment drug use. Lower intentions to use are correlated with lower levels of actual posttreatment drug use. Data from Spear and Skala (unpublished observations) suggest that adolescents who did not return to their pretreatment level of drug use were more likely to be involved in a 12-step program, engage in leisure activities where drugs were not present, and stay in school. They were less likely to cut school and to maintain friendships or engage in activities with pretreatment friends. In contrast, the factors associated with relapse included lack of involvement in productive activities (work, school, leisure activities), return to the environment where the adolescent previously used drugs, failure to establish social contact with nonusing adolescents (DeJong and Henrich 1980), and less family involvement in adolescent's treatment (Shoemaker and Sherry 1991).

Implications for Posttreatment Services

Data on outcome correlates suggest posttreatment services for adolescents must address the same basic tasks as those for adults. For example, recovery correlates such as staying in school, functioning effectively at school or work, engaging in nondrug-related leisure activities, and having more effective coping strategies suggest the importance of facilitating effective functioning in the larger community during adolescents' posttreatment transition. Other correlates of recovery such as establishing friendships with nondrug-using adolescents, not associating with drug-using pretreatment friends, or participating in 12-step programs increase the likelihood that the adolescent will build a social support group for a drug-free lifestyle. Thus, it would appear that adolescents face the same key tasks as adults when they return to the larger community and try to remain drug free.

Returning to the Larger Community

Regardless of whether a drug-dependent individual is an adult or adolescent, the recovery process includes returning to drug-free functioning in the larger community. Returning to the larger community may pose difficulties unique to the adolescent (De Leon and Deitch 1985). Many adolescents complete primary treatment while they are under the age of 18 (Brown et al. 1989; Grenier 1985; Spear and Skala 1991). Because they are legally minors, these adolescents do not choose where they will live after completing primary treatment. The majority of adolescents return to the pretreatment home, school, and neighborhood. These environments may pose significant risks for relapse.

Data collected during treatment indicate that adolescents most often report using drugs at home, at a friend's home, or at school (Brown et al. 1989; Grenier 1985; Spear and Skala 1992). Anecdotal data from a study of drug-dependent adolescents utilizing posttreatment services indicate that virtually all of the adolescents returning to their old school report being offered drugs on the first day back in the school (Spear and Skala 1992).

The home environment may also reflect the complex difficulties the adolescent faces in remaining drug free. A number of studies suggest that the home environment may increase the difficulties of the adolescent to remain drug free. Adolescents who use drugs are more likely to have parents and siblings who use drugs (Cotton 1979; Goodwin 1985; Hawkins et al. 1987, Kumpfer and DeMarsh 1986; Vaillant 1983). Spear and Skala (1992) found that among adolescents in treatment for drug dependency, 80 percent of the adolescents and 71 percent of the parents indicated that an immediate family member, other than the adolescent in treatment, had a problem with chemical dependency.

Adolescent drug use is also associated with higher levels of family conflict and poor communication between adolescents and their parents (Baumrind 1985; Braucht et al. 1973; Hawkins et al. 1987; Kumpfer 1987; Kumpfer and DeMarsh 1986; Spear and Skala 1992; Toray et al. 1991) as well as lack of stability in the home environment, multiple residential moves (Catalano et al. 1989; Hawkins et al. 1987; Kaplan et al. 1984; Kumpfer 1987; Vaillant and Milofsky 1982), unstructured environments, and multiple changes in parental marital status (Kumpfer 1987; Kumpfer and DeMarsh 1986; Spear and Skala 1992; Vaillant and Milofsky 1982). Unless the home environment changes or the adolescent relates to the environment in new ways, the factors that increased the risk of drug use may increase the risk of relapse.

PROMISING POSTTREATMENT SERVICE MODALITIES

For lasting behavioral change to occur, researchers agree that it is not sufficient to treat adolescent substance abusers in residential facilities and then return them to environments that supported their drug use. Some form of transition services are needed. Postresidential treatment services are based on the assumption that continuing assistance can reduce the impact of factors associated with relapse and strengthen those factors associated with recovery (Brown and Ashery 1979; De Leon 1991; Hawkins and Catalano 1985). Although there is currently little research or literature on postresidential treatment services for adolescents, the complex recovery process, adolescent characteristics, and possible factors associated with relapse suggest that timing and intensity of services are critically important given the adolescent tendency to early relapse. Research into the environmental characteristics recovering substance abusers most often reenter upon discharge from primary inpatient treatment is related to the issues of timing and intensity. Thompson and colleagues (1984) pointed out that, in the posttreatment environment, illegal behavior and substance use are often the most immediate and potent sources of gratification available to recovering substance abusers. While prosocial activities such as entering school or getting a job can serve to disrupt the drug user's former sources of gratification (Vaillant 1988), the positive reinforcement potential of these activities is weaker, generally delayed, and possibly even negative (e.g., punishment for inappropriate behavior in school). Thus, it is no easy task for the recovering adolescent to establish prosocial networks or function effectively in the larger community, even with the necessary skills. Posttreatment services must be timely and initially intense to support and help the adolescent create linkages with positive drug-free support structures within the community (Jenson et al. 1986).

A number of specific treatment modalities show promise in helping the adolescent sustain the recovery process. In particular, they have potential in helping adolescents address the tasks and issues associated with returning to the wider community. These posttreatment service modalities include cognitive-behavioral skill training, intensive outpatient treatment, family-based interventions, and case management.

Skills Training

Adolescents who frequently use drugs often lack a range of skills that seem to be important to success in creating new patterns of interaction with nondrug-using others (Catalano et al. 1989; Shoemaker and Sherry 1991). These skills include impulse control, anger management, problem solving, assertiveness, time management, and coping with anxiety or stress. Cognitive-behavioral skill training focuses on developing new ways of interpreting and responding to interpersonal and intrapersonal situations. Despite disappointing results among adult substance abusers receiving skills training (Hawkins et al. 1989), studies of skills training interventions targeting adolescents suggest that the acquisition of cognitive-behavioral skills shows promise in helping to maintain treatment gains and to negotiate the posttreatment environment.

Shoemaker and Sherry (1991) reported on a 3-month followup study of 144 adolescents who had completed primary inpatient treatment.

Adolescents who used active behavioral and cognitive coping strategies in response to crises were more likely to remain abstinent while those who used avoidant coping responses were more likely to relapse.

Jenson and colleagues (1993) examined the relationship between cognitive-behavioral skills, intentions to use drugs, and later drug and alcohol use among 130 delinquent adolescents who had completed treatment in a juvenile facility. Interviews at 12-month followup indicated results were different for males and females. For females, a higher skills level was directly and positively related to the number of drug-free months and inversely related to marijuana use and variety and severity of drug use. The same skills did not have a statistically significant direct effect on any measured drug outcomes for males. However, higher skills levels did lower male subjects' intentions to use drugs or alcohol. Less drug and alcohol use was associated with decreased intentions to use. This suggests an indirect relationship between skills and reductions in drug and alcohol use among males.

Shoemaker and Sherry (1991) also noticed gender differences with regard to abstinence, with females being more likely to remain abstinent than males. While no mention was made of gender in relation to use of cognitive-behavioral coping skills, a higher skills level was related to abstinence.

Preliminary analysis of the Spear and Skala (unpublished) data on posttreatment service effectiveness suggests results similar to those of Jenson and colleagues (1993). At 1 year following completion of primary treatment, girls randomized to the skills training group were significantly less likely to return to their pretreatment level of drug use than those in the traditional talk therapy aftercare. No significant differences were found between boys randomized to the two different posttreatment service modalities. However, adolescents in the skills training group were more likely to stay in school, spend less time with old friends, and more likely to engage in leisure activities with new friends. These studies suggest that interventions directed at increasing cognitive-behavioral skills and intentions to remain drug-free may positively impact recovery among adolescents.

Skills training has been evaluated among conduct-disordered, predelinquent, delinquent, and drug-abusing adolescents. Skills were both maintained after training and generalized to nontraining situations (Catalano et al. 1990-1991). The similar profiles of delinquent and drug-abusing adolescents suggest that approaches effective with one group may be as effective as the other (Elliott et al. 1985).

Outpatient

Review of the literature yielded no specific information on outpatient treatment as a posttreatment modality. By and large the information available on outpatient treatment services defies easy summary due to the heterogeneity of the client populations served and the heterogeneity of modalities classified as outpatient (Gerstein and Harwood 1990). However, it is clear that both inpatient and outpatient treatment are conceived of as alternative freestanding services, not sequential services providing a continuity of care. Nevertheless, information provided by Filstead and Anderson (1983) suggested that outpatient treatment services can be effective provided clients meet certain criteria (e.g., not mentally ill, willing to abstain from mood altering chemicals) and the services are sufficiently intense over an adequate span of time. Intensive outpatient treatment services seem to be logical for those adolescents who are at greater risk of returning to their pretreatment level of drug use particularly during the first few months after completing primary treatment.

Family Interventions

The impact of family functioning on recovery of adults and adolescents is well established (Finney et al. 1980; Hawkins and Catalano 1985; Shoemaker and Sherry 1991). For the adolescent, especially, the role of the family can be critical in either supporting or undermining recovery. While most family interventions are viewed as adjuncts to primary inpatient treatment, these services hold promise as part of posttreatment interventions because they shift the focus from the drug-abusing adolescent to the larger systems that support dysfunctional behavior (Szapocznik et al. 1983). Though research on the effectiveness of posttreatment family services is virtually nonexistent, indications are that family interventions have shown promise as outpatient treatment services despite widely varying modalities (e.g., conjoint family therapy, one patient family therapy, family-oriented drug education programs) (Kaufman 1985; Lewis et al. 1990; Stanton 1991; Szapocznik et al. 1983).

However, family-oriented interventions of all types are unfortunately plagued by the same problem: How to engage the family in treatment.

Arguing that treatment resistance is symptomatic of family dysfunction in much the same way as drug abuse, Szapocznik and colleagues (1988) demonstrated that effective engagement procedures increase not only engagement but treatment completion. Kaufman (1985, 1986) maintained that posttreatment family services are rare but necessary, and effective provided the intervention is delivered by a therapist who has a firm knowledge of substance abuse and its effect on the family, has established a workable system of family therapy (most therapists are eclectic in approach), and is able to engage the family in treatment.

Case Management

Case management is an intervention strategy that holds promise for treatment populations that present multiple problems such as seriously emotionally disturbed children (Behar 1985), children with HIV infection (Woodruff and Sterzin 1988), and drug abusers (Fertman and Toca 1989; Ridgely and Willenbring 1992; Thompson et al. 1984). Various models of case management exist, but all involve helping the client implement personal reentry plans, monitoring the client's progress, intervening in client and family crises, and most importantly helping the client to create links with prosocial support structures within the larger drug-free community.

When case management is part of the posttreatment continuum of care, the case manager works to reintegrate the adolescent with the family or an out-of-home placement, coordinates care with treatment staff and staff from other support agencies, helps the adolescent enroll in school and coordinates support with school personnel, and assists the adolescent in finding work and/or appropriate drug-free social and leisure activities. The contact between the case manager and the adolescent should be most intense during the critical 2-month period after discharge from primary treatment. Contact should be less frequent as the case manager continues to assist the client in creating and establishing links with prosocial networks and supportive persons within the community, and plans are made with the adolescent for termination of treatment services (Haggerty et al. 1989). Case management provides continuity of care while simultaneously working to increase the client's independence from that care (Dennis et al. 1992; Ridgely and Willenbring 1992).

Although the need for case management in substance abuse treatment has been recognized for more than a decade, case management interventions in this field have been accompanied by little research concerning its effectiveness. One study indicated that case management services may be very effective in treating an adolescent population. Amini and colleagues (1982) compared adolescent drug abusers randomly assigned to either psychodynamically oriented residential treatment or an intervention similar to case management at 1-year followup. No significant differences in social functioning and drug or alcohol use were found despite the intensive nature of the inpatient treatment. These results, the results of studies with adults assigned to community supervision (Gerstein and Harwood 1990; Vaillant 1988), and the dimensions of continuity inherent in case management suggest it may be an effective posttreatment service for recovering adolescents.

These four approaches to posttreatment services are often used in primary treatment as well. Each approach has potential in helping the adolescent establish a social network to support a drug-free lifestyle and/or assist in increasing effective functioning in the wider community. It is likely that for some, if not all adolescents, some combination of these posttreatment modalities rather than any single type of intervention will be needed to significantly alter the high relapse rates in this population (Hester and Miller 1988).

IMPLICATIONS FOR FUTURE RESEARCH

Throughout this review there has been an attempt to identify the implications of existing research for designing posttreatment services for adolescents. Concurrent with such discussions has been the recognition of the scarcity of scientifically sound research in that area. Therefore, research in this area needs to address two basic tasks. First, it must clarify the relapse/recovery rates and patterns for the adolescent population. Second, it must identify posttreatment modalities or combinations of these modalities that significantly alter those rates and patterns.

Relapse and Recovery

Clarifying the nature of the relapse and recovery processes is essential to strengthening posttreatment services for adolescents. The fact that nearly all adolescents engage in some drug use suggests a number of research questions. What patterns of abstinence and use are associated with the long-term prospects for recovery? How do relapse patterns vary with such characteristics as gender, coexisting morbidities, and/or type of drug of dependence? What useful outcome measures can reflect small but real changes in drug use and behavior associated with drug use? Data on these questions are basic to defining who and what are the targets of posttreatment services.

Posttreatment Services

In focusing on posttreatment service modalities, the key issue is which modality or combination of modalities maximize the likelihood of sustaining recovery in the home environment. At this point, the discussion is not about fine tuning interventions but rather identifying which posttreatment modalities have a significant impact on relapse rates for which adolescents.

In a recent set of articles reviewing randomized clinical trials (RCTs) of primary treatment, Ashery and McAuliffe (1992) discussed the problem of detecting small differences in impact likely to be associated with any particular outpatient treatment modality. The problems discussed in regard to RCTs of primary treatment modalities are likely to apply to RCTs of posttreatment modalities as well. The importance of RCTs as a means of attributing outcome to a specific intervention is not in dispute. Rather, the issue is how to detect small outcome differences given the small number of subjects in RCTs.

In addition to maximizing the number of subjects, Ashery and McAuliffe (1992) suggested maximizing the differences between the interventions being compared. This latter suggestion provides some direction to research on posttreatment services for adolescents. That is, posttreatment intervention research must focus on modalities or combinations of modalities that have a significant impact on recovery rates and behavior associated with establishing a drug-free lifestyle. Maximizing outcome differences may require randomizing subjects to conditions with multiple intervention sets versus single modalities. If significantly different outcomes result, statistical analysis and additional research can be used to determine the differential impact of each intervention.

While such an approach is not ideal from a research design perspective, there is currently no clear-cut evidence that any single posttreatment modality significantly lowers relapse rates. Research needs to focus on differences in posttreatment service outcome for different subgroups of adolescents. Research must also examine the impact of various posttreatment modalities on behavior associated with relapse or recovery.

Such behaviors include participation in posttreatment, changes in effectiveness in functioning in the wider community, and interacting with social groups supportive of a drug-free lifestyle.

The importance of posttreatment services is widely recognized (Gerstein and Harwood 1990; Hawkins and Catalano 1985; Marlatt and George 1984). A research base that focuses on relapse, posttreatment services that impact relapse, and relapse-related behavior is essential to sustaining the recovery process begun in primary treatment. Nevertheless, the complexity of the target population, the relapse and recovery processes, and research design issues suggest that building a scientifically sound basis for designing effective posttreatment services will require significant time, effort, and funding. However, this investment is long overdue. A significant investment in research effort and funding to determine how to initiate recovery without equal investment in determining how to sustain that process is neither logical nor cost effective.

REFERENCES

Amini, F.; Zilberg, N.J.; Burke, E.L.; and Salesnek, S. A controlled study of inpatient vs. outpatient treatment of delinquent drug abusing adolescents: One year results. *Compr Psychiatry* 23(5):436-444, 1982.

Ashery, R.S., and McAuliffe, W.E. Implementation issues and techniques in randomized trials of outpatient psychosocial treatments of drug abusers: Recruitment of subjects. *Am J Drug Alcohol Abuse* 18(3):305-329, 1992.

Baumrind, D. Familial antecedents of adolescent drug use: A developmental perspective. In: Jones, C.L., and Battjes, R.J., eds. *Etiology of Drug Abuse: Implications for Prevention.* National Institute on Drug Abuse Research Monograph No. 56. DHHS Publication No.(ADM)85-1335. Washington, DC: Supt. of Docs., U.S. Govt. Print. Off., 1985. pp. 13-44.

Behar, L. Changing patterns of state responsibility: A case study of North Carolina. *J Clin Child Psychol* 14(3):188-195, 1985.

Booth, R. Alcohol halfway houses: Treatment, length and treatment outcome. *Int J Addict* 16:927-934, 1981.

Braucht, G.N.; Brakarsh, D.; Follingstad, D.; and Berry, K.L. Deviant drug use in adolescence: A review of psychosocial correlates. *Psychol Bull* 79:92-106, 1973.

Brown, B.S., and Ashery, R.S. Aftercare in drug abuse programming. In: Dupont, R.L.; Goldstein, A.; and O'Donnell, J., eds. *Handbook on Drug Abuse.* Washington, DC: Supt. of Docs., U.S. Govt. Print. Off., 1979. pp. 165-174.

Brown, S.A.; Vik, P.W.; and Creamer, V.A. Characteristics of relapse following adolescent substance abuse treatment. *Addict Behav* 14:291-300, 1989.

Catalano, R.F., and Hawkins, J.D. Project skills: Preliminary results from a theoretically based aftercare experiment. In: Ashery, R.S., ed. *Progress in the Development of Cost-Effective Treatment for Drug Abusers.* National Institute on Drug Abuse Research Monograph No. 58. DHHS Pub. No.(ADM)85-1401. Washington, DC: Supt. of Docs., U.S. Govt. Print. Off., 1985. pp. 157-181.

Catalano, R.F.; Hawkins, J.D.; Wells, E.A.; Miller, J.; and Brewer, D. Evaluation of the effectiveness of adolescent drug abuse treatment, assessment of risks for relapse, and promising approaches for relapse prevention. *Int J Addict* 25(9A/10A):1085-1140, 1990-91.

Catalano, R.F.; Wells, E.A.; Jenson, J.M.; and Hawkins, J.D. Aftercare services for drug-using institutionalized delinquents. *Soc Service Rev* 63(4):553-577, 1989.

Cotton, N.S. The familial incidence of alcoholism. *J Stud Alcohol* 40(1):89-116, 1979.

DeJong, R., and Henrich, G. Follow-up results of a behavior modification program for juvenile drug addicts. *Addict Behav* 5:49-57, 1980.

De Leon, G. Aftercare in therapeutic communities. *Int J Addict* 25(9A/10A):1225-1237, 1990-91.

De Leon, G., and Deitch, D. Treatment of the adolescent substance abuser in a therapeutic community. In: Friedman, A.S., and Beschner, G.M., eds. *Treatment Services for Adolescent Substance Abusers.* DHHS Pub. No.(ADM)85-1342. Washington, DC: Supt. of Docs., U.S. Govt. Print. Off., 1985. pp. 209-217.

De Leon, G., and Jainchill, N. Circumstance, motivation, readiness and suitability as correlates of treatment tenure. *J Psychoactive Drugs* 18(3):203-208, 1986.

Dembo, R.; Williams, L.; LaVoie, L.; Berry, E.; Gertreu, A.; Wish, E.D.; Schmeidler, J.; and Washburn, M. Physical abuse, sexual victimization, and illicit drug use: Replication of a structural analysis among a new sample of high-risk youths. *Violence Vict* 4(2):121-138, 1989.

Dembo, R.; Williams, L.; LaVoie, L.; Schmeidler, J.; Kern, J.; Gertreu, A.; Estrellita, B.; Genung, B.; and Wish, E. A longitudinal study of the relationships among alcohol use, marijuana/hashish use, and emotional/psychological problems in a cohort of high-risk youth. *Int J Addict* 25(11):1341-1382, 1990.

Dembo, R.; Williams, L.; Gertreu, A.; Genung, L.; Schmeidler, J.; Berry, E.; Wish, E.; and LaVoie, L. Recidivism among high-risk youths: Study of a cohort of juvenile detainees. *Int J Addict* 26(2):121-177, 1991.

Dennis, M.L.; Karuntzos, G.T.; and Rachal, J.V. Application of case management to drug abuse treatment: Overview of models and research issues. In: *Progress and Issues in Case Management.* National Institute on Drug Abuse Research Monograph No. 127. DHHS Pub. No.(ADM)92-1946. Washington, DC: Supt. of Docs., U.S. Govt. Print. Off., 1992. pp. 54-78.

Elliott, D.S.; Huizinga, D.; and Ageton, S.S. *Explaining Delinquency and Drug Use.* Beverly Hills, CA: Sage, 1985.

Fertman, C.I., and Toca, O.A. A drug and alcohol aftercare service: Linking adolescents, families, and schools. *J Alcohol Drug Educ* 34(2):46-53, 1989.

Filstead, W.J., and Anderson, C.L. Conceptual and clinical issues in the treatment of adolescent alcohol and substance misusers. *Child Youth Services* 6(1-2):103-116, 1983.

Finney, J.W.; Moos, R.H.; and Mewborn, C.R. Posttreatment experiences and treatment outcome of alcoholic patients six months and two years after hospitalization. *J Consult Clin Psychol* 48(1):17-29, 1980.

Friedman, A.S.; Glickman, N.W.; and Morrissey, M.R. Prediction to successful treatment outcome by client characteristics and retention in treatment in adolescent drug treatment programs: A large scale cross validation study. *J Drug Educ* 16:149-165, 1987.

Gerstein, D.R., and Harwood, H.J., eds. *Treating Drug Problems.* Vol. 1. Washington, DC: National Academy Press, 1990.

Goodwin, D.W. Alcoholism and genetics: The sins of the fathers. *Arch Gen Psychiatry* 6:171-174, 1985.

Grenier, C. Treatment effectiveness in an adolescent chemical dependency treatment program: A quasi-experimental design. *Int J Addict* 20(3):381-391, 1985.

Haggerty, K.P.: Wells, E.A.; Jenson, J.M.; Catalano, R.F.; and Hawkins, J.D. Delinquents and drug use: A model program for community reintegration. *Adolescence* 24(94):439-456, 1989.

Hall, S.M.; Wasserman, D.A.; and Havassy, B.E. Relapse prevention. In: Pickens, R.W.; Leukefeld, C.G.; and Schuster, C.R., eds. *Improving Drug Abuse Treatment*. National Institute on Drug Abuse Research Monograph No. 106. DHHS Pub. No.(ADM)91-1754. Washington, DC: Supt. of Docs., U.S. Govt. Print. Off., 1991. pp. 279-292.

Harrison, P.A., and Hoffman, N.G. *CATOR 1987 Report: Adolescent Residential Treatment Intake and Follow-Up Findings*. St. Paul, MN: CATOR, 1987.

Harrison, P.A.; Hoffman, N.G.; and Edwall, G.G. Sexual abuse correlates: Similarities between male and female adolescents in chemical dependency treatment. *J Adolesc Res* 4:385-399, 1989.

Hart, L.E.; Mader, L.; Griffith, K.; and Demendonca, M. Effects of sexual and physical abuse: A comparison of adolescent inpatients. *Child Psychiatry Hum Dev* 20:49-57, 1989.

Hawkins, J.D., and Catalano, R.F. Aftercare in drug abuse treatment. *Int J Addict* 20:917-945, 1985.

Hawkins, J.D.; Catalano, R.F.; Gillmore, M.R.; and Wells, E.A. Skills training for drug abusers: Generalization, maintenance, and effects on drug use. *J Consult Clin Psychol* 57(4):559-563, 1989.

Hawkins, J.D.; Lishner, D.M.; Jenson, J.M.; and Catalano, R.F. Delinquents and drugs: What the evidence suggests about prevention and treatment programming. In: Brown, B.S., and Mills, A.R., eds. *Youth at Risk for Substance Abuse*. DHHS Pub. No.(ADM)90-1537. Washington, DC: Supt. of Docs., U.S. Govt. Print. Off., 1987. pp. 81-135.

Hester, R.K., and Miller, W.R. Empirical guidelines for optimal client-treatment matching. In: Rahdert, E.R., and Grabowski, J., eds. *Adolescent Drug Abuse: Analyses of Treatment Research*. National Institute on Drug Abuse Research Monograph No. 77. DHHS Pub. No.(ADM)88-1523. Washington, DC: Supt. of Docs., U.S. Govt. Print. Off., 1988. pp. 27-38.

Hubbard, R.L.; Cavanaugh, E.R.; Craddock, S.G.; and Rachal, J.V. Characteristics, behaviors, and outcomes for youth in the TOPS. In: Friedman, A.S., and Beschner, G.M., eds. *Treatment Services for Adolescent Substance Abusers*. DHHS Pub. No.(ADM)85-1342. Washington, DC: Supt. of Docs., U.S. Govt. Print. Off., 1985. pp. 49-65.

Hunt, W.A.; Barnet, L.W.; and Branch, L.G. Relapse rates in addiction programs. *J Clin Psychol* 27:455-456, 1971.

Jenson, J.M.; Hawkins, J.D.; and Catalano, R.F. Social support in aftercare services for troubled youth. *Child Youth Services Rev* 8(4):323-347, 1986.

Jenson, J.M.; Wells, E.A.; Plotnick, R.D.; Hawkins, J.D.; and Catalano, R.F. The effects of skills and intentions to use drugs on posttreatment drug use of adolescents. *Am J Drug Alcohol Abuse* 19(1):1-18, 1993.

Kandel, D.; Simcha-Fagan, O.; and Davies, M. Risk factors for delinquency and illicit drug use from adolescence to young adulthood. *J Drug Issues* 16(1):67-90, 1986.

Kanfer, F.H., and Goldstein, A.P. *Maximizing Treatment Gains: Transfer Enhancement in Psychotherapy.* New York: Academic Press, 1979.

Kaplan, H.; Martin, S.; and Robbins, C. Pathways to adolescent drug use: Self-derogation, peer influence, weakening of controls and early substance use. *J Health Soc Behav* 25:270-289, 1984.

Kaufman, E. Critical issues in family research in drug abuse. *J Drug Issues* (Fall):463-475, 1985.

Kaufman, E. A contemporary approach to the family treatment of substance abuse disorders. *J Drug Alcohol Abuse* 12:199-211, 1986.

Kumpfer, K. Special populations: Etiology and prevention of vulnerability to chemical dependency in children of substance abusers. In: Brown, B.S., and Mills, A.R., eds. *Youth at Risk for Substance Abuse.* DHHS Pub. No.(ADM)90-1537. Washington, DC: Supt. of Docs., U.S. Govt. Print. Off., 1987. pp. 1-80.

Kumpfer, K.L., and DeMarsh, J. Family environmental and genetic influences on children's future chemical dependency. In: Ezekoye, S.; Kumpfer, K.; and Bukowski, W., eds. *Childhood and Chemical Abuse: Prevention and Intervention.* New York: Haworth Press, 1986. pp. 49-91.

Leukefeld, C.G., and Tims, F.M. Relapse and recovery in drug abuse: Research and practice. *Int J Addict* 24(3):189-201, 1989.

Lewis, R.A.; Piercy, F.P.; Sprenkle, D.H.; and Trepper, T.S. Family-based interventions for helping drug-abusing adolescents. *J Adolesc Res* 5(1):82-95, 1990.

Marlatt, G.A., and George, W.H. Relapse prevention: Introduction and overview of the model. *Br J Addict* 79:261-273, 1984.

Marlatt, G.A., and Gordon, J.R. Determinants of relapse: Implications for maintenance of behavior change. In: Davidson, P., and Davidson, S., eds. *Behavioral Medicine: Changing Health Lifestyles.* New York: Brunner/Mazel Publishers, 1980. pp. 410-452.

McAuliffe, W.E. From theory to practice: The planned treatment of drug abusers. *Int J Addict* 24(6):527-608, 1989.

McAuliffe, W.E., and Gordon, R.A. A test of Lindesmith's theory of addiction: The frequency of euphoria among long-term addicts. *Am J Sociology* 79(4):795-840, 1974.

McLellan, A.T.; Luborsky, L.; O'Brien, C.P.; Barr, H.L.; and Evans, F. Alcohol and drug abuse treatment in three different populations: Is there improvement and is it predictable? *Am J Drug Alcohol Abuse* 12(1 & 2):101-120, 1986.

Mummé, D. Aftercare: Its role in primary and secondary recovery of women from alcohol and other drug dependence. *Int J Addict* 26(5):549-564, 1991.

O'Brien, C.P.; Childress, A.R.; and McLellan, A.T. Conditioning factors may help to understand and prevent relapse in patients who are recovering from drug dependence. In: Pickens, R.W.; Leukefeld, C.G.; and Schuster, C.R. *Improving Drug Abuse Treatment.* National Institute on Drug Abuse Research Monograph No. 106. DHHS Pub. No.(ADM)91-1754. Washington, DC: Supt. of Docs., U.S. Govt. Print. Off., 1991. pp. 293-312.

Ridgely, M.S., and Willenbring, M.L. Application of case management to drug abuse treatment: Overview of models and research issues. In: Ashery, R.S., ed. *Progress and Issues in Case Management.* National Institute on Drug Abuse Research Monograph No. 127. DHHS Pub. No.(ADM)92-1946. Washington, DC: Supt. of Docs., U.S. Govt. Print. Off., 1992. pp. 12-33.

Rounsaville, B.J. Clinical implications of relapse research. In: Tims, F.M., and Leukefeld, C.G., eds. *Relapse and Recovery in Drug Abuse.* National Institute on Drug Abuse Research Monograph No. 72. DHHS Pub. No.(ADM)86-1473. Washington, DC: Supt. of Docs., U.S. Govt. Print. Off., 1986. pp. 172-184.

Sells, S.B., and Simpson, D.D. Evaluation of treatment outcome for youths in the Drug Abuse Reporting Program (DARP): A follow-up study. In: Beschner, G.M., and Friedman, A.S., eds. *Youth Drug Abuse: Problems, Issues and Treatments.* Lexington, MA: Lexington Books, 1979. pp. 571-628.

Shoemaker, R.H., and Sherry, P. Posttreatment factors influencing outcome of adolescent chemical dependency treatment. *J Adolesc Chem Dependency* 2(1):89-105, 1991.

Spear, S.F., and Skala, S.Y. "Gender Differences among Chemically Dependent Adolescents. Public Health and a National Health Care Program." Paper presented at the meeting of the American Public Health Association, Atlanta, GA, November 10-14, 1991.

Spear, S.F., and Skala, S.Y. "A Comparative Study of Abused and Non-abused Adolescents Treated for Chemical Dependency. Uniting for Health Committees." Paper presented at the meeting of the American Public Health Association, Washington, DC, November 8-12, 1992.

Stanton, M.D. "Recent Outcome Studies on Family Treatment of Drug Abuse." Paper presented at National Institute on Drug Abuse National Conference on Drug Abuse Research and Practice: An Alliance for the 21st Century. Washington, DC, January 12-15, 1991.

Szapocznik, J.; Kurtines, W.M.; Foote, F.H.; Perez-Vidal, A.; and Hervis, O. Conjoint versus one-person family therapy: Some evidence for the effectiveness of conducting family therapy through one person. *J Consult Clin Psychol* 51:889-899, 1983.

Szapocznik, J.; Perez-Vidal, A.: Brickman, A.L.; Foote, F.H.; and Kurtines, W.M. Engaging adolescent drug abusers and their families in treatment: A strategic structural systems approach. *J Consult Clin Psychol* 56(4):552-557, 1988.

Thompson, T.; Koerner, J.; and Grabowski, J. Brokerage model rehabilitation system for opiate dependence: A behavioral analysis. In: Grabowski, J.; Stitzer, M.L.; and Henningfield, J.E., eds. *Behavioral Intervention Techniques in Drug Abuse Treatment.* National Institute on Drug Abuse Research Monograph No. 46. DHHS Pub. No.(ADM)84-1846. Washington, DC: Supt. of Docs., U.S. Govt. Print. Off., 1984. 131-146.

Toray, T.; Coughlin, C.; Vuchinich, S.; and Patricelli, P. Gender differences associated with adolescent substance abuse: Comparisons and implications for treatment. *Fam Rel* 40:338-344, 1991.

Vaillant, G.E. *The National History of Alcoholism.* Cambridge, MA: Harvard University Press, 1983.

Vaillant, G.E. What can long-term follow-up teach us about relapse and prevention of relapse in addiction? *Br J Addict* 83:1147-1157, 1988.

Vaillant, G.E., and Milofsky, E.G. The etiology of alcoholism: A prospective viewpoint. *Am Psychol* 37:494-503, 1982.

Woodruff, G., and Sterzin, E.D. The transagency approach: A model for serving children with HIV infection and their families. *Child Today* 17(3):9-14, 1988.

Zackon, F.; McAuliffe, W.E.; and Chien, J.M. *Addict Aftercare: Recovery Training and Self-help.* DHHS Pub. No.(ADM)85-1341. Washington, DC: Supt. of Docs., U.S. Govt. Print. Off., 1985.

AUTHORS

Sherilynn F. Spear, Ph.D.
Associate Professor

Sharon Y. Skala, M.A., M.S.
School of Allied Health Professions
Northern Illinois University
Williston Hall 212
DeKalb, IL 60115

National Institute on Drug Abuse Research Monograph Series

While limited supplies last, single copies of the monographs may be obtained free of charge from the National Clearinghouse for Alcohol and Drug Information (NCADI). Please also contact NCADI for information about availability of coming issues and other publications of the National Institute on Drug Abuse relevant to drug abuse research.

Additional copies may be purchased from the U.S. Government Printing Office (GPO) and/or the National Technical Information Service (NTIS) as indicated. NTIS prices are for paper copy; add $3.00 handling charge for each order. Microfiche copies also are available from NTIS. Prices from either source are subject to change.

Addresses are:

NCADI
National Clearinghouse for Alcohol and Drug Information
P.O. Box 2345
Rockville, MD 20852
(301) 468-2600
(800) 729-6686

GPO
Superintendent of Documents
U.S. Government Printing Office
P.O. Box 371954
Pittsburgh, PA 15220-7954
(202) 738-3238
FAX (202) 512-2233

NTIS
National Technical Information Service
U.S. Department of Commerce
Springfield, VA 22161
(703) 487-4650

For information on availability of NIDA Research Monographs from 1975-1993 and those not listed, write to NIDA, Community and Professional Education Branch, Room 10A-39, 5600 Fishers Lane, Rockville, MD 20857.

26 THE BEHAVIORAL ASPECTS OF SMOKING.
Norman A. Krasnegor, Ph.D., ed. (Reprint from 1979 Surgeon General's Report on Smoking and Health.)
NCADI#M26   NTIS PB #80-118755/AS (A09) $27.00

42 THE ANALYSIS OF CANNABINOIDS IN BIOLOGICAL FLUIDS. Richard L. Hawks, Ph.D., ed.
NCADI #M42   NTIS PB #83-136044/AS (A07) $27.00

50 COCAINE: PHARMACOLOGY, EFFECTS, AND TREATMENT OF ABUSE. John Grabowski, Ph.D., ed.
NCADI #M50   NTIS PB #85-150381/AS (A07) $27.00

52 TESTING DRUGS FOR PHYSICAL DEPENDENCE POTENTIAL AND ABUSE LIABILITY. Joseph V. Brady, Ph.D., and Scott E. Lukas, Ph.D., eds.
NCADI #M52   NTIS PB #85-150373/AS (A08) $27.00

53 PHARMACOLOGICAL ADJUNCTS IN SMOKING CESSATION. John Grabowski, Ph.D., and Sharon M. Hall, Ph.D., eds.
NCADI #M53   NTIS PB #89-123186/AS (A07) $27.00

54 MECHANISMS OF TOLERANCE AND DEPENDENCE.
Charles Wm. Sharp, Ph.D., ed.
NCADI #M54   NTIS PB #89-103279/AS (A19) $52.00

56 ETIOLOGY OF DRUG ABUSE: IMPLICATIONS FOR PREVENTION. Coryl LaRue Jones, Ph.D., and Robert J. Battjes, D.S.W., eds.
NCADI #M56   NTIS PB #89-123160/AS (A13) $36.50

61 COCAINE USE IN AMERICA: EPIDEMIOLOGIC AND CLINICAL PERSPECTIVES. Nicholas J. Kozel, M.S., and Edgar H. Adams, M.S., eds.
NCADI #M61   NTIS PB #89-131866/AS (A11) $36.50

62 NEUROSCIENCE METHODS IN DRUG ABUSE RESEARCH.
Roger M. Brown, Ph.D., and David P. Friedman, Ph.D., eds.
NCADI #M62   NTIS PB #89-130660/AS (A08) $27.00

63 PREVENTION RESEARCH: DETERRING DRUG ABUSE AMONG CHILDREN AND ADOLESCENTS. Catherine S. Bell, M.S., and Robert J. Battjes, D.S.W., eds.
NCADI #M63   NTIS PB #89-103287/AS (A11) $36.50

64 PHENCYCLIDINE: AN UPDATE. Doris H. Clouet, Ph.D., ed.
NCADI #M64   NTIS PB #89-131858/AS (A12) $36.50

65 WOMEN AND DRUGS: A NEW ERA FOR RESEARCH.
Barbara A. Ray, Ph.D., and Monique C. Braude, Ph.D., eds.
NCADI #M65   NTIS PB #89-130637/AS (A06) $27.00

69 OPIOID PEPTIDES: MEDICINAL CHEMISTRY.
Rao S. Rapaka, Ph.D.; Gene Barnett, Ph.D.; and
Richard L. Hawks, Ph.D., eds.
NCADI #M69   NTIS PB #89-158422/AS (A17) $44.50

70 OPIOID PEPTIDES: MOLECULAR PHARMACOLOGY,
BIOSYNTHESIS, AND ANALYSIS. Rao S. Rapaka, Ph.D., and
Richard L. Hawks, Ph.D., eds.
NCADI #M70   NTIS PB #89-158430/AS (A18) $52.00

72 RELAPSE AND RECOVERY IN DRUG ABUSE.
Frank M. Tims, Ph.D., and Carl G. Leukefeld, D.S.W., eds.
NCADI #M72   NTIS PB #89-151963/AS (A09) $36.50

74 NEUROBIOLOGY OF BEHAVIORAL CONTROL IN DRUG
ABUSE. Stephen I. Szara, M.D., D.Sc., ed.
NCADI #M74   NTIS PB #89-151989/AS (A07) $27.00

78 THE ROLE OF NEUROPLASTICITY IN THE RESPONSE TO
DRUGS. David P. Friedman, Ph.D., and Doris H. Clouet, Ph.D.,
eds.
NCADI #M78   NTIS PB #88-245683/AS (A10) $36.50

79 STRUCTURE-ACTIVITY RELATIONSHIPS OF THE
CANNABINOIDS. Rao S. Rapaka, Ph.D., and
Alexandros Makriyannis, Ph.D., eds.
NCADI #M79   NTIS PB #89-109201/AS (A10) $36.50

80 NEEDLE SHARING AMONG INTRAVENOUS DRUG
ABUSERS: NATIONAL AND INTERNATIONAL
PERSPECTIVES.
Robert J. Battjes, D.S.W., and Roy W. Pickens, Ph.D., eds.
NCADI #M80   NTIS PB #88-236138/AS (A09) $36.50

82 OPIOIDS IN THE HIPPOCAMPUS. Jacqueline F. McGinty,
Ph.D., and David P. Friedman, Ph.D., eds.
NCADI #M82   NTIS PB #88-245691/AS (A06) $27.00

83 HEALTH HAZARDS OF NITRITE INHALANTS.
Harry W. Haverkos, M.D., and John A. Dougherty, Ph.D., eds.
NCADI #M83   NTIS PB #89-125496/AS (A06) $27.00

84 LEARNING FACTORS IN SUBSTANCE ABUSE.
Barbara A. Ray, Ph.D., ed.
NCADI #M84   NTIS PB #89-125504/AS (A10) $36.50

85 EPIDEMIOLOGY OF INHALANT ABUSE: AN UPDATE.
Raquel A. Crider, Ph.D., and Beatrice A. Rouse, Ph.D., eds.
NCADI #M85   NTIS PB #89-123178/AS (A10) $36.50

87 OPIOID PEPTIDES: AN UPDATE. Rao S. Rapaka, Ph.D., and
Bhola N. Dhawan, M.D., eds.
NCADI #M87   NTIS PB #89-158430/AS (A11) $36.50

88 MECHANISMS OF COCAINE ABUSE AND TOXICITY.
Doris H. Clouet, Ph.D.; Khursheed Asghar, Ph.D.; and
Roger M. Brown, Ph.D., eds.
NCADI #M88   NTIS PB #89-125512/AS (A16) $44.50

89 BIOLOGICAL VULNERABILITY TO DRUG ABUSE.
Roy W. Pickens, Ph.D., and Dace S. Svikis, B.A., eds.
NCADI #M89   NTIS PB #89-125520/AS (A09) $27.00

92 TESTING FOR ABUSE LIABILITY OF DRUGS IN HUMANS.
Marian W. Fischman, Ph.D., and Nancy K. Mello, Ph.D., eds.
NCADI #M92   NTIS PB #90-148933/AS (A17) $44.50

94 PHARMACOLOGY AND TOXICOLOGY OF AMPHETAMINE
AND RELATED DESIGNER DRUGS. Khursheed Asghar, Ph.D.,
and Errol De Souza, Ph.D., eds.
NCADI #M94   NTIS PB #90-148958/AS (A16) $44.50

95 PROBLEMS OF DRUG DEPENDENCE, 1989. PROCEEDINGS
OF THE 51st ANNUAL SCIENTIFIC MEETING. THE
COMMITTEE ON PROBLEMS OF DRUG DEPENDENCE, INC.
Louis S. Harris, Ph.D., ed.
NCADI #M95   NTIS PB #90-237660/AS (A99) $67.00

96 DRUGS OF ABUSE: CHEMISTRY, PHARMACOLOGY,
IMMUNOLOGY, AND AIDS. Phuong Thi Kim Pham, Ph.D., and
Kenner Rice, Ph.D., eds.
NCADI #M96   NTIS PB #90-237678/AS (A11) $36.50

97 NEUROBIOLOGY OF DRUG ABUSE: LEARNING AND
MEMORY. Lynda Erinoff, Ph.D., ed.
NCADI #M97   NTIS PB #90-237686/AS (A11) $36.50

98 THE COLLECTION AND INTERPRETATION OF DATA
FROM HIDDEN POPULATIONS.
Elizabeth Y. Lambert, M.Sc., ed.
NCADI #M98   NTIS PB #90-237694/AS (A08) $27.00

99 RESEARCH FINDINGS ON SMOKING OF ABUSED
SUBSTANCES. C. Nora Chiang, Ph.D., and
Richard L. Hawks, Ph.D., eds.
NCADI #M99   NTIS PB #91-141119 (A09) $27.00

100 DRUGS IN THE WORKPLACE: RESEARCH AND
EVALUATION DATA. VOL II. Steven W. Gust, Ph.D.;
J. Michael Walsh, Ph.D.; Linda B. Thomas, B.S.;
and Dennis J. Crouch, M.B.A., eds.
NCADI #M100   GPO Stock #017-024-01458-3 $8.00

101 RESIDUAL EFFECTS OF ABUSED DRUGS ON BEHAVIOR.
John W. Spencer, Ph.D., and John J. Boren, Ph.D., eds.
NCADI #M101   NTIS PB #91-172858/AS (A09) $27.00

102 ANABOLIC STEROID ABUSE. Geraline C. Lin, Ph.D., and Lynda Erinoff, Ph.D., eds.
NCADI #M102   NTIS PB #91-172866/AS (A11) $36.50

106 IMPROVING DRUG ABUSE TREATMENT. Roy W. Pickens, Ph.D.; Carl G. Leukefeld, D.S.W.; and Charles R. Schuster, Ph.D., eds.
NCADI #M106   NTIS PB #92-105873(A18) $50.00

107 DRUG ABUSE PREVENTION INTERVENTION RESEARCH: METHODOLOGICAL ISSUES. Carl G. Leukefeld, D.S.W., and William J. Bukoski, Ph.D., eds.
NCADI #M107   NTIS PB #92-160985 (A13) $36.50

108 CARDIOVASCULAR TOXICITY OF COCAINE: UNDERLYING MECHANISMS. Pushpa V. Thadani, Ph.D., ed.
NCADI #M108   NTIS PB #92-106608 (A11) $36.50

109 LONGITUDINAL STUDIES OF HIV INFECTION IN INTRAVENOUS DRUG USERS: METHODOLOGICAL ISSUES IN NATURAL HISTORY RESEARCH. Peter Hartsock, Dr.P.H., and Sander G. Genser, M.D., M.P.H., eds.
NCADI #M109   NTIS PB #92-106616 (A08) $27.00

111 MOLECULAR APPROACHES TO DRUG ABUSE RESEARCH: RECEPTOR CLONING, NEUROTRANSMITTER EXPRESSION, AND MOLECULAR GENETICS: VOLUME I. Theresa N.H. Lee, Ph.D., ed.
NCADI #M111   NTIS PB #92-135743 (A10) $36.50

112 EMERGING TECHNOLOGIES AND NEW DIRECTIONS IN DRUG ABUSE RESEARCH. Rao S. Rapaka, Ph.D.; Alexandros Makriyannis, Ph.D.; and Michael J. Kuhar, Ph.D., eds.
NCADI #M112   NTIS PB #92-155449 (A15) $44.50

113 ECONOMIC COSTS, COST EFFECTIVENESS, FINANCING, AND COMMUNITY-BASED DRUG TREATMENT. William S. Cartwright, Ph.D., and James M. Kaple, Ph.D., eds.
NCADI #M113   NTIS PB #92-155795 (A10) $36.50

114 METHODOLOGICAL ISSUES IN CONTROLLED STUDIES ON EFFECTS OF PRENATAL EXPOSURE TO DRUG ABUSE. M. Marlyne Kilbey, Ph.D., and Khursheed Asghar, Ph.D., eds.
NCADI #M114   NTIS PB #92-146216 (A16) $44.50

115 METHAMPHETAMINE ABUSE: EPIDEMIOLOGIC ISSUES AND IMPLICATIONS. Marissa A. Miller, D.V.M., M.P.H., and Nicholas J. Kozel, M.S., eds.
NCADI #M115   NTIS PB #92-146224/ll (AO7) $27.00

116 DRUG DISCRIMINATION: APPLICATIONS TO DRUG
ABUSE RESEARCH. R.A. Glennon, Ph.D.;
Toubjörn U.C. Järbe, Ph.D.; and J. Frankenheim, Ph.D., eds.
NCADI #M116   NTIS PB #94-169471 (A20) $52.00

117 METHODOLOGICAL ISSUES IN EPIDEMIOLOGY,
PREVENTION, AND TREATMENT RESEARCH ON DRUG-
EXPOSED WOMEN AND THEIR CHILDREN.
M. Marlyve Kilbey, Ph.D., and Kursheed Asghar, Ph.D., eds.
GPO Stock #O17-024-01472-9 $12.00
NCADI #M117   NTIS PB #93-102101/LL (A18) $52.00

118 DRUG ABUSE TREATMENT IN PRISONS AND JAILS.
Carl G. Leukefeld, D.S.W., and Frank M. Tims, Ph.D., eds.
GPO Stock #O17-024-01473-7 $16.00
NCADI #M118   NTIS PB #93-102143/LL (A14) $44.50

120 BIOAVAILABILITY OF DRUGS TO THE BRAIN AND THE
BLOOD-BRAIN BARRIER. Jerry Frankenheim, Ph.D., and
Roger M. Brown, Ph.D., eds.
GPO Stock #017-024-01481-8 $10.00
NCADI #M120   NTIS PB #92-214956/LL (A12) $36.50

121 BUPRENORPHINE: AN ALTERNATIVE TREATMENT FOR
OPIOID DEPENDENCE. Jack D. Blaine, Ph.D., ed.
GPO Stock #017-024-01482-6 $5.00
NCADI #M121   NTIS PB #93-129781/LL (A08) $27.00

123 ACUTE COCAINE INTOXICATION: CURRENT METHODS
OF TREATMENT. Heinz Sorer, Ph.D., ed.
GPO Stock #017-024-01501-6 $6.50
NCADI #M123   NTIS PB #94-115433/LL (A09) $27.00

124 NEUROBIOLOGICAL APPROACHES TO BRAIN-BEHAVIOR
INTERACTION. Roger M. Brown, Ph.D., and
Joseph Fracella, Ph.D., eds.
GPO Stock #017-024-01492-3 $9.00
NCADI #M124   NTIS PB #93-203834/LL (A12) $36.50

125 ACTIVATION OF IMMEDIATE EARLY GENES BY DRUGS
OF ABUSE. Reinhard Grzanna, Ph.D., and
Roger M. Brown, Ph.D., eds.
GPO Stock #017-024-01503-2 $7.50
NCADI #M125   NTIS PB #94-169489 (A12) $36.50

126 MOLECULAR APPROACHES TO DRUG ABUSE RESEARCH
VOLUME II: STRUCTURE, FUNCTION, AND EXPRESSION.
Theresa N.H. Lee, Ph.D., ed.
NCADI #M126   NTIS PB #94-169497 (A08) $27.00

127 PROGRESS AND ISSUES IN CASE MANAGEMENT.
Rebecca S. Ashery, D.S.W., ed.
NCADI #M127   NTIS PB #94-169505 (A18) $52.00

128 STATISTICAL ISSUES IN CLINICAL TRIALS FOR TREATMENT OF OPIATE DEPENDENCE.
Ram B. Jain, Ph.D., ed.
NCADI #M128 NTIS PB #93-203826/LL (A09) $27.00

129 INHALANT ABUSE: A VOLATILE RESEARCH AGENDA.
Charles W. Sharp, Ph.D.; Fred Beauvais, Ph.D.; and Richard Spence, Ph.D., eds.
GPO Stock #017-024-01496-6 $12.00
NCADI #M129 NTIS PB #93-183119/LL (A15) $44.50

130 DRUG ABUSE AMONG MINORITY YOUTH: ADVANCES IN RESEARCH AND METHODOLOGY. Mario De La Rosa, Ph.D., and Juan-Luis Recio Adrados, Ph.D., eds.
GPO Stock #017-024-01506-7 $14.00
NCADI #M130 NTIS PB #94-169513 (A15) $44.50

131 IMPACT OF PRESCRIPTION DRUG DIVERSION CONTROL SYSTEMS ON MEDICAL PRACTICE AND PATIENT CARE.
James R. Cooper, Ph.D.; Dorynne J. Czechowicz, M.D.; Stephen P. Molinari, J.D., R.Ph.; and Robert C. Peterson, Ph.D., eds.
GPO Stock #017-024-01505-9 $14.00
NCADI #M131 NTIS PB #94-169521 (A15) $44.50

132 PROBLEMS OF DRUG DEPENDENCE, 1992: PROCEEDINGS OF THE 54TH ANNUAL SCIENTIFIC MEETING OF THE COLLEGE ON PROBLEMS OF DRUG DEPENDENCE.
Louis Harris, Ph.D., ed.
GPO Stock #017-024-01502-4 $23.00
NCADI #M132 NTIS PB #94-115508/LL (A99)

133 SIGMA, PCP, AND NMDA RECEPTORS.
Errol B. De Souza, Ph.D.; Doris Clouet, Ph.D., and Edythe D. London, Ph.D., eds.
NCADI #M133 NTIS PB #94-169539 (A12) $36.50

134 MEDICATIONS DEVELOPMENT: DRUG DISCOVERY, DATABASES, AND COMPUTER-AIDED DRUG DESIGN.
Rao S. Rapaka, Ph.D., and Richard L. Hawks, Ph.D., eds.
GPO Stock #017-024-01511-3 $11.00
NCADI #M134 NTIS PB #94-169547 (A14) $44.50

135 COCAINE TREATMENT: RESEARCH AND CLINICAL PERSPECTIVES. Frank M. Tims, Ph.D., and Carl G. Leukefeld, D.S.W., eds.
GPO Stock #017-024-01520-2 $11.00
NCADI #M135 NTIS PB #94-169554 (A13) $36.50

136 ASSESSING NEUROTOXICITY OF DRUGS OF ABUSE.
Lynda Erinoff, Ph.D., ed.
GPO Stock #017-024-01518-1 $11.00
NCADI #M136 NTIS PB #94-169562 (A13) $36.50

137 BEHAVIORAL TREATMENTS FOR DRUG ABUSE AND DEPENDENCE. Lisa Simon Onken, Ph.D.; Jack D. Blaine, M.D., and John J. Boren, Ph.D., eds.
GPO Stock #017-024-01519-9 $13.00
NCADI #M137   NTIS PB #94-169570 (A15) $44.50

138 IMAGING TECHNIQUES IN MEDICATIONS DEVELOPMENT: CLINICAL AND PRECLINICAL ASPECTS. Heinz Sorer, Ph.D., and Rao S. Rapaka, Ph.D., eds.

NCADI #M138

139 SCIENTIFIC METHODS FOR PREVENTION INTERVENTION RESEARCH. Arturo Cazares, M.D., M.P.H., and Lula A. Beatty, Ph.D., eds.

NCADI #M139

140 PROBLEMS OF DRUG DEPENDENCE, 1993: PROCEEDINGS OF THE 55TH ANNUAL SCIENTIFIC MEETING, THE COLLEGE ON PROBLEMS OF DRUG DEPENDENCE, INC. VOLUME I: PLENARY SESSION SYMPOSIA AND ANNUAL REPORTS. Louis S. Harris, Ph.D., ed.

NCADI #M140

141 PROBLEMS OF DRUG DEPENDENCE, 1993: PROCEEDINGS OF THE 55TH ANNUAL SCIENTIFIC MEETING, THE COLLEGE ON PROBLEMS OF DRUG DEPENDENCE, INC. VOLUME II: ABSTRACTS. Louis S. Harris, Ph.D., ed.

NCADI #M141

142 ADVANCES IN DATA ANALYSIS FOR PREVENTION INTERVENTION RESEARCH. Linda M. Collins, Ph.D., and Larry A. Seitz, Ph.D., eds.

NCADI #M142

143 THE CONTEXT OF HIV RISK AMONG DRUG USERS AND THEIR SEXUAL PARTNERS. Robert J. Battjes, D.S.W.; Zili Sloboda, Sc.D.; and William C. Grace, Ph.D., eds.

NCADI #M143

144 THERAPEUTIC COMMUNITY: ADVANCES IN RESEARCH AND APPLICATION. Frank M. Tims, Ph.D.; George De Leon, Ph.D.; and Nancy Jainchill, Ph.D., eds.

NCADI #M144

145 NEUROBIOLOGICAL MODELS FOR EVALUATING MECHANISMS UNDERLYING COCAINE ADDICTION. Lynda Erinoff, Ph.D., and Roger M. Brown, Ph.D., eds.

NCADI #M145

146 HALLUCINOGENS: AN UPDATE. Geraline C. Lin, Ph.D., and Richard A. Glennon, Ph.D., eds.

NCADI #M146

147 DISCOVERY OF NOVEL OPIOID MEDICATIONS. Rao S. Rapaka, Ph.D., and Heinz Sorer, Ph.D., eds.

NCADI #M147

148 EPIDEMIOLOGY OF INHALANT ABUSE: AN INTERNATIONAL PERSPECTIVE. Nicholas J. Kozel, M.S.; Zili Sloboda, Sc.D.; and Mario R. De La Rosa, Ph.D., eds.

NCADI # M148

149 MEDICATIONS DEVELOPMENT FOR THE TREATMENT OF PREGNANT ADDICTS AND THEIR INFANTS. C. Nora Chiang, Ph.D., and Loretta P. Finnegan, M.D., eds.

NCADI # M149

150 INTEGRATING BEHAVIORAL THERAPIES WITH MEDICATIONS IN THE TREATMENT OF DRUG DEPENDENCE. Lisa Simon Onken, Ph.D.; Jack D. Blaine, M.D.; and John J. Boren, Ph.D., eds.

NCADI # M150

151 SOCIAL NETWORKS, DRUG ABUSE, AND HIV TRANSMISSION. Richard H. Needle, Ph.D., M.P.H.; Susan L. Coyle, Ph.D.; Sander G. Genser, M.D., M.P.H.; and Robert T. Trotter II, Ph.D., eds.

NCADI # M151

154 MEMBRANES AND BARRIERS: TARGETED DRUG DELIVERY. Rao S. Rapaka, Ph.D., ed.

NCADI # M154

157 QUALITATIVE METHODS IN THE PREVENTION OF DRUG ABUSE AND HIV RESEARCH. Elizabeth Y. Lambert, M.Sc.; Rebecca S. Ashery, D.S.W.; and Richard H. Needle, Ph.D., M.P.H., eds.

NCADI # M157

158 BIOLOGICAL MECHANISMS AND PERINATAL EXPOSURE TO ABUSED DRUGS. Pushpa V. Thadani, Ph.D., ed.

NCADI # M158